JOURNEY
Through the
BIBLE

JOURNEY
Through the
BIBLE

365-Day Readings With Daily Devotional

Christy Coleman Schuette

XULON PRESS

Xulon Press
2301 Lucien Way #415
Maitland, FL 32751
407.339.4217

www.xulonpress.com

© 2022 by Christy Coleman Schuette

All rights reserved solely by the author. The author guarantees all contents are original and do not infringe upon the legal rights of any other person or work. No part of this book may be reproduced in any form without the permission of the author.

Due to the changing nature of the Internet, if there are any web addresses, links, or URLs included in this manuscript, these may have been altered and may no longer be accessible. The views and opinions shared in this book belong solely to the author and do not necessarily reflect those of the publisher. The publisher therefore disclaims responsibility for the views or opinions expressed within the work.

Unless otherwise indicated, Scripture quotations taken from the Holy Bible, New International Version (NIV). Copyright © 1973, 1978, 1984, 2011 by Biblica, Inc.™. Used by permission. All rights reserved.

Scripture quotations taken from the Holman Christian Standard Bible (HCSB). Copyright © 1999, 2000, 2002, 2003, 2009 by Holman Bible Publishers, Nashville Tennessee. All rights reserved.

Scripture quotations taken from the English Standard Version (ESV). Copyright © 2001 by Crossway, a publishing ministry of Good News Publishers. Used by permission. All rights reserved.

Scripture quotations taken from the New American Standard Bible (NASB). Copyright © 1960, 1962, 1963, 1968, 1971, 1972, 1973, 1975, 1977, 1995 by The Lockman Foundation. Used by permission. All rights reserved.

Scripture quotations taken from the King James Version (KJV) – *public domain.*

Scripture quotations taken from the Christian Standard Bible. (CSB). Copyright © 2017 by Holman Bible Publishers. Used by permission. All rights reserved.

Scripture quotations taken from the International Children's Bible (ICB). The Holy Bible, International Children's Bible® Copyright© 1986, 1988, 1999, 2015 by Tommy Nelson™, a division of Thomas Nelson. Used by permission.

Scripture quotations taken from The Message (MSG). Copyright © 1993, 1994, 1995, 1996, 2000, 2001, 2002. Used by permission of NavPress Publishing Group. Used by permission. All rights reserved.

Scripture quotations taken from the Holy Bible, New Living Translation (NLT). Copyright ©1996, 2004, 2007 by Tyndale House Foundation. Used by permission of Tyndale House Publishers, Inc.

Paperback ISBN-13: 978-1-66284-581-9
Ebook ISBN-13: 978-1-66284-582-6

I WOULD LIKE to dedicate this book to my family. My husband, Brian, who is my strongest supporter. You encourage me and push me to pursue Christ and His plans for my life. To my two amazing daughters, Emily and Hannah. You are my inspiration for writing. I know that my most important calling in life is to pass on my faith to the next generation and it is a great joy to see you both seeking to please God and follow Him. To my two sons-in-law, Logan and Ryan. I could not have picked better husbands for my daughters. I am so proud of both of you. To my beautiful grandbaby, Hadley, who brings so much joy to my life. I look forward to teaching you all about Jesus. And to my mother, Sandra, who is my prayer warrior and constant source of encouragement. I love you all dearly. Thank you for giving me the freedom and time to write. And lastly to my beloved dog Asher who sat faithfully by my side as I wrote every page of this book but passed away before it was published. You are greatly missed, and your absence will be felt in my future writing projects.

Through the Bible in a Year Plan

__January 1	Genesis 1-2	Matthew 1	Ps. 1	Proverbs 1:1-4
__January 2	Genesis 3-4	Matthew 2	Ps. 2:1-6	Proverbs 1:5-6
__January 3	Genesis 5-6	Matthew 3	Ps. 2:7-12	Proverbs 1:7
__January 4	Genesis 7-8	Matthew 4	Ps. 3	Proverbs 1:8-9
__January 5	Genesis 9-10	Matthew 5:1-26	Ps. 4	Proverbs 1:10-14
__January 6	Genesis 11-12	Matthew 5:27-47	Ps. 5:1-6	Proverbs 1:15-16
__January 7	Genesis 13-14	Matthew 6:1-18	Ps. 5:7-12	Proverbs 1:17-19
__January 8	Genesis 15-16	Matthew 6:19-34	Ps. 6:1-5	Proverbs 1:20-23
__January 9	Genesis 17-18	Matthew 7	Ps. 6:6-10	Proverbs 1:24-27
__January 10	Genesis 19-20	Matthew 8:1-17	Ps. 7:1-8	Proverbs 1:28-31
__January 11	Genesis 21-22	Matthew 8:18-34	Ps. 7:9-17	Proverbs 1:32-33
__January 12	Genesis 23-24	Matthew 9:1-17	Ps. 8	Proverbs 2:1-5
__January 13	Genesis 25-26	Matthew 9:18-38	Ps. 9:1-6	Proverbs 2:6-8
__January 14	Genesis 27-28	Matthew 10:1-20	Ps. 9:7-12	Proverbs 2:9-10
__January 15	Genesis 29-30	Matthew 10:21-42	Ps. 9:13-20	Proverbs 2:11-15
__January 16	Genesis 31	Matthew 11:1-19	Ps. 10:1-11	Proverbs 2:16-19
__January 17	Genesis 32-33	Matthew 11:20-30	Ps. 10:12-18	Proverbs 2:20-22
__January 18	Genesis 34-35	Matthew 12:1-21	Ps. 11:1-3	Proverbs 3:1-2
__January 19	Genesis 36	Matthew 12:22-50	Ps. 11:4-7	Proverbs 3:3-4
__January 20	Genesis 37	Matthew 13:1-23	Ps. 12:1-4	Proverbs 3:5-6
__January 21	Genesis 38	Matthew 13:24-58	Ps. 12:5-8	Proverbs 3:7-8
__January 22	Genesis 39-40	Matthew 14:1-21	Ps. 13	Proverbs 3:9-10
__January 23	Genesis 41-42	Matthew 14:22-36	Ps. 14	Proverbs 3:11-12
__January 24	Genesis 43	Matthew 15:1-20	Ps. 15	Proverbs 3:13-14
__January 25	Genesis 44	Matthew 15:21-39	Ps. 16:1-6	Proverbs 3:15-16
__January 26	Genesis 45-46	Matthew 16	Ps. 16:7-11	Proverbs 3:17-18
__January 27	Genesis 47-48	Matthew 17	Ps. 17:1-5	Proverbs 3:19-20
__January 28	Genesis 49-50	Matthew 18	Ps. 17:6-9	Proverbs 3:21-23

___January 29	Exodus 1-2	Matthew 19	Ps. 17:10-13	Proverbs 3:24-26
___January 30	Exodus 3-4	Matthew 20	Ps. 17:14-15	Proverbs 3:27-28
___January 31	Exodus 5-6	Matthew 21:1-17	Ps. 18:1-6	Proverbs 3:29-32
___February 1	Exodus 7-8	Matthew 21:18-27	Ps. 18:7-12	Proverbs 3:33-35
___February 2	Exodus 9-10	Matthew 21:28-46	Ps. 18:13-19	Proverbs 4:1-2
___February 3	Exodus 11-12	Matthew 22:1-22	Ps. 18:20-24	Proverbs 4:3-4
___February 4	Exodus 13-14	Matthew 22:23-46	Ps. 18:25-29	Proverbs 4:5-6
___February 5	Exodus 15-16	Matthew 23:1-22	Ps. 18:30-36	Proverbs 4:7-9
___February 6	Exodus 17-18	Matthew 23:23-39	Ps. 18:37-42	Proverbs 4:10-13
___February 7	Exodus 19-20	Matthew 24:1-14	Ps. 18:43-50	Proverbs 4:14-17
___February 8	Exodus 21-22	Matthew 24:15-35	Ps. 19:1-6	Proverbs 4:18-19
___February 9	Exodus 23-24	Matthew 24:36-51	Ps. 19:7-14	Proverbs 4:20-22
___February 10	Exodus 25-26	Matthew 25:1-13	Ps. 20	Proverbs 4:23-24
___February 11	Exodus 27	Matthew 25:14-30	Ps. 21:1-7	Proverbs 4:25-27
___February 12	Exodus 28	Matthew 25:31-46	Ps. 21:8-13	Proverbs 5:1-2
___February 13	Exodus 29-30	Matthew 26:1-25	Ps. 22:1-5	Proverbs 5:3-6
___February 14	Exodus 31-32	Matthew 26:26-51	Ps. 22:6-10	Proverbs 5:7-8
___February 15	Exodus 33-34	Matthew 26:52-75	Ps. 22:11-15	Proverbs 5:9-10
___February 16	Exodus 35-36	Matthew 27:1-23	Ps. 22:16-21	Proverbs 5:11-14
___February 17	Exodus 37-38	Matthew 27:24-44	Ps. 22:22-26	Proverbs 5:15-17
___February 18	Exodus 39	Matthew 27:45-66	Ps. 22:27-31	Proverbs 5:18-20
___February 19	Exodus 40	Matthew 28	Ps. 23	Proverbs 5:21-23
___February 20	Leviticus 1-2	Mark 1:1-20	Ps. 24	Proverbs 6:1-3
___February 21	Leviticus 3-4	Mark 1:21-45	Ps. 25:1-7	Proverbs 6:4-5
___February 22	Leviticus 5-6	Mark 2	Ps. 25:8-15	Proverbs 6:6-8
___February 23	Leviticus 7-8	Mark 3:1-12	Ps. 25:16-22	Proverbs 6:9-11
___February 24	Leviticus 9-10	Mark 3:13-35	Ps. 26:1-7	Proverbs 6:12-15
___February 25	Leviticus 11-12	Mark 4:1-20	Ps. 26:8-12	Proverbs 6:16-19
___February 26	Leviticus 13-14	Mark 4:21-41	Ps. 27:1-6	Proverbs 6:20-22
___February 27	Leviticus 15	Mark 5:1-20	Ps. 27:7-14	Proverbs 6:23-26
___February 28	Leviticus 16	Mark 5:21-43	Ps. 28:1-5	Proverbs 6:27-29
___March 1	Leviticus 17-18	Mark 6:1-20	Ps. 28:6-9	Proverbs 6:30-31
___March 2	Leviticus 19-20	Mark 6:21-56	Ps. 29:1-6	Proverbs 6:32-33
___March 3	Leviticus 21-22	Mark 7:1-16	Ps. 29:7-11	Proverbs 6:34-35
___March 4	Leviticus 23-24	Mark 7:17-37	Ps. 30:1-6	Proverbs 7:1-3

__March 5	Leviticus 25	Mark 8	Ps. 30:7-12	Proverbs 7:4-5
__March 6	Leviticus 26	Mark 9:1-29	Ps. 31:1-8	Proverbs 7:6-8
__March 7	Leviticus 27	Mark 9:30-41	Ps. 31:9-18	Proverbs 7:9-12
__March 8	Numbers 1	Mark 9:42-10:12	Ps. 31:19-24	Proverbs 7:13-17
__March 9	Numbers 2	Mark 10:13-31	Ps. 32:1-7	Proverbs 7:18-20
__March 10	Numbers 3	Mark 10:32-52	Ps. 32:8-11	Proverbs 7:21-23
__March 11	Numbers 4-5	Mark 11:1-11	Ps. 33:1-9	Proverbs 7:24-27
__March 12	Numbers 6	Mark 11:12-33	Ps. 33:10-17	Proverbs 8:1-3
__March 13	Numbers 7	Mark 12:1-27	Ps. 33:18-22	Proverbs 8:4-5
__March 14	Numbers 8-9	Mark 12:28-44	Ps. 34:1-7	Proverbs 8:6-7
__March 15	Numbers 10-11	Mark 13:1-23	Ps. 34:8-14	Proverbs 8:8-9
__March 16	Numbers 12-13	Mark 13:24-37	Ps. 34:15-22	Proverbs 8:10-13
__March 17	Numbers 14	Mark 14:1-26	Ps. 35:1-8	Proverbs 8:14-16
__March 18	Numbers 15	Mark 14:27-42	Ps. 35:9-16	Proverbs 8:17-19
__March 19	Numbers 16-17	Mark 14:43-72	Ps. 35:17-21	Proverbs 8:20-21
__March 20	Numbers 18	Mark 15:1-20	Ps. 35:22-28	Proverbs 8:22-24
__March 21	Numbers 19-20	Mark 15:21-47	Ps. 36:1-6	Proverbs 8:25-26
__March 22	Numbers 21-22	Mark 16	Ps. 36:7-12	Proverbs 8:27-29
__March 23	Numbers 23-24	Luke 1:1-25	Ps. 37:1-6	Proverbs 8:30-31
__March 24	Numbers 25	Luke 1:26-56	Ps. 37:7-13	Proverbs 8:32-33
__March 25	Numbers 26	Luke 1:57-80	Ps. 37:14-22	Proverbs 8:34-36
__March 26	Numbers 27-28	Luke 2:1-20	Ps. 37:23-29	Proverbs 9:1-2
__March 27	Numbers 29-30	Luke 2:21-38	Ps. 37:30-34	Proverbs 9:3-6
__March 28	Numbers 31	Luke 2:39-52	Ps. 37:35-40	Proverbs 9:7-9
__March 29	Numbers 32	Luke 3:1-20	Ps. 38:1-8	Proverbs 9:10-12
__March 30	Numbers 33-34	Luke 3:21-38	Ps. 38:9-15	Proverbs 9:13-15
__March 31	Numbers 35-36	Luke 4:1-21	Ps. 38:16-22	Proverbs 9:16-18
__April 1	Deut. 1	Luke 4:22-44	Ps. 39:1-6	Proverbs 10:1-2
__April 2	Deut. 2-3	Luke 5	Ps. 39:7-13	Proverbs 10:3-5
__April 3	Deut. 4	Luke 6:1-26	Ps. 40:1-5	Proverbs 10:6-8
__April 4	Deut. 5-6	Luke 6:27-49	Ps. 40:6-10	Proverbs 10:9-11
__April 5	Deut. 7-8	Luke 7:1-23	Ps. 40:11-17	Proverbs 10:12-14
__April 6	Deut. 9-10	Luke 7:24-50	Ps. 41:1-6	Proverbs 10:15-17
__April 7	Deut. 11-12	Luke 8:1-18	Ps. 41:7-13	Proverbs 10:18-21
__April 8	Deut. 13-14	Luke 8:19-39	Ps. 42	Proverbs 10:22-24
__April 9	Deut. 15-16	Luke 8:40-56	Ps. 43	Proverbs 10:25-27

__April 10	Deut. 17-18	Luke 9:1-17	Ps. 44:1-8	Proverbs 10:28-30
__April 11	Deut. 19-20	Luke 9:18-36	Ps. 44:9-16	Proverbs 10:31-32
__April 12	Deut. 21-23	Luke 9:37-62	Ps. 44:17-26	Proverbs 11:1-3
__April 13	Deut. 24-25	Luke 10:1-24	Ps. 45:1-5	Proverbs 11:4-6
__April 14	Deut. 26-27	Luke 10:25-42	Ps. 45:6-12	Proverbs 11:7-8
__April 15	Deut. 28	Luke 11:1-28	Ps. 45:13-17	Proverbs 11:9-11
__April 16	Deut. 29-30	Luke 11:29-54	Ps. 46	Proverbs 11:12-13
__April 17	Deut. 31	Luke 12:1-21	Ps. 47	Proverbs 11:14-15
__April 18	Deut. 32	Luke 12:22-34	Ps. 48:1-7	Proverbs 11:16-18
__April 19	Deut. 33-34	Luke 12:35-59	Ps. 48:8-14	Proverbs 11:19-21
__April 20	Joshua 1-3	Luke 13:1-17	Ps. 49:1-9	Proverbs 11:22-23
__April 21	Joshua 4-6	Luke 13:18-35	Ps. 49:10-15	Proverbs 11:24-26
__April 22	Joshua 7-8	Luke 14	Ps. 49:16-20	Proverbs 11:27-29
__April 23	Joshua 9-10	Luke 15:1-10	Ps. 50:1-6	Proverbs 11:30-31
__April 24	Joshua 11-12	Luke 15:11-32	Ps. 50:7-15	Proverbs 12:1-3
__April 25	Joshua 13-14	Luke 16:1-13	Ps. 50:16-23	Proverbs 12:4-5
__April 26	Joshua 15-16	Luke 16:14-31	Ps. 51:1-5	Proverbs 12:6-7
__April 27	Joshua 17-18	Luke 17	Ps. 51:6-10	Proverbs 12:8-10
__April 28	Joshua 19	Luke 18:1-23	Ps. 51:11-15	Proverbs 12:11-12
__April 29	Joshua 20-21	Luke 18:24-43	Ps. 51:16-19	Proverbs 12:13-14
__April 30	Joshua 22-23	Luke 19:1-27	Ps. 52	Proverbs 12:15-16
__May 1	Joshua 24	Luke 19:28-48	Ps. 53	Proverbs 12:17-18
__May 2	Judges 1-2	Luke 20:1-26	Ps. 54	Proverbs 12:19-21
__May 3	Judges 3-4	Luke 20:27-47	Ps. 55:1-8	Proverbs 12:22-24
__May 4	Judges 5	Luke 21:1-19	Ps. 55:9-15	Proverbs 12:25-26
__May 5	Judges 6-7	Luke 21:20-38	Ps. 55:16-23	Proverbs 12:27-28
__May 6	Judges 8-9	Luke 22:1-23	Ps. 56:1-7	Proverbs 13:1-2
__May 7	Judges 10-11	Luke 22:24-46	Ps. 56:8-13	Proverbs 13:3-4
__May 8	Judges 12-14	Luke 22:47-71	Ps. 57:1-6	Proverbs 13:5-6
__May 9	Judges 15-16	Luke 23	Ps. 57:7-11	Proverbs 13:7-8
__May 10	Judges 17-18	Luke 24	Ps. 58:1-5	Proverbs 13:9-10
__May 11	Judges 19-21	John 1	Ps. 58:6-11	Proverbs 13:11-12
__May 12	Ruth 1-2	John 2	Ps. 59:1-5	Proverbs 13:13-14
__May 13	Ruth 3-4	John 3	Ps. 59:6-13	Proverbs 13:15-16
__May 14	I Samuel 1-3	John 4	Ps. 59:14-17	Proverbs 13:17-18
__May 15	I Samuel 4-5	John 5	Ps. 60:1-5	Proverbs 13:19-21
__May 16	I Samuel 6-7	John 6	Ps. 60:6-12	Proverbs 13:22-23
__May 17	I Samuel 8-10	John 7	Ps. 61	Proverbs 13:24-25
__May 18	I Samuel 11-12	John 8	Ps. 62:1-8	Proverbs 14:1-2
__May 19	I Samuel 13-14	John 9	Ps. 62:9-12	Proverbs 14:3-4

__May 20	I Samuel 15	John 10	Ps. 63:1-5	Proverbs 14:5-7
__May 21	I Samuel 16-17	John 11	Ps. 63:6-11	Proverbs 14:8-10
__May 22	I Samuel 18-19	John 12	Ps. 64:1-6	Proverbs 14:11-12
__May 23	I Samuel 20-21	John 13	Ps. 64:7-10	Proverbs 14:13-14
__May 24	I Samuel 22-23	John 14	Ps. 65:1-8	Proverbs 14:15-16
__May 25	I Samuel 24-25	John 15	Ps. 65:9-13	Proverbs 14:17-19
__May 26	I Samuel 26-28	John 16	Ps. 66:1-9	Proverbs 14:20-21
__May 27	I Samuel 29-31	John 17	Ps. 66:10-15	Proverbs 14:22-23
__May 28	2 Samuel 1-2	John 18	Ps. 66:16-20	Proverbs 14:24-25
__May 29	2 Samuel 3-4	John 19	Ps. 67:1-4	Proverbs 14:26-27
__May 30	2 Samuel 5-6	John 20	Ps. 67:5-7	Proverbs 14:28-30
__May 31	2 Samuel 7-9	John 21	Ps. 68:1-6	Proverbs 14:31-32
__June 1	2 Samuel 10-11	Acts 1	Ps. 68:7-14	Proverbs 14:33-35
__June 2	2 Samuel 12-13	Acts 2:1-13	Ps. 68:15-18	Proverbs 15:1-2
__June 3	2 Samuel 14-15	Acts 2:14-46	Ps. 68:19-27	Proverbs 15:3-4
__June 4	2 Samuel 16-17	Acts 3	Ps. 68:28-35	Proverbs 15:5-7
__June 5	2 Samuel 18-19	Acts 4:1-22	Ps. 69:1-4	Proverbs 15:8-9
__June 6	2 Samuel 20-21	Acts 4:23-37	Ps. 69:5-12	Proverbs 15:10-12
__June 7	2 Samuel 22-24	Acts 5:1-16	Ps. 69:13-18	Proverbs 15:13-14
__June 8	1 Kings 1-2	Acts 5:17-42	Ps. 69:19-28	Proverbs 15:15-17
__June 9	1 Kings 3-4	Acts 6:1-13	Ps. 69:29-36	Proverbs 15:18-19
__June 10	1 Kings 5-7	Acts 6:14-7:50	Ps. 70	Proverbs 15:20-21
__June 11	1 Kings 8	Acts 7:51-60	Ps. 71:1-8	Proverbs 15:22-23
__June 12	1 Kings 9-10	Acts 8	Ps. 71:9-16	Proverbs 15:24-26
__June 13	1 Kings 11-12	Acts 9	Ps. 71:17-24	Proverbs 15:27-28
__June 14	1 Kings 13-14	Acts 10	Ps. 72:1-7	Proverbs 15:29-30
__June 15	1 Kings 15-16	Acts 11	Ps. 72:8-11	Proverbs 15:31-33
__June 16	1 Kings 17-18	Acts 12	Ps. 72:12-16	Proverbs 16:1-3
__June 17	1 Kings 19-20	Acts 13	Ps. 72:17-20	Proverbs 16:4-5
__June 18	1 Kings 21-22	Acts 14	Ps. 73:1-3	Proverbs 16:6-7
__June 19	2 Kings 1-2	Acts 15	Ps. 73:4-12	Proverbs 16:8-9
__June 20	2 Kings 3-4	Acts 16:1-15	Ps. 73:13-20	Proverbs 16:10-11
__June 21	2 Kings 5-6	Acts 16:16-40	Ps. 73:21-28	Proverbs 16:12-13
__June 22	2 Kings 7-8	Acts 17	Ps. 74:1-4	Proverbs 16:14-15
__June 23	2 Kings 9-10	Acts 18	Ps. 74:5-11	Proverbs 16:16
__June 24	2 Kings 11-12	Acts 19	Ps. 74:12-17	Proverbs 16:17-19
__June 25	2 Kings 13-14	Acts 20	Ps. 74:18-23	Proverbs 16:20-21
__June 26	2 Kings 15-16	Acts 21	Ps. 75:1-5	Proverbs 16:22-23
__June 27	2 Kings 17-18	Acts 22	Ps. 75:6-10	Proverbs 16:24-25
__June 28	2 Kings 19-20	Acts 23	Ps. 76:1-6	Proverbs 16:26-27

__June 29	2 Kings 21-23	Acts 24	Ps. 76:7-12	Proverbs 16:28-29
__June 30	2 Kings 24-25	Acts 25	Ps. 77:1-6	Proverbs 16:30-31
__July 1	1 Chron. 1-2	Acts 26	Ps. 77:7-15	Proverbs 16:32-33
__July 2	1 Chron. 3-5	Acts 27	Ps. 77:16-20	Proverbs 17:1-2
__July 3	1 Chron. 6-7	Acts 28	Ps. 78:1-8	Proverbs 17:3-4
__July 4	1 Chron. 8-9	Romans 1	Ps. 78:9-16	Proverbs 17:5-6
__July 5	1 Chron. 10-12	Romans 2	Ps. 78:17-31	Proverbs 17:7-8
__July 6	1 Chron. 13-15	Romans 3	Ps. 78:32-39	Proverbs 17:9-11
__July 7	1 Chron. 16-17	Romans 4	Ps. 78:40-55	Proverbs 17:12-13
__July 8	1 Chron. 18-19	Romans 5	Ps. 78:56-64	Proverbs 17:14-15
__July 9	1 Chron. 20-22	Romans 6	Ps. 78:65-72	Proverbs 17:16-17
__July 10	1 Chron. 23-24	Romans 7	Ps. 79:1-4	Proverbs 17:18-20
__July 11	1 Chron. 25-26	Romans 8:1-17	Ps. 79:5-8	Proverbs 17:21-22
__July 12	1 Chron. 27-29	Romans 8:18-39	Ps. 79:9-13	Proverbs 17:23-24
__July 13	2 Chron. 1-2	Romans 9	Ps. 80:1-3	Proverbs 17:25-26
__July 14	2 Chron. 3-5	Romans 10	Ps. 80:4-7	Proverbs 17:27-28
__July 15	2 Chron. 6-7	Romans 11	Ps. 80:8-11	Proverbs 18:1-2
__July 16	2 Chron. 8-9	Romans 12	Ps. 80:12-19	Proverbs 18:3-5
__July 17	2 Chron. 10-12	Romans 13	Ps. 81:1-5	Proverbs 18:6-8
__July 18	2 Chron. 13-15	Romans 14	Ps. 81:6-10	Proverbs 18:9-10
__July 19	2 Chron. 16-18	Romans 15	Ps. 81:11-16	Proverbs 18:11-12
__July 20	2 Chron. 19-20	Romans 16	Ps. 82:1-4	Proverbs 18:13-14
__July 21	2 Chron. 21-23	Romans Road	Ps. 82:5-8	Proverbs 18:15-16
__July 22	2 Chron. 24-25	1 Cor. 1	Ps. 83:1-8	Proverbs 18:17-18
__July 23	2 Chron. 26-28	1 Cor. 2	Ps. 83:9-12	Proverbs 18:19-21
__July 24	2 Chron. 29-30	1 Cor. 3	Ps. 83:13-18	Proverbs 18:22-24
__July 25	2 Chron. 31-32	1 Cor. 4	Ps. 84:1-7	Proverbs 19:1-2
__July 26	2 Chron. 33-34	1 Cor. 5	Ps. 84:8-12	Proverbs 19:3-4
__July 27	2 Chron. 35-36	1 Cor. 6	Ps. 85:1-7	Proverbs 19:5-6
__July 28	Ezra 1-2	1 Cor. 7:1-16	Ps. 85:8-13	Proverbs 19:7
__July 29	Ezra 3-4	1 Cor. 7:17-40	Ps. 86:1-4	Proverbs 19:8-9
__July 30	Ezra 5-6	1 Cor. 8	Ps. 86:5-10	Proverbs 19:10-11
__July 31	Ezra 7-8	1 Cor. 9	Ps. 86:11-17	Proverbs 19:12-14
__August 1	Ezra 9-10	1 Cor. 10	Ps. 87	Proverbs 19:15-16
__August 2	Nehemiah 1-3	1 Cor. 11	Ps. 88:1-5	Proverbs 19:17-18
__August 3	Nehemiah 4-5	1 Cor. 12	Ps. 88:6-12	Proverbs 19:19-20
__August 4	Nehemiah 6-7	1 Cor. 13	Ps. 88:13-18	Proverbs 19:21-23
__August 5	Nehemiah 8-9	1 Cor. 14:1-25	Ps. 89:1-7	Proverbs 19:24-25
__August 6	Nehemiah 10-11	1 Cor. 14:26-40	Ps. 89:8-18	Proverbs 19:26-27
__August 7	Nehemiah 12-13	1 Cor. 15:1-19	Ps. 89:19-26	Proverbs 19:28-29

__August 8	Esther 1-2	1 Cor. 15:20-34	Ps. 89:27-37	Proverbs 20:1-2
__August 9	Esther 3-5	1 Cor. 15:35-58	Ps. 89:38-45	Proverbs 20:3-4
__August 10	Esther 6-7	1 Cor. 16	Ps. 89:46-52	Proverbs 20:5-6
__August 11	Esther 8-10	2 Cor. 1:1-14	Ps. 90:1-6	Proverbs 20:7-9
__August 12	Job 1-3	2 Cor. 1:15-2:17	Ps. 90:7-12	Proverbs 20:10-11
__August 13	Job 4-5	2 Cor. 3	Ps. 90:13-17	Proverbs 20:12-13
__August 14	Job 6-7	2 Cor. 4	Ps. 91:1-8	Proverbs 20:14-15
__August 15	Job 8-10	2 Cor. 5:1-15	Ps. 91:9-16	Proverbs 20:16-18
__August 16	Job 11-12	2 Cor. 5:16-21	Ps. 92:1-7	Proverbs 20:19
__August 17	Job 13-14	2 Cor. 6:1-13	Ps. 92:8-15	Proverbs 20:20-21
__August 18	Job 15-17	2 Cor. 6:14-18	Ps. 93	Proverbs 20:22-23
__August 19	Job 18-19	2 Cor. 7	Ps. 94:1-7	Proverbs 20:24-25
__August 20	Job 20-21	2 Cor. 8	Ps. 94:8-15	Proverbs 20:26-28
__August 21	Job 22-24	2 Cor. 9	Ps. 94:16-23	Proverbs 20:29-30
__August 22	Job 25-27	2 Cor. 10	Ps. 95:1-5	Proverbs 21:1-2
__August 23	Job 28-29	2 Cor. 11	Ps. 95:6-11	Proverbs 21:3-4
__August 24	Job 30-31	2 Cor. 12	Ps. 96:1-6	Proverbs 21:5-6
__August 25	Job 32-33	2 Cor. 13	Ps. 96:7-13	Proverbs 21:7-8
__August 26	Job 34-35	Galatians 1	Ps. 97:1-5	Proverbs 21:9-10
__August 27	Job 36-37	Galatians 2	Ps. 97:6-12	Proverbs 21:11-12
__August 28	Job 38-39	Galatians 3	Ps. 98:1-3	Proverbs 21:13-15
__August 29	Job 40-42	Galatians 4	Ps. 98:4-9	Proverbs 21:16-17
__August 30	Eccles. 1-2	Galatians 5	Ps. 99:1-5	Proverbs 21:18-19
__August 31	Eccles. 3-5	Galatians 6	Ps. 99:6-9	Proverbs 21:20-21
__September 1	Eccles. 6-8	Ephesians 1	Ps. 100	Proverbs 21:22-24
__September 2	Eccles. 9-10	Ephesians 2:1-10	Ps. 101:1-4	Proverbs 21:25-26
__September 3	Eccles. 11-12	Ephesians 2:11-22	Ps. 101:5-8	Proverbs 21:27-28
__September 4	Song of Sol. 1-2	Ephesians 3	Ps. 102:1-11	Proverbs 21:29-31
__September 5	Song of Sol. 3-4	Ephesians 4:1-16	Ps. 102:12-14	Proverbs 22:1-2
__September 6	Song of Sol. 5-6	Ephesians 4:17-32	Ps. 102:15-22	Proverbs 22:3-4
__September 7	Song of Sol. 7-8	Ephesians 5:1-20	Ps. 102:23-28	Proverbs 22:5-6
__September 8	Isaiah 1-2	Ephesians 5:21-33	Ps. 103:1-5	Proverbs 22:7-8
__September 9	Isaiah 3-5	Ephesians 6:1-9	Ps. 103:6-10	Proverbs 22:9-11
__September 10	Isaiah 6-8	Ephesians 6:10-23	Ps. 103:11-14	Proverbs 22:12-13
__September 11	Isaiah 9-10	Philippians 1:1-20	Ps. 103:15-22	Proverbs 22:14-16
__September 12	Isaiah 11-13	Philippians 1:21-30	Ps. 104:1-9	Proverbs 22:17-21
__September 13	Isaiah 14-16	Philippians 2:1-11	Ps. 104:10-15	Proverbs 22:22-23
__September 14	Isaiah 17-19	Philippians 2:12-30	Ps. 104:16-26	Proverbs 22:24-25
__September 15	Isaiah 20-22	Philippians 3:1-11	Ps. 104:27-35	Proverbs 22:26-27
__September 16	Isaiah 23-25	Philippians 3:12-21	Ps. 105:1-6	Proverbs 22:28-29

__September 17	Isaiah 26-27	Philippians 4	Ps. 105:7-11	Proverbs 23:1-3
__September 18	Isaiah 28-29	Colossians 1:1-14	Ps. 105:12-22	Proverbs 23:4-5
__September 19	Isaiah 30-31	Colossians 1:15-29	Ps. 105:23-36	Proverbs 23:6-8
__September 20	Isaiah 32-33	Colossians 2	Ps. 105:37-45	Proverbs 23:9-11
__September 21	Isaiah 34-36	Colossians 3:1-17	Ps. 106:1-5	Proverbs 23:12-14
__September 22	Isaiah 37-38	Colossians 3:18-4:1	Ps. 106:6-12	Proverbs 23:15-16
__September 23	Isaiah 39-41	Colossians 4:2-18	Ps. 106:13-18	Proverbs 23:17-18
__September 24	Isaiah 42-43	1 Thess. 1	Ps. 106:19-27	Proverbs 23:19-21
__September 25	Isaiah 44-46	1 Thess. 2	Ps. 106:28-39	Proverbs 23:22-23
__September 26	Isaiah 47-48	1 Thess. 3	Ps. 106:40-48	Proverbs 23:24-25
__September 27	Isaiah 49-50	1 Thess. 4	Ps. 107:1-9	Proverbs 23:26-28
__September 28	Isaiah 51-53	1 Thess. 5:1-11	Ps. 107:10-16	Proverbs 23:29-35
__September 29	Isaiah 54-55	1 Thess. 5:12-28	Ps. 107:17-22	Proverbs 24:1-2
__September 30	Isaiah 56-57	2 Thess. 1	Ps. 107:23-32	Proverbs 24:3-4
__October 1	Isaiah 58-59	2 Thess. 2	Ps. 107:33-43	Proverbs 24:5-6
__October 2	Isaiah 60-61	2 Thess. 3	Ps. 108:1-6	Proverbs 24:7
__October 3	Isaiah 62-64	1 Timothy 1	Ps. 108:7-13	Proverbs 24:8-9
__October 4	Isaiah 65-66	1 Timothy 2	Ps. 109:1-8	Proverbs 24:10-12
__October 5	Jeremiah 1-2	1 Timothy 3	Ps. 109:9-20	Proverbs 24:13-14
__October 6	Jeremiah 3-4	1 Timothy 4	Ps. 109:21-31	Proverbs 24:15-16
__October 7	Jeremiah 5-6	1 Timothy 5	Ps. 110	Proverbs 24:17-18
__October 8	Jeremiah 7-8	1 Timothy 6:1-10	Ps. 111	Proverbs 24:19-20
__October 9	Jeremiah 9-10	1 Timothy 6:11-21	Ps. 112:1-5	Proverbs 24:21-22
__October 10	Jeremiah 11-12	2 Timothy 1	Ps. 112:6-10	Proverbs 24:23-25
__October 11	Jeremiah 13-14	2 Timothy 2	Ps. 113:1-3	Proverbs 24:26-27
__October 12	Jeremiah 15-16	2 Timothy 3	Ps. 113:4-9	Proverbs 24:28-29
__October 13	Jeremiah 17-18	2 Timothy 4	Ps. 114	Proverbs 24:30-34
__October 14	Jeremiah 19-21	Titus 1	Ps. 115:1-8	Proverbs 25:1-3
__October 15	Jeremiah 22-23	Titus 2	Ps. 115:9-18	Proverbs 25:4-5
__October 16	Jeremiah 24-26	Titus 3	Ps. 116:1-11	Proverbs 25:6-7
__October 17	Jeremiah 27-29	Philemon 1	Ps. 116:12-19	Proverbs 25:8-10
__October 18	Jeremiah 30-31	Hebrews 1	Ps. 117	Proverbs 25:11-12
__October 19	Jeremiah 32-33	Hebrews 2	Ps. 118:1-4	Proverbs 25:13
__October 20	Jeremiah 34-36	Hebrews 3	Ps. 118:5-14	Proverbs 25:14-15
__October 21	Jeremiah 37-38	Hebrews 4:1-13	Ps. 118:15-21	Proverbs 25:16-17
__October 22	Jeremiah 39-41	Hebrews 4:14-16	Ps. 118:22-29	Proverbs 25:18-19
__October 23	Jeremiah 42-43	Hebrews 5	Ps. 119:1-8	Proverbs 25:20-22
__October 24	Jeremiah 44-45	Hebrews 6:1-12	Ps. 119:9-16	Proverbs 25:23-24
__October 25	Jeremiah 46-47	Hebrews 6:13-20	Ps. 119:17-24	Proverbs 25:25-26
__October 26	Jeremiah 48-49	Hebrews 7:1-10	Ps. 119:25-32	Proverbs 25:27-28

__October 27	Jeremiah 50	Hebrews 7:11-28	Ps. 119:33-40	Proverbs 26:1-2
__October 28	Jeremiah 51-52	Hebrews 8:1-6	Ps. 119:41-48	Proverbs 26:3
__October 29	Lam. 1-2	Hebrews 8:7-13	Ps. 119:49-56	Proverbs 26:4-7
__October 30	Lam. 3-5	Hebrews 9:1-10	Ps. 119:57-64	Proverbs 26:8-10
__October 31	Ezekiel 1-3	Hebrews 9:11-28	Ps. 119:65-72	Proverbs 26:11-12
__November 1	Ezekiel 4-6	Hebrews 10:1-18	Ps. 119:73-80	Proverbs 26:13-15
__November 2	Ezekiel 7-8	Hebrews 10:19-39	Ps. 119:81-88	Proverbs 26:16
__November 3	Ezekiel 9-11	Hebrews 11:1-16	Ps. 119:89-96	Proverbs 26:17
__November 4	Ezekiel 12-13	Hebrews 11:17-12:3	Ps. 119:97-104	Proverbs 26:18-19
__November 5	Ezekiel 14-16	Hebrews 12:4-13	Ps. 119:105-112	Proverbs 26:20-22
__November 6	Ezekiel 17-18	Hebrews 12:14-29	Ps. 119:113-120	Proverbs 26:23-25
__November 7	Ezekiel 19-20	Hebrews 13	Ps. 119:121-128	Proverbs 26:26-28
__November 8	Ezekiel 21-22	James 1:1-18	Ps. 119:129-136	Proverbs 27:1-2
__November 9	Ezekiel 23-24	James 1:19-27	Ps. 119:137-144	Proverbs 27:3-4
__November 10	Ezekiel 25-27	James 2:1-13	Ps. 119:145-152	Proverbs 27:5-6
__November 11	Ezekiel 28-29	James 2:14-26	Ps. 119:153-160	Proverbs 27:7-8
__November 12	Ezekiel 30-31	James 3:1-12	Ps. 119:161-168	Proverbs 27:9-10
__November 13	Ezekiel 32-33	James 3:13-18	Ps. 119:169-176	Proverbs 27:11-12
__November 14	Ezekiel 34-36	James 4:1-12	Ps. 120	Proverbs 27:13-14
__November 15	Ezekiel 37-38	James 4:13-17	Ps. 121	Proverbs 27:15-16
__November 16	Ezekiel 39-40	James 5:1-12	Ps. 122	Proverbs 27:17-18
__November 17	Ezekiel 41-42	James 5:13-20	Ps. 123	Proverbs 27:19-20
__November 18	Ezekiel 43-44	1 Peter 1:1-12	Ps. 124	Proverbs 27:21-22
__November 19	Ezekiel 45-46	1 Peter 1:13-25	Ps. 125	Proverbs 27:23-24
__November 20	Ezekiel 47-48	1 Peter 2:1-10	Ps. 126	Proverbs 27:25-27
__November 21	Daniel 1-2	1 Peter 2:11-25	Ps. 127	Proverbs 28:1-2
__November 22	Daniel 3-4	1 Peter 3:1-12	Ps. 128	Proverbs 28:3-5
__November 23	Daniel 5-6	1 Peter 3:13-22	Ps. 129	Proverbs 28:6-7
__November 24	Daniel 7-8	1 Peter 4	Ps. 130	Proverbs 28:8-9
__November 25	Daniel 9-10	1 Peter 5	Ps. 131	Proverbs 28:10-11
__November 26	Daniel 11-12	2 Peter 1	Ps. 132:1-10	Proverbs 28:12
__November 27	Hosea 1-3	2 Peter 2	Ps. 132:11-18	Proverbs 28:13
__November 28	Hosea 4-5	2 Peter 3	Ps. 133	Proverbs 28:14-15
__November 29	Hosea 6-7	1 John 1	Ps. 134	Proverbs 28:16-17
__November 30	Hosea 8-9	1 John 2	Ps. 135:1-7	Proverbs 28:18-19
__December 1	Hosea 10-11	1 John 3	Ps. 135:8-14	Proverbs 28:20-21
__December 2	Hosea 12-14	1 John 4	Ps. 135:15-21	Proverbs 28:22-23
__December 3	Joel 1:1-2:11	1 John 5	Ps. 136:1-12	Proverbs 28:24-26
__December 4	Joel 2:12-3:21	2 John 1	Ps. 136:13-26	Proverbs 28:27-28
__December 5	Amos 1-2	3 John 1	Ps. 137	Proverbs 29:1-3

__December 6	Amos 3-4	Jude 1	Ps. 138:1-3	Proverbs 29:4-6
__December 7	Amos 5-6	Revelation 1	Ps. 138:4-8	Proverbs 29:7-8
__December 8	Amos 7-9	Revelation 2	Ps. 139:1-6	Proverbs 29:9-10
__December 9	Obadiah 1	Revelation 3	Ps. 139:7-12	Proverbs 29:11-12
__December 10	Jonah 1-2	Revelation 4	Ps. 139:13-18	Proverbs 29:13-14
__December 11	Jonah 3-4	Revelation 5	Ps. 139:19-24	Proverbs 29:15-17
__December 12	Micah 1-2	Revelation 6	Ps. 140:1-5	Proverbs 29:18-19
__December 13	Micah 3-4	Revelation 7	Ps. 140:6-13	Proverbs 29:20-21
__December 14	Micah 5-6	Revelation 8	Ps. 141:1-6	Proverbs 29:22-23
__December 15	Micah 7	Revelation 9	Ps. 141:7-10	Proverbs 29:24-25
__December 16	Nahum 1	Revelation 10	Ps. 142	Proverbs 29:26-27
__December 17	Nahum 2-3	Revelation 11:1-10	Ps. 143:1-6	Proverbs 30:1-6
__December 18	Hab. 1:1-2:3	Revelation 11:11-19	Ps. 143:7-12	Proverbs 30:7-10
__December 19	Hab. 2:4-3:19	Revelation 12	Ps. 144:1-8	Proverbs 30:11-14
__December 20	Zephaniah 1-2	Revelation 13:1-10	Ps. 144:9-15	Proverbs 30:15-17
__December 21	Zephaniah 3	Revelation 13:11-18	Ps. 145:1-7	Proverbs 30:18-20
__December 22	Haggai 1-2	Revelation 14:1-14	Ps. 145:8-13	Proverbs 30:21-23
__December 23	Zechariah 1-2	Revelation 14:15-20	Ps. 145:14-21	Proverbs 30:24-28
__December 24	Zechariah 3-4	Revelation 15	Ps. 146:1-4	Proverbs 30:29-33
__December 25	Zechariah 5-6	Revelation 16	Ps. 146:5-10	Proverbs 31:1-5
__December 26	Zechariah 7-8	Revelation 17	Ps. 147:1-9	Proverbs 31:6-9
__December 27	Zechariah 9-10	Revelation 18	Ps. 147:10-20	Proverbs 31:10-14
__December 28	Zechariah 11-12	Revelation 19	Ps. 148:1-6	Proverbs 31:15-19
__December 29	Zechariah 13-14	Revelation 20	Ps. 148:7-14	Proverbs 31:20-23
__December 30	Malachi 1-2	Revelation 21	Ps. 149	Proverbs 31:24-27
__December 31	Malachi 3-4	Revelation 22	Ps. 150	Proverbs 31:28-31

Introduction

I AM CONVINCED that the Bible is God's Word to us. It is not just a book written a long time ago that gives us good advice. It's not a self-help book. It is the very words of the God of the Universe given to us to show us how to live. It is the basis for our understanding of life. Its words are the standard that shapes our worldview, our actions, and our destiny. It is impossible to give it too much weight. Our view of scripture determines how much influence it will have over our lives. It is not a book that we can read through once and have it figured out. And it is not a book that we can just randomly pick out passages that we like and ignore the rest. It requires reading it, meditating on it, studying it, and then reading it again. The more we read it, the more we will understand it. And the more we read it, we realize how much we don't understand. He wants to speak to us through the pages of His Word. He wants to give us insight into the mysteries it holds. This depth of understanding doesn't come naturally or casually. It comes to those who are seeking. It is not an intellectual pursuit. There are many biblical scholars who know all about the Bible and can quote it extensively, who never get this depth of knowledge. My grandmother was not an educated woman. She did not complete high school and yet she understood God's Word far more than most people. Her Bible was worn, and the pages were bent from constant use. Jeremiah 29:13 says, "You will seek Me and find Me when you search for Me with all your heart. I will be found by you." (HCSB)

As a teenager, I was blessed to be a part of a very active youth group in my church and to have several youth ministers that gave me a solid foundation to build my faith. Then I went away to college and was a part of the Baptist Student Union. Instead of my college years being a time of straying from my faith, those years were times of growth and building on that foundation. One of the consistent messages from youth and campus ministers was that of the importance of a quiet time. They stressed the significance of spending time with Jesus every day. I believed what they were saying, but I can't say that I followed their advice consistently. Those days were busy and there seemed to be other priorities. Then I went away to seminary, got married, began a career, had children, and life happened. There were seasons when I was consistent and then other seasons when I was more sporadic in spending time with the Lord. I was serving faithfully in my church, leading Bible studies, and walking with the Lord, but not consistently spending time in His presence every day. I can't tell you exactly when it happened or why, but a little over 10 years ago I started a Read

Through the Bible in a Year plan and I did it. I read my Bible every day for a year and finished the plan. At that point, I was hooked. I began to long for that time every day. I have tried several different plans. I read straight through the Bible a couple of years, read it chronologically a couple of times, and then I found a plan that went through it by doing a passage in the Old Testament, a passage in the New Testament, a Psalm, and a Proverb. And I have done this for the last 7 years. I love this system because I don't get bogged down in the Old Testament and I get some praise time in the Psalms, and some wisdom in Proverbs that always seems to apply to my day.

As I get older, I am spending more time in reflection. Looking back over my life, I can see a difference in the seasons when I was more consistent in my daily quiet time. Those times were not circumstantially different. There were good times and bad times, pain and suffering, celebrations, and accomplishments. The difference was in me. In those seasons, I was more at peace, and more content. My reactions were more consistently faithful. I can tell that I was being led by the Holy Spirit and I was listening (well most of the time anyway). Starting my day off with Jesus puts me in a position to face whatever my day holds. He can prepare me for what lies ahead and then I am more likely to turn to Him immediately during the day. Often, I will read a passage in the morning that doesn't speak to me, but later in the day I will be reminded of it when I am talking with a friend or when something happens that is unexpected. Sometimes in my prayer time, He will prompt me to call or pray for someone that I would have missed if I had not been listening. It is during my time with Him that He leads me, guides me, chastens me, corrects me, comforts me, encourages me, and helps me. But even more significantly, it is in that time that I am getting to know Him. I am experiencing His love and mercy toward me and my head knowledge about Him is developing into intimacy with Him. I long for that time with Him now. It is no longer something to check off my list that I have completed. If you are in the season when it is something you do because you know you should, I encourage you to keep it up. Be consistent and persistent. God honors our faithfulness. It will become a habit and then it will become an essential part of your day.

Several years ago, I began writing this devotional book to help believers develop a consistent, daily walk with Jesus. My goal is to point people to Jesus through His Word. I developed a reading plan that can be done in just a few minutes each day so that you have time for meditation and prayer. My prayer is that God will use the daily readings and the devotional that goes along with them to speak to you and help you grow in your relationship with Jesus. And that as you grow in your knowledge of His Word that you will "be able to comprehend with all the saints what is the length and width, height and depth of God's love and to know the Messiah's love that surpasses knowledge, so that you may be filled with all the fullness of God." Ephesians 3:18-19 (HCSB)

January 1

Genesis 1-2
Psalm 1
Proverbs 1:1-4
Matthew 1

Creator God

"In the beginning, God created the heavens and the Earth." Genesis 1:1 NIV

"In the beginning, God created..." Those first words in Genesis 1 lay the groundwork for the entire history of the world. It says so much about our Creator. God is love and out of that love, He created. John 1:3 says, "Through Him all things were made, without Him nothing was made that has been made." (NIV) God created everything that has been created. The Latin phrase, *ex nihilo*, means creating something out of nothing. Only God can do that. He looked at the nothingness around Him and spoke everything we see into existence. You can't look at the world we live in and not come to the same conclusion as David did when he wrote Psalm 19:1. "The heavens declare the glory of God; the skies declare the work of His hands." (NIV)

Although man would argue that the world was just some cosmic accident, I think it takes a lot more faith to believe that all the beauty of this world and the intricate details of His creation just happened one day out of a big bang. When we examine the vastness of the universe and at the same time look at the detail and complexity of even the smallest creature, it is incomprehensible to deny or even doubt that it was a loving, powerful, sovereign God who created all things. It is fitting that we begin this year, acknowledging that God created and sustains all things. Acts 17:28 says, "In Him we live and move and have our being." (NIV) Let us keep our eyes and attention focused on God as we approach the year before us.

Genesis 3-4
Psalm 2:1-6
Proverbs 1:5-6
Matthew 2

January 2

Accepting Responsibility

"Then the man replied, 'The woman You gave to be with me—she gave me some fruit from the tree, and I ate.' So, the Lord God asked the woman, 'What is this you have done?' And the woman said, 'It was the serpent. He deceived me, and I ate.'" Genesis 3:12-13 HCSB

SINCE THE BEGINNING of time, humans have never been very good at accepting responsibility for our actions. We are no different from Adam and Eve. We blame our parents for the way they raised us. We blame the circumstances of our past for our present lack of responsibility. We excuse our sins as character flaws and things we can't change. (That's just the way God made me.) Philippians 3:13-14 says, "Forgetting what is behind and straining toward what is ahead, I press on toward the goal to win the prize for which God has called me heavenward in Christ Jesus." (NIV) No matter what your past may have looked like, this is a new day, a new year. You cannot continue to blame others for the problems you are facing, or for your own sinful actions.

The past is in the past and there is nothing you can do to change it. God can and will use the things that have happened to you leading up to this point in your life to make you into the person He wants you to be. He did not cause the bad things to happen to you, but He can use them for His glory and your good if you allow Him to do so. If you choose to continue wallowing in self-pity or blaming others for your own poor choices, you will continue to reap the consequences. Romans 8:28 says, "And we know that in all things God works for the good of those who love Him, who have been called according to His purpose." (NIV) Let us be quick to accept responsibility and ask for forgiveness from God and anyone we might have hurt. "So, I strive always to keep my conscience clear before God and man." Acts 24:16 (NIV)

Genesis 5-6
Psalm 2:7-12
Proverbs 1:7
Matthew 3

January 3

Obedience

"Noah was a righteous man, blameless among the people of his time, and he walked faithfully with God. He did everything just as God commanded Him." Genesis 6:9, 22 NIV

NOAH WAS BLAMELESS among his contemporaries, and he did everything God had commanded him to do. That is amazing. I would love for that to be said about me, but I'm afraid I am a long way from that being true. Too often my obedience is dependent on whether I like what I am being told to do or whether it seems to make sense. I go to God with a plan and ask Him to bless it instead of going to God and asking what His plan is. Proverbs 3:5-6 says, "Trust in the Lord with all your heart and lean not on your own understanding. In all your ways submit to Him, and He will make your paths straight." (NIV) If I lean on my limited understanding, what He is telling me often doesn't make sense. But He has a much broader perspective and knows what is best.

A few years ago, I overheard my oldest daughter tell her younger sister that delayed obedience is disobedience. That hit home with me because, unfortunately, if I think God is telling me to do something I don't really like, I often wait and see if He will change His mind or I rationalize that I must have heard Him wrong and I wait for Him to tell me again. When I do this, I miss out on the blessing I would have received by obeying Him immediately. His purposes will be accomplished, but He may use someone else to do it instead of me. It is interesting to note that there is no mention of rain in the Bible until the flood. So, when God told Noah there was going to be a flood there had never even been rain. He could not have understood what God was telling Him and yet He obeyed. If Noah had waited to start building the ark, it might not have been done by the time the flood came. His timing and His will are perfect. One of my goals as I start this New Year is to be so connected to Him that I immediately respond to His promptings without even hesitating. He really does know best and if I obey Him, He will make my paths straight.

January 4

Genesis 7-8
Psalm 3
Proverbs 1:8-9
Matthew 4

The Sword of The Spirit

"But He answered, 'It is written...' Jesus told him, 'It is also written...' Then Jesus told him, 'Go away, Satan! For it is written:" Matthew 4:4, 7, 10 HCSB

When tempted in the desert by Satan, Jesus did not try to reason with him or argue with him out of His own reasoning and understanding. Each time Satan tempted Him, He responded with scripture. 2 Timothy 3:16-17 tells us that, "All scripture is God-breathed and is useful for teaching, rebuking, correcting and training in righteousness, so that the servant of God may be thoroughly equipped for every good work." (NIV) If Jesus inspired every word that was written, it seems logical that He didn't need to quote Himself. He could have just given Satan an answer to each temptation. Instead, He purposefully and intentionally quoted scripture each time. I believe He did this as an example to us of how we should respond when tempted by Satan.

Unlike Jesus, our own reasoning and understanding is no match for Satan's attacks. He is smarter than we are, and He knows our weaknesses better than we do. We are ill-equipped to stand up to his schemes and pretensions. Fortunately, we do not stand alone. We stand in the power of the Holy Spirit who dwells within us. We have been equipped with the armor of God found in Ephesians 6 that includes "a shield of faith with which we can extinguish the flaming arrows of the evil one...and the Sword of the Spirit, which is the Word of God." (NIV) When faced with Satan's arrows of temptation or accusation, Jesus modeled the perfect response. The more time we spend reading, meditating, and memorizing God's Word, the better we will be able to respond to Satan's attacks.

Genesis 9-10
Psalm 4
Proverbs 1:10-14
Matthew 5:1-26

January 5

Salt and Light

"You are the salt of the Earth… You are the light of the world… In the same way, let your light shine before men, so that they may see your good works and give glory to your Father in Heaven." Matthew 5:13, 14, 16 HCSB

JESUS SAYS THAT we are to be salt and light in the world. We are to be different. The people around us, those who know us well and those who are just acquainted with us, should be able to see a difference in us immediately. The first time my daughter, Emily, swam in the ocean she was three years old. The first thing she said to me after going under and getting a mouthful of the water was, "Mommy, it tastes just like pretzels." She immediately recognized the saltiness of the water. She recognized that there was a difference between this water and the pool water she was used to swimming in. Salt is used for flavoring, but it is also used for preserving. We should not only provide a better flavor to the world around us, but we should also help to preserve the world from the evil that is so prevalent in our culture.

Jesus also describes us as light. Light dispels the darkness. The world we live in can be a very dark place. Even the smallest light drives out the darkness. We are very fortunate to live near Mammoth Cave and have been there many times over the years. I am always amazed when they turn the lights out during the tour to show us what complete darkness is like. I am not afraid of the dark, but this is always unsettling to me, and I am relieved when the lights come back on. Our world can seem very dark and evil, and if we look around, it may seem that Satan is succeeding in turning out the lights. But we know that is not true, because we are the light of the world. God's love and righteousness shine through us to a dark world. Let your light shine before men today that they may praise your Father in Heaven.

January 6

Genesis 11-12
Psalm 5:1-6
Proverbs 1:15-16
Matthew 5:27-47

Love My Enemies?

"But I tell you: Love your enemies and pray for those who persecute you..."
Matthew 5:44 HCSB

I don't really think of myself as someone who has a lot of enemies. I get along with most everyone. Recently, however, God has shown me that there are some people in my life to whom I have been harboring bad feelings and unforgiveness. These people don't even know that I feel this way about them and quite frankly, I wasn't even aware of it myself in most cases. As I began to examine my heart and my thoughts when confronted with situations involving these individuals, I didn't like what I saw. I often expected them to respond negatively to me or say something offensive even before they did. And I was quick to grumble and complain about having to be around them. There was very little of God's love and mercy flowing out of me toward them. I felt justified in my feelings and thoughts toward them and didn't see any need to deal with it. After all, since they did not know how I felt, it was better to just ignore it, right?

Psalm 139:23-24 says, "Search me, God, and know my heart, test me and know my anxious thoughts. See if there is any offensive way in me and lead me in the way everlasting." (NIV) God rarely lets me get by with doing things the easy way. I am spending a lot of time right now praying for them. It is amazing how difficult it is to continue to feel negatively toward someone I am earnestly praying for daily. I'm also asking God to show me if I need to go to them and ask for forgiveness. If they do not know how I feel it may not be a good idea to address it with them so I'm earnestly seeking God to give me wisdom about this. I do know that I need to let God change my heart toward them. The best way to do that is to pray for them. I don't mean praying that God will make them be nice to me or act the way I want them to, but prayers for their wellbeing and that God would bless them. If I am truly praying God's blessings on someone, my attitude toward them changes. I'm not as likely to be as easily offended and assume they will act negatively toward me, and even when they do, it is easier to let it roll off my back. I would encourage you to ask God to show you if there is anyone in your life that you need to forgive or with whom you need to restore relationship.

January 7

Genesis 13-14
Psalm 5:7-12
Proverbs 1:17-19
Matthew 6:1-18

Looking Out for Number One

"Then Abram said to Lot, 'Please let's not have quarreling between you and me, or between your herdsmen and my herdsmen, since we are relatives. Isn't the whole land before you? Separate from me: if you go to the left, I will go to the right; if you go to the right, I will go to the left." Genesis 13:8-9 HCSB

THE WORLD TEACHES us that if we don't look out for our own best interests, no one will. We have to look out for number one. We have to get all we are entitled to. We have rights and we should fight for them. Philippians 2:3-4 teaches us a very different concept. "Do nothing out of selfish ambition or vain conceit, rather, in humility value others above yourselves, not looking to your own interests, but each of you to the interests of others." (NIV) Abram exhibited this type of unselfish attitude in his dealings with Lot. He let Lot choose which land he wanted. Abram was Lot's uncle and the leader of the family. He had every right to pick what he wanted and give what was left over to Lot or to take it all for himself and tell Lot to go find his own land. But in humility, he considered Lot's interests before his own and let Lot choose first.

Abram trusted God and knew that God would look out for his interests. He didn't have to fight to get what was owed him. He trusted God to give him what He wanted him to have, and that whatever God chose to give him would be what was best for him. We can trust God just as Abram did. God has our back. He will defend our cause. We can approach others in love and reverence and trust God to look out for us. It seems that the more I focus on serving others and looking out for the interests of others instead of focusing on getting what I want and think I deserve, the happier I am.

January 8

Genesis 15-16
Psalm 6:1-5
Proverbs 1:20-23
Matthew 6:19-34

Taking Matters into My Own Hands

"Sarai said to Abram, 'Since the Lord has prevented me from bearing children, go to my slave: perhaps through her I can build a family.' And Abram agreed to what Sarai said." Genesis 16:2 HCSB

God had promised Abram that his descendants would be as numerous as the stars in the sky. He had promised to make Abram into a great nation. At the time God made the promise to Abram, Sarai was already very old and past childbearing years. She must have come to grips over the years with the fact that she was barren and would not have children. Then God gave her hope. He promised that she would have descendants. But a long time passed and still she was childless. She grew impatient and decided to take matters into her own hands. Instead of trusting God to fulfill His promise to her, she came up with a plan to help God out. She did what seems unthinkable to us. She gave her husband to another woman.

Sarai's actions seem crazy to us. Unfortunately, too often we are just like Sarai. When we think God is taking too long and we begin to doubt if He is going to come through, we come up with plans to help Him out. Instead of waiting and trusting, we come up with our own solutions. Taking matters into our own hands is extremely dangerous. The byproduct of Sarai and Abram's impatience was a baby named Ishmael. Ishmael is the father of the Arab nation. The promised child of Abram and Sarai was Isaac, whose descendants are the Jewish nation. Centuries of conflict between the Arab and Israeli people have resulted.

Yes and no answers to our prayers are much easier to deal with than when God tells us to wait. Waiting on God's timing can be so difficult. Knowing what to do while we wait, not giving up hope, and the fear of disappointment are very real concerns. The only way to navigate the waiting is by staying in constant connection with God. Staying in His Word and seeking Him through prayer allows us to trust in His timing and have faith that He loves us so much that He will always bring about what is best for us. The consequences of taking matters into our own hands can be disastrous to us and to those around us.

January 9

Genesis 17-18
Psalm 6:6-10
Proverbs 1:24-27
Matthew 7

Beyond Our Imagination

"The Lord said, 'I will surely return to you about this time next year and Sarah, your wife, shall have a son.' So, Sarah laughed to herself, saying, 'After I am worn out, and my lord is old, shall I have this pleasure.' 'Is anything too hard for the Lord?'" Genesis 18:10, 12, 14 ESV

"Ask and it will be given to you; seek and you will find; knock and the door will be opened to you. For everyone who asks receives; the one who seeks finds; and to the one who knocks, the door will be opened. Which of you, if your son asks for bread, will give him a stone? Or if he asks for a fish, will give him a snake? If you, then, though you are evil, know how to give good gifts to your children, how much more will your Father in Heaven give good gifts to those who ask Him!" Matthew 7:7-11 NIV

Is anything too hard for the Lord? Our immediate response to this question is no, of course not! But do we really believe that? Do our actions and our prayer life reflect that we believe that? Ephesians 3:20-21 tells us that God can do immeasurably more than all we ask or imagine, and I Corinthians 2:9 says, "No eye has seen, no ear has heard, no mind has conceived the things God has prepared for those who love Him." (NIV) God's plans for us are beyond our wildest imagination. Sarah had wanted a child for as long as she could remember. She had asked and sought and knocked and had finally given up. Then, when she heard the Lord tell Abraham that she would have a son in a year, she laughed. She couldn't let herself believe her dream might finally come true. She couldn't face the disappointment if she believed, and it didn't happen.

Do we limit God because we don't want to be disappointed? Do we fail to experience the fullness of all the plans God has for us because we fail to ask? As we spend time with the Lord in prayer and in His Word, we get to know Him more fully. The more we get to know Him, the more we realize how incomprehensible He is. He is transcendent, way beyond our capacity to imagine. When we begin to recognize who He is and who we are in Christ, it changes the way we pray. Our Father is the King of the universe. He is limitless in power and in His love for us. He not only wants what is best for us, but He has the ability to make it happen. Is anything too hard for the Lord?

Genesis 19-20
Psalm 7:1-8
Proverbs 1:28-31
Matthew 8:1-17

January 10

Great Faith

"The centurion replied, 'Lord, I do not deserve to have you come under my roof. But just say the word, and my servant will be healed'... When Jesus heard this, He was amazed and said to those following Him, 'Truly I tell you, I have not found anyone in Israel with such great faith." Matthew 8:8, 10 NIV

WHEN THE CENTURION asked Jesus to heal his servant, Jesus agreed to come with him and heal the servant. I would have been thrilled. Jesus said yes to my request. I had His full attention, and He was coming to my house. I would get to watch Him perform a miracle right in front of my eyes. But the centurion reacted very differently than I would have. He even responded differently than Jesus thought he would. He told Jesus that he didn't want to bother Him to come all that way. He was completely and totally convinced that Jesus was the Son of God and if He was the Son of God, then He didn't have to touch the servant or be in his presence. All He had to do to heal the man was speak and it would be done from wherever He was. Jesus was astonished. I am guessing it takes a lot to astonish Jesus. He has seen everything and heard everything. But the Bible says He was astonished by the man's faith. He told the centurion to go home, and it would be done as he had asked. He left Jesus and returned home. He didn't have a cell phone so that he could call home and make sure the servant was healed. And just in case he wasn't well, maybe he could get Jesus to go ahead and come with him. He just trusted that it was done and left to go home. And when he arrived, he found that the servant had been healed right when Jesus said he would be.

When we receive an answer to our prayers, do we believe it will be done? Do we thank Him and wait expectantly to see it fulfilled or do we continue to worry and fret and try to handle it ourselves until we see the answer. Jesus told Thomas in John 20:29, "Because you have seen me, you have believed; blessed are those who have not seen and yet have believed." (NIV) Lord, let me be like the centurion who believed without seeing. "Let us hold unswervingly to the hope we profess, for He who promised is faithful." Hebrews 10:23 (NIV)

Genesis 21-22
Psalm 7:9-17
Proverbs 1:32-33
Matthew 8:18-34

The Measure of our Faith is Obedience

"Then God said, 'Take your son, your only son, whom you love, Isaac, and go to the region of Moriah. Sacrifice him there as a burnt offering on a mountain I will show you.' Early the next morning Abraham got up and loaded his donkey. He took with him two of his servants and his son Isaac. When he had cut enough wood for the burnt offering, he set out for the place God had told him about." Genesis 22:2-3 NIV

As a parent, I cannot fathom being asked to do what God asked Abraham to do. But it is even more amazing when we look back at Abraham's history. God chose him, set him apart to be the father of a great nation. God told Abraham that He was going to make his descendants as numerous as the stars. Many years passed and still Abraham did not have any children, so Sarah decided to take matters into her own hands and arranged for her servant Hagar to have a child for Abraham. God told Abraham that Ishmael was not the child through whom God would fulfill His promise. Then, when Abraham was 99 years old, Sarah became pregnant and gave birth to a son, Isaac. Abraham had been waiting for this child his whole life. He must have cherished him and loved him dearly. This child was the fulfillment of God's promise to him. God had told him so and he believed God completely. "After waiting patiently, Abraham received what was promised." Hebrews 6:15 (NIV)

Then one day, out of the blue, God tells him to take Isaac to the top of a mountain and sacrifice him as a burnt offering. Abraham must have been absolutely heart broken, confused, angry, and devastated. And yet the Bible says that early the next morning he got up, saddled his donkey, chopped the wood, and set out on his journey. I don't know about you, but when God tells me to do something I don't want to do, I don't typically get up early and start doing it. I like my sleep. I do not like to get up early to do things I enjoy doing, much less something I don't want to do. Not Abraham. He so fully trusted God that he got up early and obeyed. Hebrews 11:19 says, "Abraham reasoned that God could even raise the dead." (NIV) God had told him that through Isaac he would be a great nation with descendants as numerous as the stars, so he believed that somehow, someway God would make it happen. He did what God told him to do, even though it didn't make sense. Fortunately, because of his immediate obedience, God spared Isaac and provided a ram for the sacrifice. If God had not intervened, Abraham would have killed his only son in obedience to God. The measure of our faith is our obedience.

January 12

Genesis 23-24
Psalm 8
Proverbs 2:1-5
Matthew 9:1-17

Majestic

"O Lord, our Lord, how majestic is Your name in all the Earth! When I consider Your heavens, the work of Your fingers, the moon, and the stars, which You have set in place, what is man that You are mindful of him, the son of man that You care for him?" Psalm 8:1, 3-4 ESV

From the time I was six weeks old my mother worked for NASA and when she retired from there, she worked for a space contractor for several years. Needless to say, I have been surrounded by planets, stars, and space exploration my entire life. Growing up it was almost commonplace because I heard about it all the time, but as an adult I have come to recognize and be fascinated by just how amazing the universe really is. I have heard people say that they feel closest to God when they are at the beach looking out over the crystal-clear ocean and listening to the waves beat against the shore. Some feel the Lord's presence hiking in the mountains breathing in the crisp, fresh air and listening to the gentle breeze blowing through the towering trees. But I think I agree with the psalmist; there is nothing that ushers me into the presence of the Lord like staring into the night sky. When I look up on a clear night and see millions of stars lighting up the darkness, I am mesmerized.

David did not have the knowledge that we have today. He could only see the sky with his naked eye. We have the benefit of years of research, satellite technology, space exploration and actual photographic images taken from outer space. We can see the vastness and splendor of God's creation in a way that David couldn't even imagine. But he understood that the God who created the sun, moon, planets, and stars and who continues to keep them in motion cared about him. And He cares about you and me as well. I am only one of nearly seven billion people on a tiny planet called Earth and yet He cares about every detail of my life. "Are not five sparrows sold for two pennies? Yet not one of them is forgotten by God. Indeed, the very hairs on your head are all numbered. Don't be afraid; you are worth more than many sparrows." Luke 12:6-7 (NIV) The majesty of God and the intimacy of God seem to be contradictory and yet both are completely true. Thank You, Jesus, for being mindful of me, a sinner.

Genesis 25-26
Psalm 9:1-6
Proverbs 2:6-8
Matthew 9:18-38

January 13

Like Father, Like Son

"When the men of that place asked him about his wife, he said, 'She is my sister,' because he was afraid to say, 'She is my wife.' He thought, 'The men of this place might kill me on account of Rebekah, because she is beautiful.'" Genesis 26:7 NIV

In Genesis 12:10-20, we find Abraham in Egypt. When the men of the area asked him about Sarai, he lied and told them she was his sister. He was afraid the men would kill him so they could take her. Again, in Genesis 20:1-18, Abraham told Abimelech that Sarah was his sister to protect himself from harm. Abraham had seen God's power and he trusted God completely, but for some reason he felt he had to lie to protect himself from men who might want to kill him to take his wife. In our reading today, we find Isaac, Abraham's beloved son repeating his father's behavior and lying to Abimelech (probably the son or grandson of the king Abraham lied to). Isaac was not born when Abraham and Sarah were in Egypt or when they met Abimelech, but he repeated the sin of his father. He did not trust God to protect him against the men in the area.

I can remember several times when my children were little that they said or did things that I couldn't imagine where they had learned. Unfortunately, I usually could trace it back to something either my husband or I had done. Whether I realized it or not, they were watching everything we did and modeling their behavior after ours. As Christians, we are being watched, not only by our children, but by people all around us. Friends, relatives, co-workers, fellow Christians, and lost people are watching to see how we deal with the joys, sorrows, difficulties, and disappointments of everyday life. They are watching to see if the presence of Jesus in our life makes a difference. They want to know if we are different because the Holy Spirit lives within us. We will mess up sometimes and act in ways that do not please God. We aren't perfect, but there should be a difference. Do people see a difference in you?

Genesis 27-28
Psalm 9:7-12
Proverbs 2:9-10
Matthew 10:1-20

January 14

The Right Words

"Do not worry about what to say or how to say it. At that time, you will be given what to say, for it will not be you speaking, but the Spirit of your Father speaking through you." Matthew 10:19-20 NIV

So often we do not share with people about Jesus because we think we don't know what to say. We are afraid we will not say the right thing, leave something out, or say something that isn't accurate. We are afraid we won't have all the answers to their questions, so we just don't say anything. If we are doing the talking and answering their questions out of our reasoning and understanding, then we will not be effective. The Holy Spirit gives us the words to speak, and the Holy Spirit prepares their heart to hear what we have to say. "This is what we speak, not in words taught us by human wisdom, but in words taught by the Spirit, explaining spiritual realities with spirit-taught words." I Corinthians 2:13 (NIV)

The more time we spend in God's Word and in prayer, the more prepared we will be to share about Jesus with others. We are not better prepared because we have more knowledge and know more Bible verses to tell them, because we have memorized the plan of salvation, or because we have a speech ready to recite whenever someone asks us about Jesus. We are better prepared because we know Jesus better and we have our eyes focused on Him as we go through our day. We are more aware of opportunities to share and His Spirit overflows from within us. When someone asks me about my husband, I can tell them all about him. I can tell them the things he likes and doesn't like, what makes him happy, and what makes him mad. I can tell them how much I love him and how much he loves me. I spend time with him and know him well, so I am excited to tell anyone about him. The more time we spend with Jesus, the easier it is to tell others about Him. Keep your focus on Jesus and when He gives you opportunities to tell others about Him, He will give you the words they need to hear.

January 15

Genesis 29-30
Psalm 9:13-20
Proverbs 2:11-15
Matthew 10:21-42

Unlovely

"Leah conceived, gave birth to a son, and named him Reuben, for she said, 'The Lord has seen my affliction; surely my husband will love me now. She conceived again, gave birth to a son, and said, 'The Lord heard that I am unloved and has given me this son also.' So she named him Simeon. Genesis 29:32-33 HCSB

It breaks my heart to read this passage and hear the pain and heartache in Leah's voice. Her father tricked Jacob into marrying her when he did not love her. He loved her sister, Rachel. She was obviously very well aware of his feelings toward her sister. Jacob had been living in their home for seven years and working to earn the right to marry Rachel. Then when the time came, instead of giving Rachel to him, their father gave him Leah instead. This must have been horrible for all of them. Rachel thought she was going to be married to the man she loved. She was excited and waited for her wedding with great anticipation. Then her father betrayed her and gave her sister what she had longed for. Leah probably wasn't any happier about the situation. She deserved a man who loved her and would cherish her, not one that wished he was with her sister. Talk about sibling rivalry. I've made mistakes as a parent, but this was foolish. You can't really blame Jacob either. This was not what he had agreed to do. He didn't love Leah. He loved Rachel and had worked long and hard for the right to marry her. He was tricked into marrying Leah. He reluctantly agreed, but wasn't happy about it.

Leah felt unloved. She tried desperately to get Jacob to love her by giving him children. Each time she thought, "Surely he will love me now." And each time she was disappointed. She based her worth and dignity on what other people thought of her and how they valued her. God loved Leah and blessed her greatly with six sons and a daughter. He made her the mother of half of the children of Israel, his beloved people. She has a very special place in history and her Heavenly Father loved her very much. We may find ourselves in an unfair situation. We did nothing to get there and can do nothing to get out of it. It is what it is. We may feel unloved and unwanted. But we are not unloved. Our Heavenly Father loves us. He may not remove us from the situation, but He will take care of us, comfort us, provide for us and will accomplish his purposes in and through us. Our value is not based on what other people think of us. Our value is found in who we are in Christ. The Creator of the universe loves us and cares for us. We are of great value, and we are loved more than we can even imagine.

January 16

Genesis 31
Psalm 10:1-11
Proverbs 2:16-19
Matthew 11:1-19

God Has My Back

"For twenty years I have worked in your household—fourteen years for your two daughters and six years for your flocks—and you have changed my wages ten times! If the God of my father, the God of Abraham, the Fear of Isaac, had not been with me, certainly now you would have sent me off empty-handed. But God has seen my affliction and my hard work, and He issued His verdict last night." Genesis 31:41-42 HCSB

WE LIVE IN a world where we have a right to justice and to be treated fairly. Our legal system, while not perfect, is designed to provide an environment where everyone is treated the same. Whether we are rich or poor, young or old, no matter what our race, religion, or sex, we are supposed to have the same rights, protections, and responsibilities under the law. We have come to expect this. Please don't get me wrong, I feel very blessed to have been born in a country where I am afforded this protection under the law. However, we are not always treated fairly. Just like Jacob in the passage above, sometimes we are promised one thing and receive another. Bad things sometimes happen to us through no fault of our own. We will, at some time in our lives, be cheated, lied to, and mistreated. Jesus himself tells us in John 16:33 that in this world we will have trouble. How we react to it is of utmost importance.

My husband is an attorney and spends much of his time helping his clients receive what they are entitled to receive. There is nothing wrong with that. We have an entire system of justice set up for that purpose. The problem comes when we react in ways that are inappropriate and ungodly. Our natural instinct when we have been mistreated is to get angry and demand our rights. We often say and do things in our anger that we later regret. Demanding our way rarely gets the desired result. Our first reaction should be to take our case to God. Our worldly system is not perfect, but His system always gets the right result. It may not be exactly the result we want all the time, but we can be confident that God will bring about justice in one way or another. We need to take our concerns to God and then let Him guide our actions. After we have done what He has led us to do, then we have to leave it in His hands. Exodus 14:14 tells us, "The Lord will fight for you; you need only to be still." (NIV) In Isaiah 41:13 we are assured, "I am the Lord, your God, who takes hold of your right hand and says to you, do not fear; I will help you." (NIV)

Genesis 32-33
Psalm 10:12-18
Proverbs 2:20-22
Matthew 11:20-30

January 17

Burn Out

"Come to Me, all you who are weary and burdened, and I will give you rest. Take my yoke upon you and learn from Me, for I am gentle and humble in heart, and you will find rest for your souls. For My yoke is easy and My burden is light." Matthew 11:28-30 NIV

His yoke is easy and His burden is light. So why is it that we are so weary and burdened? Most of the time we are stressed, overwhelmed, frustrated, and tired. Our lives are not characterized by rest and peace. We are busy people. Most of the things we fill our days with are not bad things. Many of them are even good things. If you look at your calendar in a typical week, you might find work, Bible study, volunteering at your child's school, exercise (that probably wouldn't be on my calendar), attending your child's ballgame, taxiing children to soccer practice, piano lessons, youth group activities, a committee meeting at church, grocery shopping, cleaning house, another Bible study, church on Sunday, church on Wednesday night, doctor's appointment, lunch with a friend, choir practice, date night with your spouse, and the list goes on and on and on and on. If you take any of those things by themselves, they are harmless. They don't take a lot of time and energy and seem to be good things. But when we put them all together, we end up exhausted and burned out. We fill up every minute in our calendar and when someone asks us to do something else, we squeeze it in, too.

Why do we do that? I hate to admit it, but for me I think I have equated busyness with significance. The more responsibility I have, the more things I am involved in, then the more important I am and the more significance my life has. Ouch! Did I just put that on paper? If you asked me, I would argue vehemently that my significance and importance is based on my relationship with Jesus Christ and His work in and through me. Unfortunately, I am afraid my calendar might suggest something else. I think it is time for me (and maybe you) to take a long, hard look at the things I am doing with my time. While they may very well be good things, are they the best things? Am I using my time in the way that God wants me to use my time? This verse promises that His yoke is easy, and His burden is light, so if I am filling my time with the things He wants me to be doing, I will be rested, and my life will be characterized by peace. There may be periods of busyness and stress, but overall, my life will not be so hectic. There is a little two-letter word I seemed to have forgotten how to use---NO!

Genesis 34-35:15
Psalm 11:1-3
Proverbs 3:1-2
Matthew 12:1-21

January 18

Memorials

"Jacob set up a stone pillar at the place where God had talked with him, and he poured out a drink offering on it, and he also poured oil on it. Jacob called the place where God had talked with him Bethel." Genesis 35:14-15 NIV

I LOVE HISTORY. It absolutely fascinates me. I love to visit historic sites and learn about the events that took place there. My idea of a vacation is one in which I have been to a new place and learned something new. My family does not have the same idea of a vacation. They love to go lie on a beach somewhere, sleep late every day and not have an agenda. I have learned to compromise over the years and do enjoy relaxing with a good book. But I still insist on some historical/educational enrichment every now and then. Several years ago, my mother, my daughter, and I went to Paris. We visited typical tourist attractions in the city, but one of my favorite things we did on the trip was visiting Normandy. We rented a car and drove through the French countryside to the beaches at Normandy and the American War Memorial where 9,694 American soldiers are buried. The scene was tranquil and the view over the English Channel was breathtaking. It seems that is the case with most memorials I have visited. They are places of quiet reflection. Those who visit, even small children, seem to sense respect and reverence.

Throughout the Old Testament we find the children of God setting up memorials, places of remembrance. This was usually done after God had acted in a miraculous way on their behalf. They wanted to remember what God had done for them and they wanted everyone who saw the memorial to know that their God was the one true God and that He provides for His children. We have such short memories. God performs in a mighty way in our lives and for a while our faith is strong, but then the worries of our everyday lives creep back in. We forget about all the times He has proven Himself able to handle anything that comes our way. Very early in our marriage, my husband and I learned about Memorial Boxes and decided to make one for our home. The concept comes from these passages and the idea is to set up a memorial to remind us of the times when God has shown Himself faithful to us in an extraordinary way. We have a large shadow box filled with objects/pictures that represent each of those times hanging in our house. It is not only a reminder to us about those times, but also a wonderful teaching opportunity for our children. We have had countless opportunities to share with others who ask about the box filled with strange objects and tell them about our God who loves us and has proven Himself over and over.

Genesis 35:16-36
Psalm 11:4-7
Proverbs 3:3-4
Matthew 12:22-50

January 19

Careless Words

"The good man brings good things out of the good stored up in him, and the evil man brings evil things out of the evil stored up in him. But I tell you that everyone will have to give account on the day of judgment for every empty word they have spoken. For by your words you will be acquitted, and by your words you will be condemned." Matthew 12:35-37 NIV

Jesus Himself tells us that our words are important. The childhood chant that says, "Sticks and stones may break my bones, but words can never hurt me," is far from true. We all remember hurtful things said to us carelessly by others. They may not have even meant the things they said, but the words cut deep, and we can still recall them word for word. 100 people can compliment us and tell us something positive, but if we hear one criticism, we dwell on that and play their words over and over in our mind. The tongue is a powerful weapon, and it is extremely difficult to tame. "All kinds of animals, birds, reptiles and sea creatures are being tamed and have been tamed by mankind, but no human being can tame the tongue. It is a restless evil, full of deadly poison." James 3:7-8 (NIV)

Having personally experienced the destructive power of negative words spoken to or about us, we should be sensitive to the effect our words have on others. "Therefore, encourage one another and build each other up." I Thessalonians 5:11 (NIV) My grandmother used to tell me that if you don't have anything good to say, you shouldn't say anything at all. She was a wise woman. "When words are many, sin is unavoidable, but the one who controls his lips is wise." Proverbs 10:19 (HCSB) Taming the tongue can only be accomplished through prayer and intentional effort. Our natural tendency is to blurt out whatever comes to our mind. It takes deliberate effort to think before we speak. "May the words of my mouth and the meditation of my heart be acceptable to You, Lord, my Rock and my Redeemer." Psalm 19:14 (HCSB)

January 20

Genesis 37
Psalm 12:1-4
Proverbs 3:5-6
Matthew 13:1-23

Trust

"Trust in the Lord with all your heart and lean not on your own understanding; in all your ways submit to Him and He will make your paths straight." Proverbs 3:5-6 NIV

This is a passage that is familiar to most Christians. Many of us even have it memorized. It can be found on plaques, bookmarks, and bumper stickers. Myriad sermons have been preached on the topic and numerous books have been written on it. But how many of us put it into practice? Do we really trust in the Lord with all our hearts? Do we rely on the guidance of the Holy Spirit even when we don't understand? Do we acknowledge Him in ALL our ways? Our God is completely faithful and trustworthy. He knows everything. He knows what is going on around us that we cannot see. He knows our past and our future. He truly knows what is best for us. And He wants us to know what that is. He's not trying to keep it from us. But we must ask. We must submit to Him in all our ways, and He will make our paths straight.

Nothing is too small to talk to God about. If we ask Him about all the little things, we can often avoid bigger problems arising. Whenever we have a decision to make, our first order of business should be to pray and ask for God's guidance. Acknowledging Him in every situation makes us receptive to His guidance. When we focus our eyes and our mind on Jesus, He can lead us and help us make the right decisions in every circumstance. Our part is to trust and acknowledge. He will do the rest.

Genesis 38
Psalm 12:5-8
Proverbs 3:7-8
Matthew 13:24-58

January 21

Side By Side

"But while everyone was sleeping his enemy came and sowed weeds among the wheat and went away. When the wheat sprouted and formed heads, then the heads also appeared... The weeds are the sons of the evil one, and the enemy who sows them is the devil." Matthew 13:25, 26, 38-39 NIV

Sometimes I wish that I could just go somewhere and shut myself away with my Christian friends and family members and be apart from the corruption and evil I see in the world. I used to be an avid news junkie. I watched the news all the time. It was the first thing I turned on in the morning and I watched it before I went to bed at night. I even set my computer to alert me of breaking news stories. But I found that it made me depressed, so I have slowly backed off. I still turn it on for the headlines, but it does not consume me. Watching all the stories about murders, wars, riots, politicians involved in immoral or illegal activities, and so on and so on makes me ask God when will enough be enough. When my girls were little, I remember times when they would be arguing, and I would tell them to stop. They would keep arguing and I would tell them again. After a few times I would finally get to the point where I raised my voice and would tell them that it was enough. They knew they had pushed me to the limit, and they better stop. It was over.

Fortunately, God is much more patient than I am. If I was God, I would have returned long ago to put an end to all the evil in the world and set up a "new Heaven and a new Earth." As in the parable we looked at today, all the sons of the evil one would be removed and thrown into the fire and the devil himself would be eliminated permanently. What a glorious day that will be when Satan is no longer able to influence anyone and when there will be no more sin and evil in the world. God's mercy and grace are evident as He tarries, not wanting any to perish, but all to come to repentance. "He is patient with you, not wanting anyone to perish, but everyone to come to repentance." 2 Peter 3:9 (NIV) Until that day, we must remain in the world as salt and light. We must live our lives in a way that will influence others to come to Christ. We cannot remove ourselves from the world, but we can live in a way that sets us apart from it.

Genesis 39-40
Psalm 13
Proverbs 3:9-10
Matthew 14:1-21

January 22

I Don't Understand

"Joseph's master took him and put him in prison, the place where the king's prisoners were confined. The chief cupbearer, however, did not remember Joseph; he forgot him." Genesis 39:20, 40:23 NIV

Joseph did everything right. When faced with temptation, he not only avoided the sin, but he also ran from it. Potiphar's wife was apparently not used to being told no and she decided to lie and say that Joseph had tried to force himself on her. Understandably, her husband had Joseph thrown in prison. Even there, God showed him favor and he was put in charge of the other men who were being held in prison. His true nature and his integrity were evident despite the false accusations. Genesis 39:23 tells us that "the Lord was with Joseph and gave him success in whatever he did." (NIV) Sometime later, Joseph was given the opportunity to interpret the dreams of the chief cupbearer and baker. He was hoping this would provide the way out of prison for him. Unfortunately, this was not the case because the cupbearer forgot him, and he would have to remain in prison for 2 more years.

This must have been a very difficult time for Joseph. He could not see how God was working. He couldn't see that he needed to be thrown in prison to meet the cupbearer and interpret his dream. He couldn't see that after 2 full years the cupbearer would remember him and tell Pharoah about him. He didn't know that he would have the opportunity to interpret Pharoah's dream and would be put in charge of all of Egypt or that God would use him to preserve his family during the famine and establish them into His chosen nation. Joseph could not see what was going to happen. But God could see. A couple of days ago we looked at Proverbs 3:5-6. It says to trust in the Lord and not to rely on our own understanding. If Joseph relied on his understanding, he would certainly have lost hope. He could not see that God had a plan and was working out the details. But he trusted God and God used him in a mighty way. It gives me great comfort to know that even when I don't understand, He has it all figured out.

January 23

Genesis 41-42
Psalm 14
Proverbs 3:11-12
Matthew 14:22-36

Fixing Our Eyes on Jesus

"Then Peter got out of the boat, walked on the water and came toward Jesus. But when he saw the wind, he was afraid and, beginning to sink, cried out, 'Lord, save me!'" Matthew 14:29-30 NIV

It is so easy to lose our focus. We can be in a place where we are walking with the Lord and things are going well. We step out in faith and are doing things that we never thought possible. Like Peter, we are walking on water. Then suddenly our attention is diverted. We take our eyes off Jesus and start to think about all those waves. The second that happens we start looking at the problems around us. When our eyes and our mind are focused on Jesus, our problems are still there. They haven't disappeared, but they are in perspective. We can view them through His lenses and we see that He will help us face whatever comes our way. We are also able to see His hand at work in us and in our circumstances to accomplish His purposes. We may not enjoy the process, but we can know that He will work in all things to bring about good for us. Whatever happens in our lives He will use to grow us into the person He has intended us to be. When I am facing difficulty, especially when I don't understand why or even what is going on, it is extremely comforting to know that there is a purpose. It is much easier to endure difficulties if I know that it is accomplishing something, even if I don't know what it is. If I feel that my difficulties are random and have no purpose, it is much more difficult to persevere. When I am focused on Jesus and spending time in His presence my circumstances may not change, but my perspective will be radically different. The wind was still blowing and there were waves all around Peter as He walked to Jesus. As long as he kept his eyes on Jesus, he had no trouble walking on the water, but as soon as he took his eyes off Jesus and looked at the waves, he began to sink. As soon as we begin to focus on our problems, we begin to sink further into the depths of fear and worry. Our mind will race further and further down the path of what ifs and if only.

Fortunately, we only must cry out, "Lord, save me," and He will reach out His hand to pull us up. "Let us fix our eyes on Jesus, the author and perfecter of our faith." Hebrews 12:2 (NASB1995) May we have our attention so fixed on Him that we cannot be distracted by anything.

January 24

Genesis 43
Psalm 15
Proverbs 3:13-14
Matthew 15:1-20

Integrity

"He whose walk is blameless and who does what is righteous, who speaks the truth from their heart; whose tongue utters no slander, who does no wrong to a neighbor, and casts no slur on others, who despises a vile person but honors those who fear the Lord, who keeps an oath even when it hurts, and does not change their mind; who lends money to the poor without interest; who does not accept a bribe against the innocent. Whoever does these things will never be shaken." Psalm 15:2-5 NIV

INTEGRITY IS SO rare these days that when someone acts in the manner described above, we are suspicious. We wonder what their ulterior motives might be. It is no longer normal to expect people to be honest and to do what they say they are going to do. A man's word and his handshake used to mean something. Unfortunately, it has become accepted to change our minds and do whatever best suits our needs at the time. Our commitments can be counted on until we get a better offer or as long as it is convenient for us. Worldly standards and expectations may have changed, but God's Word has not changed and His expectations of us remain. As Christians, we live by a higher standard. God expects us to be honest and blameless. He expects us to "conduct ourselves in a manner worthy of the gospel of Christ." Philippians 1:27 (NIV) If we tell someone we are going to do something, He expects us to do it even when it hurts. Psalm 15:5 tells us that he who does these things will never be shaken and Philippians 1:27 says that we will be able to stand firm. Are you easily swayed by circumstances or your own whims and desires? Or are you someone who can be trusted to do the right thing and be honest in every situation? "Search me, God, and know my heart; test me and know my anxious thoughts. See if there is any offensive way in me and lead me in the way everlasting." Psalm 139:23-24 (NIV)

Genesis 44
Psalm 16:1-6
Proverbs 3:15-16
Matthew 15:21-39

January 25

My Portion

"Lord, You are my portion and my cup of blessing; You hold my future."
Psalm 16:5 HCSB

THIS VERSE IS a source of great comfort. You, Lord, hold my future. I have no way of knowing what tomorrow will bring. I do not know how many tomorrows I have. I can plan and prepare for what I think tomorrow will hold. We are told often in scripture to be wise and plan for our future. We should be diligent and good stewards of the resources God has blessed us with today and use those resources to help plan for our future. But in doing so, we should not "lean on our own understanding, but we should submit to Him in all our decisions so that He can direct our paths." Proverbs 3:5-6 (NIV) He can see our tomorrows and He can direct our steps today to prepare us for our tomorrows. Even though we cannot know the future, by following His leading we can go into tomorrow confidently knowing that He has gone before us and prepared the way for us. He has planned each of our steps to make sure that we are fully equipped to meet the needs of tomorrow. This is true from a monetary standpoint, but it is even more true from an emotional and spiritual standpoint. He is putting things into our life today that will develop qualities and attributes that we will need to equip us for what our tomorrows hold. If, however, we are not acknowledging Him today and we are leaving Him out of our decisions and plans, we are not benefitting from His wisdom, and we will be ill-equipped to face our tomorrows. He is my portion and my cup of blessing. I do not want to miss out on what He has planned for me.

January 26

Genesis 45-46
Psalm 16:7-11
Proverbs 3:17-18
Matthew 16

Perspective

"Then Joseph said to his brothers, 'Come close to me.' When they had done so, he said, 'I am your brother Joseph, the one you sold into Egypt! And now, do not be distressed and do not be angry with yourselves for selling me here, because it was to save lives that God sent me ahead of you... So then, it was not you who sent me here, but God." Genesis 45:4-5, 8 NIV

"I keep the Lord in mind always. Because He is at my right hand, I will not be defeated." Psalm 16:8 HCSB

We have mentioned several times in the last month that God may not change our circumstances, but He will change our perspective if we keep our eyes focused on Him. There is no better example of this than is seen in today's reading. Joseph had his eyes and mind focused on God. His brothers had beaten him, thrown him in a pit and left him to die. Then they decided to make a little profit, so they sold him into slavery. Joseph could have easily been filled with anger and bitterness toward his brothers. He could have spent those years in prison plotting his revenge and planning for the day when he could get them back for what they did to him. They deserved to be put to death. They deserved the same treatment they had given him. Now, after all those years they had shown up needing help and Joseph was able to do whatever he wanted to do to them. He could have had them beaten and thrown in prison. At the very least, he could have sent them away to die in the famine. But that was not his response to them. His response was forgiveness and mercy. He was overwhelmed with joy to see them. He was able to see his life from God's perspective and not his own and to see that God had orchestrated the events, even the bad things his brothers did to him, to place him in the position to save his family from the famine in the land. That is not a natural response. He had his eyes focused on God.

Joseph, like the Psalmist kept the Lord in his mind always. God was at his right hand leading him and guiding his steps. He was able to respond to his brothers in the way that God wanted him to respond because God was constantly before him. He wasn't driven by his fleshly emotions. His actions were guided by God's still small voice. That was only possible because he maintained constant communication and blessed fellowship with his Father, and He had complete faith in God.

Genesis 47-48
Psalm 17:1-5
Proverbs 3:19-20
Matthew 17

January 27

God's Way

"Joseph said to his father, 'Not that way, my father! This one is the firstborn. Put your right hand on his head.' But his father refused and said, 'I know, my son, I know! He too will become a tribe, and he too will be great; nevertheless, his younger brother will be greater than he, and his offspring will become a populous nation." Genesis 48:18-19 HCSB

JOSEPH HAD BROUGHT his sons before their grandfather to receive a blessing. He thought he knew exactly how it would happen. As was the custom in the day, he expected his father to place his right hand on his eldest son's head and bless him first and then give the younger son, Ephraim, a "lesser" blessing. He expected Manasseh to be the greatest because he was his firstborn. This seems odd. Of all people, you would think that Joseph would understand that the firstborn son isn't always chosen to accomplish God's purposes. Joseph was the eleventh son of Jacob. So often we think we know best. We think we have it all figured out. It seems obvious to us. That is just the time when God often steps in and does something totally unexpected. "As the heavens are higher than the Earth, so are My ways higher than your ways, and My thoughts than your thoughts." Isaiah 55:9 (NIV) It is in those times that we have to step back and just trust. Even when it doesn't seem to make sense, we have to trust that He really does know best, and His ways are higher than our ways. His sovereignty and foreknowledge give Him a vantage point that we do not have. When we place our complete trust in Him, He will never lead us wrong.

Genesis 49-50
Psalm 17:6-9
Proverbs 3:21-23
Matthew 18

January 28

Forgiveness

"Then Peter came to Him and asked, 'Lord, how many times shall I forgive my brother or sister who sins against me? Up to seven times?' Jesus answered, 'I tell you, not seven times, but seventy-seven times.

"Then the master called the servant in, 'You wicked servant,' he said, 'I canceled all that debt of yours because you begged me to. Shouldn't you have had mercy on your fellow servant just as I had on you?' In anger his master handed him over to the jailers to be tortured, until he should pay back all he owed. This is how my Heavenly Father will treat each of you unless you forgive your brother or sister from your heart." Matthew 18:21-22, 32-35 NIV

THE BIBLICAL PRINCIPLE of forgiveness is very clear. It is not based on whether the person who has committed the offense is deserving of forgiveness. It has nothing to do with that. So often we get caught up in the idea that the person has done nothing to merit our forgiving them. They may not have asked for forgiveness or in any way even acknowledged that they are wrong. If our extending forgiveness to someone is based on their actions, then we would rarely have to forgive anyone. We could hold on to the bitterness and resentment toward that person indefinitely. But that is not what scripture says. We are to forgive whatever offense is done to us, because we have been forgiven by our Heavenly Father. Just as they are not deserving of our forgiveness, we are not deserving of the forgiveness God has given us. We have been forgiven much by our Master so we should be quick to forgive others.

This is much easier said than done. We have an innate desire for justice where others are concerned, but we want mercy for ourselves. We want them to pay for the sin they committed against us, and to acknowledge their wrong and beg us for forgiveness. We even make it sound more noble by saying that if they don't acknowledge their sin, then they cannot learn from their mistakes. We think that if we let them off the hook by forgiving them, then they will never learn and they will keep acting the same way. That may be true. But that is not what scripture teaches us. Jesus himself tells us to forgive over and over and over. There is no caveat that says we are to forgive when someone asks us to forgive them, or forgive when the person pays for their sin, or even to forgive when they acknowledge their wrong. We are instructed to forgive because we have been forgiven much. It has nothing to do with their actions at all. We must forgive and leave the rest to God.

Exodus 1-2
Psalm 17:10-13
Proverbs 3:24-26
Matthew 19

January 29

The Divine Architect

"God heard their groaning and He remembered His covenant with Abraham, with Isaac and with Jacob. So God looked on the Israelites and was concerned about them." Exodus 2:24-25 NIV

Exodus 1 and 2 are very comforting passages to me. At the end of chapter 2 we see the Israelites groaning to God and crying out to Him in their slavery asking Him to help. This came as no surprise to Him. He wasn't up in Heaven carrying on His daily routine and all the sudden heard them cry out to Him. He didn't suddenly have to come up with a plan to save them. He had been preparing for it all along. Forty years earlier a baby was born in Egypt to a Hebrew woman. His mother placed him in a basket and put him in the Nile to avoid being killed along with all the other Hebrew boys. He was found by Pharaoh's daughter and raised in Pharaoh's palace. God was preparing Moses from birth to deliver His people from the bondage of slavery. He had a blueprint, and He worked His divine plan so that at the time that the Israelites cried out to Him in their bondage, He had Moses ready to step in and deliver them. His plan and His timing are always perfect.

It is no less that way in our lives today. God knows what my needs are today, and He has prepared for all of them. He also knows what my needs will be in the future, and He is preparing events and circumstances in my life today to meet those needs. I can go forward in confidence knowing that the Divine Architect has gone before me and that His timing and plan is perfect.

January 30

Exodus 3-4
Psalm 17:14-15
Proverbs 3:27-28
Matthew 20

God With Us

"And God said, 'I will be with you.' God said to Moses, 'I Am Who I Am.' This is what you are to say to the Israelites; 'I Am has sent me to you.' God also said to Moses, 'Say to the Israelites, The Lord, the God of your fathers—the God of Abraham, the God of Isaac, and the God of Jacob—has sent me to you. This is my name forever, the name by which I am to be remembered from generation to generation." Exodus 3:12, 14-15 NIV

Whatever God calls us to do, we can know that He will be with us. The task before Moses, seemed impossible. It must have seemed crazy. He had fled Egypt because he murdered an Egyptian and Pharaoh was trying to kill him. Now God was asking him to go to Pharaoh and ask him to let the Israelites go. And just as crazy was the idea that the Israelites would follow him. He was born as a Hebrew boy but had been raised in the palace by Pharaoh's daughter. Why would the Israelites trust him? We look at the exchange between God and Moses now and wonder how Moses could question God. But I dare say, most of us would have had the exact same reaction. If truth be told, we often have that exact same reaction when God asks us to do something that we don't understand. We question God and tell Him that we can't possibly do what He is asking us to do. We tell Him that surely someone else can do it; surely there is someone better suited to the task.

God will never ask us to do something that He does not fully equip us to do. God does not call the equipped. He does not look at all the people in the world and decide who is best equipped to do His task. He equips the called. He decides who He wants to use and then He equips them. And He goes even further. He does not prepare us, give us a good pep talk, and send us out to do the task He has assigned to us. He prepares us spiritually, mentally, physically, and emotionally and then He goes with us. He is before us leading the way, beside us holding our right hand, and behind us protecting us. Whatever task He calls us to, He gives us everything we need to accomplish that task. He is God with us.

January 31

Exodus 5-6
Psalm 18:1-6
Proverbs 3:29-32
Matthew 21:1-17

Expectation

"Then the Lord said to Moses, 'Now you will see what I will do to Pharaoh. Because of My mighty hand, he will let them go; because of My mighty hand he will drive them out of his country...Moreover, I have heard the groaning of the Israelites, who the Egyptians are enslaving, and I have remembered My covenant. Therefore, say to the Israelites: I am the Lord, and I will bring you out from under the yoke of the Egyptians. I will free you from being slaves to them and I will redeem you with an outstretched arm and with mighty acts of judgment." Exodus 6:1, 5-6 NIV

"In my distress I called to the Lord; I cried to my God for help. From His temple He heard my voice; my cry came before Him, into His ears." Psalm 18:6 NIV

WE SERVE A God who hears us. Throughout scripture, we see accounts of God hearing His people and answering their cries. He is not a far-off God who does not care about the concerns of His people. He listens for us. He hears us when we call. And when He hears us, He answers. The answer may be to do what we asked, it may be to tell us to wait a while until He has finished His work in and around us, or it may be no. We may not like the answer, but He will answer us. When we have presented our requests to God, we are to wait in hopeful anticipation of His answer. So often we present our requests to God and then we continue to hold on to the problem and try to fix it ourselves, or we wait anxiously and fearfully.

The Lord told Moses that now he would see what He would do to Pharaoh. Now he would see. They had suffered and labored under Pharaoh for many years and now it was time to see what God was going to do. We can have that same confidence when God has answered our prayer. Even when we can't see the answer, we can wait in hopeful expectation knowing that God will hear from Heaven and will act on our behalf. His timing is often different from what we want, but it is always what is best for us.

February 1

Exodus 7-8
Psalm 18:7-12
Proverbs 3:33-35
Matthew 21:18-27

Faith to Move a Mountain

> "Jesus replied, 'Truly I tell you, if you have faith and do not doubt, not only can you do what was done to the fig tree, but also you can say to this mountain, 'Go throw yourself into the sea,' and it will be done. If you believe, you will receive whatever you ask for in prayer." Matthew 21:21-22 NIV

THERE ARE LOTS of possible theological meanings that can be drawn from the incident with Jesus and the fig tree. A fig tree that was filled with leaves should be bearing fruit. It looked good from a distance, but when Jesus got close and looked for something to eat, there was no fruit on it. He had just left the temple that was filled with religious leaders who looked great on the outside. They had the appearance of being very spiritual and godly, but when you looked closely, they had no fruit. This seems to be an obvious lesson He could teach His disciples, but He chose to talk to them about faith. He told His disciples that if they believed, whatever they asked for in prayer would be accomplished. He wanted them to bear fruit. He wanted their faith to be substantive and have depth and power. He did not want them to be like the religious leaders who looked good on the outside, but whose prayers were meaningless because they lacked faith. He got down to the real heart of the matter. He wanted them to understand that performing miracles and seeing God accomplish amazing things in and through your life has nothing to do with how spiritual and religious you look on the outside. It comes through faith and faith alone. And that kind of faith comes through intimate, personal knowledge of Him through prayer. That kind of faith can say to a mountain, "Go throw yourself into the sea," and it will be done.

February 2

Exodus 9-10
Psalm 18:13-19
Proverbs 4:1-2
Matthew 21:28-46

Freedom

"He brought me out into a spacious place; He rescued me because He delighted in me." Psalm 18:19 NIV

"He brought me out into a spacious place" seems like a strange use of words until we consider where David had been. For some time, David had been hiding in the wilderness of Judea. This was a desolate area, with bare hills and deep, rough valleys. There were steep cliffs of rocks in many shapes and sizes with caves and plenty of hiding places. David and his men spent almost six years hiding from Saul. I always enjoyed playing hide and seek as a kid, but I remember one time when I was playing with some friends that I did not enjoy it very much. There were some bushes and trees along the fences that separated our houses in the back. I had decided to crawl in between them to hide. It took some effort to get back in there where I was hidden, but I was quite proud of myself for finding the best hiding place ever. I waited and waited very quietly. I could hear my friends searching, but I kept quiet. After a while, they all went to other yards to search. I tried to get out to run to "home base" where I would be safe, but I was stuck. No matter how hard I tried, I could not free myself from between the bushes and the fence. I began to yell but found out later that my friends had all been called home for lunch and thought I had gone home as well. After several hours of sitting there crying (well ok, it was only about 30 minutes, but it felt like hours) my grandmother came looking for me and helped me escape the bushes. I was so relieved to be free after being cramped up in that little space that I ran all the way home. I cannot imagine being cramped up in caves and hiding behind rocks afraid for my life for six years. David must have felt tremendous joy and relief when God brought him into a wide-open space where he didn't have to worry about being attacked. He was safe. When God rescues us from our enemies and from the fear and anxiety that entangles us, we are free. We can be exposed and laid bare before Him because we are safe in His hands. He desires to rescue us because He delights in us and wants us to experience freedom and peace.

Exodus 11-12
Psalm 18:20-24
Proverbs 4:3-4
Matthew 22:1-22

February 3

Obedience

> "All the Israelites did just what the Lord had commanded Moses and Aaron. And on that very day the Lord brought the Israelites out of Egypt by their divisions."
> Exodus 12:50-51 NIV

THE ISRAELITES FOLLOWED the Lord's instructions completely. They did exactly as He told them, and they were rescued. After 430 years in Egypt, God brought 600,000 men plus women and children out from the bondage of slavery. They did not have to fight Pharaoh's army or sneak away in the middle of the night. They were begged to leave, and they didn't leave empty-handed. The Egyptians gave them gold and silver, clothing, and everything they were going to need to build and furnish the tabernacle in the desert. After years of living in bondage to these people, the Egyptians were now giving them everything they owned just to get them to leave. The Israelites obeyed God's instructions and then sat back and watched in amazement as God performed a miracle on their behalf. It must have seemed impossible that God could rescue them, but they did as they were told. How often do we miss out on the miracles God wants to perform in our lives because we fail to obey His instructions to us? When we don't understand what He is saying, it just doesn't make sense to us or we don't like what He is telling us we stall, rationalize, or ignore Him hoping He will change His mind. Then when things don't turn out right, we blame Him, or we run to Him to clean up the mess. In this instance the Israelites obeyed. As we read further, we will see that there were many times when they followed their own way and got into trouble. Whenever they were obedient, God was with them, and their path was smooth. May we always be obedient to His leading.

February 4

Exodus 13-14
Psalm 18:25-29
Proverbs 4:5-6
Matthew 22:23-46

The Greatest Commandment

"Jesus replied, 'Love the Lord your God with all your heart and with all your soul and with all your mind. This is the first and greatest commandment.' Matthew 22:37-38 NIV

As Christians, we are often so concerned with doing great things for God and accomplishing things in His name that we forget about loving Him. We get so caught up in serving and doing that we have very little time and energy left for Him. It is easier I think to do things for God than to be with Him. In the last year, God has shown me that my busyness has often been a substitute for intimacy with Him. I am a type A personality and very goal oriented. Give me a task and I will get it done. Although I probably would not have admitted it, spending lengthy times in prayer and fellowship with God seemed a waste of my time. I felt almost guilty when I spent long periods of time in prayer because I had so many other things I needed to be doing. And if I am totally honest, most of my time with God was rushed and lacking in true intimacy. He has shown me that He is far more interested in spending time with me and revealing Himself to me than He is in any task or act of service I might do for Him. He is teaching me that time spent with Him is the best and most productive use of my time. Time alone with Him will prepare me to serve Him. If He is not preparing me then I am struggling to accomplish things on my strength and abilities. The only way I can love God with all my heart, soul and mind is to get to know Him and the only way to get to know Him is to spend time with Him every day.

My husband and I met at church. We did things with our singles group for a couple of months before we started dating. We knew a lot about each other, but we did not really know each other. When we started dating, we spent time alone together talking and getting to know each other. We both knew very quickly that we wanted to get married and believed that God brought us together. When we got married a few short months later, I know I loved him, but after thirty-one years together I love him so much more. I know him deeply and intimately. I know what he likes and what he doesn't like. I know what makes him happy and what makes him angry. We have been through good times and bad times. The time together has developed our love for each other. This is true of our relationship with God as well. We cannot truly love God without spending time to get to know Him.

Exodus 15-16
Psalm 18:30-36
Proverbs 4:7-9
Matthew 23:1-22

February 5

Humility

"The greatest among you will be your servant. For those who exalt themselves will be humbled, and those who humble themselves will be exalted." Matthew 23:11-12 NIV

THIS VERSE SEEMS to be in direct conflict with what we are taught in our society. We are told that we deserve the best, we should demand our rights, and we have to do whatever it takes to get ahead. If we don't toot our own horn, then who will? The idea of humility, especially for women, is demeaning and degrading. Everyone is concerned about having healthy self-esteem and we have mistakenly equated humility with low self-esteem. Our value and worth is not based on our accomplishments or abilities. It is not based on who we are, but on whose we are. As Christians, we are children of the King. The God of the universe is our Father. We haven't done anything to deserve to be called His children and yet He has adopted us as His own. As we humbly accept our position, we can see others in the way God sees them. And love them with the love that God has for them.

Jesus, who Himself was God the Son, said, "For even the Son of Man did not come to be served, but to serve, and to give his life as a ransom for many." Mark 10:45 (NIV) Jesus spent His time on Earth serving others. If anyone had the right to demand to be served, it was Him. He was God Almighty and yet He put that aside because of His love for us. As we draw close to Him, we can see ourselves for the sinful beings that we are. If we look around us, we may think that we measure up ok until we realize that our standard is Jesus. When we recognize our own sinfulness, we can grasp what He has done for us and humbly seek to share that with others so that they too can know His amazing love.

February 6

Exodus 17-18
Psalm 18:37-42
Proverbs 4:10-13
Matthew 23:23-39

Support

"As long as Moses held up his hands, the Israelites were winning, but whenever he lowered his hands, the Amalekites were winning. When Moses' hands grew tired, they took a stone and put it under him, and he sat on it. Aaron and Hur held his hands up—one on one side, one on the other—so that his hands remained steady till sunset." Exodus 17:11-12 NIV

I FEEL SO blessed to have many precious, godly friends. Looking back over my life, I can see that God placed different people in my life at just the right time to help me through whatever I was experiencing. And He has allowed me the privilege of being available at just the right time to help friends who needed me. He does not expect us to go through this journey alone. God provided Moses with Aaron to help him lead the people in the wilderness. David had Jonathan. Even Jesus had twelve disciples to walk with Him in ministry. We are here to hold each other's arms up. It may take the form of hours of prayer on behalf of a friend who has strayed, a shoulder to cry on when her marriage is falling apart, or holding her hand as she battles cancer or faces the death of a loved one. It may be a gentle reminder to seek God's wisdom before making a decision, or a Bible verse to help guide her in the right direction. It may be hours spent in God's Word together trying to figure out what He is telling you to do. Ecclesiastes 4:10 tells us "If either of them falls down, one can help the other up. But pity anyone who falls and has no one to help them up." (NIV)

Thank God today for the friends He has given you. Ask Him to show you ways you can hold up the arms of your friends to help them accomplish God's purposes. When God calls us to complete a task for Him, He will provide other people to help us along the way. Sometimes that may mean setting aside our own agenda for a while to help someone else, or it may mean putting aside our pride and accepting help from others.

Exodus 19-20
Psalm 18:43-50
Proverbs 4:14-17
Matthew 24:1-14

February 7

The Ten Commandments

"You shall have no other gods before Me. You shall not make for yourself an image in the form of anything... You shall not misuse the name of the Lord your God... Remember the Sabbath Day and keep it holy...Honor your father and mother... You shall not murder...You shall not commit adultery... You shall not steal... You shall not give false testimony against your neighbor... You shall not covet." Exodus 20:3-17 NIV

So much controversy surrounds the Ten Commandments. For decades they were proudly displayed in courthouses throughout our country as the principles on which our legal system was founded. Now they have been taken down and cast aside as narrow-minded and offensive. If we examine them, we see that they pretty much cover everything. The first four deal with our relationship with God. If we recognize that He and He alone is God, we are not to allow anything to come before Him, we respect Him and His name, and set aside time regularly to spend worshipping and seeking Him, then most everything else will fall into place.

The next six commandments deal with our relationships with other people. If we honor others and treat them with respect, do not take what does not belong to us, and are always honest, our lives will be much simpler and happier. The principles God gave the Israelites are not a set of rules that we must follow to be saved. Rather, they are guidelines He has given us that will help us live a full and meaningful life that is filled with joy and peace. John 10:10 says, "I am come that they may have life, and have it to the full." (NIV) We would do well to examine them and apply them to our lives and not discard them as antiquated or only intended for the children of Israel.

February 8

Exodus 21-22
Psalm 19:1-6
Proverbs 4:18-19
Matthew 24:15-35

Glory

"The heavens declare the glory of God; the skies proclaim the work of His hands. Day after day they pour forth speech; night after night they display knowledge. They have no speech; they use no words. Their voice goes out into all the Earth; their words to the ends of the world." Psalm 19:1-4 NIV

As I write this, I am sitting on the balcony in my hotel room overlooking the ocean. A tropical storm came through over the weekend and the outer bands are now making their way north. Violent winds have blown over trees and scattered debris over the normally pristine beaches. The winds are still heavy, and the waves are crashing against the shore with amazing intensity. I love the ocean. I could sit for hours watching the waves roll in and out. Even with the winds blowing fiercely around me, it is strangely peaceful. I think it is because I feel the Lord's presence. The waves and the wind seem to shout the glory of the Lord just as today's verses tell us that the heavens and the sky declare the glory of God. All creation testifies to the power and majesty of the God who created it. He is above all, over all, and beyond all. The waves and wind do not need speech to tell of His awesome power. The sun, moon and stars do not need speech to testify to his brilliant majesty. How much more has He done for us? He sent His beloved Son to Earth to die on a cross to pay for my sins. He has forgiven all my sin and I stand before Him purified and washed clean. May my words declare His glory and testify to what He has done for me.

February 9

Exodus 23-24
Psalm 19:7-14
Proverbs 4:20-22
Matthew 24:36-51

Wisdom

"The law of the Lord is perfect, refreshing the soul. The statutes of the Lord are trustworthy, making wise the simple. The precepts of the Lord are right, giving joy to the heart. The commands of the Lord are radiant, giving light to the eyes. The fear of the Lord is pure, enduring forever. The decrees of the Lord are firm, and all of them are righteous. They are more precious than gold, than much pure gold; they are sweeter than honey, than honey from the honeycomb. By them your servant is warned; in keeping them there is great reward." Psalm 19:7-11 NIV

God's Word is our guidebook, our instruction manual if you will. I really like instructions. I am very organized and methodical so if you give me step-by-step directions, I can usually figure them out. I don't skip ahead past the instructions I think I already know. I follow them precisely. This sometimes takes longer, but in the end, it is done right. Often, God's instructions to us are difficult. He rarely lets us take short cuts. He doesn't let us skip over the parts we think are unnecessary. The process is just as important as the result. By following His statutes and commands, He is molding us into the person He wants us to be. He is shaping us and teaching us to trust Him and to obey Him.

As Christians, we have the benefit of the Word of God to guide our way. The Old Testament believers had the scriptures to follow as well. But we also have the Holy Spirit, who lives within us to lead and guide us. "But the Advocate, the Holy Spirit, whom the Father will send in My name, will teach you all things and will remind you of everything I have said to you." John 14:26 (NIV) We have God's Word and the Holy Spirit with us continually to lead and guide us through any situation we may face. So often, unfortunately we do not take the time to read the manual. We rush ahead thinking we know what we are doing, and we find ourselves in a mess. We need to be in the Word daily and we need to be constantly listening to that still small voice. "Whether you turn to the right or to the left, your ears will hear a voice behind you, saying, 'This is the way; walk in it.'" Isaiah 30:21 (NIV) He rarely shouts to get our attention. We have to seek Him and slow down long enough to listen for the answer.

February 10

Exodus 25-26
Psalm 20
Proverbs 4:23-24
Matthew 25:1-13

Where Do I Place My Trust?

"Some trust in chariots and some in horses, but we trust in the name of the Lord our God. They are brought to their knees and fall, but we rise up and stand firm. Lord, give victory to the king! Answer us when we call!" Psalm 20:7-9 NIV

THESE VERSES HAVE really come home to me in the last several months. I have had to examine my life and let the Lord reveal to me that I place far too much trust in the horses and chariots that this world offers. Peace and joy do not come from things. I would have told you I believed that before, but He has graciously shown me that I put too much emphasis on financial security. I believe it is important to be good stewards of the money He has entrusted to us, but we cannot place our security and trust in anything other than Christ. The things of this world can be taken away in an instant. A global pandemic, economic lockdowns, racial and political unrest, fear, and uncertainty have rocked our world this year. Our relationship with the Lord is the only thing that cannot be taken from us. "The Lord is my rock, my fortress and my deliverer; my God is my rock, in whom I take refuge, my shield and the horn of my salvation, my stronghold." Psalm 18:2 (NIV) He alone is worthy of my trust. Nothing I face surprises Him. He has either allowed it or has caused it to come into my life and He will help me deal with it. Peace and joy come from giving Him control, allowing Him to guide my steps, and trusting that He knows what He is doing. He loves me completely and unconditionally and will always make the decisions that are in my best interest.

February 11

Exodus 27
Psalm 21:1-7
Proverbs 4:25-27
Matthew 25:14-30

The Straight Path

"Let your eyes look straight ahead; fix your gaze directly before you. Give careful thought to the paths for your feet and be steadfast in all your ways. Do not turn to the right or the left; keep your foot from evil." Proverbs 4:25-27 NIV

My prayer has often been, "Lord please keep me on Your path. I do not want to be even one step off. I want to be right in the center of Your will." I love this passage because it perfectly conveys my prayer. Hebrews 12:1 tells us to fix our eyes on Jesus, the author and perfecter of our faith. We are so easily distracted. We so often take our eyes off Jesus and look at the problems around us. When Peter was walking on the water, as long as he was looking at Jesus, he was fine, but when he began to look at the waves around him, he began to sink. When we keep our focus on Jesus and trust Him to help us with whatever we are facing, we are able to stay above the water, but when we begin to look around, we get stressed and anxious and begin to sink.

We are also easily distracted by the things of the world around us. Satan knows exactly how to make sin enticing. It rarely looks evil with skull and crossbones warning us not to go near. He dresses it up to look harmless so that we follow him down the path and end up at a place we never thought we would go. Proverbs 3:5-6 tells us "Trust in the Lord with all your heart and lean not on your own understanding; in all your ways submit to Him and He will make your paths straight." (NIV) Staying close to Him and seeking Him in all our ways will keep us on the path God has marked out for us. The path that leads to the abundant, full life He has planned for us.

February 12

Exodus 28
Psalm 21:8-13
Proverbs 5:1-2
Matthew 25:31-46

The Least of These

"For I was hungry and you gave me something to eat, I was thirsty and you gave me something to drink, I was a stranger and you invited me in, I needed clothes and you clothed Me, I was sick and you looked after Me, I was in prison and you came to visit Me...The King will reply, 'Truly I tell you, whatever you did for one of the least of these brothers and sisters of Mine, you did for Me." Matthew 25:35-36, 40 NIV

KINDNESS DOES NOT come naturally. Most of us go through our days struggling to meet our needs and the needs of our loved ones. We barely find the time to feed, clothe, and care for those we are responsible for. We occasionally make a meal for a sick friend and at Christmas we buy presents for an angel tree child and think we have fulfilled our responsibility. Have we? Is this what He is referring to here? When we stand before our Lord will He look at our lives and say that we were kind and compassionate to the least of these brothers? Please don't misunderstand me, I do not believe that we have to work and be kind and give to others to earn our salvation. "For it is by grace you have been saved, through faith—and this not from yourselves, it is the gift of God." Ephesians 2:8 (NIV) However, I believe that when we have received God's grace and have been forgiven and redeemed, we are filled with a love and gratitude for what He has done for us. This overflows in us and we will want to share this love with others. A kindness and compassion flow out of us that is not natural. It comes from the work of the Holy Spirit in us. I have begun to ask the Lord daily to make me aware of the needs around me and to show me ways that I can show love to the least of these. Sometimes it takes me out of my comfort zone, but I am always amazed at the blessing I receive from obeying His leading.

February 13

Exodus 29-30
Psalm 22:1-5
Proverbs 5:3-6
Matthew 26:1-25

My Best

"Do not make any incense with this formula for yourselves; consider it holy to the Lord." Exodus 30:37 NIV

"A woman came to Him with an alabaster jar of very expensive perfume, which she poured on His head as He was reclining at the table." Matthew 26:7 NIV

Two of the passages we read today deal with spices, incense, and perfume. God gave Moses instructions on how to mix the spices into an incense to be used in sacrificing to the Lord. This particular formula was to be set apart as holy to the Lord and they were not to use it for their own purposes. They were to set aside the best of what they had for God. Likewise, in the Matthew passage we find Mary Magdalene pouring a very expensive jar of perfume over Jesus' head. The disciples criticized her for wasting the perfume, but Jesus knew that she had sacrificed the best of what she had for Him. He tells the disciples that she has prepared Him for burial. They did not understand that in just a few short hours He would be betrayed by one of His own and would give His life as a sacrifice for them. Scripture repeatedly instructs us to give God the first and the best of what we have. So often we give Him what is left after we have used what we wanted. This applies not only to our financial and physical resources, but also to our time, abilities, energy, etc. Everything I am and have I owe to Him. How can I give Him less than my best in gratitude for what He has done for me?

February 14

Exodus 31-32
Psalm 22:6-10
Proverbs 5:7-8
Matthew 26:26-51

Good Intentions vs. Weak Flesh

"Peter replied, 'Even if all fall away on account of you, I never will.' 'Truly I tell you,' Jesus answered, 'This very night—before the rooster crows, you will disown Me three times. Then He returned to His disciples and found them sleeping. 'Couldn't you men keep watch with Me for one hour?' He asked Peter. 'Watch and pray so that you will not fall into temptation. The spirit is willing, but the body is weak.'"
Matthew 26:33, 40-41 NIV

I BELIEVE THAT Peter had good intentions. He never meant to deny Jesus. He had every intention of following Jesus to His death. And he did not intend to fall asleep. He meant to stay awake and pray. I'm sure that when Jesus came and found him sleeping, he promised to do better and to stay awake, but his body was weak, and he quickly fell asleep again. How like Peter we are. We have good intentions. We fully expect that we will not yield to that temptation, we will stay alert and pray. But, like Peter, too often we fall that very night. If we examine Peter's life a little further, we find that just a few weeks later he stood boldly before the Sanhedrin and proclaimed that Jesus was the Messiah. He spent the rest of his life proclaiming Jesus as Lord and he died a martyr's death. What was the difference? Peter received the power and indwelling of the Holy Spirit at Pentecost. From that time forth, he no longer had to rely on his weak flesh, but he could rely on the work of the Holy Spirit in him to accomplish God's purposes. We have that same power in us. When we accept Jesus as our Lord and Savior, we receive the Holy Spirit and have full access to His power and guidance. We do not have to rely on our weak flesh. He does not expect us to carry out His plans and purposes on our strength and power. He has given us everything we need.

Exodus 33-34
Psalm 22:11-15
Proverbs 5:9-10
Matthew 26:52-75

February 15

God's Presence

"Then Moses said to Him, 'If Your Presence does not go with us, do not send us up from here. How will anyone know that You are pleased with me and with Your people unless You go with us? What else will distinguish me and Your people from all the other people on the face of the Earth?" Exodus 33:15-16 NIV

THIS IS MY sincere prayer for both my life individually and for this nation. Moses knew that unless God went with them, the children of Israel were doomed to fail. God's presence was their protection, their provision, and their deliverance and without it they would not survive the wilderness. They would never enter and possess the land that had been promised to Abraham, Isaac, and Jacob. I do not want to go one step forward without God's presence and guidance in my life as well. His protection, provision and deliverance have sustained me, and I cannot imagine being outside of His presence. As I watch the news and see the direction in which America is heading, I cannot help but think that we have gotten outside of His presence. The principles on which this nation was founded have been almost forgotten and revisionist historians have tried to make us believe that our founding fathers never intended for this to be a Christian nation. If we look back at the original documents, it is amazing to see the clear references to Jesus Christ, the Bible, and God as not only important, but the foundation on which this country was built. The founding fathers were men of strong faith in God who were not ashamed of the gospel and who talked openly and unapologetically about their beliefs. Today we cannot say the name of Jesus Christ without being criticized as elitist and intolerant. May the presence of the Lord go before us and may we, as Christians, boldly proclaim Christ as our forefathers did. What else will distinguish us from all the other people on the Earth?

February 16

Exodus 35-36
Psalm 22:16-21
Proverbs 5:11-14
Matthew 27:1-23

More Than Enough

"And everyone who was willing and whose heart moved them came and brought an offering to the Lord for the work on the Tent of Meeting, all its service and for the sacred garments... 'So Bezalel, Oholiab and every skilled person to whom the Lord has given skill and ability to know how to carry out all the work of constructing the sanctuary are to do the work just as the Lord has commanded'...They received from Moses all the offerings the Israelites had brought to carry out the work of constructing the sanctuary...And so the people were restrained from bringing more, because what they already had was more than enough to do all the work." Exodus 35:20, 36:1, 3, 6-7 NIV

MORE THAN ENOUGH. Moses had to tell the people to stop bringing their offerings because they already had more than enough to complete the job God had given them. I don't think I have ever heard of a church or ministry asking people to stop giving because they already have more than enough to do what God has called them to do. If we look at the Israelite's history, we see that they were not consistent in their dedication to the Lord. They had periods when they were following Him wholeheartedly and then in the next instant, they were making a calf idol to worship. But at this time, they were all in unison, committed to God and to building His tabernacle. "Everyone who was willing and whose heart moved him came." Moses did not have to stand up and give them a guilt trip to get them to give. He did not beg and plead or threaten them. He told them God's plan and He left it up to God to prompt them to give. If God gives us a task, He will provide the resources needed to accomplish that task. God provided not only the physical resources they needed, but He also provided the skills and knowledge they would need. He does not expect us to carry out a task on our own. He expects us to be available and willing to be used by Him to accomplish His purposes. Did you catch that? His purposes, not our purposes. Too often I think we come up with great ideas and plans and ask Him to provide the resources for us to carry out our plans. That isn't how it works. He is the master, and we are the servants. We don't come up with the agenda. We just make ourselves available to Him and watch as He carries out His plans. Within the body God has gifted us each in different ways to carry out His purposes. He has provided people with the abilities and skills to do everything He has called us to do. It is our responsibility to be attentive to His leading and sensitive to His moving in our hearts.

Exodus 37-38
Psalm 22:22-26
Proverbs 5:15-17
Matthew 27:24-44

February 17

Self-Control

"In the same way the chief priests, the teachers and the elders mocked Him. 'He saved others,' they said, 'but He can't save Himself! He's the King of Israel! Let Him come down now from the cross, and we will believe in Him. He trusts in God. Let God rescue Him now if He wants Him, for He said, 'I am the Son of God.'" Matthew 27:41-43 NIV

THROUGHOUT HIS MINISTRY, Jesus exhibited incredible self-control, but it was never as evident as when He hung on the cross. In agonizing pain and unbearable sorrow, He listened as He was mocked and insulted. He quietly watched as His family, His disciples, and His followers had to endure the pain of seeing their leader murdered and their hopes and dreams dashed. He could have called 10,000 angels to come down and put an end to it all. He could have taken over as an earthly king and shown them that everything He said was true. He could have spoken a word and all the chief priests, teachers and elders would have dropped dead. But that was not His Father's plan. Jesus was completely and wholly committed to obeying His Father. The satisfaction of being proven right was not as important as providing salvation for a lost and dying world. Taking away the pain His friends and family were experiencing was not as important as providing a way through which you and I might be redeemed. Easing His own pain and agony was not as important as exhibiting His love for us through His sacrificial death.

Not defending yourself and keeping your mouth shut is often criticized as being weak and cowardly. Jesus provides an excellent example of the strength and love exhibited by self-control. May we follow Jesus' example of being completely and wholly committed to obeying God.

February 18

Exodus 39
Psalm 22:27-31
Proverbs 5:18-20
Matthew 27:45-66

Every Knee Shall Bow

"All the ends of the Earth will remember and turn to the Lord, and all the families of the nations will bow down before Him, for dominion belongs to the Lord and He rules over the nations." Psalm 22:27-28 NIV

THIS PASSAGE REMINDS me of the passage in Philippians 2:9-11. "Therefore, God exalted Him to the highest place and gave Him the name that is above every name, that at the name of Jesus every knee should bow, in Heaven and on Earth and under the Earth, and every tongue confess that Jesus Christ is Lord, to the glory of God the Father." (NIV) If we listen to the news about wars and riots, corrupt politicians and evil dictators, greedy businessmen and economic doom, it is easy to forget that God is in control. We may not understand His ways or His timing. We may not understand why He lets our leaders get away with what they do and why He does not intervene when we think He should. But we can be assured that He is in control. He is watching and aware of everything happening in our country and the countries throughout the world. He is in every boardroom, in every meeting, on every battlefield and is intimately aware of the events that alter the course of human history. He is Lord and He rules over the nations whether we acknowledge it or not. One day, probably in the not-too-distant future, all the Earth will remember and turn to the Lord, and every knee will bow, and tongue confess that Jesus is Lord of all. Spend some time today praying for our nation and its leaders.

February 19

Exodus 40
Psalm 23
Proverbs 5:21-23
Matthew 28

Never Alone

"In all the travels of the Israelites, whenever the cloud lifted from above the tabernacle, they would set out; but if the cloud did not lift, they did not set out—until the day it lifted. So, the cloud of the Lord was over the tabernacle by day, and fire was in the cloud by night, in the sight of all the house of Israel during their travels." Exodus 40:36-38 NIV

"And surely I am with you always, to the very end of the age." Matthew 28:20 NIV

WE DO NOT serve a God who created the world, set it into motion and then left it to fend for itself. Many world religions serve "gods" who are far off and who rule from a lofty throne somewhere "above." Their followers are constantly trying to please a "god" who does not exist. They have no evidence or reason to base their belief on because there is none. We serve the only true God, and we know He exists because He is with us. From the beginning of history, He has been intimately involved in the lives of men. There is ample evidence of His existence because we can see Him at work in our lives. He was with the Israelites in the wilderness in a cloud by day and a ball of fire at night. He came to Earth and walked around as a man so that He could share in our suffering and understand our temptations. He is Immanuel, God with us. And when He was taken up to Heaven, He sent His Holy Spirit to live in us and walk with us always, to the very end of the age. I have no doubt that He is with me because I have personally experienced Him working in my life. I love the old hymn, "In the Garden." The beautiful chorus says it all, "He walks with me, and talks with me, and tells me I am His own. And the joy we share as we tarry there, none other has ever known."[1] I am so thankful for my Savior who walks with me and talks with me and tells me I am His own and who is intimately involved in every part of my life.

February 20

Leviticus 1-2
Psalm 24
Proverbs 6:1-3
Mark 1:1-20

Fishers of Men

"Come, follow Me,' Jesus said, 'and I will make you fishers of men.' At once they left their nets and followed Him." Mark 1:17-18 NIV

JESUS WAS TALKING to fishermen and used language they would understand. If He was talking to a doctor, He might tell them to follow Him and He would make them healers of the sick. If He was talking to a lawyer, He might tell them to follow Him and He will make them defenders of the oppressed. God wants to use each of us right where we are to bring people to Him. We are not all called to be pastors or ministers, but we are all called to be witnesses. Wherever we are, God has called us to tell others about Him. Whether we are at work, at school, on the ball field, or at the gym, He expects us to tell others about Him. We do not have to be biblical scholars to proclaim what He has done for us. We are to be fishers of men wherever we are. We do not have to convince—that is the work of the Holy Spirit. We are called to proclaim. These verses tell us that Peter and Andrew at once left their nets and followed Him. When we are given opportunities to witness, we often hesitate and think about how the other person will react and we miss the chance to share Jesus with them. Take a few moments now to pray that God will give you an opportunity today to share what Jesus has done in your life and that you will immediately respond to His leading.

February 21

Leviticus 3-4
Psalm 25:1-7
Proverbs 6:4-5
Mark 1:21-45

Quiet Time

"Very early in the morning, while it was still dark, Jesus got up, left the house and went off to a solitary place, where He prayed." Mark 1:35 NIV

Jesus knew the value of spending time alone with God. Jesus was God. He was fully God and fully man. He was sinless and yet He took time every day to spend with His Father. During His ministry, He knew that He would have no time alone during the day. He was surrounded by crowds everywhere He went. There were people to heal, crowds to be fed, and multitudes to be taught the truth of God's love and grace. From morning till night, He was busy. Instead of hitting the snooze button and closing His eyes for just a few more minutes, Jesus got up, and went to a solitary place to pray. He longed for time with His Father. He enjoyed the sweet fellowship They shared and did whatever was necessary to make it happen, even if He had to get up while it was still dark and seek out a place to be alone. This causes me to pause and consider how much I long for that sweet fellowship. To what lengths do I go to spend time with my Savior? How much more do I need time alone with Him for instruction, for teaching, for training in righteousness and just for intimate fellowship to get to know Him more?

February 22

Leviticus 5-6
Psalm 25:8-15
Proverbs 6:6-8
Mark 2

Bring Them to Jesus

"Then they came to Him bringing a paralytic, carried by four men. Since they were not able to bring him to Jesus because of the crowd, they removed the roof above where He was. And when they had broken through, they lowered the stretcher on which the paralytic was lying." Mark 2:3-4 HCSB

THESE FOUR MEN give us a beautiful picture of true friendship. They brought their friend who was paralyzed to Jesus because they heard that Jesus could heal him. When they arrived at the house where Jesus was teaching, there were so many people that they couldn't even get in the door. Instead of just leaving and coming back another day, they climbed on the roof, lifted the man on the stretcher onto the roof, broke through the ceiling and lowered the man down in front of Jesus. Jesus healed the man and he walked out in front of everyone. They were all astounded and gave glory to God. These men did whatever it took to bring their friend to Jesus. They couldn't help him, but they knew the One who could. Often, we are in a similar situation. We have friends who bring their concerns to us, but we are powerless to help them. Fortunately, we know the One who can. Whether it is by physically bringing them to church or bringing them before the Lord in prayer we have access to the only One who can make a difference.

February 23

Leviticus 7-8
Psalm 25:16-22
Proverbs 6:9-11
Mark 3:1-12

Hope

"Turn to me and be gracious to me, for I am lonely and afflicted. Relieve the troubles of my heart and free me from my anguish. Look upon my affliction and my distress and take away all my sins. See how numerous are my enemies and how fiercely they hate me! Guard my life and rescue me; do not let me be put to shame, for I take refuge in You. May integrity and uprightness protect me because my hope, Lord, is in You." Psalm 25:16-21 NIV

My hope is in You, Lord. Some days I feel like everything is crashing in around me. I can hardly breathe. Not only are my troubles bearing down on me from the outside, but I feel turmoil on the inside as well. I react in ways that I know are not pleasing to You. I am anxious and worried. I am afraid and I can't seem to stop my mind from wandering to all the what ifs and if onlys that make me more depressed and scared. I want to turn all my problems over to You and leave them there, but I keep picking them back up time and time again. I carry them around with me like an albatross around my neck. I keep trying to figure out how to solve my problems. If I just think about it a little bit more, I am sure I can come up with the perfect solution. I know that You tell me that You already have it all figured out, and I just need to trust You. But I feel guilty not doing anything. I feel like I should be doing something, after all I got myself into this situation so I should get myself out. Right? I know that's not how it works. You tell me to "cast all my anxiety on You because You care for me." I Peter 5:7 (NIV) "Do not be anxious about anything, but in everything, by prayer and petition, with thanksgiving, present your requests to God." Philippians 4:6 (NIV) The peace and joy that I know You have for me seem just beyond my grasp. Please help me, Lord. Please guard my life and rescue me. Let me not be put to shame, for I take refuge in You and You alone. Please help me to conduct myself with integrity and uprightness. My hope is in You.

February 24

Leviticus 9-10
Psalm 26:1-7
Proverbs 6:12-15
Mark 3:13-35

Dishonesty

"A troublemaker and a villain, who goes about with a corrupt mouth, who winks with his eye, signals with his feet and motions with his fingers, who plots evil with deceit in his heart—he always stirs up conflict." Proverbs 6:12-14 NIV

DISHONESTY HAS BECOME so commonplace in our culture that we almost expect it. Little white lies are no big deal and when we get caught, we just tell another one to cover it up. Unfortunately, we are all guilty of it. We ease our conscience by rationalizing that we don't want to hurt anyone's feelings or that we aren't really lying, we just aren't telling the whole truth. I grew up in the Deep South so it was drilled into me very early that you are to always be nice and never say something that would hurt someone's feelings. We like our tea sweet, and we like our words even sweeter. Don't get me wrong. I am not advocating rudeness. We all know people who say whatever comes into their mind without regard to how it might make others feel. My mother used to always tell me that if I couldn't say something nice, I shouldn't say anything at all. Maybe better advice would be that if we can't say something honest, we shouldn't say anything at all. We are so used to not telling the whole truth that we often don't even realize it. "The Lord detests lying lips, but He delights in people who are trustworthy." Proverbs 12:22 (NIV) "Then you will know the truth and the truth will set you free." John 8:32 (NIV) "Therefore each of you must put off falsehood and speak truthfully to his neighbor." Ephesians 4:25 (NIV) Ask the Lord to reveal to you when you are not being honest and begin to speak the truth in love.

February 25

Leviticus 11-12
Psalm 26:8-12
Proverbs 6:16-19
Mark 4:1-20

What the Lord Hates

"There are six things the Lord hates, seven that are detestable to Him: haughty eyes, a lying tongue, hands that shed innocent blood, a heart that devises wicked schemes, feet that are quick to rush into evil, a false witness who pours out lies, and a man who stirs up conflict in the community." Proverbs 6:16-19 NIV

WE DEALT WITH two of these yesterday. The Lord hates a lying tongue and a false witness who pours out lies. Two of the seven things listed as the things God hates the most deal with dishonesty. We don't think of lying as being as bad as murder, but it is listed right there alongside it. God places an extremely high value on telling the truth. These verses also tell us that the Lord hates haughty eyes. Psalm 10:4 helps to explain why pride and arrogance are detestable to Him. "In his pride the wicked man does not seek Him, in all his thoughts there is no room for God." (NIV) In pride, we think we have it all under control and we don't need God. Obviously, that is incorrect, and that attitude is not pleasing to Him.

A heart that devises wicked schemes and feet that are quick to rush into evil seem to go hand in hand. Sometimes we have the idea that if we didn't come up with the idea, we shouldn't get in as much trouble. In the legal system, those who go along with the plan are held just as responsible as those who plan the crime. The person driving the get-away car is just as culpable as the one who held the hostages at gunpoint. In God's eyes, laughing along when someone makes fun of the shy girl is just as bad as saying the words yourself. Going along with the crowd is never acceptable in God's eyes.

The last one is interesting to me. Unfortunately, I think we see this far too much in the body of believers. This passage tells us the Lord hates people who just like to cause trouble. They grumble and complain and are never satisfied. They don't like the songs we sang in church, or the pastor said something that made them mad. The pastor's wife wore a skirt that was too short, or their Bible Study leader didn't call to see why they weren't there on Tuesday. (Of course, they got mad two weeks before because she was calling and hounding them about not being there.) May we not be ones who stir up dissension, but those who seek peace.

February 26

Leviticus 13-14
Psalm 27:1-6
Proverbs 6:20-22
Mark 4:21-41

No Faith?

"He said to His disciples, 'Why are you afraid? Do you still have no faith?'"
Mark 4:40 NIV

AFTER A LONG day of teaching, Jesus and His disciples got into boats to cross to the other side of the Sea of Galilee. The Sea of Galilee is surrounded by mountains and is normally very calm, but at night, cool air from the mountains is known to come down and meet the warm air from the sea and violent storms can come up quickly. This is what happened this particular night. Jesus was sound asleep below deck and His disciples ran downstairs to wake Him and ask if He didn't care that they were all going to drown. Jesus spoke to the wind, and it immediately stopped. Notice that He did not pray and ask God to stop the storm. He spoke to the wind Himself and it responded. He showed the disciples that He was not only someone sent to them by God; He was God. Only the Creator of the wind and the seas has control over them. He then rebuked them for their lack of faith.

There are several lessons that can be drawn from this account. Following Jesus does not mean that we will be free from storms. Actually, we can be right in the middle of God's plan for us, on the path, following Him and we can encounter very difficult times. In John 16:33, Jesus tells us that in this world we will have trouble. The storms we face often expose our lack of faith. I can certainly relate to this. I can be going along fine and out of nowhere a storm hits me that is not even as bad as the one the disciples were facing, and I am gripped with fear and dread. I feel all alone and overwhelmed, and I run to Jesus asking if He is going to let me drown. My faith is exposed as very weak. Fortunately, He teaches me another important lesson. He did not tell the disciples to come back when their faith is stronger and then He would calm the sea. He calmed the sea and then He showed them their lack of faith. He used it to teach them more of who He was and helped to increase their faith. Thankfully, that is also how He responds to me. He calms my storms, sometimes immediately taking them away and sometimes by calming me so I can face them. The object of my faith is much more important than the strength of my faith. He does not help me because my faith is great, and I deserve His help. He helps me because He loves me. He is in the process of teaching me to trust Him fully even in the midst of the storm.

February 27

Leviticus 15
Psalm 27:7-14
Proverbs 6:23-26
Mark 5:1-20

Eyewitness Testimony

"Go home to your people and tell them how much the Lord has done for you, and how He has had mercy on you.' So, the man went away and began to tell in the Decapolis how much Jesus had done for him. And all the people were amazed."
Mark 5:19-20 NIV

Jesus did not tell the demon-possessed man to go quote scripture to the people and tell them great theological truths. He told him to go tell his friends and family what He had done for him. He told him to explain to them how Jesus had mercy on him. We are afraid to talk to people about Jesus because we are afraid they are going to ask us questions we can't answer. We don't want to invite our coworker to church because they might ask us what we believe, and we aren't sure we can explain it in a way they will understand. We try to make it far more complicated than it is. Jesus instructs us to just tell people what He has done for us and how He has had mercy on us. We don't have to be able to quote a lot of scripture or explain biblical principles to them. We just tell them our story. An eyewitness in a courtroom who gives a testimony is supposed to tell the truth about what they saw. Expert witnesses give explanations about the testimony and its ramifications. Both sides in a case call their own experts to give testimony that supports their interpretation of the facts. The jury must decide which expert they want to believe, but they give much more weight to an eyewitness of the events. When someone tells you how Jesus has made a difference in their life, it is hard to ignore. This is what happened to me. I can't tell you how or why, but Jesus came into my life, and He has given me peace. He forgave me for the bad things I have done. He helps me face the difficulties in my life. I know I can get through whatever comes, because He is there to help me and walk beside me every step of the way. Be an eyewitness today.

February 28

Leviticus 16
Psalm 28:1-5
Proverbs 6:27-29
Mark 5:21-43

The Lord Hears

"To You, Lord, I call; You are my Rock; do not turn a deaf ear to me. For if You remain silent, I will be like those who go down to the pit." Psalm 28:1 NIV

WE ARE REMINDED over and over in scripture that God hears the cries of His people. "The righteous cry out, and the Lord hears them; He delivers them from all their troubles." Psalm 34:17 (NIV) "In my distress I called to the Lord; I called out to my God. From His temple, He heard my voice; my cry came to His ears." 2 Samuel 22:7 (NIV) "For the eyes of the Lord are on the righteous and His ears are attentive to their prayer." I Peter 3:12 (NIV) "In the morning, Lord, You hear my voice; in the morning I lay my requests before You and wait expectantly." Psalm 5:3 (NIV) "Know that the Lord has set apart His faithful servant for Himself; the Lord hears when I call to Him." Psalm 4:3 (NIV) "But as for me, I watch in hope for the Lord, I wait for God my Savior; my God will hear me." Micah 7:7 (NIV) My God does not turn a deaf ear to me. He hears every cry that comes out from my mouth and every prayer that is in my heart. Thank You, Jesus, that I can know You will answer when I call. The answer may not come in the way or the time that I want, but I am assured that You hear and will respond to me.

Leviticus 17-18
Psalm 28:6-9
Proverbs 6:30-31
Mark 6:1-20

Following God's Rules

"You must not do as they do in Egypt, where you used to live, and you must not do as they do in the land of Canaan, where I am bringing you. Do not follow their practices. You must obey My laws and be careful to follow My decrees. I am the Lord your God. Keep My decrees and laws, for the man who obeys them will live by them. I am the Lord." Leviticus 18:3-5 NIV

In the world we live in, it is becoming increasingly more unpopular to follow God's rules. In this age of political correctness and not wanting to offend anyone, many Christians tiptoe around God's standards. Unfortunately, even many Christian churches have watered down the gospel to such an extent that it is barely recognizable. God's standards and rules are just as applicable to our lives today as they were when they were written. We cannot blatantly ignore Him and His Word and expect to receive His blessing.

The morals and standards of the culture around us are constantly changing. The world would have us believe that truth is relative and therefore subject to individual interpretation. The Bible tells us differently. "Jesus Christ is the same yesterday, and today and forever." Hebrews 13:8 (NIV) "All Your words are true; all Your righteous laws are eternal." Psalm 119:160 (NIV) The standards set forth in scripture are not arbitrary. They have a purpose and are meant to help us live a peaceful, joyful life. Deviating from God's plan brings consequences. He knows what is best for us and He loves us so much that He wants us to "have life and have it to the full." John 10:10 (NIV) Do not do as they do in the land where you live; follow God's rules, keep His statutes, and walk in them.

March 2

Leviticus 19-20
Psalm 29:1-6
Proverbs 6:32-33
Mark 6:21-56

Rest

"He said to them, 'Come with Me by yourselves to a quiet place and get some rest.' So they went away by themselves in a boat to a solitary place...After leaving them, He went up on a mountainside to pray." Mark 6:31-32, 46 NIV

Jesus knew the importance of rest. Even He, in His human state, needed to rest. Everywhere He turned there was someone who needed Him: a blind man who wanted to receive sight, a leper who needed to be healed, a prostitute who needed forgiveness, or a crowd that needed to be fed. He always had compassion on them and met their need. But this had been a very difficult day. In the midst of ministering, His disciples came to tell Him that His beloved cousin, John, had been beheaded. In His sorrow, Jesus told His disciples that He wanted to go away with them to a quiet place to rest. Unfortunately, they were followed by a crowd of people and He, as always, met their needs. At the end of the day, we are told that He sent His disciples ahead in a boat and He went away to the mountain to pray. He needed time with His Heavenly Father. He needed the love and peace and strength of His Father to deal with the loss of His loved one.

We can learn some important lessons from this passage. First, we need the love and support of our brothers and sisters in Christ. Jesus wanted to be with His dearest friends, His disciples, to grieve the loss of John. While ministering and carrying out our daily responsibilities, it is important to take time for fellowship and rest with friends. Second, we need time alone with our Heavenly Father to gain the peace and strength necessary for each day. If we are too busy to spend time with our Father, then we are too busy. Third, we shouldn't feel guilty for resting. If Jesus needed time to rest, then we certainly do. Our minds and our bodies need down time. Work hard, do your best and then take time to rest and have some fun.

March 3

Leviticus 21-22
Psalm 29:7-11
Proverbs 6:34-35
Mark 7:1-16

Far Away Hearts

"He replied, 'Isaiah was right when he prophesied about you hypocrites; as it is written: "These people honor Me with their lips, but their hearts are far from Me. They worship Me in vain; their teachings are merely human rules." Mark 7:6-7 NIV

I became a Christian as a little girl. I do not remember a time when I was not in church at least once, if not several times, a week. At various times in my walk with the Lord, I have realized that I had let church activity and service temporarily take the place of a personal, intimate relationship with my Savior. I believe that this is one of Satan's most devious schemes. He gets us so busy doing good things that we neglect doing the best thing, which is spending time with Jesus. During those times I honor Him with my lips, but my heart is far away. I am following the rules and usually making sure others follow them as well, but my heart is not sensitive to His leading. I am not listening for His voice prompting me to give words of encouragement to my weary friend or tell my lost neighbor about His love and grace. I am not getting much needed strength and nourishment from time in His Word, and I am not experiencing victory in overcoming temptation. My heart is far away.

In those times I often have to ask Him to give me a burning desire for Him; not for the things He can do for me, but for intimacy with Him. I believe that He honors my desire to desire Him even if my effort is weak, and He makes me aware of the void that can only be filled by His presence. My prayer is that I will be like David in Psalm 42:1-2, "As the deer pants for streams of water, so my soul pants for You, my God. My soul thirsts for God, for the living God." (NIV)

March 4

Leviticus 23-24
Psalm 30:1-6
Proverbs 7:1-3
Mark 7:17-37

Morning Joy

"Weeping may stay for the night but rejoicing comes in the morning." Psalm 30:5b NIV

In this life, we will experience difficulty. There will be long nights filled with weeping and sadness. We will have to deal with the death of loved ones, hurtful words by a family member, and rejection by a dear friend. There will be moments of fear, heartache, loneliness, and mourning. But as children of God, we have the assurance that "Because of the Lord's great love we are not consumed, His compassions never fail. They are new every morning; great is Your faithfulness, Lord." Lamentations 3:22-23 (NIV) No matter what we are experiencing we know that our Heavenly Father loves us and will take us through to the other side. There may be difficult days, but there is hope because joy comes in the morning.

Things often seem worse during the night. I lay awake at night worrying about things that many times never happen. In the darkness my imagination tends to run away with me, and my mind goes down paths of fear and dread that have very little basis in reality. Satan loves the darkness because he knows that truth is revealed in the light. He can convince me of things in the night that I would never believe in the light of day. I have found that even when the things I have feared actually happen they are often not as bad as I had imagined they would be. And I know that in everything that happens, I am never alone. My loving Lord is with me each step of the way to help me, guide me, comfort me, and see me through whatever happens. Weeping may last for the night, but joy comes in the morning.

March 5

Leviticus 25
Psalm 30:7-12
Proverbs 7:4-5
Mark 8

Who do you say I am?

"But what about you," He asked. "Who do you say I am?' Peter answered, "You are the Messiah." Mark 8:29 NIV

THERE ARE MANY people who say that Jesus was a good man, a teacher, or even a prophet. They would say that they believe what He taught was good and that we should try to live our lives following the guidelines He set out. They would agree that we should love others and be honest. We should treat others the way we want to be treated and we should not be judgmental. The problem is that we can't pick and choose the things that we want to believe and ignore the rest of His teaching.

Jesus went right to the heart of the matter. He asked His disciples the question that we must ask ourselves. Who do you say that He is? Jesus left no doubt about His identity. He made it very clear that He is the Son of God. He is the Messiah. He is Lord of all. If He is who He says He is, then He deserves our complete and total commitment. We should do everything He says to do. If He is not who He says He is, then He is not a good man. He is either a liar or He is crazy, and we should not follow His teachings or listen to anything He says. There is no middle ground. He is either Lord, or He is not. It is a matter of authority. If He is the Son of God, we must acknowledge that He is in control. Not only is He in control of the world, but He is in control of our lives. He should be a part of every decision we make and every plan we pursue. "Trust in the Lord with all your heart and lean not on your own understanding; In all your ways submit to Him, and He will make your paths straight." Proverbs 3:5-6 (NIV) Who do you say that He is?

March 6

Leviticus 26
Psalm 31:1-8
Proverbs 7:6-8
Mark 9:1-29

Idols

"Do not make idols or set up an image or a sacred stone for yourselves, and do not place a carved stone in your land to bow down before it. I am the Lord your God. Observe My Sabbaths and have reverence for My sanctuary. I am the Lord."
Leviticus 26:1-2 NIV

NOT MANY OF us have golden idols or bronze images in our homes that we bow down to. We don't have pillars or figured stones in our churches that we worship. As a matter of fact, we pride ourselves in not bowing to anyone or anything. But we are fooling ourselves if we believe we don't have idols in our lives that we worship. "For where your treasure is, there your heart will be also." Matthew 6:21 (NIV) Where is your treasure? What do you value the most? What takes up most of your time and energy? Is anything more important to you than your relationship with Jesus? Even good things can become idols when we allow them to consume us. "If anyone comes to Me and does not hate his father and mother, wife and children, brothers and sisters---yes, even their own life---He cannot be My disciple." Luke 14:26 (NIV) Jesus is not telling us to hate anyone. He is telling us that nothing and no one can be more important to us than Jesus.

Being a good wife and mother is important and pleases God, but when those relationships take precedence in our life and distract us from spending time with Jesus, it does not please Him. We are commanded to honor our father and mother, but not if it keeps us from honoring our commitment to God. We are told to be a good employee and to work at everything as we are working for the Lord, but our jobs should not keep us from worshipping and serving God. Houses, cars, clothes, beauty, fitness and exercise, fame, prestige, power, and any number of other things can become idols in our life if we get our priorities out of order. Ask the Lord to reveal to you any idols you have allowed to creep into your life and to help you put them back into their proper place of importance.

March 7

Leviticus 27
Psalm 31:9-18
Proverbs 7:9-12
Mark 9:30-41

Servant Leadership

"Sitting down, Jesus called the twelve and said, 'Anyone who wants to be first must be the very last, and the servant of all.' He took a little child whom He placed among them. Taking the child in His arms, He said to them, 'Whoever welcomes one of these little children in My name welcomes Me; and whoever welcomes Me does not welcome Me but the One who sent Me." Mark 9:35-37 NIV

THE DISCIPLES JUST didn't get it. Over and over, Jesus told them to humble themselves, to be like little children, to serve others and to consider others as more important than themselves. It must have been frustrating to Him that after all the time He had spent with them, they were arguing about who was the most important among them. They were still waiting for Jesus to set up an earthly kingdom and put them in charge. They weren't really listening to His words.

Before we are too critical of the disciples, let's evaluate our own lives. We have the benefit of the whole picture. We know what He meant because we can read about His sacrificial death on the cross and how He willingly submitted to being beaten, spit upon, mocked and humiliated to pay the penalty for our sins. We know what the plan was and that the reason He was willing to humble Himself was because of His amazing love for us. We see over and over in scripture the dramatic, life-changing results of putting the needs of others first and serving others in love. Yet how different are we from the disciples. We want to be important and for others to recognize and acknowledge that. We get our feelings hurt when we are not treated with respect. We are more concerned with being served and having our needs met than we are with the needs of those around us.

> "In your relationships with one another, have the same mindset as Christ Jesus: Who, being in very nature God, did not consider equality with God something to be used to His own advantage, rather, He made himself nothing by taking the very nature of a servant, being made in human likeness. And being found in appearance as a man, He humbled himself by becoming obedient to death---even death on a cross!" Philippians 2:5-8 (NIV)

March 8

Numbers 1
Psalm 31:19-24
Proverbs 7:13-17
Mark 9:42-10:12

Divine Protection

"How great is Your goodness that You have stored up for those who fear You and accomplished in the sight of everyone for those who take refuge in You. You hide them in the protection of Your presence; You conceal them in a shelter from the schemes of men, from quarrelsome tongues. May the Lord be praised, for He has wonderfully shown His faithful love to me in a city under siege. Be strong and courageous, all you who put your hope in the Lord." Psalm 31:19-21, 24 HCSB

DAVID HAD EXPERIENCED first-hand the divine protection of the Lord. He was being hunted by Saul and forced to hide in caves to avoid being killed. God had, on more than one occasion, delivered him from certain death. The words David chose paint a beautiful picture of a loving Father who loves and protects His children. He stores up abundant goodness for those who fear Him. Not only does He dispense goodness to us; He stores it up for us so that it is available when we need it. He hides us from the plots of men. When we are completely unaware that someone is plotting against us or scheming to cause trouble for us, God knows and is placing a cover of protection over us. He is working on our behalf to bring about good and to "make all things work together for our good." Romans 8:28 (NIV) When we are in distress and we cry out to God for help, He hears us and answers. We can be strong and take courage because our hope is in the Lord and His steadfast love.

In the midst of difficulty, it is easy to become discouraged and lose hope. David provides an excellent example for us to follow. When he was afraid, he cried out to the Lord. When he was discouraged, he reminded himself of all the times God had been faithful to him in the past. When he was weary, he prayed for God's strength. And when he experienced God's power and protection, he spent time in praise and thanksgiving. David knew God intimately. He had a deep, abiding, personal relationship with His Lord and he was confident that God would take care of him no matter what happened. We have that same assurance of His love and protection.

March 9

Numbers 2
Psalm 32:1-7
Proverbs 7:18-20
Mark 10:13-31

As Little Children

"People were bringing little children to Jesus to have Him touch them, but the disciples rebuked them. When Jesus saw them, He was indignant. He said to them, 'Let the little children come to Me and do not hinder them, for the kingdom of God belongs to such as these. Truly I tell you, anyone who will not receive the kingdom of God like a little child will never enter it.' And He took the children in His arms, put His hands on them and blessed them." Mark 10:13-16 NIV

"And He said, 'Truly I tell you, unless you change and become like little children, you will never enter the kingdom of Heaven. Therefore, whoever takes the lowly position of this child is the greatest in the kingdom of Heaven." Matthew 18:3-4 NIV

WHAT DOES IT mean to become like a little child? Children are innocent and trusting. They put their complete confidence in their father because they know that he loves them and wants what is best for them. When my children were little and we were teaching them to swim, my husband would put them on the side of the pool and have them jump into his arms. They were afraid to jump into my arms or anyone else's arms, but they always readily jumped into their Daddy's arms. They had complete confidence that he would catch them and would not let them go under. They trusted him. They didn't worry about how the bills were going to be paid or where their next meal was going to come from. They didn't worry about who would take care of their needs or who would protect them. A few years ago, there was a police standoff with a mentally ill man a couple of blocks from our house. We were in no immediate danger, the police had him surrounded and yet my children wanted their Daddy, and they didn't relax until he got home. They felt safe when he was with them.

I believe that is what Jesus meant when He said that we are to be like little children. We are to have complete confidence and trust in our Heavenly Father. He loves us and promises to take care of us. He is always with us to protect us. He knows what is best for us and will do whatever it takes to bring that about. He will meet our needs and He will never let us down. As adults we like to think that we are self-sufficient. We can take care of ourselves. Children recognize that they are helpless and in need of their father's constant care. May we recognize our helplessness and become like little children.

March 10

Numbers 3
Psalm 32:8-11
Proverbs 7:21-23
Mark 10:32-52

Stubborn as a Mule

"I will instruct you and teach you in the way you should go; I will counsel you with My loving eye on you. Do not be like the horse or the mule, which have no understanding but must be controlled by bit and bridle or they will not come to you."
Psalm 32:8-9 NIV

GOD IS PATIENT and gracious with me. He gently instructs me and teaches me. He gives me counsel and He watches over me. Unfortunately, too often I act like the mule who has no understanding. I try to go my own way instead of listening to His wise instruction. I pull and fight on the reins instead of willingly submitting to His leading. Inevitably, I get myself in trouble and figure out that His way really was best. After a while, the mule will submit to the bit and do what it is told. But the next day, it will resist again, try to go its own way, and will have to be forced to obey. How like the mule I am. I go along my own way, following my plans and doing what I think is best. Then I get myself in trouble and realize I should have listened to His still, small voice guiding me. I repent and submit to Him for a time, but then I start thinking I know what I am doing and so I decide to go my own way again. It is a vicious cycle. I don't want to be like the stubborn, ignorant mule, but I find myself repeating the pattern over and over.

The only way to avoid this destructive tendency is to stay in constant communication with God. When I am spending time with Him daily, seeking His face and listening for and to His voice, I am much less likely to go my own way. I am more like the prophet Isaiah who wrote in Isaiah 30:21, "Whether you turn to the right or to the left, your ears will hear a voice behind you saying, 'This is the way, walk in it.'" (NIV) I hear and heed His voice.

March 11

Numbers 4-5
Psalm 33:1-9
Proverbs 7:24-27
Mark 11:1-11

He Spoke

"For He spoke, and it came to be; He commanded, and it stood firm." Psalm 33:9 NIV

Wow! God spoke and it came to be. Creatio ex nihilo is the Latin phrase for the attribute of God that tells us that He can create something out of nothing. Man is capable of amazing things. We can send a man to the moon. We can speak into a small metal object called a cell phone and someone on the other side of the planet can hear us and respond immediately. We can even take a baby out of its mother's womb, perform surgery on it and return it to the womb to complete gestation. Man is very creative. We can make a beautiful picture using paint on a canvas. We can create masterpieces out of fabric, wood, plastic, yarn, steel, and clay. But no man can create something out of nothing. With all our technology and intellectual capability no one has ever figured out how to make something out of nothing. Only God can do that. And if that doesn't completely amaze you, consider that God doesn't even have to lift a finger to create something out of nothing. He only has to speak, and it is done. This is a very important theological principle. Nothing comes from nothing. There must be a divine architect who set everything in motion. All creation had a beginning and before that beginning, there was God. This verse makes me think of my favorite hymn, "How Great Thou Art." There are many versions of it available on the internet and I would encourage you to find it and listen carefully to the words as you worship our Creator God.

March 12

Numbers 6
Psalm 33:10-17
Proverbs 8:1-3
Mark 11:12-33

Fruit

> "The next day as they were leaving Bethany, Jesus was hungry. Seeing in the distance a fig tree in leaf, He went to find out if it had any fruit. When He reached it, He found nothing but leaves, because it was not the season for figs. Then He said to the tree, 'May no one ever eat fruit from you again.' ... In the morning, as they went along, they saw the fig tree withered from the roots." Mark 11:12-14, 20 NIV

FIG TREES IN the Mediterranean are typically just beginning to get leaves in March or April, but do not produce figs until their leaves are all out in June. This tree was an exception because it was already full of leaves at the time of the Passover. When Jesus saw the tree, it appeared to be in full bloom, and He expected to find it full of figs. But when He reached it, He found no fruit. It looked good but had nothing of substance to offer. When He reached Jerusalem, He went to the temple and found the same thing. The leaders in the temple were very religious. They followed the rules, they knew the scriptures, and they looked good on the outside. But they had nothing of substance to offer. They had no fruit. The only times in scripture we find that Jesus became angry or used harsh words are when He was confronting hypocrisy. He dealt with many people in varying kinds of sinful situations. He approached them in love and forgiveness and encouraged them to repent and turn away from their sin. But He cursed hypocrites calling them whitewashed sepulchers, vipers, fools, and blind guides. The evidence of spiritual depth and maturity is not outward appearances; it is fruit. Galatians 5:22-23 tells us, "The fruit of the spirit is love, joy, peace, patience, kindness, goodness, faithfulness, gentleness and self-control. Against such things there is no law." (NIV) Are you fruitful or just leafy?

March 13

Numbers 7
Psalm 33:18-22
Proverbs 8:4-5
Mark 12:1-27

Common Sense

> "You who are simple, gain prudence; you who are foolish, set your hearts on it."
> Proverbs 8:5 NIV

MERRIAM-WEBSTER DEFINES "SIMPLE" as "lacking in knowledge or expertise, lacking in intelligence, not wise."[2] The person who is simple often acts precipitously because they lack knowledge and experience. A simple-minded fool doesn't even realize how little he knows. He has an inflated view of his own wisdom. Solomon is advising us not to act foolishly, but to exercise common sense. Many of the problems we experience are a result of our failure to just be prudent. It is interesting that we often have difficulty seeing the foolishness of our own decisions but can clearly look at someone else's choices and see that they are hasty and rash. As children of God, we have access to the One who is the source of all wisdom. We do not have to make decisions on our own. In fact, we should not make any decision on our own. We should never act hastily. Before making any decision, we need to seek God through prayer and reading His Word. We should also seek counsel from godly Christian brothers who will pray with and for us about the matter. If forced to decide before we have time to pray and seek the Lord about what we should do, then we should say no. If it is God's plan, He will always give us the opportunity to evaluate and make a wise choice. Instead of asking if it would be ok to do something, ask if it would be wise to do it. It may be ok to buy that new dress, but is it wise? It may be ok to hang out with that friend, but is it wise? It may be ok to watch that TV program, but is it wise? "If any of you lacks wisdom, you should ask God, who gives generously to all without finding fault, and it will be given to you." James 1:5 (NIV)

March 14

Numbers 8-9
Psalm 34:1-7
Proverbs 8:6-7
Mark 12:28-44

Deliverance

"I will extol the Lord at all times; His praise will always be on my lips. I will glory in the Lord; let the afflicted hear and rejoice. Glorify the Lord with me; let us exalt His name together. I sought the Lord, and He answered me; He delivered me from all my fears...The angel of the Lord encamps around those who fear Him, and He delivers them." Psalm 34:1-4, 7 NIV

DAVID BEGINS THIS Psalm with praise, glorifying his Father in Heaven and recognizing that God alone is worthy of our praise. David knew from experience that only God could deliver him. He had intimate acquaintance with his God, and he knew that He alone had the power and authority to bring about deliverance not only from his circumstances, but from his fears. I heard an acrostic for fear several years ago that has stuck with me. It is **F**alse **E**vidence **A**ppearing **R**eal. Obviously, there are good fears that protect us from danger and alert us to impending harm. But many fears in our lives are Satan's tactics to debilitate us and keep us from experiencing the peace and joy God has for us. For years I struggled with fear about my health. I had a melanoma that was found very early and removed without requiring any further treatment. While I experienced no physical side effects, I was left with a fear that gripped me and would not let go. For years, every discomfort, pain or ache was magnified in my mind so that I believed I had cancer. I spent many nights worrying about whatever twinge I happened to be feeling at the time. I let my mind wander down dark paths of fear and dread. I knew in my mind that this was unproductive, and that Satan was using this to distract me and keep me from fulfilling God's purposes in my life, but I felt powerless to do anything about it. I can't really explain what happened, but one night in a church service I knew I had had enough. I knew that God would deliver me from this fear, but I had to acknowledge it and give it to Him once and for all. That night I went to the altar and left my fear there. My pastor and the elders of our church prayed for me, and I was delivered from my fear. Since that day, I have not experienced that gripping, paralyzing weight that had been my constant companion. Occasionally, when I have one of those aches and pains that seem to come more frequently as I age, I have a passing thought about cancer, but I do not let my mind wander down that path. God has replaced my fear with peace. He has my life in His hands. I can testify with David that I sought the Lord and He delivered me from my fears. The Lord encamps around those who fear Him, and He delivers them. "For God has not given us a spirit of fearfulness, but one of power, love and sound judgment." 2 Timothy 1:7 (HCSB)

March 15

Numbers 10-11
Psalm 34:8-14
Proverbs 8:8-9
Mark 13:1-23

El Shaddai

"The Lord answered Moses, 'Is the Lord's arm too short? Now you will see whether or not what I say will come true for you.'" Numbers 11:23 NIV

"The lions may grow weak and hungry, but those who seek the Lord lack no good thing." Psalm 34:10 NIV

I LOVE TO compare different translations of the Bible. Numbers 11:23 in The Message says, "God answered Moses, 'So, do you think I can't take care of you? You'll see soon enough whether what I say happens for you or not.'" Several years ago, I made it a practice to write Bible verses on index cards that speak to me so I can refer to them often. I just wrote that one down. That verse pretty much sums it up. No matter what problem I may be facing, what question I may have, or what need I have, that is my answer. God can take care of me. Whatever He has promised me will happen. Over the last few years, my prayer has been that God will reveal Himself to me because I want to get to know Him better. I have spent much of my life seeking Him for what He can do for me, but I just want to get to know Him for who He is now. In the Old Testament we find many names for God. They all reflect different aspects of His character. One of my favorites is EL Shaddai. It means "All sufficient one, the God of the mountains, God Almighty, the Enough." God is the all-sufficient source of all our blessings. He is all-powerful. Our problems are not too big for God to handle. He is Enough.

Isaiah 59:1 says, "Surely the arm of the Lord is not too short to save, nor His ear too dull to hear." (NIV) Several years ago, my mother, my daughter, Emily, and I went to The Vatican and toured the Sistine Chapel. One of the images Michelangelo painted on the ceiling is of God's Hand reaching down from Heaven and Adam's hand reaching up to God. When I read these verses, that image came to my mind. Surely, God's arm is not too short to reach us. My arms cannot possibly reach all the way to Heaven, but His loving arms can reach down to Earth to help me whenever I am in need. He hears me and He answers me. He is EL Shaddai.

March 16

Numbers 12-13
Psalm 34:15-22
Proverbs 8:10-13
Mark 13:24-37

Be Alert

"At that time people will see the Son of Man coming in clouds with great power and glory. And He will send His angels and gather His elect from the four winds, from the ends of the Earth to the ends of Heaven. Now learn this lesson from the fig tree: As soon as its twigs get tender and its leaves come out, you know that summer is near. Even so, when you see these things happening, you know that it is near, right at the door." Mark 13:26-27 NIV

THERE HAVE ALWAYS been people who have believed they had figured out the date that Jesus would return and rapture His church beginning the period of tribulation spoken of in Revelation. Up until this time they have been wrong. Jesus Himself tells us that no one knows the day and the hour. But the verse above tells us that we can know the season. As we see world events lining up and as prophecies are fulfilled, we can see the day approaching. Make no mistake, there will come a day when Jesus will appear in the sky. On that day, those of us who know Him, who are called by His Name will go to be with Him. Those who have rejected Him will perish. We don't need to worry about when it will happen. We just need to make sure we are ready now. Are you ready? What about those around you? Are you afraid they might think you are a religious fanatic if you tell them about Jesus? What if it is today?

March 17

Numbers 14
Psalm 35:1-8
Proverbs 8:14-16
Mark 14:1-26

The Lord is With Us

"Joshua son of Nun and Caleb son of Jephunneh, who were among those who had explored the land, tore their clothes, and said to the entire Israelite assembly, 'The land we passed through and explored is exceedingly good. If the Lord is pleased with us, He will lead us into that land, a land flowing with milk and honey, and will give it to us. Only do not rebel against the Lord. And do not be afraid of the people of the land, because we will devour them. Their protection is gone, but the Lord is with us. Do not be afraid of them." Numbers 14:6-9 NIV

THE PEOPLE IN Canaan were giants and they were numerous. The spies who went into Canaan realistically saw their opposition. They accurately described what they had seen, but they did not have an accurate interpretation of their circumstance. They were leaving God out of the equation. They had watched as God delivered them from Egypt, through the Red Sea, fed them with manna, and led them to the land He had promised to give them. Now they thought they were on their own to possess it. God promised Abraham that His descendants would possess that land and God is faithful to all His promises. Joshua and Caleb alone recognized that "the Lord is with us." They believed that God would do what He had promised to do. They were ready to go in and possess the land. Unfortunately, the Israelites refused to listen to them and spent the next 40 years wandering around in the desert. Joshua and Caleb were the only ones who had the privilege of stepping foot into the promised land and receiving their inheritance.

How often do we leave God out of the equation? We have seen God do amazing things. We have watched as He provided for us, delivered us, and answered our prayers. And yet when we are asked to step out in faith and believe He will accomplish His purposes in our lives, we look at our giants and shrink back. We accurately see our circumstances as we view the mountain of difficulty before us, but we leave God out of the equation. We fail to recognize that "the Lord is with us." Step out in faith today and do not be afraid.

March 18

Numbers 15
Psalm 35:9-16
Proverbs 8:17-19
Mark 14:27-42

WILLING BUT WEAK

"Peter declared, 'Even if all fall away, I will not.' 'Truly I tell you,' Jesus answered, 'Today—yes, tonight---before the rooster crows twice you yourself will disown Me three times.' 'Watch and pray so that you will not fall into temptation. The spirit is willing, but the flesh is weak.'" Mark 14:29-30, 38 NIV

EVEN WITH THE best of intentions, sometimes we fail. Like Paul, we find ourselves saying, "I do not understand what I do. For what I want to do I do not do, but what I hate, I do... For I have the desire to do what is good, but I cannot carry it out. For I do not do the good I want to do, but the evil I do not want to do—this I keep on doing... So, I find this law at work: Although I want to do good, evil is right there with me... What a wretched man I am! Who will rescue me from this body that is subject to death? Thanks be to God, who delivers me through Jesus Christ our Lord." Romans 7:15-25 (NIV) I'm sure Peter believed he would never deny Jesus. Jesus was his best friend and he loved Him very much. When Jesus told him that they were all going to fall away and that he was going to deny Him three times that night, Peter couldn't imagine a scenario where that could possibly happen. And yet it did. Just a few hours later the disciples scattered, and Peter denied knowing Him to a servant girl. He didn't deny Jesus at gunpoint or to a Roman guard. He couldn't even tell a lowly servant girl that he was one of Jesus' followers. How disappointed he must have been in himself. He must have felt like a complete failure.

Have you ever been there? I certainly have. That sin I promised never to do, I did---again. That lie that just came out of my mouth before I even realized it. The angry words that spewed out of me like venom. I don't even know why I did it. It didn't make sense. I knew better. My intentions were good, but I succumbed to temptation again. What a wretched man I am! After the resurrection, the Gospel of Mark tells us that the young man at the tomb instructs the ladies who came to anoint Jesus' body to go and tell the disciples and Peter that Jesus had risen just as He said He would. He made sure that they told Peter. Jesus wanted Peter to know that He loved him and forgave him. The Gospel of John tells us of a conversation Jesus had with Peter before He ascended into Heaven in which He predicted Peter's future ministry. Even after Peter denied Him, Jesus still loved him and had a purpose and a plan to fulfill through him. Even though we may fail Him, He loves us and wants to forgive us and fulfill His purposes in us.

Numbers 16-17
Psalm 35:17-21
Proverbs 8:20-21
Mark 14:43-72

March 19

I Am

"Again, the High Priest asked Him, 'Are You the Messiah, the Son of the Blessed One?' 'I Am,' said Jesus, 'And you will see the Son of Man sitting at the right hand of the Mighty One and coming on the clouds of Heaven." Mark 14:61-62 NIV

IN THIS ONE small verse Jesus answers the question that had been on everyone's mind. He answered the question that is still on the minds of so many today. He said unequivocally that He is the Christ, the Son of God. If there was any doubt as to who He claimed to be, it was gone. Jesus told them that He is the Messiah. I love His answer because He didn't just say, "Yes, I am the Messiah." He said, "I Am." This ties in the Old Testament account of when Moses asked God what he should tell the Israelites when they asked him who had sent him. God told him to tell the people that "I Am sent him." It also ties in the prophecy about the Messiah found in Isaiah 7:14 which refers to the Messiah as Immanuel. The Hebrew word for Immanuel is translated "God with us" or "I Am." Matthew 1:23 tells us that this prophecy was fulfilled at Jesus' birth. Jesus then goes on to say that they will see the Son of Man seated next to God and coming on the clouds of Heaven. Jesus refers to Himself as the "Son of Man" 81 times in the Gospels. This is His most common title for Himself and no one else uses this title for Him. Another prophecy about the Messiah is found in Daniel 7:13. "In my vision at night I looked, and there before me was one like a Son of Man coming with the clouds of Heaven." (NIV) Jesus is leaving no doubt as to His identity. He wants them to know that He is the Messiah. The members of the Sanhedrin refused to believe Him and turned Him over to be crucified. Do you believe Him?

March 20

Numbers 18
Psalm 35:22-28
Proverbs 8:22-24
Mark 15:1-20

Going Along with the Crowd

"Wanting to satisfy the crowd, Pilate released Barabbas to them. He had Jesus flogged and handed Him over to be crucified." Mark 15:15 NIV

VERSE 10 TELLS us that Pilate knew Jesus was not guilty of any crime and that the only reason the chief priests had handed Jesus over to him was because they were jealous. He tried several times to get them to change their mind, but in the end, he refused to stand up and do what was right. He went along with the crowd. It is difficult to do the right thing when everyone around you is doing something else. It becomes even more difficult when they begin to mock you and ridicule you for standing up for what you believe. We find a perfect example of a man who stood up for what he believed in the face of much opposition in the life of Daniel. Throughout his lifetime there are instances in which it would have been much easier and even understandable to go along with the crowd, but Daniel stood firm. When he was first brought to Babylon, he refused to eat the choice food and wine of the king that went against the dietary restrictions God had placed over the Jews. God blessed him and he was healthier and better nourished than any of the young men who had eaten the king's food. When the king issued a decree that everyone must bow down and worship him only, Daniel refused to obey and continued praying every day to God and worshipping Him alone. He was thrown into the lion's den and God brought him out completely unharmed. In the book of Daniel, we also see the account of Shadrach, Meshach and Abednego who refused to bow down and worship anyone but God. They were thrown into the fiery furnace and came out without even smelling like smoke. In each of these instances they faced the ridicule and mocking of the crowd, and they also faced the very real possibility of death. Yet they remained faithful. They did not bow to peer pressure. Are you willing to satisfy the crowd, or will you remain faithful even when it is difficult? Will you do the right thing even if you are alone?

March 21

Numbers 19-20
Psalm 36:1-6
Proverbs 8:25-26
Mark 15:21-47

A Better Way

"The Lord said to Moses, 'Take your staff, and you and your brother Aaron gather the assembly together. Speak to that rock before their eyes and it will pour out its water. You will bring water out of the rock for the community so they and their livestock can drink.' So, Moses took the staff from the Lord's presence, just as He commanded him. He and Aaron gathered the assembly together in front of the rock and Moses said to them. 'Listen, you rebels, must we bring you water out of this rock?' Then Moses raised his arm and struck the rock twice with his staff. Water gushed out, and the community and their livestock drank. But the Lord spoke to Moses and Aaron, 'Because you did not trust in Me enough to honor Me as holy in the sight of the Israelites, you will not bring this community into the land I give them.'" Numbers 20:7-12 NIV

THIS PASSAGE IS evidence that God takes our obedience seriously. When He tells us to do something, He expects us to do it. If we do not do what He tells us we will face consequences. The consequence of disobedience for Moses and Aaron was not getting to enter the promised land. God instructed Moses to speak to the rock and water would pour forth. Moses decided to strike the rock with his staff instead. This doesn't seem like that big of a deal on the surface. The water still poured forth. We don't know exactly what was going on in Moses' mind or in his heart, but God knew. God had used this very staff 40 years earlier to bring water out of the rock. That time God told Moses to strike the rock and water poured forth. Maybe this time he thought God forgot to tell him to strike the rock. Striking the rock had worked before. He had seen it work the last time so he would do the same thing again and it should work. Right? He didn't trust God's instructions. He took matters into his own hands. He had to try to help God out. Or maybe it was pride. If he just spoke to the rock, he wasn't really participating. God did everything. If he struck the rock, his action of striking the rock is the thing that brought forth the water, so he got part of the glory. It also could have been anger. He was clearly angry with the people for their grumbling and complaining yet again. He had put up with it for 40 years wandering around in the desert so maybe he had had enough and striking the rock was lashing out in anger. Whatever Moses' motive was for disobeying God's instructions, it was still disobedience. God gave Moses a specific instruction and he did not do what God said. He thought he had a better way. The end does not justify the means. Just because he got the same result does not mean that he had been obedient. When God gives us instructions, do we obey Him, or do we think we have a better way?

March 22

Numbers 21-22
Psalm 36:7-12
Proverbs 8:27-29
Mark 16

The Shadow of His Wing

"God, Your faithful love is so valuable that people take refuge in the shadow of Your wings." Psalm 36:7 HCSB

THIS BEAUTIFUL IMAGERY is found numerous times in scripture. Psalm 17:8, 36:7, 57:1, 61:4, 63:7, and Ruth 2:12 all give us a picture of God stretching out His protective arms over us like an eagle stretching out its wing over her eaglets. The eagle protects her young from the oppressive heat of the sun. As a little girl in Alabama, I can relate to the scorching summer heat. Working in my grandmother's garden, picking vegetables, planting seeds, or hoeing the weeds out from around the tender plants with sweat pouring into my eyes, I couldn't wait till I got to the south end of the rows. At that end stood a grove of trees, so the last third of the row I would get to work in the shade. The difference was amazing. The temperature was the same, but the covering of the shade made all the difference in the world. The shadow of the eagle's wing also protected the young eaglets from the wind and storms. High in the trees there was little protection against the buffeting of strong winds and heavy rains. The eagle stands strong as the winds blow and the rain pelts her, but her precious little ones are warm and dry beneath her wings. There is peace and calm in the midst of the storm. They are not worried or afraid because they know they are safe.

If we remain under the shadow of the Almighty, beneath the protection of His mighty wings, the storms still come and the winds buffet all around us, but we remain safe and dry under His wings. He protects us from the dangers around us and from the scorching heat of oppression. If the eaglets venture out on their own path, away from the eagle, they must face the heat, wind, and storms on their own. "He who dwells in the shelter of the Most High will rest in the shadow of the Almighty. I will say of the Lord, 'He is my refuge and my fortress, my God, in whom I trust. Surely, He will save you from the fowler's snare and from the deadly pestilence. He will cover you with His feathers and under His wings you will find refuge; His faithfulness will be your shield and rampart." Psalm 91:1-4 (NIV)

Numbers 23-24
Psalm 37:1-6
Proverbs 8:30-31
Luke 1:1-25

March 23

Delight

"Take delight in the Lord and He will give you the desires of your heart. Commit your way to the Lord; trust in Him and He will do this: He will make your righteous reward shine like the dawn, your vindication like the noonday sun." Psalm 37:4-6 NIV

WE LIKE THE sound of the last part of verse 4. God will give me the desires of my heart. Yay!! Let's see, what do I want? A new house? A new wardrobe? Hum? Maybe I should make a list like I do for Santa each year. Unfortunately, we tend to gloss over the first part of the verse. Delight yourself in the Lord. What does that mean? Delighting in something means that we derive our pleasure from it. I cannot honestly say that I derive my pleasure from Him. It doesn't say I derive some pleasure from Him, but that I derive my pleasure from Him. Is He the greatest source of my pleasure? Would I rather be spending time with Him than doing anything else? Do I yearn for time with Him? If I am delighting myself in Him and He is my greatest source of delight, then what will be the desires of my heart? It will be to know Him more intimately and to seek Him more and more. The promise here is not that He will give me the things of this world if I delight in Him, but that He will give me Himself and in doing that He is giving me the greatest blessing He can possibly give me. The next verse tells us to commit my way to the Lord and trust in Him and He will make my righteousness shine like the dawn. Righteousness does not refer to perfection. I am far from perfect. It refers to being righteous in His sight because I am in right standing with Him. The reason I am in right standing with Him is not because of my own actions, but because of my relationship with Jesus. He has taken the penalty for my sin and has left me in right standing before God. Matthew 6:33 tells us to "seek first His kingdom and His righteousness, and all these things will be given to me as well." (NIV) If I am seeking Him and the righteousness I have because of my relationship with Jesus, then I don't have to worry about anything else, He will take care of it all for me.

March 24

Numbers 25
Psalm 37:7-13
Proverbs 8:32-33
Luke 1:26-56

Do Not Fret

"Be still before the Lord and wait patiently for Him; do not fret when people succeed in their ways, when they carry out their wicked schemes. Refrain from anger and turn from wrath; do not fret—it leads only to evil." Psalm 37:7-8 NIV

THIS ONE HITS a little too close to home. I find myself fretting a lot more than I would like to admit. I can be having a great day and then something happens, someone says something to me, or I find out about something that really isn't that big of a deal, but I spend hours fretting over it. I get all caught up in the injustice of it and rehearse over and over in my head how I should respond. I let myself get more and more upset to the point that I say or do something I shouldn't. Often when I look back on it, I realize that my fretting was completely unnecessary. I either didn't have all the facts and so it wasn't as bad as I thought or my getting upset didn't make one bit of difference in the outcome. I am not the kind of person that can just sit back and do nothing when I see a problem. Sometimes this is a good thing because I get things done. But I am learning that I need to seek God before I act. There is a big difference in the outcome of a situation when I take the time to be still before the Lord and seek His guidance and when I just react with my own plan of action. First, my attitude is different. Instead of fretting myself into a state of anger about the situation, God gives me a peace and calm that helps me to think more clearly and react with more love and grace. Sometimes He makes me just keep my mouth shut and let Him deal with it. Although it is frustrating, I must admit that it always turns out better. At other times He gives me permission to intervene, but because He has calmed me down, I am able to respond with a godlier approach and the result is always better than if I had gone in like a bull in a china shop demanding the outcome I think is just. Secondly, when I take the time to pray about the situation and turn it over to God, He intervenes in the hearts of the other people involved so that their reaction is often different. The end of yesterday's reading said, "and the justice of your cause will shine like the noonday sun." He has our back. We can trust Him. When we leave the results to Him, He will bring about the right result. We may not immediately see the result we want, but He assures us "that in all things He works for the good of those who love Him, who have been called according to His purpose." Romans 8:28 (NIV)

Numbers 26
Psalm 37:14-22
Proverbs 8:34-36
Luke 1:57-80

March 25

Consequences

> "Not one of them was among those counted by Moses and Aaron the priest when they counted the Israelites in the Desert of Sinai. For the Lord had told those Israelites they would surely die in the wilderness, and not one of them was left except Caleb son of Jephunneh and Joshua son of Nun." Numbers 26:64-65 NIV

In Numbers 14:27-35, God told Moses that not one of the Israelites who were 20 years or older at the time would enter the promised land except for Caleb and Joshua. They did not trust God to take care of them and bring them into the land He had promised them. He told them that they would have to wander around in the desert for forty years, one year for each of the forty days they explored Canaan. In today's passage we find the fulfillment of that promise by God. At the end of forty years of wandering, they took another census and found that not one person included on that earlier census was still alive except for Joshua, Caleb, and Moses. We know that Moses was not allowed to enter the promised land because of his disobedience in bringing the water out of the rock. There are consequences for our sin. Sometimes the punishment is swift and complete and at other times the consequences last for years. Unfortunately, as the Israelites found out, sometimes we are not the only ones who have to suffer the consequences for our actions. The Israelite men and women had to wander in the desert for forty years, but their children also had to wander in the desert. They would eventually get to enter the promised land, but only after years of wandering and watching their parents die in the desert. If their parents had trusted God, they could have spent those years living in the land flowing with milk and honey and experiencing God's blessings. Whether we are the one who has brought the consequences of our actions onto others, or we are the one who is living with the consequences of someone else's actions, we can be assured that if we turn to Him, He will use those consequences to bring about good in our lives. He will use them to train us and teach us and to give us the joy of ministering to others who are facing similar circumstances. God used their experiences in the desert to prepare the children of Israel to enter the promised land and He will do the same for you. You can't do anything about the past, but you can go forward committed to obeying God now.

Numbers 27-28
Psalm 37:23-29
Proverbs 9:1-2
Luke 2:1-20

Awe

"But Mary treasured up all these things and pondered them in her heart."
Luke 2:19 NIV

MARY WAS A simple young girl who had been chosen by God to be the mother of His Son. She didn't understand why God had chosen her or even how it could possibly be real. She was a participant in the single most important event in the history of the world. Did she understand the importance of what was taking place? Did she have any idea that her Son would be the Savior of the world? This verse tells us that she was just taking it all in. She trusted God completely and was submitted to His will in her life, so she was just sitting back watching the events unfolding before her. I have to believe she was in awe as the shepherds found them and worshipped Jesus and as the wise men brought Him gifts from afar. I can't even imagine the conversations that she and Joseph must have had deciding how to go about raising God's Son. She must have been watching Him throughout His childhood and pondering in her heart how different He was from her other children. There is no indication in scripture that she told others that He was God's Son. We don't even find that Mary explained herself to Joseph. An angel came to Joseph in a dream and told him that the child Mary was carrying was conceived through the Holy Spirit. There must have been talk around town when Mary began to show and it was obvious that she was pregnant, but we are not told that she tried to explain to everyone that the baby was God's Son. She just quietly accepted God's will for her life. It was enough that she knew what God was doing in her life. She didn't have to tell everyone else. Sometimes I feel like that, too. Obviously, in a much different way, but when God speaks to me or does something amazing in my life, I just need time to treasure it in my heart and ponder it before I tell anyone else. I am so in awe that He would intervene in my life or that He would speak to me that I just want time to think about it and let it sink in for a while. And sometimes it takes a little while to grasp the reality of what He has done and to fathom the mystery of the King of the Universe using me to carry out His purposes here on Earth.

March 27

Numbers 29-30
Psalm 37:30-34
Proverbs 9:3-6
Luke 2:21-38

The Value of God's Word

"The mouths of the righteous utter wisdom; and their tongue speaks what is just. The law of their God is in their heart; their feet do not slip." Psalm 37:30-31 NIV

MANY OF THE problems we face are a result of poor choices and a lack of wisdom. The righteous man seeks God and spends time studying God's Word. He has the law of God in his heart, and he does what it says. Obedience to God's Word protects us from many of the snares that cause us to stumble. "I have hidden Your Word in my heart that I might not sin against You." Psalm 119:11 (NIV) "Your Word is a lamp for my feet and a light on my path." Psalm 119:105 (NIV) "All scripture is God-breathed and is useful for teaching, rebuking, correcting and training in righteousness, so that the servant of God may be thoroughly equipped for every good work." 2 Timothy 3:16-17 (NIV) God is the source of all wisdom. "If any of you lacks wisdom, he should ask God, who gives generously to all without finding fault, and it will be given to you." James 1:5 (NIV) "The fear of the Lord is the beginning of knowledge; but fools despise wisdom and instruction." Proverbs 1:7 (NIV) "Oh, how I love Your law! I meditate on it all day long. Your commands are always with me and make me wiser than my enemies. I have more insight than all my teachers, for I meditate on Your statutes. I have more understanding than the elders, for I obey Your precepts. I have kept my feet from every evil path so that I might obey Your Word. I have not departed from Your laws, for You Yourself have taught me. How sweet are Your words to my taste, sweeter than honey to my mouth! I gain understanding from Your precepts; therefore, I hate every wrong path." Psalm 119:97-104 (NIV) We cannot expect to have wisdom unless we spend time seeking the One who is the source of all wisdom. Our decisions, our actions and the words that come out of our mouth will be the evidence of the time and attention we give to God's Word.

March 28

Numbers 31
Psalm 37:35-40
Proverbs 9:7-9
Luke 2:39-52

Wisdom and Humility

"Do not rebuke mockers or they will hate you; rebuke the wise and they will love you. Instruct the wise and they will be wiser still; teach the righteous and they will add to their understanding." Proverbs 9:8-9 NIV

THE PASSAGE TODAY in Proverbs follows nicely our passage yesterday in Psalm. Yesterday we saw that all wisdom comes from God and that the way to gain wisdom is to seek the One who is the source of wisdom through prayer and studying His Word. The passage today gives us insight into the heart of the wise. "When pride comes, then comes disgrace, but with humility comes wisdom." Proverbs 11:2 (NIV) "Who is wise and understanding among you? Let them show it by their good life, by deeds done in the humility that comes from wisdom." James 3:13 (NIV) A wise man welcomes correction and rebuke because he knows that is the way to gain deeper understanding and more wisdom. None of us likes to be rebuked. We do not enjoy correction and reproof, but the humble man recognizes that without it we cannot grow and mature into the person God designed for us to be. Pride keeps us from acknowledging our sin and the areas where we need to change. "Where there is strife, there is pride, but wisdom is found in those who take advice." Proverbs 13:10 (NIV) How do you react when someone corrects you? Do you get angry and think, "How dare they tell me what I should do?" Or do you listen to what they have to say and respond by seeking God and asking Him to reveal to you changes that you need to make. They may not be entirely accurate in their rebuke, but there is usually something that God can use to teach you through their words. There is always room to grow in our wisdom and usually a need for a little more humility as well.

March 29

Numbers 32
Psalm 38:1-8
Proverbs 9:10-12
Luke 3:1-20

We're All in This Together

"He said to them, 'If the Gadites and Reubenites, every man armed for battle, cross over the Jordan with you before the Lord, then when the land is subdued before you, you must give them the land of Gilead as their possession." Numbers 32:29 NIV

As they approached the promised land this time, they were about to cross the Jordan and take possession of the land God had promised them. The Reubenites and Gadites surveyed the land and decided that this land would be good for them because they had large herds and flocks. The land on this side of the Jordan was good for grazing their livestock, so they went to Moses and asked if they could stay and take possession of this land. The problem was that Moses needed every able-bodied man to help them take possession of the land that had been promised to them. They agreed to go with Moses and fight alongside their brothers to take control of the land and after all the land had been conquered, they could return and live in Gilead. A few years ago, *High School Musical* was the most popular movie for preteen and teen girls and both of my daughters loved it. It played so often on my TV that without even realizing it I memorized the words to all the songs. When I read today's passage, I couldn't help thinking of the words to one of the songs, "We're All in This Together." I think if they did a remake of the *Ten Commandments* when they came to this scene Moses might break out into his own version of this song to convince the tribes of Gad and Reuben that they needed to help their brothers out. Can't you just picture it? Before the scene is over, they would all be singing and dancing together and ready to go over and conquer anybody in their way.

God created us to live in community. We are all in this together. We need each other. We need other Christians for support, encouragement, guidance, and strength. We are designed to function within a body of believers. We have a role and purpose within that body. Are you fulfilling that role? Are you serving others? Are you providing encouragement, support, guidance, and strength to others? Ask the Lord to show you ways that you can step up and work together with other believers.

March 30

Numbers 33-34
Psalm 38:9-15
Proverbs 9:13-15
Luke 3:21-38

Clean House

"Speak to the Israelites and say to them, 'When you cross the Jordan into Canaan, drive out all the inhabitants of the land before you. Destroy all their carved images and their cast idols and demolish all their high places. Take possession of the land and settle in it, for I have given you the land to possess… But if you do not drive out the inhabitants of the land, those you allow to remain will become barbs in your eyes and thorns in your sides.'" Numbers 33:51-53, 55 NIV

I WAS RAISED in Alabama where football is a part of who you are. It is not just a game. You are either an Auburn fan or an Alabama fan. You CANNOT be both. I am an Auburn fan. Win or lose they are my team. Fall is my favorite time of year and on any Saturday you will either find me at a game or in front of my TV yelling for Auburn or whatever team is playing Alabama that day. I know that sounds ugly, but that is just how it is. Growing up with football, I understand the game pretty well. I have watched as coaches have come and gone and I have come to understand something that didn't used to make sense to me. Whenever a new coach comes in, they almost always get rid of everyone on the staff before them. They call it "cleaning house." I used to think that was unnecessary. In any other business, if you hire a new leader, you keep most of the other staff so that you have an easy transition. They can help and tell you how they do things there. But this doesn't work in football. Each coach has his own style, his own way of doing things. If you leave the old staff, they tend to want to keep things the way they were. We don't like change, so we resist doing things differently. When a new coach comes in, he doesn't have much time. He only has a few months to get everyone on his program, working as a team with his game plan. He doesn't have time to deal with resistance. It is better to just start fresh.

God was telling the Israelites the same thing. They needed to clean house. This was going to be a new day for them. They had a fresh start. He wanted them working together as a team on His game plan. He didn't want them to be influenced by the people living in the land now because they worshipped other gods and had evil practices that God didn't even want them to know about. He wanted them to be a people set apart for His purposes. He wants the same thing for us. He wants to get rid of anything in your life that isn't on His game plan. Ask Him today to reveal to you anything you need to drive out of your life so that you can be set apart for Him.

Numbers 35-36
Psalm 38:16-22
Proverbs 9:16-18
Luke 4:1-21

March 31

Tempted by the Devil

"Jesus, full of the Holy Spirit, left the Jordan, and was led by the Spirit in the wilderness, where for forty days He was tempted by the devil." Luke 4:1-2 NIV

This passage clearly tells us that Jesus was led by the Spirit into the desert where He was tempted. It doesn't say that Satan followed Him or that Jesus just happened to be there so Satan tempted Him. It says that the Spirit led Him there. This was a planned encounter between Jesus and Satan. It gives us the perfect example of how to deal with Satan when he tempts us. We have the privilege of watching as Jesus skillfully and without hesitation fends off every attempt by Satan to cause Him to stumble. He counters every argument from Satan with scripture. Instead of getting into a lengthy argument, He simply quotes scripture. Satan responds by moving on to some other tactic. He knows he cannot argue with scripture. This also introduces truth into the situation. Satan is the father of lies and will say anything to get us to go along with him. Quoting scripture reinforces in our minds what God's Word says and reminds us of His promises.

This passage also shows us that temptation is not evidence of something we are doing wrong. Actually, it may be evidence that we are doing exactly what we are supposed to be doing. Satan will not bother us if we are following his path in the wrong direction. We are exactly where he wants us to be. We get his attention when we start doing what God wants us to do. The fact that we are being tempted is not the issue, it is how we deal with the temptation that can be the problem. This encounter is indicative of the most common tactics Satan uses to tempt us. 1. He makes us question whether God can or will provide for our needs. 2. He tries to get us to follow our own plans and dreams instead of God's plan. 3. He makes us impatient so that instead of waiting on God's timing we take matters into our own hands. Satan's message hasn't changed much in the last two thousand years and like Jesus, we can stand firm on the truth of God's Word to defend against his attacks.

Deuteronomy 1
Psalm 39:1-6
Proverbs 10:1-2
Luke 4:22-44

Turn and Go

"The Lord our God said to us at Horeb, 'You have stayed long enough at this mountain. Break camp and advance into the hill country of the Amorites; go to all the neighboring peoples in the Arabah, in the mountains, in the western foothills, in the Negev, and along the coast, to the land of the Canaanites and to Lebanon, as far as the great river, the Euphrates." Deuteronomy 1:6-7 NIV

This command to the Israelites is one that I think we need to hear as well. "You have been here long enough: Turn and go!" My Bible is an NIV. That is the one I have gotten used to, but I like to look at other translations as well because it gives me a clearer picture of the meanings of words. I think sometimes we lose something in the translation from Greek or Hebrew to English. The NIV says "break camp and advance." The RSV and ESV both say, "turn and take your journey." The Message expounds on the command here. It says "On your way now! Get moving!" God is not saying to the children of Israel, "I guess you have wandered around long enough. Go ahead and get your stuff and let's go on over the Jordan. Take your time, when you are ready, we will move on." He is telling them, "Ok, let's go! You have been here long enough! It is time you got out of here. Go now!"

Are you stuck in the wilderness? Sometimes we wander around so long we don't even realize we are wandering. God has a plan and a purpose for us. He uses time in the wilderness to prepare us, cleanse us, test us, and purify us. But when He tells us it is time to move forward, it is time, and we need to go! Is He telling you that you have been wandering around long enough? On your way, now! Get moving! Go now!

April 2

Deuteronomy 2-3
Psalm 39:7-13
Proverbs 10:3-5
Luke 5

Sufficient

"When He had finished speaking, He said to Simon, 'Put out into deep water, and let down the nets for a catch.' Simon answered, 'Master, we've worked hard all night and haven't caught anything. But because You say so, I will let down the nets.' When they had done so, they caught such a large number of fish that their nets began to break." Luke 5:4-6 NIV

Can't you just picture this exchange between Jesus and Peter? Jesus, the carpenter turned preacher, is telling Peter, the fisherman, how to fish. Peter's reaction is priceless. I would love to have heard the words he spoke because I'll bet they had some skepticism, maybe even a little sarcasm in their tone. "Ok Jesus, we have been fishing all night and haven't caught anything. We are tired and ready to go home. You know we've been doing this a long time and we are pretty good at it, but if You say so, we'll put our nets back out." I don't mean to be critical of Peter. Believe me, I am sure I would have reacted the same way. And at least Peter obeyed Jesus. I might have been tempted to explain to Him why there were no fish in that area and how we would be better off waiting a couple of days or going to a different spot. Peter said, "At Your word, I will let down the nets."

While we can learn from Peter's obedience, I don't want us to miss another important lesson from this story. Let's examine why Jesus chose to do this miracle. This was not an afterthought. When He finished speaking, I don't think He suddenly decided He was hungry and wanted some fish, so He told them to go fishing. Jesus knew His time was limited. He was purposeful about everything He did, and I believe this is no exception. Jesus was showing the disciples that He alone is sufficient to meet all their needs. We know we need His help in the areas where we are weak, but in the areas where we are strong, the things that we are good at, we think we don't really need His help. We will let Him focus on our weaknesses. We don't want to ask Him for too much. After all, He might get tired of us asking so we better save up for the times we really need Him. Right? Jesus was showing Peter and his friends that even in the things we think we are good at, He is better. He wants to help us in everything. Even in the areas where we think we are sufficient; we are going to have a bad night when we don't catch any fish. But He is sufficient to meet all our needs. Always!

Deuteronomy 4
Psalm 40:1-5
Proverbs 10:6-8
Luke 6:1-26

Don't Forget

"Only be careful and watch yourselves closely so that you do not forget the things your eyes have seen or let them fade from your heart as long as you live. Teach them to your children and to their children after them." Deuteronomy 4:9 NIV

MOSES IS GIVING the Israelites the secret to overcoming fear and standing against Satan's attacks. "Be careful, don't forget the things your eyes have seen or let them fade from your heart." Focus on God. If we are reminding ourselves of the faithfulness of God and everything we have seen Him do in our lives and in the lives of others, we will not faint. We will not grow weary. We will be able to stand firm against the lies that Satan hurls at us. Remembrance is a theme we see throughout scripture. We are constantly told to remember what God has done for us and to tell others. It is true that we should remember so we can give Him the praise and thanksgiving that He deserves. That is very important and should not be neglected, but there is another reason as well. Remembering increases our faith. We have very short memories. When we are in a crisis or a struggle we wonder if God will help us. God delivered the children of Israel from one crisis after another and yet the next time they found themselves in a difficulty they became anxious, fearful, and worried that He wouldn't come through for them again. Moses had to remind them repeatedly of all the things God had done for them. Here he is telling them they do not need to forget what they have seen. He is also telling them to tell their children and grandchildren about God's faithfulness.

My husband and I have a memorial box in our house. It is a shadow box that hangs on our wall that contains small tokens, pictures, symbols that remind us of the things God has done for us and the times He has acted in unequivocal ways in our lives. Unless you know the stories behind each thing in the box, it looks like a random hodgepodge of unrelated things. It reminds us of God's faithfulness, but it also gives us the opportunity to share those stories of God's faithfulness with our children and with others who visit in our home. It has been a tremendous source of blessing to us, and an avenue to share our testimony with others. I encourage you to do something to remind you of God's faithfulness in your life.

April 4

Deuteronomy 5-6
Psalm 40:6-10
Proverbs 10:9-11
Luke 6:27-49

After God's Heart

"I desire to do Your will, my God; Your law is within my heart. I proclaim Your saving acts in the great assembly; I do not seal my lips, as you know. I do not hide Your righteousness in my heart; I speak of Your faithfulness and Your saving help; I do not conceal Your love and Your faithfulness from the great assembly." Psalm 40:8-10 NIV

WE ARE NOT told the circumstances that David faced as he wrote this Psalm. He begins by praising God for His faithfulness in the past and will conclude by asking for help with his current situation. But before he asks for help, he tells God that he desires to do His will. He will boldly ask God to intervene on his behalf but is submitting to God's wisdom and authority. He is acknowledging that God knows best, so above all else he desires God's will. He can boldly profess to God that he has been faithful. He has told others about God's protection and provision. He has proclaimed God's love and His truth to others. He was well acquainted with God's law and has hidden it within his heart. David knew God intimately and he trusted Him completely. This gives us a glimpse of the one who God calls "a man after My own heart, he will do everything I want him to do." Acts 13:22 (NIV) Adultery and murder in David's history prevent us from thinking that he was somehow more holy than the rest of us. David was not a perfect man and yet God Himself called David "a man after My own heart." David loved and trusted God. I believe that love and trust are what God desires the most from us. He knows we are human and that we are not perfect. He knows that we are going to mess up. But His desire for us is that we love Him and trust Him as David did. Even during David's greatest failures, He sought God. He did not try to run away. When confronted with his sin, he confessed, repented, and turned to God. He trusted God to deal with him in the most loving and just way and he left the outcome to God. David sought God when he faced his greatest troubles and fears. He poured his heart out to God and then trusted Him enough to leave the outcome in His hands. That is God's desire for us as well. He wants us to love Him and trust Him. Oh, how I desire that God would say I am "a woman after His own heart."

April 5

Deuteronomy 7-8
Psalm 40:11-17
Proverbs 10:12-14
Luke 7:1-23

Power and Riches

"You may say to yourself, 'My power and the strength of my hands have produced this wealth for me.' But remember the Lord your God, for it is He who gives you the ability to produce wealth, and so confirms His covenant, which He swore to your ancestors, as it is today. If you ever forget the Lord your God and follow other gods and worship and bow down to them, I testify against you today that you will surely be destroyed. Like the nations the Lord destroyed before you, so you will be destroyed for not obeying the Lord your God." Deuteronomy 8:17-20 NIV

IN THE CULTURE we live in, we are encouraged to work hard, pay our own way, and do whatever it takes to get ahead. We work long hours, and even put in overtime to provide for our family. We instill this mentality into our children as well. We fill every waking minute with sports, school, homework, dance, gymnastics, boy scouts, etc. We work and strive and stress to get more and more and more stuff. We want the best house, the newest car, and the latest fashions. We do whatever it takes to make sure our kid is the best basketball player on the team, the smartest girl in her class, or the prettiest toddler in a tiara. But at what cost? Families are falling apart, staggering numbers of children and adults are on antidepressants or anxiety medications, drugs and alcohol are being used at alarming rates to help people escape from their everyday lives. Self-help books line the shelves of bookstores, and it is difficult to get an appointment with therapists because they are booked weeks in advance. We have bought into the message of this verse. We believe that our power and the strength of our hands has produced whatever we have so we must keep working harder and harder to maintain it. Let me interject here that I believe that hard work is a good thing, and we should not sit around and let others work to pay our way. That is not what this is about. What this passage is telling us is that we must never forget that God is the one who deserves the praise and thanksgiving for any accomplishments we may have. He created us and it is His blessing on our life that provides all that we need. We are utterly dependent on Him for our very lives and if we forget this, we will face the consequences. Pride and self-reliance are very dangerous. The secret to finding fulfillment and joy in our lives is not in getting more wealth and power. It is in finding balance and ordering our lives around His priorities instead of our worldly desires and passions. The gods of power, wealth, status, popularity, and fame are just as destructive to us today as the gods Baal and Ashtoreth were to the Israelites. If we bow down to them, we will suffer the consequences.

Deuteronomy 9-10
Psalm 41:1-6
Proverbs 10:15-17
Luke 7:24-50

April 6

Fear and Reverence

> "And now, Israel, what does the Lord your God ask of you, but to fear the Lord your God, to walk in obedience to Him, to love Him, to serve the Lord your God with all your heart and with all your soul, and to observe the Lord's commands and decrees that I am giving you today for your good?" Deuteronomy 10:12 NIV

EARLIER THIS WEEK, we talked about loving and trusting God. To be "a man after God's own heart" there is something else that we cannot forget. King David knew God intimately and loved Him dearly, but He never forgot that He alone is God. David never lost his sense of awe and reverence for the Creator of the universe. His close, personal relationship with God never allowed him to think they were peers, buddies, or pals. David recognized who God is and never tried to elevate his own position in the relationship. I cringe when I hear people calling God "the man upstairs" or speaking about Him in ways that are too familiar and fail to acknowledge His absolute supremacy and complete authority. The Bible tells us over and over that we are to fear God and be in awe of Him. "For great is the Lord and most worthy of praise; He is to be feared above all gods. For all the gods of the nations are idols, but the Lord made the heavens." I Chronicles 16:25-26 (NIV) "Let all the Earth fear the Lord, let all the people of the world revere Him. For He spoke and it came to be. He commanded, and it stood firm." Psalm 33:8-9 (NIV) "I tell you, my friends, do not be afraid of those who kill the body and after that can do no more. But I will show you whom you should fear; Fear Him who, after the killing of the body, has the authority to throw you into Hell. Yes, I tell you, fear Him." Luke 12:4-5 (NIV) God is our loving, merciful, gracious Father, but He is also the holy, just, righteous Lord of the universe. We cannot begin to reconcile those two things in our minds, and yet we cannot ignore either reality. The holy, majestic, all-powerful, Lord of lords and King of kings loves me and wants to have a relationship with me. He desires to spend time with me and help me. He cares about what concerns me. As I grow closer to Him, my reverence and fear of Him are increasing. Intimate knowledge of Him reveals my own shortcomings. Recognition of who I am reveals His mercy and grace and fills me with love and thanksgiving. Fear and reverence go hand in hand with love and trust.

April 7

Deuteronomy 11-12
Psalm 41:7-13
Proverbs 10:18-21
Luke 8:1-18

Thorns

> "Other seed fell among thorns, which grew up with it and choked the plants. The seed that fell among thorns stands for those who hear, but as they go on their way they are choked by life's worries, riches and pleasures, and they do not mature."
> Luke 8:7, 14 NIV

JESUS OFTEN USED parables to teach difficult concepts. He used things they were familiar with, that they were around every day to help them understand deep, spiritual matters. Although the story itself is easy to understand, there were often hidden meanings in His words. Those who were sincere and were seeking spiritual understanding would be able to figure them out, but those who were not seeking would not understand His meaning. This is one of the few parables that Jesus explained to His disciples. The seed is the Word of God. This could take many forms. It could be a sermon, a Bible study, a song, a book or meditating on scripture. We are fortunate today to have an abundance of avenues to receive God's Word. The question is what we do with it after we have heard it. Unfortunately, I think many of us allow God's Word to fall among the thorns. We go to church, attend Bible studies, listen to Christian radio, but then we go on our way allowing worries, fears, busyness, etc. to keep us from applying its truths. Those things are not necessarily bad. We can so fill our time with activity, even good activity, that we have no time left to seek God. We never mature in our faith because we never allow the truths of God's Word to make a difference in our lives. There is no change in our hearts. We let the truths go in one ear and out the other. We have good intentions, but then we get busy and forget what we heard. Ask God to show you the thorns in your life that need to be removed so that you can mature and develop into the person He wants you to be.

April 8

Deuteronomy 13-14
Psalm 42
Proverbs 10:22-24
Luke 8:19-39

Listen

> "The Lord your God is testing you to find out whether you love Him with all your heart and all your soul. It is the Lord your God you must follow and Him you must revere. Keep His commands and obey Him; serve Him and hold fast to Him."
> Deuteronomy 13:3-4 NIV

As I have told you before, I love to look at different translations of God's Word because it gives us a fuller understanding of the meaning of a passage. When I looked up this passage in several other versions, verse 4 is translated a little differently than in the NIV. The HCSB says, "Keep His commands and listen to His voice." Several other versions say, "Keep His commands and obey His voice." I have had several conversations lately with people about hearing God's voice. This is a difficult concept to explain to people. Obviously, God's voice is not audible so how do we know that it is Him talking to us and not just our imagination? How do we know that we aren't just hearing what we want to hear? In John 10:3-5, 14, Jesus Himself tells us, "The gatekeeper opens the gate for him, and the sheep listen to His voice. He calls His own sheep by name and leads them out. When He has brought out all His own, He goes on ahead of them, and His sheep follow Him because they know His voice. But they will never follow a stranger; in fact, they will run away from him because they do not recognize a stranger's voice... I am the good shepherd; I know My sheep and My sheep know Me." (NIV) In Isaiah 30:21 we are told, "Whether you turn to the right or to the left, your ears will hear a voice behind you, saying, 'This is the way, walk in it.'" (NIV) Scripture is very clear that God does speak to us. He speaks through His Word, but He also speaks to us in our hearts as well. The Holy Spirit is living in us, guiding us, leading us, and showing us which way to go. He is there to help us make decisions and to show us God's will. Unfortunately, His voice isn't the only one trying to get our attention. Satan is trying to convince us to follow his path and our own desires and will are vying for our attention as well. The only way that we can hear and recognize God's voice is by spending time with Him. We must get still and quiet long enough to seek His face and truly listen to His voice. He does not play hide the ball with us. He wants us to hear His voice and follow His path. He wants to show us the best way, but He will not force us to listen. He usually does not put up a flashing billboard that says, "Go this way, not that way." He expects us to seek Him. We recognize His voice when we know Him. If we want to hear His voice, we cannot have a superficial relationship with Him. Recognition of His voice comes from intimacy and intimacy comes from time spent with Him.

Deuteronomy 15-16
Psalm 43
Proverbs 10:25-27
Luke 8:40-56

Vengeance

"Vindicate me, my God, and plead my cause against an unfaithful nation; rescue me from those who are deceitful and wicked... Send me Your light and Your faithful care, let them lead me." Psalm 43:1, 3 NIV

WHEN WE FEEL that we have been wronged or misunderstood, it is our natural tendency to want to set things straight. We want everyone to know the truth. We want to be proven right. Sometimes that is possible. Unfortunately, often it doesn't work out that way. Life is just messy. Our intentions are not always understood. Feelings are hurt. There is not always a good resolution. As a social worker I dealt with lots of messy situations. If there is one thing I learned, it is that there are two sides to every story. There are often more than two sides. People perceive things in different ways. If two people see the exact same event, they will give you different versions of what happened. We come to a situation from the perspective of where we have been. It is not possible to be completely objective and neutral. This is especially true when emotions get involved. Paul gives us good advice in Romans 12:19. "Do not take revenge, my dear friends, but leave room for God's wrath, for it is written: 'It is Mine to avenge; I will repay,' says the Lord." (NIV) We are told instead to forgive. We are not told to forgive if someone asks for forgiveness or if they deserve forgiveness. We are just told to forgive. Jesus Himself tells us in Matthew 18:22 that we are to forgive seventy-seven times. This is not a specific number that we have to keep track of so that on the seventy-eighth time it is ok not to forgive. Rather Jesus is telling us that we are to forgive an unlimited number of times. Whenever someone wrongs us, we are to forgive them. And then we are to leave it in God's hands to deal with them appropriately. This doesn't mean that God will necessarily punish them in the way that we think they need to be punished. But that also means that He will not deal with us in the way that someone we have wronged may want us to be punished. By leaving it in God's hands we are allowing Him to be God. We are submitting to Him with the knowledge that He really does know best, and He will deal with the situation in the best possible way for everyone. It is hard to let go of hurt and pain, but if we don't, we are allowing bitterness and resentment to take root in our heart. God doesn't expect us to do it on our own. He will give us the strength and the will to forgive. Ask Him to search your heart and reveal to you anyone you need to forgive. Then turn it over to Him.

April 10

Deuteronomy 17-18
Psalm 44:1-8
Proverbs 10:28-30
Luke 9:1-17

Do Not Go Back!

"However, he must not acquire many horses for himself, or send the people back to Egypt to acquire many horses, for the Lord has told you, 'You are never to go back that way again.'" Deuteronomy 17:16 HCSB

THIS SEEMS LIKE an odd instruction. Why would God tell them to never go back to Egypt again? After all, it had been forty years. What would be so bad about just going back to buy some horses? They aren't going back to live, just visit. Maybe they could see a few old friends, let the overseers who ruled over them see what God had done for them and how well they are doing. It seems harmless, right? Not on your life. God knew their hearts. They had been wandering around for forty years in the wilderness grumbling and complaining. On numerous occasions they had lamented ever leaving Egypt. They had longed for the food in Egypt and said they would have been better off if they had stayed there. They seemed to have forgotten the torment they experienced in Egypt. They were just remembering the good things and forgetting all the bad. God knew that if they went back, they could easily get sucked back in and find themselves in slavery again.

This is a powerful lesson for us as well. There are things in all our pasts that God has warned us never to go back to again. It may have been an addiction, a relationship, a lifestyle, a place, or a sin God has freed you from. Whatever it is, it needs to remain in the past. After a while, we can begin to think that it doesn't have a hold on us any longer. It would be harmless just to visit it briefly. We can go there just to prove that we can withstand the temptation. A little bit is ok, right? Definitely not! God knows your heart as well. He knows how easily we can get sucked back in. We tend to forget the torment we experienced and remember the good times forgetting all the bad. Do you want to find yourself in slavery again? Heed God's warning. "Never go that way again!"

April 11

Deuteronomy 19-20
Psalm 44:9-16
Proverbs 10:31-32
Luke 9:18-36

The Right Words

"The mouth of the righteous produces wisdom, but a perverse tongue will be cut out. The lips of the righteous know what is appropriate, but the mouth of the wicked, only what is perverse." Proverbs 10:31-32 HCSB

I CANNOT TELL you how many times I have prayed for the right words to say in a situation and God gave me exactly the right thing to say. I have found myself quoting scripture or giving advice that I knew was not coming from me. There have been many times that something I read that morning in my quiet time, or something I heard in a sermon have come to my mind and I am able to give sound biblical advice to someone who is struggling with what they should do. There have also been times when I wanted to say something, and the Holy Spirit has shut my mouth. I don't always know why. Sometimes it is because I am not the right one to deliver the message. The person may need to hear what I am saying, but not from me. Or it may be that it is not the right time or that my heart is not right so I would not speak the truth in love. Unfortunately, I can also recount many times when I have not prayed before speaking and have said things I later regretted. "The mouth of the righteous brings forth wisdom...the lips of the righteous know what is appropriate." Wisdom comes from the Holy Spirit living within us. Knowing what to say, when to say it and how to say it is not something we just learn. It isn't a skill we can practice and get better at. There is no book that can teach you how to speak wisely. "If any of you lacks wisdom, you should ask God, who gives generously to all without finding fault, and it will be given to you." James 1:5 (NIV) God is the only source of true wisdom. Spending time meditating on God's Word, in Bible study and prayer will help you grow closer to the source of wisdom and knowledge. "For the mouth speaks what the heart is full of." Luke 6:45b (NIV)

Deuteronomy 21-23
Psalm 44:17-26
Proverbs 11:1-3
Luke 9:37-62

April 12

Follow Me

"As they were walking along the road, a man said to Him, 'I will follow You wherever You go.' Jesus replied, 'Foxes have dens and birds have nests, but the Son of Man has no place to lay His head.' He said to another man, 'Follow Me.' But the man replied, 'Lord, first let me go and bury my father.' Jesus said to him, 'Let the dead bury their own dead, but you go and proclaim the kingdom of God.' Still another said, 'I will follow You, Lord, but first let me go back and say goodbye to my family.' Jesus replied, 'No one who puts his hand to the plow and looks back is fit for service in the kingdom of God.'" Luke 9:57-62 NIV

EACH OF THESE men said they would follow Jesus, but when it came down to it, they had an excuse. The first man said he would go wherever Jesus went. Jesus looked into his heart and responded by telling the man that following would mean that he would not have material wealth and he might not even have a place to lay his head at night. The second man asked to go bury his father. This seems reasonable, but if the man's father had died, he would already be attending to the funeral arrangements. This man was most likely telling Jesus that he had family matters to attend to and when he finished taking care of all his other responsibilities, then he would follow Jesus. The third man wanted to go back and tell his family goodbye. Jesus looked into his heart and saw that the man had divided loyalties. Jesus told the man that he had to choose. He couldn't follow Jesus if he was going to be constantly looking back to what he was leaving behind. What is your excuse? Is the cost of following Him too great? Do you want to wait until you have taken care of all your other responsibilities before you give yourself fully to following Him? Do you have a divided heart? Jesus wants our wholehearted devotion. If we are to follow Him, we must be willing to do whatever He says, go wherever He leads, and trust Him completely.

April 13

Deuteronomy 24-25
Psalm 45:1-5
Proverbs 11:4-6
Luke 10:1-24

Harvest

"He told them, 'The harvest is plentiful, but the workers are few. Ask the Lord of the harvest, therefore, to send out workers into His harvest field.'" Luke 10:2 NIV

THERE WERE MULTITUDES of people who listened to Jesus' teaching. Everywhere He went crowds surrounded Him. People wanted to hear what He had to say. In our reading yesterday, Jesus explained to them the cost of following Him. Shortly after that, Jesus sent out those who were willing to pay the price. He tells them that the harvest is plentiful, but the workers are few. There are multitudes of people who need to know about Jesus, but very few people to tell them. That is just as true today as it was in Jesus' day. Everywhere we look, we can find people who need to know that God loves them. We don't have to go to Africa or India or the other side of the world to find people who need to hear about Jesus. We are not all called to be missionaries or preachers or evangelists, but we are all called to tell others about Jesus. There are people around us every day who desperately need to know what God is doing in our life. They need to see the difference He makes and hear how He can make a difference in their life, too. Pray that God will provide opportunities for you to talk to your coworker who is having problems in her marriage, or that friend at school whose parents are getting a divorce. Pray for a chance to ask that friend you met at the gym or that soccer mom you see at the ball field each week to come to church with you. God will provide opportunities for us to tell others and He will give us the words to say. All we have to do is be willing.

Deuteronomy 26-27
Psalm 45:6-12
Proverbs 11:7-8
Luke 10:25-42

April 14

Better

> "Martha, Martha,' the Lord answered, 'you are worried and upset about many things, but few things are needed, or indeed only one. Mary has chosen what is better, and it will not be taken from her." Luke 10:41-42 NIV

MARY HAS CHOSEN what is better. This verse plays over and over in my head. The Lord is teaching me to choose what is better. And believe me, it is not an easy task. Thankfully, He is patient and longsuffering because I am a slow learner. I am Martha. Give me a task and I can get it done. I will plan it out, make my list and methodically cross things off that list until the task is complete. Being organized and getting things done is not a bad thing. After all, things need to get done. We can't just sit around all the time praying and reading our Bible. We have responsibilities we cannot neglect and Jesus Himself tells us that we are to serve others and serve Him. The problem comes when we neglect our relationship with Him to serve Him and meet our responsibilities. He equips us for service and gives us the wisdom and strength to fulfill our responsibilities. Spending time at His feet prepares us to face whatever lies ahead. For many years my time alone with Him was sporadic and hurried. I served Him vigorously and willingly, but I was too busy to just sit at His feet and enjoy His presence. When I read my Bible, it was for a purpose. A Bible study I needed to complete and check off my list, a question I needed to answer so that I could give a friend sound, biblical advice, or a daily Bible reading/devotional so a could say I had my quiet time that day. I cannot say that I longed for or just enjoyed spending time in His presence. I had tasks I needed to do. I almost felt guilty for just sitting quietly with Him. He has changed me. I'm not exactly sure how He did it or even when, but He has given me a yearning for time alone with Him. I love sitting at His feet and just enjoying His presence. Instead of longing to be doing tasks when I am alone with Him, I now find myself longing for time alone with Him when I am completing a task. An amazing thing has happened in this process. I find that I am doing fewer things than I used to do, but the things I am doing are accomplishing more. I am learning to do the things that He has chosen for me to do instead of doing everything that I see that needs to be done. There are always going to be things that need to be done. Finding something to do will never be a problem. The difficulty is choosing what is better. When I spend time at His feet, He helps me choose those things that He wants me to do and gives me the strength and ability to do them. My challenge to you is to ask God to give you a yearning for Him. Ask Him today to fill you with desire to know Him more.

April 15

Deuteronomy 28
Psalm 45:13-17
Proverbs 11:9-11
Luke 11:1-28

Good Gifts

"Which of you fathers, if your son asks for a fish, will give him a snake instead? If he asks for an egg, will give him a scorpion? If you then, though you are evil, know how to give good gifts to your children, how much more will your Father in Heaven give the Holy Spirit to those who ask Him!" Luke 11:11-13 NIV

ONE OF THE most difficult things about being a parent is giving your children what they need instead of what they want. It is much easier to give them what they want. It is easier to let them eat french fries and chicken nuggets for every meal instead of making them eat vegetables. It is easier to go ahead and buy the candy bar at the grocery store instead of listening to the tantrum at the checkout counter. It is easier to let your daughter go to that party where you don't know what will be happening than to say no and listen to her screaming and pouting about how you don't trust her. When we are entrusted with the responsibility of caring for one of God's precious children, we must make hard choices. We have to think of their future and do what is best for them. We know that they need the vitamins and nutrients that vegetables provide. We know that if we give in to a tantrum this time at the grocery, then every time they don't get their way, they will throw a tantrum. And we know from experience, the things that can happen at parties. It is our responsibility to protect them from those dangers. Unfortunately, we don't always make the right choices. Sometimes we give in and do the easy thing instead of the right thing. We cave to the pressure or just make unwise decisions. Our intentions are good. We love our children and want what is best for them, but we are human. Fortunately, our Heavenly Father doesn't make bad choices. He always does what is best for us. We do not always understand what He is doing. Thankfully, He does not always give us what we ask for. He doesn't give us french fries when we need vegetables. And even if we throw a tantrum when we don't get our way, He doesn't give in to us. He always does what is best because He loves us. Thank Him today for His loving protection and care and for knowing when to say no.

Deuteronomy 29-30
Psalm 46
Proverbs 11:12-13
Luke 11:29-54

April 16

Life or Death: The Choice is Yours

"This day I call the heavens and the Earth as witnesses against you that I have set before you life and death, blessings and curses. Now choose life, so that you and your children may live and that you may love the Lord your God, listen to His voice and hold fast to Him. For the Lord is your life, and He will give you many years in the land He swore to give to your fathers, Abraham, Isaac and Jacob." Deuteronomy 30:19-20 NIV

"He says, 'Be still and know that I am God; I will be exalted among the nations, I will be exalted in the Earth.' The Lord Almighty is with us; the God of Jacob is our fortress." Psalm 46:10-11 NIV

THE CHOICE IS clear: life or death. He is God. Whether or not we acknowledge Him and submit to Him does not change the fact that He is God. He is sovereign and His will is going to be done. He will be exalted. He has set before us the choice. If we choose to love Him and listen to His voice and hold fast to Him, we will experience life and peace. He has a very specific plan and purpose for us. When we choose to follow His leading, we can expect Him to take care of us, protect us, provide for us, and give us an abundant, full life. "'For I know the plans I have for you,' declares the Lord, 'plans to prosper you and not to harm you, plans to give you hope and a future.'" Jeremiah 29:11 (NIV) "I have come that they may have life and have it to the full." John 10:10b (NIV) If we choose to ignore Him and follow our own path, we cannot expect to experience His blessing. "Do not be deceived: God cannot be mocked. A man reaps what he sows. Whoever sows to please their flesh, from the flesh will reap destruction; whoever sows to please the Spirit, from the Spirit will reap eternal life." Galatians 6:7-8 (NIV) There is no middle ground. The choice is between God's way and any other way. It doesn't matter what other path we may choose, if it is not God's way, it will lead to destruction. "Enter through the narrow gate. For wide is the gate and broad is the road that leads to destruction, and many enter through it. But small is the gate and narrow the road that leads to life and only a few find it." Matthew 7:13-14 (NIV) Choose for yourselves this day whom you will serve.

April 17

Deuteronomy 31
Psalm 47
Proverbs 11:14-15
Luke 12:1-21

Guidance

"For lack of guidance a nation falls, but victory is won through many advisors."
Proverbs 11:14 NIV

A COMMON THEME in the book of Proverbs is the importance of wise counsel. Proverbs 12:15 tells us "The way of fools seem right to them, but the wise listen to advice." (NIV) Proverbs 15:22 says "Plans fail for lack of counsel, but with many advisors they succeed." (NIV) Verses 31-33 tell us "Whoever heeds life-giving correction will be at home among the wise. Those who disregard discipline despise themselves, but the one who heeds correction gains understanding. Wisdom's instruction is to fear the Lord, and humility comes before honor." (NIV) Proverbs 19:20-21 says "Listen to advice and accept discipline, and in the end, you will be counted among the wise. Many are the plans in a person's heart, but it is the Lord's purpose that prevails." (NIV) Proverbs 28:26 says, "Those who trust in themselves are fools, but those who walk in wisdom are kept safe." (NIV) Solomon was the wisest man who ever lived and yet he knew the importance of listening to the counsel of others. He knew what the prophet tells us in Jeremiah 17:9, "The heart is deceitful above all things and beyond cure. Who can understand it?" (NIV) We can convince ourselves of whatever we want to hear. We rationalize, manipulate the truth, and justify what we want to do. It may be easier to see this principal at work in the lives of others. We can all point to examples of people who would not listen to those around them and made really bad decisions. They were warned numerous times, but they ignored the advice of others and now are suffering the consequences. I am not saying that others are always right, and you should do whatever they say. I am suggesting that you should seek the counsel of those who you respect and trust. You should talk to several people that you know care about you and want what is best for you; people who will pray with you and for you to help you discern God's will about the decision you have to make. Listening to their reasoning and their concerns will help you make an informed decision. It is important to look at different perspectives and weigh them against the truth of God's Word.

April 18

Deuteronomy 32
Psalm 48:1-7
Proverbs 11:16-18
Luke 12:22-34

Do Not Worry

"Therefore, I tell you, do not worry about your life, what you will eat; or about your body, what you will wear… Consider the ravens: They do not sow or reap; they have no storeroom or barn; yet God feeds them. And how much more valuable you are than birds!… Consider how the wildflowers grow. They do not labor or spin. Yet I tell you, not even Solomon in all his splendor was dressed like one of these. If that is how God clothes the grass of the field, which is here today and tomorrow is thrown into the fire, how much more will He clothe you, you of little faith!… For the pagan world runs after all such things, and your Father knows that you need them. But seek His kingdom, and these things will be given to you as well." Luke 12:22-31 NIV

THESE WORDS ARE hitting home to me right now. God is teaching me not to worry. It seems that the only way He can teach me is to put me in situations where I must trust Him, over and over and over. He is stretching my faith and testing me to see if I really do trust Him or if I will fall back into my old patterns of worry and fear. I wish there was an easier way. But I don't think there is. I know it doesn't do any good to worry. It doesn't change my circumstance in any way, but it seems to be my default setting. I am not there yet, but He has brought me a long way. Slowly, but surely, He is teaching me a better way. Instead of stressing out and panicking, my first reaction now is to take my concern to Him. Instead of going over and over it in my mind trying to figure out how to fix the problem, I am learning to "take every thought captive and make it obedient to Christ." Instead of focusing on the problem I am facing, I am learning to "fix my eyes on Jesus, the author and perfector of my faith" and to remember all the times He has been faithful to me in the past with confidence that He will not let me down now. Instead of manipulating and trying to fix the problem myself, I am learning to leave it in His hands and wait. Instead of sinking into despair I am learning to say, "Lord I don't see how this problem can be fixed, but I trust you. I know you are faithful, and I believe you will take care of me." I must admit that I still find myself worrying occasionally, but I am catching myself much sooner and not allowing myself to go down that long, dark path of fear. For years I have used the excuse that I am just a worrier, and I can't do anything about it. That is just who I am. That is a lie from Satan. Worrying is sin. It is a lack of faith, and it is not pleasing to God. He is ridding my life of this sin and He is in the process of perfecting my faith. I cannot manufacture or develop faith. I can only cooperate as He develops it in me. I pray you will cooperate as He perfects your faith as well.

Deuteronomy 33-34
Psalm 48:8-14
Proverbs 11:19-21
Luke 12:35-59

April 19

Entrusted

> "From everyone who has been given much, much will be demanded; and from the one who has been entrusted with much, much more will be asked." Luke 12:48 NIV

MERRIAM WEBSTER DEFINES the word entrusted as "to commit to another with confidence."[3] This implies a trust and faith that the person who receives it will handle it with care and will do what they need to do with it. The Bible is clear that we are held accountable for the knowledge that we have. I had the privilege of being raised in a Christian home. I cannot remember a time when I was not involved in church. My parents and grandparents were strong Christians and gave me a firm foundation in my faith. I asked Jesus into my heart at the age of nine, so I have been walking with Him for forty-seven years. After numerous Bible studies, classes in seminary, countless sermons, and personal Bible reading, I have been given a lot of biblical instruction. This verse reminds me that I will be held accountable for that knowledge. The closer I get to Jesus, the more I realize just how little I know, but I am responsible for the knowledge I have been given. The definition of the word entrusted gives us insight into the extent of my responsibility. Knowledge is not given to us just for the sake of intellectual pursuit. It is not given so that we can impress others with how many Bible verses we know. We are entrusted with knowledge for care and protection. The knowledge is to be used to teach, equip, and prepare us to live the life God has prepared for us. We are expected to be obedient to the truths that have been entrusted to us. It is also given to us so that we can pass that knowledge on to others. We are expected to entrust what is given to us to others so that they can then pass it on to others as well.

April 20

Joshua 1-3
Psalm 49:1-9
Proverbs 11:22-23
Luke 13:1-17

BE STRONG AND COURAGEOUS

"Be strong and courageous, for you will distribute the land I swore to their fathers to give them as an inheritance. Above all, be strong and very courageous to carefully observe the whole instruction My servant Moses commanded you. Do not turn from it to the right or to the left, so that you will have success wherever you go. This book of instruction must not depart from your mouth: you are to recite it day and night, so that you may carefully observe everything written in it. For then you will prosper and succeed in whatever you do. Haven't I commanded you: Be strong and courageous? Do not be afraid or discouraged, for the Lord your God is with you wherever you go." Joshua 1:6-9 HCSB

THREE TIMES IN these four verses Joshua was encouraged to be strong and courageous. He was about to lead the children of Israel to take possession of the promised land. In Numbers 13 we find a description of the people of the land of Canaan. They are described as "powerful' and "very large." Joshua was very familiar with the people because he was one of the twelve spies who went into the land forty years earlier. He saw them and remembered them well. Now, all these years later, he was given the task of leading the children of Israel to defeat them and finally take possession. Joshua and Caleb were the only two of the twelve spies who believed they could take over the land because they knew that God had the power to do whatever He promised. But Joshua knew how large and powerful the people were, and how difficult it would be to conquer them. He believed God would go with them and protect them, but he must have been frightened. In these verses God is giving Joshua encouragement. He looked into Joshua's heart and met him where he was. He told him to be strong and courageous and assured him he was not alone. God told Joshua the importance of reading and obeying the book of instruction because it would lead them to success in whatever they did. God's Word is our source of encouragement and instruction as well. It gives us strength and hope when we are afraid. It leads and guides us and if we follow its teaching, we can expect to experience success. God knows our hearts and He meets us where we are. We do not have to be ashamed to admit that we are afraid. Franklin Delano Roosevelt was President of the United States during the Great Depression and World War 2. During that time there was legitimate reason to be afraid. The world was a scary place. In one of his "Fireside Chats" he said something that has become very familiar: "Courage is not the absence of fear, but rather the assessment that something else is more important than fear."[4] Without fear there is no need for courage. We can be in situations where we should be afraid and yet we can respond with courage because we know that God is with us and will take care of us. Joshua knew that obeying God was more important than any fear he might have, and that taking possession of the promised land was the task set before him. He chose to obey God and believe in His promises.

Joshua 4-6
Psalm 49:10-15
Proverbs 11:24-26
Luke 13:18-35

Following Directions

"On the seventh day, they got up at daybreak and marched around the city seven times in the same manner, except on that day they circled the city seven times. The seventh time around, when the priests sounded the trumpet blast, Joshua commanded the people, 'Shout! For the Lord has given you the city!' When the trumpets sounded, the army shouted, and at the sound of the trumpet, when the men gave a loud shout, the wall collapsed; so, every man charged straight in and they took the city. They devoted the city to the Lord and destroyed with the sword every living thing in it." Joshua 6:15-16, 20-21 NIV

JOSHUA AND THE children of Israel were preparing to go to war. They had to defeat the giants in the promised land to take possession. They were ready to go in and fight. They must have been surprised when God gave them the battle plan. They were expecting swords and spears, but God told them to march around the city with their trumpets. I'm sure it didn't make any sense to them, and they did not understand. Their adrenaline was pumping, and they were ready to go in and claim the victory. But God had a different plan. He slowed them down. For six days they marched to Jericho and walked around the city once blowing their trumpets and then went back to their camp. That must have been the longest six days of their lives. On the seventh day they marched around seven times, shouted, blew their trumpets and the walls came down. There was absolutely no mistake that God delivered the city into their hands. They had nothing to do with it. They could not take any of the credit. The Israelites could not believe that their great military strength or their tactical skills helped them defeat Jericho. God delivered on His promise to give them the land east of the Jordan. They followed God's directions exactly. They obeyed Him in every detail, and they were victorious. Joshua trusted God even when it didn't make sense. "Trust in the Lord with all your heart and lean not on your own understanding. In all your ways submit to Him and He will make your paths straight." Proverbs 3:5-6 (NIV) We don't always understand God's instructions to us. Sometimes what God tells us to do doesn't make sense. God expects us to trust Him and obey even when we don't understand.

April 22

Joshua 7-8
Psalm 49:16-20
Proverbs 11:27-29
Luke 14

Not Following Directions

"The Israelites, however, were unfaithful regarding the things set apart for destruction; Achan son of Carmi, son of Zabdi, son of Zerah, of the tribe of Judah, took some of what was set apart, and the Lord's anger burned against the Israelites. The men of Ai struck down about thirty-six of them and chased them from outside the gate to the quarries, striking them down on the descent. As a result, the people's hearts melted and became like water. The Lord then said to Joshua, 'Stand up! Why are you on the ground? Israel has sinned. They have violated My covenant that I appointed for them. They have taken some of what was set apart. They have stolen, deceived, and put the things with their own belongings. This is why the Israelites cannot stand against their enemies.'" Joshua 7:1, 5, 10-12 HCSB

As long as the Israelites obeyed God and followed His directions, they were able to defeat the people and take possession of the land that had been promised to them. However, when they were disobedient and decided to take matters into their own hands, they were unsuccessful. Achan stole some of the items that were set apart for the Lord's house. He not only stole something that didn't belong to him; he stole from God. It seems harsh that God punished all of them for the sins of one. I cannot pretend to understand that, but it demonstrates a truth that is undisputed. Our actions affect others. When we sin, we are not the only ones that suffer the consequences. Often, our loved ones also experience the pain and embarrassment of our poor choices and sinful decisions. Thirty-six men lost their lives because of Achan's sin.

There was an interesting omission from the story of the Israelites defeat at Ai. Before they went into Jericho, the children of Israel sought the Lord. They asked Him for His guidance, and they followed His battle plan. We see no mention in these verses that they sought God before going into Ai. Actually, it seems that they thought they didn't really need God's help with this one. They saw that Ai was small and thought they could handle this one on their own. "Pride goes before destruction, a haughty spirit before a fall." Proverbs 16:18 (NIV) Obviously, they were wrong. They needed God's guidance and His protection every step of the way if they were going to take possession of the land. They had to follow His directions completely. They repented of their sin and asked for God's guidance. God gave them the battle plan which they followed exactly, and they were able to destroy Ai.

April 23

Joshua 9-10
Psalm 50:1-6
Proverbs 11:30-31
Luke 15:1-10

The Sun Stood Still

"So, the sun stopped in the middle of the sky and delayed its setting almost a full day. There has been no day like it before or since, when the Lord listened to the voice of a man, because the Lord fought for Israel." Joshua 10:13-14 HCSB

GOD'S PURPOSES WILL be accomplished. When God makes a promise, He will make sure that it comes to pass. The Lord told Joshua that He was going to hand the five Amorite kings over to him. To bring that about, Joshua asked God to keep the sun in the sky for an extra twenty-four hours. Can you imagine? The sun did not set that day. Knowing what we know now about the rotation of the Earth around the sun, that means that the Earth stopped. The Earth stood still for 24 hours and then it started again as if nothing had happened. Gravity was not disturbed; the other planets didn't fall out of the sky and the ocean tides were not altered. Only the One who set the Earth in motion could stall it. God is faithful. No matter what it takes, He will fulfill His promises. Nothing is too difficult for Him. "Ah, Sovereign Lord, You, have made the heavens and the Earth by Your great power and outstretched arm. Nothing is too hard for You." Jeremiah 32:17 (NIV) "The Lord answered Moses, 'Is the Lord's arm too short? You will now see whether or not what I say will come true for you." Numbers 11:23 (NIV)

April 24

Joshua 11-12
Psalm 50:7-15
Proverbs 12:1-3
Luke 15:11-32

He Ran

> "But while he was still a long way off, his father saw him and was filled with compassion for him; he ran to his son, threw his arms around him and kissed him."
> Luke 15:20 NIV

THIS IS A beautiful picture of forgiveness, mercy, and grace. The most touching part of this parable is that the father did not make the son come crawling back. He didn't wait at the house and watch out the window as his son walked slowly up the driveway, scared and embarrassed. He didn't make him come in, apologize, and beg for forgiveness. He didn't reluctantly tell him that he could come back, but he had to agree to a list of conditions and if he messed up again, he was out for good. Instead, we are given a very different picture. The father saw his son when he was a long way off. I know I am reading between the lines, but I have an image in my mind of a father sitting by the window for days watching the driveway hoping to see his long-lost son. He was worried and afraid he would never see his son again. Then suddenly, off at a distance he saw something coming up the road. He was so excited that he just ran out the door as fast as he could. The son had been feeding pigs. He was bound to be dirty and smelly, but his father didn't care. He threw his arms around him and kissed him. He welcomed him back with no questions asked and threw a party to celebrate.

Thankfully, this is a picture of our Heavenly Father's love for us. No matter how far we stray or what we may do, He will always welcome us back. He is waiting and watching for us and as soon as He sees us coming, He runs to meet us. No matter how dirty or smelly we may be when we turn back to Him, He doesn't care. He will throw His arms around us, kiss us, and throw a party to celebrate. His love for us is boundless. "For I am convinced that neither death nor life, neither angels nor demons, neither the present nor the future, nor any powers, neither height nor depth, nor anything else in all creation, will be able to separate us from the love of God that is in Christ Jesus our Lord." Romans 8:38-39 (NIV)

Joshua 13-14
Psalm 50:16-23
Proverbs 12:4-5
Luke 16:1-13

April 25

Rest

"Now these are the areas the Israelites received as an inheritance in the land of Canaan, which Eleazar the priest, Joshua son of Nun, and the heads of the tribal clans of Israel allotted to them. Then the land had rest from war." Joshua 14:1, 15b NIV

THE ISRAELITES HAD been wandering around in the desert for forty years. They had been living on manna and quail and sleeping in tents. Then they entered the promised land and had to go to war against the inhabitants of the land to obtain their inheritance. It had been a long period of struggle for them. Now it was time to divide up the land and rest. This passage is very encouraging to me. It gives me hope. Ecclesiastes 3:1, 8 tells us "There is a time for everything and a season for every activity under Heaven; a time for war and a time for peace." (NIV) During difficult times, it is hard to believe that there will be a time for peace and rest again. This is especially true when the struggle has lasted for a long time. Satan wants to convince us that the pain will never end and there will never again be a time when we are happy, and things are going well. He wants us to be discouraged and lose hope. In those times it is important to focus on the promises God has given us in His Word. It is crucial that we remember all the times He has been faithful to us in the past and rely on what we know about Him and His character. He will not let us down. "And the God of all grace, who called you to His eternal glory in Christ, after you have suffered a little while, will Himself restore you and make you strong, firm and steadfast." I Peter 5:10 (NIV)

April 26

Joshua 15-16
Psalm 51:1-5
Proverbs 12:6-7
Luke 16:14-31

Confession

"Have mercy on me, O God, according to Your unfailing love; according to Your great compassion blot out my transgressions. Wash away all my iniquity and cleanse me from my sin. For I know my transgressions, and my sin is always before me. Against You, You only, have I sinned and done what is evil in Your sight, so that You are right in Your verdict, and justified when You judge." Psalm 51:1-4 NIV

There is cleansing power in the act of confession. When we completely "come clean" there is a weight that is lifted that cannot be minimized. This is true when we confess our sins to those people we have sinned against, but it is especially true in confessing our sins before God. We have an obligation to do both. When we do wrong to someone, it is our responsibility to go to that person, confess our sin and ask them for forgiveness. Their reaction may be favorable, and the relationship restored. If they refuse to accept our apology and forgive us, then we have done our part. We should continue to pray for the person and pray that God will soften their heart and restore the relationship, but we should not continue to feel the weight of guilt. But our responsibility does not end there. Whenever we sin against another person, we are also sinning against God. We have an obligation to confess our sins to Him and ask for His forgiveness. God will always accept our apology, forgive us and cleanse us of all unrighteousness. "If we confess our sins, He is faithful and just and will forgive us our sins and purify us from all unrighteousness." I John 1:9 (NIV)

Too often, however, we do not "come clean." We make excuses and fail to take responsibility for our actions. We blame other people or say, "that's just how I am, and I can't help it." There is no cleansing without confession. The Psalmist David acknowledged his sin before God. He had committed adultery and murder and had been confronted by Nathan for his sin. He had sinned against a married woman and her husband and had disgraced his position, but in this Psalm, he says to God, "against You, You only have I sinned." We know that he acknowledged his sin to Nathan. We are not told that he confessed and asked forgiveness from Bathsheba, but knowing David's character, I have to believe that he did. David knew that he had to restore his relationship with God. He knew he had sinned against the One who had protected him, cared for him, and put him on the throne as King of Israel. He had betrayed God. He didn't make excuses or blame anyone else. He confessed. As soon as we become aware of our sin, we need to confess it and ask for forgiveness.

April 27

Joshua 17-18
Psalm 51:6-10
Proverbs 12:8-10
Luke 17

Whiter Than Snow

"Cleanse me with hyssop, and I will be clean; wash me and I will be whiter than snow. Let me hear joy and gladness; let the bones You have crushed rejoice. Hide Your face from my sins and blot out my iniquity. Create in me a pure heart, O God, and renew a steadfast spirit within me." Psalm 51:7-10 NIV

"Cleanse me with hyssop." Hyssop is a common herb that grew in biblical times and can still be found in many varieties today. It has beautiful purple flowers and a strong mint smell. In the days before there was a whole aisle at the grocery store dedicated to cleaning supplies, herbs and other things found in nature were used for cleaning. Hyssop has detergent properties and was often used in cleaning sacred places such as temples. It is interesting that we find hyssop mentioned in Exodus 12:22. It was used to apply the blood of the Passover lamb to the doorposts so that the Angel of the Lord would pass over the homes of the Israelites as He struck down the first born in all of Egypt. It is mentioned in Leviticus 14:1-8 where it was used to dip into the blood of a bird and sprinkle over a person to cleanse them from leprosy.

We see hyssop used again in John 19:29 to lift the sponge of wine vinegar to Jesus lips as He hung on the cross. David was using something that would have been familiar to everyone in his day. It would be like us saying "cleanse me with bleach so that I can be clean." The next phrase says, "wash me and I will be whiter than snow." The word used here for wash me is the one used for washing clothes in his day, which was done by beating and pounding the dirt out of the clothes. David is asking God to do whatever it takes to beat the sin out of him and make him whiter than snow. He was deeply remorseful and heartsick over his sin and was begging God to forgive him. He didn't just want a quick shower; he wanted a good "scrubbin" so that the filth and dirt of his sin could be removed. He wanted to be able to stand before his Father and enjoy the intimacy of their relationship as he once had. As we saw with the prodigal son, our Heavenly Father is always waiting with open arms to welcome us back and restore our relationship.

April 28

Joshua 19
Psalm 51:11-15
Proverbs 12:11-12
Luke 18:1-23

Guilt

"Deliver me from the guilt of bloodshed, O God, You who are God my Savior, and my tongue will sing of Your righteousness." Psalm 51:14 NIV

I AM CONVINCED that one of the most dangerous schemes of Satan is guilt. Please hear me out. I understand the role of the Holy Spirit in convicting us of our sin. I understand the importance of our conscience telling us that what we are doing is wrong and that we should stop. It is vital that we listen to those voices in our head telling us to repent. The problem is that so often we are convicted of sin, we respond appropriately by confessing our sin to God and asking for His forgiveness, but we continue to feel guilty. We are haunted by the weight of what we have done, and we cannot move on because we have not accepted God's forgiveness and cleansing. Satan uses our sin against us. He throws our past sins in our face to keep us from being effective in our service to God. He tries to make us believe that no one will listen to someone who has done what we have done, or God can't possibly use someone who sins. He can even make us doubt that God has really forgiven us. He tries to convince us that we have to prove ourselves to God before He will be willing to use us again. That is a lie. We are not on probation to see if we can be good before we are given responsibility again. God is not our parole officer who is watching to see if we are going to mess up and sin. He is our loving Father who wants what is best for us and is willing to help us. There is no cleansing without confession, but once confession is made, God removes the weight of guilt from us and "as far as the east is from the west, so far has He removed our transgressions from us." Psalm 103:12 (NIV) We may have to face the consequences of our sin, but the guilt of our sin is removed when we confess and repent. Accept God's forgiveness and move on. God wants to use you today as a testimony to His mercy and grace.

Joshua 20-21
Psalm 51:16-19
Proverbs 12:13-14
Luke 18:24-43

April 29

He Keeps His Promises

"Not one of all the Lord's good promises to the house of Israel failed; every one was fulfilled." Joshua 21:45 NIV

For God to go back on a promise would be against His very nature. The character of God is behind His promises. Since He knows what will happen in the future, He can make promises based on what will be done. When I make promises to people, I have every intention of carrying them out. I do not make promises that I do not plan to keep. But I cannot control all the variables. When I am making a promise, I am saying that if I can in any way bring it about, I will. Unfortunately, sometimes things change that are beyond my control; things that I had no way of knowing when I made the promise. That does not happen to God. He does not get surprised. He knows everything that will happen in the future so He knows that He will bring about what He has promised. For Him to make a promise and not keep it, He would have to be lying because He knows He will not fulfill it. We know that God does not lie. He is truth. "Let us hold unswervingly to the hope we profess, for He who promised is faithful." Hebrews 10:23 (NIV) "For no matter how many promises God has made, they are 'Yes' in Christ. And so, through Him the 'Amen' is spoken by us to the glory of God." 2 Corinthians 1:20 (NIV) "Your kingdom is an everlasting kingdom, and Your dominion endures through all generations. The Lord is faithful to all His promises and loving toward all He has made." Psalm 145:13 (NIV) God fulfilled every promise He made to Abraham, Isaac, and Jacob. He gave the children of Israel all the land that He had promised to give them. He handed it over into their hands. He made them into a great nation and through Jesus all nations would be blessed through the seed of Abraham. God was faithful to His promises then and He is just as faithful to His promises today.

April 30

Joshua 22-23
Psalm 52
Proverbs 12:15-16
Luke 19:1-27

Changed

"When Jesus reached the spot, He looked up and said to him, 'Zacchaeus, come down immediately! I must stay at your house today.' So, he came down at once and welcomed Him gladly. All the people saw this and began to mutter, 'He has gone to be the guest of a sinner.' But Zacchaeus stood up and said to the Lord, 'Look, Lord! Here and now I give half of my possessions to the poor, and if I have cheated anybody out of anything, I will pay back four times the amount." Luke 19:5-8 NIV

AFTER MEETING JESUS, Zacchaeus was a changed man. Jesus didn't come into his house, sit down, and tell him all the things he needed to do to change. He didn't give him a list of requirements to follow. He didn't tell him to clean up his act and then He would consider whether to accept him. He didn't condemn him or even point out all his sin. Jesus looked up in the tree and had compassion on the man He saw. He just accepted Zacchaeus as he was. Jesus wasn't worried about what the people around would think about Him going to Zacchaeus' house. He wasn't worried about His reputation or if people would think He was sinful because He was hanging out with a sinner. Jesus loved Zacchaeus. As a result, Zacchaeus became a changed man. He repented of his former ways. He stood up and told Jesus that he was going to give half his possessions to the poor and pay back four times what he owed to anyone he had cheated. Jesus didn't even have to suggest to him that he should do that. When he met Jesus, his sin was exposed, and he immediately changed. This should be a lesson to us. Are we changed because we have been with Jesus? Are we different just because we have been in His presence? This should be true of us following our initial acceptance of Jesus into our hearts, but it should also be true as we daily walk with Him. We should be different from the world around us. We should exhibit His love and the joy and peace of His presence. People should be drawn to us because of our connection to Jesus. If not, then why not?

Joshua 24
Psalm 53
Proverbs 12:17-18
Luke 19:28-48

Whom Will You Serve?

"Now fear the Lord and serve Him with all faithfulness. Throw away the gods your ancestors worshipped beyond the Euphrates River and in Egypt and serve the Lord. But if serving the Lord seems undesirable to you, then choose for yourselves this day whom you will serve, whether the gods your ancestors served beyond the Euphrates River, or the gods of the Amorites, in whose land you are living. But as for me and my household, we will serve the Lord." Joshua 24:14-15 NIV

IN THE NIV the first word in this passage is "now." In several other translations it is the word "therefore." Whenever you see the word "therefore" you should always look back at the passage before it to see what the "therefore" is "there for." Joshua had given a farewell speech to the leaders of the tribes of Israel and now had assembled all the tribes of Israel together to address them one last time before he died. This is his dying declaration. It is the thing he wants to leave them with and the most important thing he wants them to know. He knows he will soon die and go to be with his Heavenly Father, so he is using this opportunity to give them his last words of advice. He has recounted for them the things that God has done for them reminding them of the faithfulness and love of their God and now he is drawing a line in the sand. He is saying, "I have made my choice. I choose to serve the Lord. I have seen His power and experienced His protection. I know He is the one true God and I choose to serve Him and follow Him only." He tells the Israelites that they must make a choice. They cannot continue to blend into the crowd, to be swayed by the culture and religions around them. They must make a choice. They cannot continue to serve two masters.

We face the same choice. It is much easier to blend in, and be swayed by our culture and popular opinion, than to stand up and choose to follow God. We cannot serve two masters. We must follow Him wholeheartedly and faithfully. Failure to make a choice is the same as choosing to follow the world. Our choice is between Jesus and any other path. "Jesus answered, 'I am the way, the truth, and the life. No one comes to the Father except through Me." John 14:6 (NIV) Neglect and inattention will inevitably lead us down another path. Choose for yourself this day whom you will serve.

Judges 1-2
Psalm 54
Proverbs 12:19-21
Luke 20:1-26

May 2

Set Apart

"The Angel of the Lord went up from Gilgal to Bokim and said, 'I brought you up out of Egypt and led you into the land that I swore to give to your ancestors.' I said, 'I will never break My covenant with you, and you shall not make a covenant with the people of this land, but you shall break down their altars. Yet you have disobeyed Me. Why have you done this?' And I have also said, 'I will not drive them out before you; they will become traps for you and their gods will become snares to you.'" Judges 2:1-3 NIV

IN JUDGES CHAPTER 1 we see that when the people of Israel took over the promised land, they did not drive out all the inhabitants of the land. They let them live there among them. On the surface this seems harmless, even humanitarian. After all, they were taking over land and possessions that they did not earn, they did not work for, and they didn't deserve so it only seems fair that they should let the people who did work for the land at least stay there. The problem is that God told them not to let anyone remain. He instructed them very clearly on several occasions to drive out all the inhabitants of the lands they were to possess. They were a separate people. God had given them very specific instructions about how they were to live. They had laws and principles and customs they were to follow. God knew that if they allowed the inhabitants of the land to remain, they would likely be affected by their customs and beliefs and would not continue to follow all of God's commandments. And this is exactly what happened. They were affected by the culture around them and even began to follow the gods of those people. The last line of our passage today is particularly sobering. "They will become traps for you and their gods will become snares to you."

The Israelites had the opportunity to live completely apart from the rest of the world. They could be a "separate" people. As Christians today, we cannot completely separate ourselves from the world around us and we should not. We should, however, be distinct and different. Jesus himself is our example. He was a part of the world He lived in. He ate with tax collectors and sinners. He talked to prostitutes and His best friends were working class, ordinary, sinful men. And yet He was completely without sin. He affected the culture instead of letting the culture affect Him. That is the example we are to follow. The gods of this world can be very alluring and can easily become a snare for us. And the people and things of this world are often thorns in our side, especially when we seek to live a godly, pure life. Only by remaining close to Jesus and being obedient to Him can we be distinct and different from the world around us: set apart.

Judges 3-4
Psalm 55:1-8
Proverbs 12:22-24
Luke 20:27-47

Running Away

"I said, 'Oh, that I had the wings of a dove! I would fly away and be at rest. I would flee far away and stay in the desert. I would hurry to my place of shelter, far from the tempest and storm." Psalm 55:6-8 NIV

THERE ARE TIMES in all our lives when we just want to run away. Troubles seem to be coming at us from all directions, our relationships are falling apart, people we trusted have let us down, bills are piling up, we can't seem to do anything right, and we just want to run away. In the moment it feels like there is no end to the struggle and we can see no light at the end of the tunnel. We just want to leave it all and get a fresh start. Maybe if we start over we can get it right this time. Unfortunately, it isn't that easy. We see this attitude all around us. If we aren't happy in our marriage, we get a divorce. If we don't like our boss or our coworkers, we quit our job. If we get mad at our pastor, we change churches. Quitting has become acceptable in our self-focused, "don't worry, be happy" society. When our priority is being happy in the moment, we take the easy way out. We ignore our responsibilities and discount the effects our actions have on those around us. We justify and rationalize. God rarely lets us take the easy way out when we are seeking and following His guidance. He is much more concerned with our character than our comfort. Even when we make commitments that were not in His will for us, He doesn't let us walk away until we have fulfilled our responsibility.

My children have gotten frustrated with me over the years because I will not let them quit things. They have joined sports teams and realized after a short time that they did not enjoy it. My husband and I never let them quit. They made a commitment to the team, and they had to stick it out for the season. They did not have to do it again next season, but they could not quit in the middle of a season. Piano lessons, dance, and cheerleading have all come and gone with complaining, grumbling and a few tears. We didn't make them stick it out because we wanted to be mean and torture them or because we wanted them to learn to play the piano or dance or be a professional softball player. We made them stick it out because we wanted them to learn to honor their commitments. We don't want them to be quitters. We are more concerned with their character than their comfort. There are times that we all want to run away and join the circus. Unfortunately, we may discover that the circus has a lot of the same problems because we were a big part of the problem. When we allow God to take over, He most often will make us stay where we are and deal with it as He molds us and changes us into the person He wants us to be.

May 4

Judges 5
Psalm 55:9-15
Proverbs 12:25-26
Luke 21:1-19

An Anxious Heart

"Anxiety weighs down the heart, but a kind word cheers it up." Proverbs 12:25 NIV

In Philippians 4:6-7, Paul gives us the solution to an anxious heart. "Do not be anxious about anything, but in everything, by prayer and petition, with thanksgiving, present your requests to God. And the peace of God, which transcends all understanding, will guard your hearts and your minds in Christ Jesus." (NIV) This sounds too good to be true. You may respond that it is easier said than done and yet, it is a promise we can claim. We are promised that if we turn over our concerns to God, He will give us peace that is beyond our understanding. We will experience a peace that doesn't make sense. We will not experience this peace if we do not give our concerns to Him and leave them there. Too often, we pray about something, we offer it up as a concern to God, but then we take it back with us. We continue to think about it, worry about it, try to come up with ways to fix it and it continues to weigh our hearts down. We feel obligated to worry about it because if we don't then we are being irresponsible. Ultimately, we don't trust that He will deal with it, or we are afraid He will deal with it in a way we don't like so we keep trying to take care of it ourselves.

Worry is a lack of faith. It is not a badge of honor or an act of love. I have had people tell me that they worry about their children because they love them. They spend their days anxious and afraid for their children's safety, their choices, what they are doing and who they are spending time with. Their anxiety doesn't change anything. It doesn't make their circumstances better and it causes friction in their relationship with their children as they are constantly nagging and complaining. Many of the things we spend our time worrying about never come to pass. And the things that do happen are often less severe than we expected, or God has prepared us to deal with it when it comes. Worrying about it doesn't change the outcome and it just makes us miserable in the meantime. We can trust God to take care of us. He has invited us to bring our concerns to Him, all our concerns. He cares about everything we are facing, and He wants us to give Him control and let Him carry the burden. It is not irresponsible. Turning our problems over to the One who can bring about the best solution for us and all concerned is the most responsible, practical thing we can do.

Judges 6-7
Psalm 55:16-23
Proverbs 12:27-28
Luke 21:20-38

May 5

The Impossible

"The Lord said to Gideon, 'You have too many men. I cannot deliver Midian into their hands, or Israel will boast against Me, 'My own strength has saved me.' The Lord said to Gideon, 'With the three hundred men that lapped I will save you and give the Midianites into your hands. Let all the others go home.'" Judges 7:2, 7 NIV

MIDIAN HAD SO impoverished the Israelites that they cried out to the Lord for help. He heard them and sent an angel to Gideon. The angel called him a mighty warrior and instructed him to deliver Israel. Gideon's response to him is priceless. "Are you crazy, I'm not a mighty warrior. My clan is the weakest in Manasseh and I am the least in my family." (My paraphrase) After the Lord assured Gideon of His presence and promised him victory, Gideon gathered all the men he could find to go to battle. He and 32,000 men prepared to fight Midian, but God told him he had too many men. He weeded it down to 10,000, but that was still too many. Gideon and three hundred men went to battle. Gideon must have thought this was crazy. He wasn't sure he could win with 32,000 men, but he knew it would be impossible to defeat the enemy with only three hundred. God usually doesn't give us the reason behind His actions. He just expects us to be obedient and do what He says even if we don't understand, but here He chose to tell Gideon why He wanted him to go to battle with only three hundred men. He did not want Israel to think they did it on their own. He created an impossible situation so there would be no doubt that God and God alone brought about their deliverance.

"Jesus looked at them and said, 'With man this is impossible, but with God all things are possible.'" Matthew 19:26 (NIV) When God moves in our lives, He often takes us out of our comfort zone and puts us in situations that are seemingly impossible. If God is calling us to do something, I believe that most of the time it will be something we cannot do on our own. His call is rarely something we feel comfortable and capable of doing. It is usually something that will stretch us beyond what we think we can do and take us places we never even imagined. He wants to get the glory and honor. He wants to accomplish the impossible. Are we willing to step out in faith and be obedient? Are we willing to go into battle with only three hundred men?

Judges 8-9
Psalm 56:1-7
Proverbs 13:1-2
Luke 22:1-23

May 6

In God We Trust

"In God, whose word I praise—In God I trust and am not afraid. What can mere mortals do to me?" Psalm 56:4 NIV

"They left and found things just as Jesus had told them. So, they prepared the Passover." Luke 22:13 NIV

IN THE PASSAGE in Luke, Jesus gave the disciples specific instructions about where and how to prepare for the Passover and they followed them exactly. They found things just as Jesus had told them. He had worked out all the details. They didn't need to worry about anything, all they had to do was obey His instructions. The disciples followed Jesus' instructions because they trusted Him. Their faith was far from perfect. They had the privilege of walking with Jesus, seeing firsthand the miracles He performed and yet we find them on a boat afraid Jesus was going to let them drown during a storm, on a hillside worried about how to feed 5,000 people and thinking they were seeing a ghost when Jesus walked out on water to them. But they were learning little by little to trust Him. By this point, they trusted Him enough to do what He said.

The Psalmist David had learned this lesson as well. He knew He could trust God. His time in the wilderness running from Saul had taught him that God is faithful, and He can be trusted. David knew that God's will and plans could not be thwarted. There was nothing that mortal men could do to Him unless God allowed it. He was not afraid because he trusted in God's goodness. He knew God loved him and that "in all things God works for the good of those who love Him and have been called according to His purpose." Romans 8:28 (NIV) David also trusted in God's greatness. He knew not only that God wanted what was best for him, but that He had the power and ability to bring it about. We have that same assurance. We can trust Him. We can obey Him and follow His instructions because we know He is faithful. We do not have to be afraid. He is working out all the details to accomplish His purposes in and through us.

Judges 10-11
Psalm 56:8-13
Proverbs 13:3-4
Luke 22:24-46

Mouth Guard

"Those who guard their lips preserve their lives, but those who speak rashly will come to ruin." Proverbs 13:3 NIV

WHEN I READ this verse, I have the mental image of an athlete with a mouth guard. Mouth guards are common in football, hockey, and boxing, but growing numbers of professional athletes in noncontact sports are wearing jaw-positioning mouth guards to improve strength, power, and accuracy. They contend that it helps them think more clearly under pressure. Recent designs not only protect the mouth, but also prevent teeth clenching which causes your body to produce the hormone cortisol. Cortisol increases the heart rate and blood pressure. They also pull the bottom jaw forward which opens the throat to allow for more efficient breathing. The combination reportedly allows the athlete to remain calm, think clearly, and perform to the best of their ability.

It isn't practical to wear a mouth guard all the time, but it would certainly be helpful to me. If I had something in my mouth that forced me to stop and think before I spoke, I could avoid a lot of the trouble my mouth gets me into. Instead of getting angry or frustrated and speaking rashly, I could remain calm, think clearly, and respond appropriately. I could even choose to not respond at all and just keep my mouth shut. In Psalm 141:3, David asks, "Set a guard over my mouth, Lord; keep watch over the door of my lips." (NIV) The Holy Spirit is ready and willing to act as our mouth guard. He is available to us, but we have to choose to listen to His prompting. His still, small voice will guide us and keep us out of trouble, but we have to listen. He doesn't shout. This is a day by day, minute by minute decision. We have to choose to utilize our mouth guard. It won't do us any good if we leave it in the drawer.

Judges 12-14
Psalm 57:1-6
Proverbs 13:5-6
Luke 22:47-71

May 8

The Kiss of Death

"While He was still speaking, suddenly a mob was there, and one of the twelve named Judas was leading them. He came near Jesus to kiss Him, but Jesus said to him, 'Judas, are you betraying the Son of Man with a kiss?'" Luke 22:47-48 HCSB

It has always struck me as odd that Jesus picked Judas to be one of the disciples. Jesus knew how this was going to end before He ever picked Judas. He knew when and how He was going to die, that Judas was going to betray Him, and that Judas was not a true believer, and yet He welcomed him into His inner circle. We don't know a lot about Judas. There are specific details about the other disciples including their former professions, where they came from and how Jesus called them to follow Him. But we don't know anything about Judas other than his name, Judas Iscariot. Jesus had hundreds of followers, so Judas may have just tagged along as one of the crowd. He may have begun following Jesus because he thought Jesus was going to be an earthly ruler who would overthrow Rome and defeat the enemies of the Jews. At some point, however, he came into the inner circle because we find the list of disciples in Matthew 10, Mark 3 and Luke 6 and Judas is listed in all three.

The only other mention of Judas is found in John 12:1-8. When Mary anointed Jesus' feet with expensive perfume, Judas complained that she should have sold the perfume and given the money to the poor. John tells us that Judas was not concerned about the poor, "but because he was a thief; as keeper of the moneybag, he used to help himself to what was put into it." (NIV) Jesus knew that Judas was not trustworthy and yet He let him oversee the money. In Matthew 6:21, Jesus taught that "where your treasure is, there your heart will be also." (NIV) Judas' treasure was found in money. Even though he looked like a disciple, hung around with disciples, spoke like a disciple, and acted like a disciple, his heart was far from God. He could fool others, but he did not fool Jesus.

Judas could have just told the religious leaders what they wanted to know, given them the testimony they needed and let them go arrest Him. They had all seen Him preaching and teaching. They all knew exactly who He was. They didn't need Judas to point Him out to them. But Judas went with them and arranged to use a kiss on the cheek as His method of identifying Him. He used the most intimate means of communication between personal friends to be his method of betrayal. He wanted Jesus to know he was the betrayer. At some point he figured out that Jesus was not going to do what he expected. His true intentions became clear. His motives were selfish. Instead of following Jesus because He was God's Son and the promised Messiah, he was following Him for what he thought Jesus could do for him. He thought Jesus was going to set up an earthly kingdom and Judas wanted to be a part of the power and prestige. When he realized this wasn't going to happen, he didn't even try to hide his betrayal. He turned on Jesus and handed Him over to be killed. Judas is evidence that you can look like you've got it all together, you can go to church and hear good sermons, and you can say all the right things, but if your heart is far from God, it doesn't do any good at all. Christianity is not about following rules and being good. Christianity is about having a personal relationship with Jesus and loving Him for who He is and not what He can do for you. You can fool others, but you can't fool Jesus. He knows the true intentions of your heart.

Judges 15-16
Psalm 57:7-11
Proverbs 13:7-8
Luke 23

May 9

Guard Your Heart

"Some time later, he fell in love with a woman named Delilah, who lived in the Sorek Valley. The Philistine leaders went to her and said, 'Persuade him to tell you where his great strength comes from, so we can overpower him, tie him up and make him helpless. Each of us will give you 1,100 pieces of silver.'" Judges 16:4-5 HCSB

Samson was anointed by God to deliver his people from the power of the Philistines. He was raised up by his parents with this anointing in mind. They had followed the instructions given them by the angel of the Lord that he should not cut his hair, drink wine or beer or eat anything unclean. God had given him incredible strength and he was able to defeat anyone who came against him. But Samson had a weakness. He had terrible taste in women. His wife betrayed him by telling her people the answer to his riddle forcing him to pay them thirty changes of clothes. You would think he would have learned his lesson about divulging secrets, but then he fell in love with Delilah. Samson made several mistakes in this relationship that had fatal consequences. Delilah was not the kind of woman he should have been with. I have to believe he knew better. He was enticed by her beauty and ignored the warning signs. Sin is like that in our lives. Satan knows just how to make it look enticing and beautiful. He makes it seem harmless and so we ignore the warning signs and let ourselves get attached to it. The Philistines promised to pay Delilah a lot of money if she found out the source of his great strength. He knew something was up when she started asking him about his strength because he lied to her twice. That should have been a flashing red light telling him to run away from her, but instead he stayed. Verse 16 tells us, "She nagged him day after day and pleaded with him until she finally wore him down." (NIV) That should have been his next clue. He wasn't married to her, but he stayed and listened to her nagging for days. Instead of fleeing from her, he made himself comfortable. If we don't flee from temptation, it will wear us down and before long we will become comfortable with our sin. It is difficult to defeat it when we are enjoying its company.

Samson should have guarded his heart. He gave his heart to two women that were not worthy of his affection. Instead of helping him fulfill the calling on his life, they lead him to destruction. It is important that we choose carefully who we allow to have our heart. This applies to friendships as well as romantic relationships. We need to spend our time and energy with people that will build us up spiritually doing things that will draw us closer to God and help us fulfill His purpose for our lives. Unlike Samson, let us heed the warning signs and flee from sinful relationships before we have to face the consequences of bad choices.

Judges 17-18
Psalm 58:1-5
Proverbs 13:9-10
Luke 24

He is Risen

"He is not here, but He has been resurrected." Luke 24:6 HCSB

THIS VERSE IS the basis of our faith. If Jesus did not raise from the dead, there is no reason for us to place our trust in Him. During His time on Earth, He lived a perfect life. He fed the hungry, healed the sick and cared for the poor. He was humble and gentle. He was a good teacher and had lots of followers everywhere He went. He was a good man. But if we look back through history, there have been a lot of good men. None of them were perfect like Jesus, but there have been many good teachers, many people who selflessly gave of their time and resources to feed the hungry, heal the sick and care for the poor, and many humble and gentle servants of God. But the thing that sets Jesus apart from every other person who has ever walked the face of the Earth is that He raised Himself from the dead.

There are 10 different accounts in the Bible of people being raised from the dead. Elijah raised the son of a widow in Zarephath, Elisha raised the Shunammite woman's son, an unnamed man was raised when his dead body was thrown into Elisha's tomb and touched his bones, Jesus raised the son of a widow from Nain, Jairus' daughter, and Lazarus. Many holy people in Jerusalem were raised from the dead when Jesus died, and the curtain was ripped in half. There was an earthquake, and many tombs were cracked open. Peter raised Tabitha from the dead and Paul raised Eutychus, the man who fell asleep in a window listening to Paul and fell three stories to his death. Being raised from the dead is certainly unusual, but we don't follow those who were risen from the dead because they eventually died again. What makes Jesus' resurrection unique is that He raised Himself from the dead. He didn't need someone else to raise Him. He raised Himself and then ascended into Heaven forty days later. He overcame death and Hell. The grave could not hold Him. No ordinary man could do that. Only the Son of God, the Messiah, could once and for all defeat death and make a way for sinful man to live eternally in Heaven with Him.

No other religion serves a living savior. No other religion claims that their god came to Earth to die to save them from their sin and make a way to bring them to Heaven. No other religion has a savior who loves them and abides in them to lead, guide, comfort, strengthen and help them. All the other world religions are based on a system of working really hard to try to be good enough to earn your way to Heaven. Our Savior knows that we cannot possibly be perfect and so He willingly bore our sins and took the punishment we deserve so that we can have a relationship with Him. This is the Savior I choose to follow.

Judges 19-21
Psalm 58:6-11
Proverbs 13:11-12
John 1

The Word

"In the beginning was the Word, and the Word was with God, and the Word was God. He was with God in the beginning. All things were created through Him, and apart from Him not one thing was created that has been created. Life was in Him and that life was the light of men. That light shines in the darkness, yet the darkness did not overcome it. But to all who did receive Him, He gave them the right to be children of God, to those who believe in His name." John 1:1-5, 12 HCSB

JOHN BEGINS HIS gospel by introducing Jesus. In this chapter John tells us who Jesus is and the purpose for which He came to Earth. He uses a term that was very familiar to the Greek and Jewish people of his day. The Greek word translated "Word" in this passage is "Logos." Logos is often used to describe the instrument through which God carries out his will. By introducing Jesus as "the Word," John is making clear that He is the revelation of God. Jesus is the instrument through which God's will would be accomplished. Not only does Jesus represent God and act as a mediator between God and man, but John is also declaring that Jesus is God. He is also proclaiming that Jesus is distinct from God. He tells us that Jesus was God and that He was with God. He was fully God, and He was also fully human. Jesus Christ is the Living Word of God who came to reveal God to man.

Verse 12 tells us that Jesus' purpose in coming was to give everyone who received Him and believed on His name the right to be children of God. He didn't come to show us how to be good so we can earn the right to be children of God. All He asks is that we receive Him and believe. Faith is the key. The Jews refused to receive Him because He didn't meet their expectations. They did not believe He was the Messiah. Let us each wholeheartedly receive Jesus as the revelation of God and believe in His Holy name.

Ruth 1-2
Psalm 59:1-5
Proverbs 13:13-14
John 2

Exceedingly Abundantly

"When the chief servant tasted the water (after it had become wine), he did not know where it came from---though the servants who had drawn the water knew. He called the groom and told him, 'Everyone sets out the fine wine first, then, after people have drunk freely, the inferior. But you have kept the fine wine until now.'"
John 2:9-10 HCSB

A FEW MONTHS ago, I watched the new series, "The Chosen." If you haven't watched it, I highly recommend it. It is a series about the life of Jesus and it is very well done. Having heard these biblical accounts my whole life, I think I often just skim through them without really thinking about the details of how these events would have played out in real life. One of the episodes gave the account of the wedding we read about in John 2. My daughter, Emily, got married in 2017, and my youngest daughter, Hannah, is getting married this summer, so I am very familiar with the excitement, planning, and stress involved in making everything perfect for that special day. In biblical times, weddings lasted for several days, and a central part of the event was wine. In the episode of "The Chosen," Mary was good friends with the mother of the bride. She had helped her plan the wedding and everything was going just as planned, until the wine ran out. I can relate to this scene so well. Over the last several years, in addition to being the mother of the bride, I have also helped several of my dear friends with their children's weddings. I can easily envision myself as Mary in this story running around trying to figure out how to solve this problem without causing embarrassment and stress to the bride and groom.

This wedding took place before Jesus began His public ministry. He was at the wedding as a family friend, not as a minister. He was one of the guests. When Mary heard that there was a problem, she knew just where to turn. She knew that Jesus could help. We can learn a lot from Mary's actions. She went to Jesus with complete confidence that He would know what to do. She didn't tell Him how to fix the problem, she just explained the problem to Him and told the servants to do whatever Jesus said to do. Too often, I go to Jesus with my problems, trying to explain to Him how He needs to fix it and giving Him ideas about the best way to handle the issue. Needless to say, He does not need my help figuring out what to do. His solutions are far better than any I could possibly come up with. My job is to present my problem to Him, leave it at His feet and trust Him to take care of it in the best way. It is also significant to note that this was a relatively minor problem. While it would have been embarrassing to run out of wine, it did not involve someone who was sick and dying or a major financial difficulty. It is comforting to know that Jesus cares about all the details of our lives. We can take any problem, big or small, to Him and ask for His help. He wants to be involved in every aspect of our lives, not just the "big" stuff. Jesus not only solved the problem by providing more wine, but He provided wine that was far superior to the wine they had been serving. Jesus' intervention in our situation will always far exceed any expectations that we have. "Now unto Him who is able to do exceedingly abundantly above all that we ask or think, according to the power that works within us, unto Him be glory in the church by Christ Jesus throughout all ages, world without end." Ephesians 3:20-21 (KJV)

Ruth 3-4
Psalm 59:6-13
Proverbs 13:15-16
John 3

May 13

Character Matters

> "Now don't be afraid, my daughter, I will do for you whatever you say, since all the people in my town know that you are a woman of noble character." Ruth 3:11 HCSB

I HAVE ALWAYS admired Ruth. The qualities we see in her life make her an excellent example to follow. As a young woman she suffered a devastating loss. She was a Moabite woman who fell in love and married a Jewish man. Before having children, her husband died leaving her a widow. Her sister-in-law and mother-in-law were also widowed. Ruth's hopes were destroyed and the life she dreamed of was not going to happen. The natural response would be to return home to her family and start over. That is exactly what her sister-in-law chose to do. In really difficult circumstances, she could have thrown herself a pity party, whined about how hard her life was and given up. No one would have blamed her if she did that, but Ruth reacted differently. Naomi tried to persuade her to go home, but Ruth refused to leave her. She didn't know what the future held so she just did the next right thing. Ruth exhibited unusual loyalty and dedication to Naomi. She went above and beyond what was expected of her. As a Moabitess, Ruth grew up worshipping the many gods of her people. When she married, she would have been introduced to the God of Israel. In chapter 1 we find Ruth's famous declaration, "For wherever you go, I will go, and wherever you live, I will live, your people will be my people, and your God will be my God." (NIV) In choosing to stay with Naomi, Ruth was also choosing to follow God. She was making a conscious choice to reject the gods of her people and choose Naomi's God. She left everything familiar and disregarded her own personal interests to care for her mother-in-law.

Ruth honored and respected Naomi in a way that made Boaz say that all the people in Bethlehem knew she was a woman of noble character. She worked hard to provide food for them and did exactly what Naomi told her to do. Character is who you are when no one is watching. Ruth had no idea that millions of people would read about her story. She lived a simple life in obscurity. She showed her true character in everything she did and as a result God took care of her. When no one else is watching, God always sees what we do. He knows our character. He knows our hearts and knows what kind of person we really are. It is useful to examine our hearts periodically and ask God to show us anything that is not pleasing to Him so we can confess, repent, and turn away from those things and live a life of integrity. It is also important to note that as Christians, people are watching us even if we don't realize it. If we bear the name Christian, we represent Christ to those around us and we want to be careful not to dishonor His name in any way.

I Samuel 1-3
Psalm 59:14-17
Proverbs 13:17-18
John 4

May 14

Attentive Listeners

> "The Lord came, stood there, and called as before, 'Samuel, Samuel!' Samuel responded, 'Speak, for Your servant is listening.'" I Samuel 3:10 HCSB

THIS IS MY prayer so often to the Lord. While I don't hear an audible voice like Samuel did in this passage, I long to be so attentive to God's presence in my life that I hear and recognize Him speaking to me. I want to be able to discern His voice so that I can distinguish between the thoughts in my head and the work of His Spirit. I find that the more time I spend with Him every day, the easier it is to recognize His voice. Sometimes He speaks to me through His Word. I will read a passage in the morning that may or may not seem significant at the time and later in the day, He will bring that passage to mind related to a situation I am facing or in response to someone I am talking to. If I had not read that passage it might not have been in my mind to recall. Sometimes during my Bible reading or prayer time He will bring someone to my mind. I have learned that means I should pray for them and then reach out to them. Often, I find out that they have a need, and I am either able to offer encouragement and prayer or provide help in some tangible way. When I ignore that prompting, I miss out on the opportunity to be a part of God's plan to help them.

A few months ago, on "The View," Joy Behar made fun of Vice President Mike Pence because in an interview he said that he prays to God every day and then waits to hear from God. She said, "It's one thing to talk to Jesus, it's another thing when Jesus talks to you...that's called mental illness...hearing voices."[5] Someone who does not know Jesus personally cannot understand that still small voice described in Isaiah 30:21, "Whether you turn to the right or the left, your ears will hear a voice behind you saying, 'This is the way, walk in it.'" (NIV) In John 10:27 Jesus tells us, "My sheep hear My voice, and I know them, and they follow Me." (HCSB) In Jeremiah 33:3 God says, "Call to Me and I will answer you, and tell you great and unsearchable things that you do not know." (NIV) We have to be very careful and prayerful in discerning God's voice because we don't want to claim we have heard from God when we haven't. But as believers we can and should hear God's voice giving us direction, guidance, correction, and instruction. It is not a sign of mental illness. It is a sign of a vibrant, personal relationship with Jesus. May we all respond to His call to us with, "Speak, for Your servant is listening."

May 15

I Samuel 4-5
Psalm 60:1-5
Proverbs 13:19-21
John 5

The Company You Keep

"The one who walks with the wise will become wise, but a companion of fools will suffer harm." Proverbs 13:20 HCSB

This verse is very clear. It matters who we hang out with. The people you choose to spend the most time with will affect your character. I Corinthians 15:33 tells us, "Do not be deceived, 'Bad company ruins good morals.'" (HCSB) The idea that we will be a good influence on them, and they won't rub off on us is wishful thinking at best and dangerous at worst. As Christians it is essential that we surround ourselves with people who will encourage us and help us on our spiritual journey. We are not meant to walk through this life alone. 2020 was a very hard year for many reasons, but one of the most difficult aspects of it was that our community was taken away. Not being able to fellowship with other believers, have Bible studies, small groups, Sunday School classes and meet for worship has had a profound impact on our society and I fear the consequences will be realized for a long time to come.

For the last fifteen or so years I have been a part of an accountability prayer group. These women are my people. I can't imagine navigating life without them. Before 2020 we met weekly. We continued to meet in 2020, but it was more challenging. Sometimes we did zoom meetings. Sometimes we met in the cul de sac of one of our members with our cars backed in a circle sitting in our hatchbacks more than six feet apart. We even met outside at our local hospital several times on the lunch hour of a nurse in our group. We didn't meet as often as usual, but we did whatever was necessary to get together because we know we need each other. During our time together we discuss our lives, our children, our families, our fears, our struggles, and our hopes. We laugh together and we cry together. We have been through the illness and death of parents, parenting teenagers, empty-nesting, weddings of our children, births of grandchildren, financial struggles, and illnesses. We don't always have the answers and we don't know how to fix all the problems we face, but we know the One who does. No matter what is going on in my life, they point me to Jesus, they pray for me, they walk beside me, and they hold me accountable. I know if I mess up, they won't let me get by with it. They won't tell me what I want to hear, they tell me what I need to hear. Because I know that they love me, I can hear their gentle and loving rebukes in a way that makes me want to repent and turn to God. If you don't have people in your life like this, get some. Do whatever you have to do to develop relationships where you can be real with people who will build you up and point you to Jesus on a regular basis. It is that important. "As iron sharpens iron, so one person sharpens another." Proverbs 27:17 (NIV)

May 16

I Samuel 6-7
Psalm 60:6-12
Proverbs 13:22-23
John 6

Leftovers

"When they were full, He told His disciples, 'Collect the leftovers so that nothing is wasted.' So, they collected them and filled twelve baskets with the pieces from the five barley loaves that were left over by those who had eaten." John 6:12-13 HCSB

THE MIRACLE OF feeding the 5,000 is the only miracle recorded in all four gospels. Jesus had been teaching all day and people had gathered in large numbers to hear Him. As evening approached, they started getting hungry. They were in the middle of nowhere with no McDonalds or Chick fila around the corner to get food. The disciples recognized that it was dinner time and approached Jesus to tell Him that He should stop teaching so the people could leave and go get something to eat. Instead, Jesus told them to feed the people. They had no food and no money to buy food and even if they had money, they had nowhere to get food. Andrew decided he would go into the crowd and see if he could find anyone with food. All he found was a small boy with two fish and five pieces of bread. The disciples knew they had no way to feed this crowd of people. They were completely helpless to meet the need before them. When we come to the place where we realize Jesus is all we have, we find out that Jesus is all we need.

If I was the little boy, I might have been tempted to hang on to my food. After all, he had planned ahead, (or more likely his mother had planned ahead) and all these other people had come unprepared. Why should he give what he had to them? Thankfully the little boy was more generous than me and he gave all he had to Jesus.

Jesus took the little amount that He had and multiplied it exponentially to provide food for everyone there to eat all they wanted. When we generously give our time and resources to God, He can multiply them and do far more than we can even imagine. Not only did Jesus provide enough for everyone to eat, but He also provided so much that there were twelve basketfuls left over. They ended up with more left over than they had to start with. A few days ago, we talked about Jesus doing exceedingly abundantly more than we ask or imagine. This is a perfect example of Jesus' abundant provision. He knows our needs and we can trust Him to provide for us. I have often heard it said that you can't outgive God. If we give Him our meager resources, we can be confident that He will meet all our needs and that He will multiply our resources for use in His kingdom.

I Samuel 8-10
Psalm 61
Proverbs 13:24-25
John 7

Be Careful What You Ask For

"The people refused to listen to Samuel. 'No,' they said, 'We must have a king over us. Then we will be like all the other nations: our king will judge us, go out before us, and fight our battles.' Samuel listened to all the people's words and then repeated them to the Lord. 'Listen to them,' the Lord told Samuel, 'Appoint a king for them.'"
I Samuel 8:19-22 HCSB

THE PEOPLE OF Israel did not need an earthly king. God was their leader and He served as their king. God gave them instructions through priests, judges, and prophets. His plan was perfect. If they had listened to Him and obeyed His instructions, they would have been successful in everything they did. With God as their leader, they were invincible. But they decided they knew better. They looked around at all the other nations and decided they wanted to be like them. The elders got together and went to Samuel to tell him that they wanted a king. Samuel presented their request to God and God told him to warn them of the consequences of having a king ruling over them. He told them how the king would take their land and their sons and their daughters for his use. He warned them that a king would make them servants and they would be treated as they had been treated in Egypt. But they refused to listen. They demanded a king, so God gave them what they wanted and appointed Saul as their king. Saul started out ok, but eventually everything Samuel predicted came true.

It is easy to read this story now and see how foolish the Israelites were. If they had listened to God and obeyed Him, they would have been very successful and would have had everything they ever wanted. But instead, they followed their own desires and plans and ended up having years of heartache and struggle during Saul's reign. Sadly, we are too often like the Israelites. We get an idea in our head, and we won't take no for an answer. We think we know best. We think if God gives us this job, or this new house, or this spouse, everything will be great. We look around and want to be like everybody else. God tries to warn us about the consequences, but we refuse to listen. He has a plan that is perfect and will give us the life that is best for us, but it isn't what we have in mind, so we keep pressuring Him to give us what we want. Unfortunately, sometimes He gives in and gives us what we want. I've done that as a parent. My kids keep asking for something I know is not a good idea and that they will regret. I warn them that they will regret it, but finally I give in to teach them a lesson and to show them that I really do know what I'm talking about, and they should listen to me. We can save ourselves a lot of heartache if we just listen to God and obey Him. He really does know best. He has a plan that is perfect for each of us.

I Samuel 11-12
Psalm 62:1-8
Proverbs 14:1-2
John 8

May 18

The First Stone

"When they persisted in questioning Him, He stood up and said to them, 'The one without sin among you should be the first to throw a stone at her!' Then He stooped down and continued writing on the ground... Only He was left, with the woman in the center. When Jesus stood up, He said to her, 'Woman, where are they? Has no one condemned you?' 'No one, Lord.' She answered. 'Neither do I condemn you,' said Jesus. 'Go, and from now on do not sin anymore.'" John 8:7-11 HCSB

THIS IS ONE of the most quoted passages in the Bible by people who do not know much about the Bible. It is too often used to excuse and take attention off the sin and accuse Christians of being judgmental. When we look at the context of the passage and not just that one verse, we get a clearer picture of the Pharisee's intentions, and we can understand Jesus' response to them in a more accurate way. John tells us exactly what was going on in verse 6. "They asked this to trap Him in order that they might have evidence to accuse Him." (HCSB) The Pharisees were doing everything they possibly could to try to trap Jesus into saying something they could use against Him. They controlled the people by their legalism and man-made laws and Jesus threatened their power. He had so many followers that they were afraid the people were going to reject them and turn to Jesus. They were desperate.

This passage does deal with being judgmental. The Pharisees were very judgmental. They had a long list of rules the people were required to follow, and the Pharisees made it their job to make sure everyone was following the rules. Some of the rules were given to them by God, but a majority of them were rules that they had made up to dictate every aspect of daily life. God gave them rules because He loved them and wanted to make sure they were protected and taken care of. The man-made rules were put in place to control the people, not out of love and concern. Jesus often went against those man-made rules. But He never disregarded God's laws. He knew the intentions of the men who brought this woman to Him, and His response was directed at them. After the men left, He gently turned to the woman. He did not tell her, "It's ok, no big deal, just forget about it." He said to her, "Go, and from now on do not sin anymore." He did not excuse her sin. He did not say it wasn't sin. He showed her grace and told her to go and sin no more. There are two important things to remember about this passage. God's rules are given to us out of love and protection. God knows the things that are bad for us. He knows the things that cause harm physically, emotionally, and spiritually to us and He wants to help us avoid those things. We obey His laws out of respect and with the understanding that if we obey God our lives will have less difficulty and problems. We must examine our lives often and ask God to show us areas of sin that we need to turn away from. When we recognize sin in our lives, we must deal with it. We cannot make excuses or laugh it off as just the way we are. Sin is very serious, and we will be held accountable for it. It is also not wrong of us to gently and lovingly correct our fellow believers who we know are engaging in sinful behavior. The important distinction is the motive of our hearts. We need to confront them in love wanting what is truly best for them and attempting to help them deal with it and turn back to God. If we approach them with condemnation, anger, and contempt we are being judgmental and that is not pleasing to God. Knowing a fellow believer is engaging in behaviors that are sinful and ignoring it is not loving. Those behaviors will lead to heartache and difficulty, and we should pray for them asking God what we can do to help.

I Samuel 13-14
Psalm 62:9-12
Proverbs 14:3-4
John 9

May 19

Now I See

> "So, a second time they summoned the man who had been blind and told him, 'Give glory to God. We know that this man is a sinner!' He answered, 'Whether or not He is a sinner, I don't know. One thing I do know: I was blind, and now I can see!'"
> John 9:24-25 HCSB

A WIDELY HELD belief among first century Jews was that if a child was born with an illness or physical deformity it was due to sin committed by his parents or by the child in the womb. When Jesus encountered the man born blind, He took the opportunity to dispel this belief. He told the disciples that neither the man nor his parents had sinned, and that He was going to use the man's blindness to display God's glory. For years this man and his parents had lived with this stigma. The religious leaders condemned them. Family and friends whispered behind their back. His parents probably spent many sleepless nights wondering what they did to cause his blindness or what their sweet child could have done to deserve to be punished this way. I imagine their guilt and grief was overwhelming. Then Jesus stepped into their lives and changed their circumstances in an instant.

The religious leaders were suspicious and called them in for questioning. The man's response to them is a great example for us. He didn't try to come up with some theological argument to explain how he was healed. He didn't defend Jesus or try to convince them He must be the Messiah. He said, "One thing I do know: I was blind and now I see!" He gave eyewitness testimony to what Jesus had done in his life. They couldn't argue with his personal experience. He didn't need to understand how Jesus did it. All he needed to know was that he had been blind all his life and then he met Jesus. In an act of love and mercy, Jesus spit on the ground, made mud from the saliva and rubbed the mud on his eyes. Jesus told him to go wash in a pool and then he could see. That must have been an amazing moment. He saw the sparkle of water as it ran down his face and through his fingers. He saw the beauty of the flowers growing beside the road and the splendor of the tall palm trees. He must have run through town soaking in every detail. And then for the first time he saw the face of his mother and father, and they rejoiced together at the miracle of sight. When people ask us about Jesus, we don't need to be able to answer deep theological questions or have a list of scriptures ready to make our case in defending Jesus to convince them to believe. All we have to do is tell them what Jesus has done for us. "I was blind, but now I see." Its ok to tell them we don't have all the answers, but we know that what Jesus did for us, He can do for them as well. All they really need to know is that Jesus loves them, and He can help them.

I Samuel 15
Psalm 63:1-5
Proverbs 14:5-7
John 10

May 20

To Obey is Better Than Sacrifice

"Then Samuel said, 'Does the Lord take pleasure in burnt offerings and sacrifices as much as in obeying the Lord? Look: to obey is better than sacrifice, to pay attention is better than the fat of rams.' Samuel mourned for Saul and the Lord regretted that He had made Saul king over Israel." I Samuel 15:22, 35 HCSB

GOD GAVE SAUL very specific instructions to attack the Amalekites and completely destroy everything they had. He was told to kill the men, women, children and infants, oxen, sheep, camels, and donkeys, not sparing any of them. Their evil ways and demonic practices would have had an influence on the children of Israel if they were allowed to survive, so God commanded him to annihilate them completely. Saul went to battle and destroyed the men, women, children, and infants, but he spared Agag their king and the best of the sheep, cattle, and choice animals. This was an act of pride and selfishness. He wanted the best animals and plunder for himself and he wanted to parade King Agag before the people to exalt himself as a great warrior. When Samuel confronted him, Saul claimed that he did obey God and that the reason he spared the animals was so that he could sacrifice them to the Lord. He thought that going through the motions of religious observance would somehow make up for the fact that he had only partially obeyed God. Are we guilty of the same mindset? Do we think that we can make up for not obeying God during the week if we go to church on Sunday? Do we think that because we read our Bible every day it will somehow make up for the fact that we fail to live according to what it says? Do we fall into the trap of believing that partial obedience is ok? Do we think that if we get the important stuff right, God will overlook the little stuff?

Saul had the idea that God wouldn't notice that he had not obeyed if he just gave part of it back to God. Can we cheat on our taxes if we give part of our savings back to God? Is it ok to gamble if we give Him a tenth of our proceeds? Will God overlook ill-gotten gain if we give Him a cut? I think the answer to these questions is found in the verses above. "To obey is better than sacrifice." God does not honor disobedience and He will not bless deceit and dishonesty. Our obedience is evidence of our faith and faith pleases Him far more than religious practices.

May 21

I Samuel 16-17
Psalm 63:6-11
Proverbs 14:8-10
John 11

After God's Heart

"But the Lord said to Samuel, 'Do not look at his appearance or his stature, because I have rejected him. Man does not see what the Lord sees, for man sees what is visible, but the Lord sees the heart." I Samuel 16:7 HCSB

SAUL WAS THE obvious choice to be king. I Samuel 9:1-2 tells us that he was the son of an influential Benjaminite. There was no one more impressive among the Israelites than Saul and he was a head taller than anyone else. David, on the other hand, was the son of Jesse, a farmer, and sheep herder from Bethlehem. God instructed Samuel to go to Jesse to anoint his son as the next king. Jesse presented seven sons to him, but none of them were God's anointed. His youngest son was out in the field tending the sheep and Jesse didn't even consider that he might be the chosen one. His brothers were much better suited to be king. Jesse sent for him and as soon as Samuel saw him, he knew that David was the one. When the people chose a king, they picked the most impressive man they could find. They looked at his background, his family, his physical stature, and his outward appearance. God picked his successor, and His criteria was very different. He was not concerned with his outward appearance, his background, or accomplishments. The only thing God was looking for in a king was someone who trusted Him. God wanted someone who would listen to Him, obey Him, and give Him the glory. Acts 13:22 tells us, "After removing Saul, He made David their king. God testified concerning him, 'I have found David son of Jesse, a man after My own heart; he will do everything I want him to do.'" (NIV)

God did not look at all the people of Israel and pick out the one that had the best qualifications to do the job. On paper Saul was the perfect choice and yet God regretted ever letting him be king. David had qualities that were not outwardly apparent, but that made him the perfect choice. David was humble, faithful to God, obedient, and he trusted God completely. God took those qualities and developed him into a godly king. David gave all the honor and glory to God. He did not seek it for himself. God's criteria haven't changed. He isn't looking for the most qualified people to carry out His plans. He still doesn't look at outward appearance and accomplishments. God is looking for people who trust Him and will obey Him. It is important that we use the same criteria for people we respect and choose to follow. Instead of being impressed with outward attributes, we should be evaluating them based on God's standards. Their true character will come through upon examination. Humility, faithfulness, obedience, and trust in God should be evident in their lives and in ours as well. May we each seek to be people after God's own heart.

I Samuel 18-19
Psalm 64:1-6
Proverbs 14:11-12
John 12

May 22

The Terror of the Enemy

"Saul was furious and resented this song, 'They credited tens of thousands to David,' he complained, 'but they only credited me with thousands. What more can he have but the kingdom?' So, Saul watched him jealously from that day forward." I Samuel 18:8-9 HCSB

"God, hear my voice when I complain. Protect my life from the terror of the enemy. Hide me from the scheming of wicked people." Psalm 64:1-2 HCSB

THE PASSAGE IN Psalm was written by David when he was fleeing from Saul. In I Samuel 18-19 we read about Saul's jealousy of David and how it incited him to attack David several times and order his death. David served Saul faithfully. He never did anything to cause Saul to question his loyalty, and yet Saul was blinded by jealousy and believed David was trying to take his throne. He did not realize that it was God who would take away his throne and give it to David as punishment for his disobedience. David wrote several Psalms during the period when he was hiding in the wilderness. The Psalms David wrote give us a peak into his heart as he allows himself to be completely vulnerable and transparent. It is evident that he was terrified of Saul. He must have been very confused. He had done nothing wrong. He lived in Saul's house and served him for many years. Saul even gave his daughter to David in marriage and Saul's son, Jonathan, was his best friend. The betrayal of someone he had grown to love must have been very painful.

In this Psalm, David is begging God to protect him from the terror of the enemy and the scheming of wicked people. He speaks of people shooting at him from concealed places, hidden traps, and secret plans. He knew God had appointed him to be Saul's successor. He was the king's son-in-law so maybe he thought Saul would appoint him king before he died. It must have been very difficult to understand why Saul would turn on him. God's plans often don't line up with our expectations. We think we know how our lives will play out and when it doesn't turn out that way, we can become confused and begin to question what we believe about God, His love for us and His plans. In the Psalms, David asks questions, he seeks answers, and he honestly lays out his fears before God, but it is evident that he has not lost faith in God. He is scared and uncertain about the future, but he trusts God to take care of him. It is comforting to know that God is ok with us being honest and open with Him. God is not upset by our questions. Like David, we can be confident that He will always take care of us. We can trust Him even when we don't understand everything that is happening.

May 23

I Samuel 20-21
Psalm 64:7-10
Proverbs 14:13-14
John 13

Dirty Feet

> "So, He got up from supper, laid aside His robe, took a towel, and tied it around Himself. Next, He poured water into a basin and began to wash the disciple's feet and to dry them with the towel tied around Him." John 13:4-5 HCSB

IN BIBLICAL TIMES, people walked everywhere on dusty, dirty roads and they wore sandals. This necessitated washing their feet whenever they entered a home. Typically, they would wash their own feet, but the wealthy had servants who performed this act. This was a chore that was reserved for the lowliest of servants. Luke tells us in his gospel that earlier in the evening Jesus had heard the disciples arguing about who was the greatest among them. The idea of humbling themselves to wash someone's feet would have probably never occurred to them. They were shocked when Jesus kneeled before them and gently, lovingly washed their feet. Even after being with Jesus for three years, they still thought that Jesus was going to establish an earthly kingdom and they wanted to be His cabinet. In this act of humble service, Jesus was once again trying to make them understand that His kingdom was very different. The last would be first, the least would be the greatest, the humble would be exalted and the proud would be humbled. His time was running out, so He needed them to understand the importance of humility and service. He decided to give them an object lesson. The Creator of the universe, the Son of God, the Messiah Himself, knelt before them, took their dirty feet in His hands, and cleansed them. This was a foreshadowing of His death on the cross that would cleanse them of their sin.

It is significant that Jesus washed Judas' feet along with the rest of the disciples. He knew what Judas was going to do later that night and yet He washed the dirt off his feet, too. "The Lord is not slow in keeping His promise, as some understand slowness. Instead, He is patient with you not wanting anyone to perish but everyone to come to repentance." 2 Peter 3:9 (NIV) Jesus was willing to humble Himself to give Judas one last chance to repent and follow Him. Judas did not take advantage of that opportunity. The other disciples didn't really understand what Jesus was trying to teach them that night, but it is evident following His death, burial, and resurrection that they figured it out. The early church, led by these men, was characterized by service and generosity. Their sacrificial love for each other and their commitment to serving others created an environment where the gospel was spread around the world. Throughout the centuries, one of the distinguishing characteristics of the body of believers is found in Philippians 2:3-4. "In humility value others above yourselves, not looking to your own interests, but each of you to the interests of others." (NIV) Following Jesus' footsteps and serving others is the greatest privilege we can have.

I Samuel 22-23
Psalm 65:1-8
Proverbs 14:15-16
John 14

The Way

"Jesus told them, 'I am the way, the truth, and the life. No one comes to the Father except through Me." John 14:6 NIV

IN THIS ONE statement, Jesus makes it absolutely clear that He is the only way to get to God. He is removing all doubt. All the other world religions that are available now and have been available since the beginning of time are attempts by Satan to distract and deceive. All other gods, (Buddha, Baal, Allah, Zeus, Shiva, Venus, etc.), are false gods made up by man under the influence of Satan. Jesus is not only saying that there is one true God; He is saying that He is the only way to get to that God. The Jewish people of His day worshipped the one true God, but they were not willing to accept that Jesus was God's Son, the Messiah. Jesus was making a definitive statement that He is the One. The idea that there are many ways to get to God is a lie. Satan does not have to convince people to worship him. All he needs to do is convince people to worship anything other than Jesus. He does not appear with a pitchfork, horns and a red suit looking evil and menacing. He comes clothed in tolerance, acceptance, "having it your way", and "getting what you deserve." His message is appealing and enticing. "Enter through the narrow gate. For wide is the gate and broad is the road that leads to destruction, and many enter through it. But small is the gate and narrow the road that leads to life, and only a few find it." Matthew 7:13-14 (NIV)

In our politically correct culture, this seems to be closed-minded and intolerant. Who are we to say that we know the right way and everyone else is wrong? This message is not culturally sensitive. But it is truth. This is not just my opinion. It is Jesus' own words. God created the universe and He created us. He gets to decide how people come to Him. We don't get a vote on what seems fair or preferable to us. He provided one way, "For God so loved the world, that He gave His only begotten Son, that whoever believes in Him should not perish, but have everlasting life." John 3:16 (KJV) We cannot be wishy washy about our beliefs. We cannot just believe what we want to and let everyone else believe what they want and not get involved. If we believe Jesus is God's Son and we believe what the Bible says then we know that anyone who does not believe these truths, no matter how nice and good they are, is going to Hell. It is not loving and accepting to let them continue to believe the lies of Satan. We have a responsibility to tell as many people as we can about Jesus. They may choose to believe Satan's lies and we cannot force them to believe the truth, but we must tell them. I know it is uncomfortable. I know it is difficult, but the alternative is eternal damnation. We cannot be content to say nothing if we truly care about them.

May 25

I Samuel 24-25
Psalm 65:9-13
Proverbs 14:17-19
John 15

Vines

"Remain in Me and I in you. Just as a branch is unable to produce fruit by itself unless it remains on the vine, so neither can you unless you remain in Me. I am the vine and you are the branches. The one who remains in Me, and I in him produces much fruit, because you can do nothing without Me." John 15:4-5 HCSB

JESUS OFTEN USED word pictures to explain concepts that were difficult to understand. He used everyday objects that those He was talking to were very familiar with. Vineyards were very common in the Middle East, and they would have understood the significance of the branches being a part of the vine. If the branch is not connected to the vine, it would die very quickly. It cannot bear grapes. In the Christian life, Jesus is the vine, and we are the branches. We must stay connected to Jesus to bear fruit. The more time we spend with Jesus in prayer and Bible study, the more intimate our relationship will be. The closer our connection, the more fruit we will bear. Galatians 5:22-23 tells us what fruit we can expect to bear if we stay close to Him. "The fruit of the Spirit is love, joy, peace, patience, kindness, goodness, gentleness, faithfulness and self-control. Against such things there is no law." (NIV) A believer who is walking in intimate fellowship with Jesus will have the benefit of these fruits overflowing from them. They will have joy in the midst of pain, peace during difficult times, patience in trials, and they will be able to extend love, kindness, and gentleness to those around them. They will exhibit goodness in the face of evil. They will be faithful and be able to control their passions and resist temptation. Those things don't come naturally. They come because of Jesus' work in our hearts. If we are not spending time with Him, He cannot accomplish that work in us. There is a direct correlation between the emphasis we give to our relationship with Jesus and the manifestation of those qualities in our lives. We are all a work in progress and there will never be a time, this side of Heaven, when all those fruits are found perfectly in us. My prayer is that I would be holding on to the vine so tightly that fruit would overflow from my branches.

May 26

I Samuel 26-28
Psalm 66:1-9
Proverbs 14:20-21
John 16

Respect

"Then Abishai said to David, 'Today God has handed your enemy over to you. Let me thrust the spear through him into the ground'... But David said to Abishai, 'Don't destroy him, for who can lift a hand against the Lord's anointed and be blameless?'"
I Samuel 26:8-9 HCSB

YESTERDAY'S READING AND today's reading in I Samuel both contain accounts of David sparing Saul's life. Saul was hunting him down to kill him. In the first account, David was hiding in the back of a cave when Saul went into the cave to use the bathroom. In the dark, David had the perfect opportunity to kill him. In the second account, Saul and his men were asleep and David and Abishai approached their camp. Abishai encouraged David to kill Saul, but David refused. He would have been justified. No one would have thought he was wrong. To be clear, David was not a pacifist. He had killed tens of thousands of people, so he was not afraid to take a life and he did not have a moral objection to killing. He made a conscious choice out of respect for Saul not to kill him. Even though God had removed His favor from Saul because of His disobedience, he was still king. God had anointed him king and he still held the office. David refused to kill God's anointed king. He respected Saul and even more importantly, He respected God. God had allowed him to serve as king. Romans 13:1 tells us, "Let everyone be subject to the governing authorities, for there is no authority except that which God has established. The authorities that exist have been established by God." (NIV)

I am writing this devotional entry on the Inauguration Day of Joe Biden. This is a very timely reminder for me. I did not vote for President Biden, and I am adamantly opposed to most of the policies he campaigned on. I believe those policies are not consistent with biblical principles and that God will not bless a nation that rejects Him. However, Joe Biden now holds the office of President of the United States. God has placed him in this position. The office of president deserves my respect and whoever holds the position deserves my respect. As Christians we have an obligation to vote for candidates that support our beliefs. We also have an obligation to pray for those in office. Because I trust in God's sovereignty, I can rest in the knowledge that God is still in control and His plans will not be thwarted. I do not know exactly how my respect will play out over the next four years. I will not support policies that are contrary to God's Word, and I will peacefully and respectfully oppose them. But I will pray for President Biden and his cabinet. My prayer is that they will turn to God and seek Him for wisdom as they lead our nation, and that as a nation we would come together, repent, and seek God. Please join me in that prayer.

I Samuel 29-31
Psalm 66:10-15
Proverbs 14:22-23
John 17

May 27

Justice and Fulfillment

> "So, on that day, Saul died together with his three sons, his armor bearer, and all his men." I Samuel 31:6 HCSB

WHILE SCRIPTURE DOES not tell us exactly how long David was in the wilderness running from Saul, scholars estimate that it was around five to seven years. I can't imagine spending that many years on the run, waiting for justice, and hoping God would make things right. The Psalms give us glimpses of the internal battle playing out in David's mind and heart. There were periods of fear and anxiety when he was convinced Saul was going to kill him. There were periods of overwhelming peace and confidence in God's protection. And then there were days when he was angry at Saul and at God for not rescuing him yet. As Americans, a sense of justice is deeply ingrained in us. We want the bad guy to be punished and the good guy to be rewarded. We want right to prevail and wrong to be defeated. As Christians, this is even more true as we recognize the spiritual battle taking place between good and evil. Thankfully, we know the end of the story. We know that one day all evil will be destroyed, justice will be done, and righteousness will prevail. Unfortunately, like in David's life, evil sometimes does prevail for a time and justice is delayed.

Scripture also does not tell us how long there was between the time when David was anointed by Samuel as the next king and when he took the throne, but it is estimated that it was around ten years. Over and over in scripture we find God making a promise to someone and then years pass before that promise is realized. Abraham waited twenty-five years from the time he was promised descendants as numerous as the stars till his son, Isaac, was born. The children of Israel wandered forty years in the desert from the time God promised to deliver them from Egypt and take them into the promised land.

There was 400 years between God's last word spoken to the prophets and the birth of Jesus, the Messiah. Waiting is not the exception in the life of the believer. Waiting is the norm. The important stuff happens during the wait. God uses that time to prepare us and equip us to receive the promise. And He uses that time to bring all the circumstances, events, and people into place to accomplish His plans. Often it seems to us like nothing is happening and we begin to wonder if we heard Him wrong or if He changed His mind. During those times it is so important to recognize that He is working on our behalf. He is not wasting time. He is doing everything that needs to be done so that at just the right time, He will do exactly what He said. David did become the king of Israel. Abraham had a son, and his descendants are as numerous as the stars in the sky. The children of Israel entered the promised land, and the long-awaited Messiah did come to save the world. God always keeps His promises.

2 Samuel 1-2
Psalm 66:16-20
Proverbs 14:24-25
John 18

Grieving for our Enemies

> "Then David took hold of his clothes and tore them, and all the men with him did the same. They mourned, wept, and fasted until the evening for those who died by the sword---for Saul, his son Jonathan, the Lord's people, and the house of Israel."
> 2 Samuel 1:11-12 HCSB

IN OUR READINGS for the last two days, we have seen David hiding in the desert, fearing for his life because Saul was trying to kill him. On two separate occasions, David had the opportunity to kill Saul, but he refused to lay a hand on the Lord's anointed. He trusted God to provide justice and did not take matters into his own hands. Yesterday Saul and his sons were killed in battle. In today's passages we see David's reaction to the deaths of Saul and Jonathan. Instead of rejoicing that his enemy had been destroyed, David tore his clothes, mourned, and wept. He wrote a beautiful lament and sang it for Saul and Jonathan. Jonathan was his dear friend so it is not surprising that David would mourn for him. But he also mourned for Saul. He praised Saul and said he was dearly loved. David was about to be king. God was fulfilling His promise to him. It would have been easy for David to gloat and be happy, but that was not his reaction. Grieving the death of your enemies is evidence of a heart that is unselfish, loving, and full of mercy. We can certainly understand why God said David was a man after His own heart. Verse 11 says that all the men with him mourned as well. These men had been in the wilderness with David for all those years, too. It would be natural for them to rejoice when Saul was killed so that they could return home. Their reaction speaks volumes about David's leadership. He could have stirred up their anger and hatred toward Saul, but apparently, he did not do that. They followed his lead and grieved for Saul and his sons, too.

Their reaction is an impressive example for us. Hopefully, we do not have anyone trying to kill us, but we each occasionally find ourselves in circumstances where we have been wronged. It is natural to want to see that person punished. We want retribution. We want them to pay for what they did to us or to someone we love. Instead of allowing God to handle that for us, sometimes we take matters into our own hands, and we get revenge. I think we know that is not pleasing to God, but David even went a step further. He waited patiently for several years, and he allowed God to bring about punishment for Saul in His time. He did everything right and then he reacted to the deaths with love, humility, and unselfishness. He was not concerned about his own rights and getting the satisfaction of being vindicated. David trusted God completely to take care of him and meet his needs which allowed him to be selfless and offer mercy and grace to others.

May 29

2 Samuel 3-4
Psalm 67:1-4
Proverbs 14:26-27
John 19

Tetelestai

> "When Jesus had received the sour wine, He said, 'It is finished.' Then bowing His head, He gave up His Spirit." John 19:30 HCSB

THE GREEK WORD "tetelestai" was the word used in this verse meaning, "It is finished." I did some research to understand what this word really means and found a very helpful article on crosswalk.com entitled "Tetelestai—It is Finished!" by Rick Renner.[6] The full meaning of this word and the implications of Jesus choosing this word to be His last word spoken is significant. The most obvious interpretation is that Jesus was saying that He had finished what His Father sent Him to do. His primary job was complete. He had accomplished His mission, so it was time to leave. The word was significant from a secular perspective as well. When a debt had been paid off, the paper on which the debt was recorded was stamped with the word, "tetelestai." When Jesus uttered this word on the cross, He was indicating that the penalty for the sins of the world had now been paid in full. When a person believes in Jesus and calls on His name, the debt of sin that they owe is removed and "tetelestai" is stamped on their heart. The debt is wiped out because Jesus paid the price for their sin.

The word also has religious significance. Once a year the high priest entered the Holy of Holies and poured blood from a spotless, sacrificial lamb on the altar. The moment the blood touched the altar, atonement was made for the people's sins for the next year. Each year they repeated that sacrifice. When Jesus hung on the cross, He offered Himself as the perfect, sacrificial lamb for the permanent removal of sin. At that moment, there was no longer a need for a yearly sacrifice. When He said, "It is finished," He was declaring the end of the sacrificial system because the perfect sacrifice had finally been made. Atonement was complete and fully accomplished once and for all. Finally, in Greek literature, the word "tetelestai" was used to depict a turning point when one period ended, and another period began. When Jesus said, "It is finished," it was a turning point in the history of the world. The Old Covenant came to an end and the New Covenant began. All the Old Testament prophecies about the Messiah had been fulfilled in Jesus. There was a new system in place by which believers could come to God. The people who heard Jesus utter those words on the cross and breathe His last probably did not understand the significance of His last words, but they no doubt figured out its meaning after His resurrection and ascension because these are foundational principles established in the early church that have had profound implications throughout church history.

May 30

2 Samuel 5-6
Psalm 67:5-7
Proverbs 14:28-30
John 20

Joyful Worship

"David was dancing with all his might before the Lord wearing a linen ephod. He and the whole house of Israel were bringing up the ark of the Lord with shouts and the sound of the ram's horn. As the ark of the Lord was entering the city of David, Saul's daughter, Michel looked down from the window and saw King David leaping and dancing before the Lord and she despised him in her heart." 2 Samuel 6:14-16 HCSB

GOD MADE A covenant with His people, the children of Israel when they were delivered from Egypt. He promised blessings to them if they obeyed His laws and He warned that they would have to face punishment and hardship if they disobeyed. The Ark of the Covenant was a sign of this covenant and represented the promise of the presence of God. It contained the stone tablets with the Ten Commandments giving the law. It contained Aaron's budded staff showing the line of priesthood through Aaron's family, the Levites. And it contained a jar of manna to remind them of the Lord's constant provision for them. The Ark was to be placed in the inner sanctum of the tabernacle in the desert and then in the Temple when it was built in Jerusalem. The lid of the Ark was called the mercy seat. Once a year the High Priest entered the Holy of Holies and poured the blood from a spotless lamb on the mercy seat. This provided atonement for their sins for the next year. Each year this sacrifice was repeated. It was the only place where this atonement could happen. The Ark is a foreshadowing of Jesus' death on the cross where He was the ultimate sacrifice for the atonement of sins once for all and now Jesus is the only place where we can go to receive forgiveness for our sins.

During Saul's reign the Ark had been stolen by the Philistines. After Saul's death there was fighting between Saul's family and David for control of the kingdom. There was division among the people, and they had become lax in their religious practices. By bringing the Ark of the Covenant back to Jerusalem, David was symbolically returning the presence of God to the temple, unifying the kingdom, and restoring religious worship. This was a wonderful day of rejoicing. There was a parade, and everyone came to celebrate. Everyone except Michel, the queen. Verse 14 tells us that David was dancing with all his might before the Lord wearing a linen ephod. It sounds like this means he was dancing around in his underwear, but that isn't exactly accurate. A linen ephod was two pieces of linen attached at the shoulders and brought together at the waist by a belt. It would not have been indecent or revealing in any way as Michel suggested. Michel was not concerned that he was dancing naked, she was concerned that he was not conducting himself in a manner worthy of a king. She was concerned with his reputation and standing and that he was not wearing his royal robes and kingly attire. When he saw the Ark, he set aside his royal robes and entered the presence of God not as a king, but as a humble servant. He was acknowledging before God and all the people present that God was the One who deserved praise and worship, not him. This was a beautiful act of humility. He was so excited to be in the presence of God that he danced with all his might. He couldn't contain his joy. I imagine this is what Heaven will be like.

There are different styles of worshiping the Lord. I do not think that one is necessarily better than the other. Some people worship through dance and exuberant movement, while others enter God's presence in a more reverent, quiet way. The condition of our heart is the significant factor. When we worship, it is important to come humbly into the presence of Almighty God. We abandon any concern about what other people will think or how we may be perceived. We set aside any ideas of our own importance and reputation. We focus all our attention on Jesus, the One who deserves all glory and honor and praise. I pray that, like David, I would come into the presence of the Lord with abandon and humility and worship Him with all my might.

2 Samuel 7-9
Psalm 68:1-6
Proverbs 14:31-32
John 21

Second Chances

"Therefore, the disciple, the one Jesus loved, said to Peter, 'It is the Lord.' When Simon Peter heard that it was the Lord, he tied his outer garment around him and plunged into the sea." John 21:7 HCSB

AFTER JESUS' DEATH, the disciples didn't know what to do. Their plans and dreams had been destroyed and they were devastated. Peter and several of the disciples did the only thing they knew. They returned to fishing. After an unsuccessful night out on their boat, they were coming back to shore when they saw a man standing on the beach. He told them to cast their net on the right side of the boat and they hauled in such a large catch they could barely get it into the boat. It is interesting to note that the first time they met Jesus was after a night of fishing without catching anything. They left everything and followed Him the first time and that was His plan for them this time as well. John recognized Jesus and told Peter it was the Lord. Impulsively, Peter plunged into the sea and ran to Jesus while the other disciples took the boat to shore.

This is the classic story of second chances. Jesus had prepared breakfast for them and when they finished Jesus approached Peter. Three times Jesus asked Peter if he loved Him and three times Peter said, "You know that I love You." Peter had denied Jesus three times on the night He died. Jesus gave him an opportunity to proclaim his love for Him three times. Jesus knew that Peter was racked with guilt. Peter needed to know he was forgiven and that there was a way forward. Thankfully, our God is the God of second chances. He is always willing to forgive us and welcome us back if we repent and turn to Him. As long as we are breathing, hope is not lost. If we turn to Him, He is always there and He can turn everything around in the blink of an eye.

When Peter told Jesus he loved Him, Jesus responded, "Feed My lambs," "Shepherd My sheep," and "Feed My sheep." Feeding sheep was not a glamorous job, it was messy business. Jesus was telling Peter that the best expression of love and gratitude to Him is through serving others. The way to reach a lost and dying world is not through religious rituals or man-made rules and regulations, but it is through sacrificial service and obedience.

2 Samuel 10-11
Psalm 68:7-14
Proverbs 14:33-35
Acts 1

June 1

Idleness

"In the spring when kings march out to war, David sent Joab with his officials and all Israel... One evening David got up from his bed and strolled around on the roof of the palace. From the roof he saw a woman bathing---a very beautiful woman. So, David sent someone to inquire about her, and he reported, 'This is Bathsheba, daughter of Eliam and wife of Uriah the Hittite.'" 2 Samuel 11:1-3 HSCB

IN THE SPRING when kings went out to war, David stayed home and sent Joab. David was a man after God's own heart. Over the last couple of weeks, we have looked at David's life and examined his heart. He was humble, faithful, and he loved God, yet today's reading is evidence that even the most faithful are capable of succumbing to temptation. For whatever reason, David decided that this spring he was not going to go out to war with his men and he found himself wandering around his castle with nothing to do. "Idle hands are the devil's workshop" is a phrase I have heard my whole life. While the phrase is not in the Bible, it is certainly a principle that can be traced back to biblical truth. 2 Thessalonians 3:11, 1 Timothy 5:13, and Proverbs 16:27 are just a few verses that talk about the dangers of idleness.

Idleness is not the same as rest. We are told in scripture that God gives rest to His children. Our bodies need periods of rest and relaxation. Idleness is laziness or doing nothing when you should be doing something. It is often a result of having no purpose or goals. God designed us to be productive. We were meant to work and contribute to society. If we have nothing to do, Satan stalks around eager to come up with things to occupy our time. When we have no purpose and responsibility, we are much more likely to be tempted to do something sinful. And that is exactly what happened to David. When he should have been out with his men, he was walking around on his roof, and he succumbed to temptation. This led him down paths he never would have dreamed he would take. Adultery, lying, cover-up and murder are things you expect to read in a mystery novel not in the Bible about someone God called, "a man after My own heart." This is a stark reminder to us that no one is immune to sin. We are all capable of giving in to temptation. 2020 was a difficult year because we were forced to stay home, not go to work, and spend long periods of time alone. Things are starting to open again, but this is a good reminder that even if we are stuck at home, we don't have to be idle. Don't allow Satan to creep in. Take up a new hobby, start a new workout routine, spend more time with God, make a meal for a sick friend, or call an elderly relative who is lonely. Ask God to show you how you can serve others. Don't spend hours watching TV or on social media. Serving others is good mentally, physically, emotionally, and spiritually for you, not to mention the benefit to those you help. Let us not allow ourselves to fall into the trap of idleness.

2 Samuel 12-13
Psalm 68:15-18
Proverbs 15:1-2
Acts 2:1-13

Repentance

"David responded to Nathan, 'I have sinned against the Lord.'" 2 Samuel 12:13 HCSB

YESTERDAY WE READ about David's sin with Bathsheba, his cover-up and murder of her husband. It would be easy to conclude that this was the end for David and that God could no longer use someone who did the things David did. Thankfully, our God never gives up on us, He never turns His back on us, and He always gives us another chance. No matter what we have done or how far we have fallen, He is always waiting with open arms to welcome us back. This passage provides several lessons for us regarding restoration after we have sinned. First, it is important to recognize that God does not let His children get away with sin. It seems that there are a lot of evil people out there who sin on a regular basis and don't get caught. They lie, cheat, steal and treat others horribly and get away with it. And then we see Christians who do the same things and they always seem to get caught. I don't think it is a coincidence and I don't think they just aren't as smart, so they get caught. I believe that God brings their sin to light. God loves us too much to let us sin and not experience consequences. He knows that sin is bad for us. His laws are intended to protect us and keep us safe, and they help us stay in right relationship with other people. If we violate those laws, some area of our life is going to suffer. In His mercy and love, God does what He must to reveal our sin so that we can repent and experience restoration. He won't let us get too far off the path before He brings us back.

There have been times in my children's lives when they have disobeyed us, and we punished them. On a few occasions they were with other children at the time who did the same thing, did not get caught, and got away with it. I remember having a conversation with Hannah about that one time. She was frustrated that she was being punished and they weren't. I explained to her that we are responsible for her and not for those other children. As her parents, we have an obligation to raise her in a way that pleases God and to help her become the person He wants her to be. I don't have that obligation to other people's children, and I don't have the right to punish them. God has that same parental relationship with us. He is responsible for us, and He does whatever is necessary to ensure that we become the person He has planned for us to be. As His children we submit to His Lordship in our lives and sometimes that involves correction and punishment. While He certainly has the right to punish anyone, He does not have the responsibility to nonbelievers that He has to His children. They have not submitted their lives to Him, so they do not have His loving protection.

David's reaction to Nathan's rebuke is also a powerful lesson for us. He did not become defensive and make excuses. He did not become indignant because he was the king so how dare anyone talk to him that way. He also did not deny his sin and keep lying to cover it up. Instead, he humbly admitted he had sinned and asked for forgiveness. Without repentance there cannot be a restoration in the relationship. Unconfessed sin is a barrier between us and God and complete fellowship cannot be restored until the sin is dealt with and removed. It is helpful to regularly ask God to reveal to us any sin that we need to deal with and when He makes us aware of it, it is best to immediately admit it, repent and ask for forgiveness. It is also important to recognize that even after we repent and our sin is forgiven, there may be consequences we have to face. A restoration of our relationship does not mean that we don't have to experience punishment. Sometimes God punishes us when we disobey Him, and sometimes He allows us to experience the natural consequences of our actions. Thankfully, He lovingly stays by our side as we deal with whatever happens and He gives us the strength and wisdom to face it. Like David, we are in the hands of a loving, Heavenly Father who is always working for our best interest.

2 Samuel 14-15
Psalm 68:19-27
Proverbs 15:3-4
Acts 2:14-46

June 3

Together

"And they devoted themselves to the apostle's teaching, to the fellowship, to the breaking of bread, and to prayer. Every day they devoted themselves to meeting together in the temple complex, and broke bread from house to house. They ate their food with a joyful and humble attitude, praising God and having favor with all the people. And every day the Lord added to their number those who were being saved." Acts 2:42, 46-47 HCSB

THIS IS A beautiful picture of unity in the Body of Christ. When we talk about the church, there are two different things we could be referring to. We may be talking about the building where we go to worship and fellowship with believers, or we may be talking about the "church" as the body of believers. It is not limited to the local congregation we are connected to, but rather the collective body of believers from around the world who are united in faith and belief in Jesus Christ as Lord. The beginning of the "church" as a body of believers is described in these verses. Before this time, there was no "church." There was a building, the temple, where the Jewish people gathered to worship God, offer sacrifices, and study the Law and the Prophets, but the people who met there were not referred to as the "church" or the "body of believers." After Pentecost, the believers began to meet together for times of worship and fellowship. Peter and the other disciples spread the news about Jesus explaining His death, burial and resurrection and thousands of people believed. On one day, 3,000 people were baptized and every day the Lord added to their number. Having so many people join them in a short amount of time must have been very difficult to manage. They did not have a huge building where they could meet, so they formed small groups. They began to meet in houses where they shared meals together, had Bible studies, prayed together, and had fellowship. That sounds exactly like small group meetings in churches around the world today. It is a wonderful model to emulate.

In large numbers, it is difficult to have accountability and meet individual needs. It is hard to get to know each other and develop relationships. But in small groups there is greater intimacy and the possibility of deeper, more meaningful interaction. Small groups are able to experience life together, face difficulties together, rejoice and mourn together. That is what happened in the early church and people noticed. They saw the unity and love they had for each other, and they wanted to be a part of it. They didn't have to knock on doors to get people to join them. People were knocking their doors down wanting to come in. That is a challenge for us today. Jesus said in John 13:35, "By this all people will know that you are My disciples, if you have love for one another." (NASB1995) When unbelievers look at the "church," what do they see? Do they see love and generosity, or division and disagreement? Do they see mercy and grace, or judgment and condemnation? They are watching how we treat each other. Do they want what we have?

2 Samuel 16-17
Psalm 68:28-35
Proverbs 15:5-7
Acts 3

Strength

"The God of Israel gives power and strength to His people. May God be praised!" Psalm 68:35 HCSB

THERE ARE OVER 350 references to God's strength and power found in Scripture. We are encouraged to "be strong in the Lord and in His mighty power." Ephesians 6:10 (NIV) Our strength is found in our relationship with Christ. He empowers us to do whatever is necessary to accomplish His will. He gives us strength to overcome temptation and to minister to others. Those who rely on God's strength day to day will find a never-ending supply of power and be able to stand under the trials and tribulations of this life. When we are feeling weak, it is helpful to remind ourselves of God's promises.

"I can do all things through Christ who gives me strength." Philippians 4:13 NIV

"He gives strength to the weary and strengthens the powerless. Youths may faint and grow weary, and young men stumble and fall, but those who trust in the Lord will renew their strength; they will soar on wings like eagles; they will run and not grow weary; they will walk and not faint." Isaiah 40:29-31 HCSB

"So do not fear, for I am with you; do not be dismayed, for I am your God. I will strengthen you and help you; I will uphold you with My righteous right hand." Isaiah 41:10 NIV

"The Lord gives strength to His people; the Lord blesses His people with peace." Psalm 29:11 NIV

"My flesh and my heart may fail, but God is the strength of my heart and my portion forever." Psalm 73:26 NIV

"I love You, Lord, my strength. The Lord is my rock, my fortress, and my deliverer; my God is my rock, in whom I take refuge, my shield, and the horn of my salvation, my stronghold." Psalm 18:1-2 NIV

"But He said to me, 'My grace is sufficient for you, for My power is made perfect in weakness.' Therefore, I will boast all the more gladly about my weaknesses, so that Christ's power may rest on me. That is why, for Christ's sake, I delight in weaknesses, in insults, in hardships, in persecutions, in difficulties. For when I am weak, then I am strong." 2 Corinthians 12:9-10 NIV

"God is our refuge and strength, an ever-present help in trouble." Psalm 46:1 NIV

"Surely God is my salvation; I will trust and not be afraid. The Lord, the Lord Himself, is my strength and my defense; He has become my salvation." Isaiah 12:2 NIV

"But the Lord is faithful, and He will strengthen and protect you from the evil one." 2 Thessalonians 3:3 NIV

"Ascribe power to God. His majesty is over Israel, His power among the clouds. God You are awe-inspiring in Your sanctuaries. The God of power gives power and strength to His people." Psalms 68:34-35 HCSB

June 5

2 Samuel 18-19
Psalm 69:1-4
Proverbs 15:8-9
Acts 4:1-22

The Jesus Factor

"When they observed the boldness of Peter and John and realized that they were uneducated and untrained men, they were amazed and recognized that they had been with Jesus...But Peter and John answered them, 'Whether it's right in the sight of God for us to listen to you rather than to God, you decide, for we are unable to stop speaking about what we have seen and heard.'" Acts 4:13, 19-20 HCSB

WHEN JESUS WAS arrested, Peter and John ran away in fear. Over the next few hours Peter denied three times that he even knew Jesus. After His death they went into hiding because they were scared. Just a short time later, these men are seen boldly telling people about Jesus in the temple complex. When confronted, they did not run away. They were arrested and brought before the rulers, elders, and scribes. Instead of shrinking in fear, Peter was filled with the Holy Spirit and unashamedly proclaimed the name of Jesus Christ, whom the Jews had crucified and whom God raised from the dead. These do not sound like the same men. When the leaders saw Peter's boldness and saw that these were uneducated and untrained men, they were amazed and recognized that they had been with Jesus. Wow! Their boldness made even their enemies admit that Jesus had made a difference in their lives.

Their relationship with Jesus and the indwelling power of the Holy Spirit changed these cowardly, scared men into bold, fearless disciples willing to put their lives on the line to tell people about Jesus. The religious leaders told them to stop preaching or teaching in the name of Jesus. Without hesitation, Peter and John told them that they had to do what God was telling them to do and they could not stop speaking about what they had seen and heard. Our relationship with Jesus and the power of the Holy Spirit living within us can give us the boldness and power to tell people about Jesus as well. Peter and John did not go to seminary. They were not trained in theology and probably couldn't win a debate over scripture with the religious leaders, but they had been with Jesus. When we spend time with Jesus, He equips us for every opportunity He gives us. We can rest in the knowledge that He will not ask us to do something that He does not prepare us to do and then He will give us the strength to carry it out. When we tell people about the things we have seen and heard, I pray they can recognize that we, too, have been with Jesus.

2 Samuel 20-21
Psalm 69:5-12
Proverbs 15:10-12
Acts 4:23-37

June 6

Generosity

"Now the large group of those who believed were of one heart and mind, and no one said that any of his possessions was his own, but instead they held everything in common...For there was not a needy person among them, because all those who owned lands or houses sold them, brought the proceeds of the things that were sold, and laid them at the apostle's feet. This was then distributed for each person's basic needs." Acts 4:32, 34-25 HCSB

THESE VERSES ARE very convicting. I'm not suggesting that we all need to sell everything we have and give it to the church, but rather that our attitude should be the same as these believers in the early church. They did not think that their possessions were their own. They believed that everything they owned belonged to God and so they were willing to give it all back to Him. God did not require them to give up all their possessions. They did it out of love and gratitude. Likewise, God does not require us to give up everything we own, but out of love and gratitude for all He has done for us, we should have a spirit of generosity. Under the law, the Jews were required to give a tenth of all they had to God. We are under a New Covenant, and we are not bound by the law. The New Testament does not specify a percentage of income Christians should give, but there are numerous verses about the importance and benefits of giving. Sometimes that means giving more than ten percent and sometimes it may mean less. It depends on the needs in the body of Christ and the ability of the believer. We should all diligently pray and ask God for wisdom about how much we need to give on a regular basis and ask Him to show us specific needs that He would like for us to meet.

"Each of you should give what you have decided in your heart to give, not reluctantly or under compulsion, for God loves a cheerful giver." 2 Corinthians 9:7 (NIV) Giving is an act of worship from a grateful heart. When we are in close fellowship with God daily, He can make us aware of the needs of others and lay it on our heart to give to meet those needs. We should also give generously to our local church to help finance its ministries. Giving is an expression of our faith. When we trust God, we can give generously with confidence that God will take care of all our needs. We should be wise and prudent in managing our money, but we don't have to fear that our Heavenly Father will leave our needs unmet. "Do not store up for yourselves treasures on Earth, where moths and rust destroy, and where thieves break in and steal. But store up for yourselves treasures in Heaven, where moths and rust do not destroy, and where thieves do not break in and steal. For where your treasure is, there your heart will be also." Matthew 6:19-21 (NIV) If we value the things of God more than we value our earthly possessions, God will take care of us. "Give and it will be given to you. Good measure, pressed down, shaken together, running over, will be poured into your lap. For with the measure you use, it will be measured to you." Luke 6:38 (NIV)

June 7

2 Samuel 22-24
Psalm 69:13-18
Proverbs 15:13-14
Acts 5:1-16

Rescue

"He reached down from Heaven and took hold of me, He pulled me out of deep waters. He rescued me from my powerful enemy and from those who hated me, for they were too strong for me. They confronted me in the day of my distress, but the Lord was my support. He brought me out to a spacious place. He rescued me because He delighted in me." 2 Samuel 22:17-20 HCSB

I LOVE THIS verse. It is so comforting to me. We do not have a God who sits up in Heaven on His throne uninvolved and disinterested in what is going on here on Earth. He is not a God who created us and then left us to take care of ourselves. He is intimately involved in every aspect of our lives. He reaches down from Heaven and takes hold of us. When David wrote this song, he was probably remembering the years he had spent hiding in the wilderness in caves running from his enemy, Saul. When God rescued him, he no longer had to look over his shoulder unsure of who he could trust, but He could go out into the open to spacious places without fear of being killed. God rescued David and set him free. He promises to do the same thing for us. He wants to bring us out into wide open spaces free from anything that holds us captive. This can take many forms: fear, worry, addiction, shame, unhealthy relationships, pride, destructive habits, etc. There are many things that bind us and keep us from living the life God intended for us. He wants us to experience the peace and joy of freedom. "Satan comes to steal, kill and destroy. I have come so that they may have life and have it in abundance." John 10:10 (HCSB) "If the Son sets you free, you will be free indeed." John 8:36 (NIV)

In other religions, their gods are far away. They are aloof and disinterested. Their followers spend all their time trying to please their god to earn his favor. If they are lucky and do enough good stuff, the god might let them into Heaven when they die, and there are often certain rituals and sacrificial acts that will help them gain access. It is very sad that they are so deceived because those gods are not real, and their efforts are in vain. Our God, the One True God, loves us so much that He left Heaven, came to Earth, and died to provide a way for us to go to Heaven with Him. And when He went back to Heaven, He left the Holy Spirit to dwell in us so that He could be with us always. He never leaves our side. He is available to help us in any situation we face. We are never alone. The trials and temptations of this life can be overwhelming and frightening, but our God reaches down from Heaven, takes hold of us, and pulls us out of deep waters.

I Kings 1-2
Psalm 69:19-28
Proverbs 15:15-17
Acts 5:17-42

June 8

Persuaded

"A Pharisee named Gamaliel, a teacher of the law who was respected by all the people, stood up in the Sanhedrin and ordered the men to be taken outside for a little while... And now I tell you, stay away from these men and leave them alone. For if this plan or this work is of men, it will be overthrown, but if it is of God, you will not be able to overthrow them. You may even be found fighting against God. So, they were persuaded." Acts 5:34, 38-39 HCSB

GAMALIEL WAS A very wise man. Throughout history there have been numerous religions and cults that have come and gone. A charismatic leader convinces a group of people to follow him, but once the leader dies, the followers fall away. If Jesus had been just another charismatic man or great teacher, Christianity would not have survived for centuries. After the crucifixion, the disciples were scared and confused. They ran away and they were hiding in fear that they would be killed for following Jesus. And yet these men who were afraid to even admit they knew Jesus were responsible for the formation of the early church. Because of them, millions of people throughout the ages have heard about Jesus and have believed that He is God's Son, the Messiah and have accepted Him as their personal Savior. In fact, each of us owe our salvation to their willingness to tell others about Jesus. Historical documents reveal that eight of the eleven disciples died as martyrs because they boldly preached the gospel and shared the good news about Jesus. John died on the Isle of Patmos after being exiled there for unashamedly proclaiming his faith. Two of them were crucified, one was stoned, and one was lanced. The method of death for the others is not given, only that they died as martyrs.

So, what happened after the night of Jesus' crucifixion that changed these frightened, cowardly men into bold, courageous apostles who were willing to put their lives on the line to proclaim that Jesus is the Messiah? Obviously, it was the resurrection of Jesus from the dead. Throughout history people have suggested that the resurrection did not happen. Some claim that the disciples stole His body and then made up a lie about His resurrection. There were numerous eyewitness accounts of people who saw Jesus after His resurrection that refute this theory. But I think even more compelling than the eyewitnesses, is the fact that these men, and many others, were completely changed. They were convinced beyond a shadow of a doubt that Jesus was who He said He was, and they risked everything to tell everyone they could about Him. If they had stolen the body and made up this elaborate hoax, they would not have spent the rest of their lives telling people about Jesus and then been willing to die to maintain the lie. The only explanation for their changed lives is that they saw for themselves that Jesus had risen Himself from the dead and they knew He was the Son of God, the Messiah, and their Savior. As Gamaliel told the Sanhedrin that day, if their work had been of men, it would have been overthrown. But the fact that Christianity is still in existence today is proof that it was indeed from God.

I Kings 3-4
Psalm 69:29-36
Proverbs 15:18-19
Acts 6

June 9

Be Careful What You Ask For!

"At Gibeon the Lord appeared to Solomon in a dream at night. God said, 'Ask. What should I give you?' Solomon replied, 'Lord my God, You have made Your servant king in my father David's place. Yet I am just a youth with no experience in leadership. So, give Your servant an obedient heart to judge Your people and to discern between good and evil. For who is able to judge this great people of Yours?'" I Kings 3:5, 7, 9 HCSB

When Brian and I had children, one of the issues we had to address was how we would deal with Santa Claus at our house. There are lots of opinions about this and I'm not going to get into all of those, but what we decided is that we would have Santa at our house, but that we did not want to put a huge emphasis on him. How we chose to deal with that is that the girls were allowed to ask Santa for one gift. It could be a nice gift, something they really wanted, but they could only ask him for one thing. Each year they had to really think about it and figure out what they wanted the most and then we would discuss it and decide if that was an appropriate thing for them to ask for. Sometimes we would steer them in a different direction, but usually the thing they wanted was ok. They knew they had to be careful what they asked for because they only got to ask for one thing. We gave them other presents, too, but Santa only brought one thing, so they wanted it to be something they really wanted.

I'm not suggesting God is like Santa in any way, so please don't misunderstand me, but this interaction between God and Solomon made me think of the girls' deliberations over Christmas presents. God asked Solomon what he wanted. He didn't put any conditions on it at all. He just said, "Ask. What should I give you?" Solomon could have asked for anything: riches, power, health, a big family, anything he wanted was his for the asking. But he was very careful what he asked for. His response suggests that he already had a measure of wisdom. Most young men raised in a palace as a prince would not have the humility that Solomon exhibits here. He recognizes that he is young and does not have leadership skills. He acknowledges that he needs help to lead God's chosen people. Instead of asking for something that would benefit him, he asked for something that would benefit others. It was an unselfish request that pleased God very much. As a result, God not only gave him wisdom, but He also gave him all the other stuff, too. He blessed Solomon with riches, power, long life, and honor. Like Solomon, we should be careful what we ask for. Thankfully, unlike Santa, God knows what is truly best for us and He loves us too much to give us anything that is not in our best interests. We do not always get what we ask for. Like a loving Father, He gives us what we need, but the more time we spend with Him and in His Word, the more closely our requests are aligned with His plans for us and the more likely we are to ask for things that please Him.

I Kings 5-7
Psalm 70
Proverbs 15:20-21
Acts 6:14-7:50

June 10

A History Lesson

"For we heard him say that Jesus, this Nazarene, will destroy this place and change the customs that Moses handed down to us. And all who were sitting in the Sanhedrin looked intently at him and saw that his face was like the face of an angel." Acts 6:14-15 HCSB

Stephen's speech changed everything. From this point forward, Christians were persecuted and martyred. They had to hide, and they risked their lives if they shared their faith. Stephen began his speech with a very succinct history of the Jewish people in fifty verses. The men in the Sanhedrin were very familiar with the history of their people and did not need to be taught anything about it. I think the reason he included this history lesson was to remind them of the rebellion of their people and their rejection of those God sent in the past to save them. He wanted them to see that just as they had turned from God before and as they had rejected Moses, now they were rejecting the Messiah, Jesus, the One God sent to save them. Time and time again they followed the same pattern: rejection of God, punishment, repentance, returning to God, falling away, rejection, punishment, etc. It was a vicious cycle that they continued to repeat. He was also trying to show them that religion as they knew it had been changed completely by the coming of Jesus. He was not preaching against the temple, rather, He was telling them that there was no longer a need for the temple. The priests and the sacrificial system pointed to the Messiah and the sacrifice that He would make. After He came there was no longer a need to continue to make animal sacrifices. He became the perfect sacrifice once for all to give us each individual access to God. We no longer have to go through a priest to gain access to God. We can each boldly go before the throne of grace personally. The religious leaders in the Sanhedrin did not want to hear this because they enjoyed the power they had over the people through the religious rules and regulations they had put in place. Instead of learning from their history and following God closely, they chose to cling to tradition and reject the Messiah.

The last year has brought a lot of changes to our world, but the most disturbing to me has been the push to erase history. I have always loved history. I love learning about our past and visiting historical sites, battlegrounds, and memorials. It is very troubling to see the push to remove the monuments and rewrite our history books to exclude the parts that are offensive. In 1905, George Santayana said, "Those who cannot remember the past are condemned to repeat it."[7] Slavery is an ugly part of our history. I agree that we do not want to celebrate it. But we also cannot deny that it ever happened. If we do not teach our children about this terrible part of our history and let them see the evil and the process by which it was abolished, they will not understand the importance of insuring that it never happens again. Satan really doesn't have any new tricks. He just keeps recycling the same ones over and over. Unfortunately, now we are seeing slavery in the form of sex trafficking. Instead of devaluing people based on their race, young girls and boys are being sold for sexual gratification. Their worth and dignity as individuals created by God and designed for a purpose has been lost in the lust for instant gratification, power, and greed. It is the same evil, just in a different form. Our history books need to teach our children the truth; the good, the bad and the ugly, so that they do not repeat it. But even more importantly, we need to teach our children to know God and follow Him closely. The closer they get to Jesus, the less likely they are to accept the lies of Satan and they will treat all people with the dignity and respect they deserve.

I Kings 8
Psalm 71:1-8
Proverbs 15:22-23
Acts 7:51-60

June 11

Persecuted

"But Stephen, filled by the Holy Spirit, gazed into Heaven. He saw God's glory, with Jesus standing at the right hand of God, and he said, 'Look! I see the heavens opened and the Son of Man standing at the right hand of God.'" Acts 7:55-56 HCSB

STEPHEN DIDN'T EVEN get to finish his speech. He began with a history lesson, but he didn't even get to the part where he told them all about Jesus' life, death, and resurrection before they became so angry at him that they stoned him to death. As I mentioned yesterday, his speech changed the course of Christianity. It began a period of terrible persecution in which Christians were forced to flee the country in all different directions and ultimately resulted in the spread of Christianity throughout the world. Throughout history, the periods of greatest growth in the church have not happened when Christianity is accepted and easy. The power of Jesus in the life of a Christian is most evident in the face of difficulty and suffering. Pain and difficulty are inevitable, and the difference Jesus makes in the life of a believer is a powerful testimony that draws others in a way that nothing else can. I had a conversation with a dear friend this morning who has had an extremely difficult year. She is a nurse and has spent the last year working at our local hospital during the pandemic. The long hours and emotional rollercoaster have taken a toll on her, and in addition to that her Daddy was diagnosed with lung cancer and she has spent the last few months juggling her job, caring for her Daddy, and welcoming a new grandbaby into the world. It has been overwhelming, but at the same time she told me that she would not trade the sweetness of the intimacy she has experienced with Jesus in these difficult days for anything. The difference Jesus has made in her life in this season is evident and her testimony is powerful.

For many years in this country, Christians have had the benefit of a culture that has been greatly influenced by Judeo-Christian values. There has been an acceptance of those values in the culture as a whole and individual Christians were generally respected and looked up to. That is changing quickly. The perception of Christians has gone from "good people" that we want to emulate to people who are intolerant, judgmental hypocrites in a frighteningly short period of time. I fear that the time of persecution is at hand for us, but I am encouraged that perhaps, if Jesus does not return to take us home before, it will result in tremendous growth and revival in the Body of Christ. The church is currently growing the fastest in Iran and China, while in the United States and Europe it is declining. There will come a time when we will be forced to decide what we truly believe. If we believe that He is who He says He is, then He will make a difference in our lives and those around us will be drawn to Him.

I Kings 9-10
Psalm 71:9-16
Proverbs 15:24-26
Acts 8

June 12

My Advocate

"For my enemies talk about me, and those who spy on me plot together, saying, 'God has abandoned him; chase him and catch him, for there is no one to rescue him.' God do not be far from me; My God, hurry to help me. May my adversaries be disgraced and destroyed; may those who seek my harm be covered with disgrace and humiliation. But I will hope continually and will praise You more and more. My mouth will tell of Your righteousness and Your salvation all day long. I come because of the mighty acts of the Lord God; I will proclaim Your righteousness, Yours alone." Psalm 71:10-16 HCSB

YESTERDAY'S PASSAGE ABOUT the stoning of Stephen reminds me of these verses in Psalm. "He saw God's glory, with Jesus standing at the right hand of God." This is the only place in Scripture where we find Jesus "standing at the right hand of God." In every other passage, He is described as "sitting at the right hand of God." We aren't told why Jesus is standing, but it brings to mind I John 2:1 that says Jesus is our advocate with the Father. When a defense attorney goes before a judge on behalf of his client, he stands up to make his case. He listens to the prosecuting attorney make the case against him and then he stands before the judge and lays out his defense of his client. I may be reaching, but I am envisioning Jesus watching the scene play out below. The Sanhedrin has made its case against Stephen, claiming he has committed blasphemy. Knowing Stephen is about to be stoned to death, Jesus stands before His Father, the ultimate judge and defends Stephen making the case on Stephen's behalf. It is important to note that Jesus is not defending Stephen because he is perfect and worthy of getting into Heaven on his own merit. We see here a man who was filled with grace and power, but he was human and sinful, just as we are. Jesus is defending him because Stephen has believed that Jesus is God's Son and has accepted Him as his Savior.

Scholars differ on the authorship of Psalm 71. Many believe that David wrote this Psalm in his old age when his son, Absalom was rebelling and seeking to steal the throne. Whoever wrote the Psalm was experiencing the pain of being falsely accused and betrayed and was begging God to come to his aid. He needed an advocate to stand up for him against his enemies and defend his cause. In humility, he acknowledges that God alone is righteous. He isn't seeking help based on his own merit, but rather he is seeking grace and mercy from God. Like the Psalmist and Stephen, we can be assured that Jesus is our Advocate before God as well if we have accepted Him. We have a defense attorney who stands before His Father on our behalf. It gives me great peace and reassurance to know that Jesus Himself will take up my cause and defend me. I don't have to defend myself or take matters into my own hands. I can entrust Him to be my advocate and bring about the right result.

June 13

I Kings 11-12
Psalm 71:17-34
Proverbs 15:27-28
Acts 9

AFTER

"But Saul grew more capable and kept confounding the Jews who lived in Damascus by proving that this One is the Messiah. Then Peter sent them all out of the room. He knelt down, prayed, and turning toward the body said, 'Tabitha, get up!' She opened her eyes, saw Peter, and sat up. This became known throughout Joppa, and many believed in the Lord." Acts 9:22, 40, 42 HCSB

IN THE ACCOUNT of the stoning of Stephen, we find this sentence, "And the witnesses laid their robes at the feet of a young man named Saul." Acts 7:58 (HCSB) This scene must have haunted Saul, who later became Paul, for the rest of his life. He stood by, giving approval, as they stoned Stephen. No one else who was there that day is mentioned, but I think this sentence is included for the same reason that the passage about Peter denying Jesus is included. In His infinite mercy, God wants us to know that no matter what we do, no matter how bad our sin, we can always come back, and He welcomes us with open arms. Not only does He accept us back when we mess up, He can still use us. God used Peter to start the early church AFTER he denied Jesus three times and He used Paul to spread the gospel to the Gentile world and to write a large part of the New Testament AFTER he persecuted Christians. Acts 9 gives us evidence of His work in the lives of both men. The chapter opens with Paul's encounter with Jesus on the road to Damascus followed by his complete transformation. It outlines his journey from persecutor to disciple and reveals a man who had a personal encounter with Jesus and then was used by God in a powerful way. The latter part of chapter 9 looks at Peter's ministry. While going from town to town telling people about Jesus, we also see that Peter was able to heal the sick and he raised a dead girl to life. AFTER his failure, we see a man who was transformed by Jesus and then was used by God in powerful ways.

If the Bible was filled with stories about all the people who were holy and followed God perfectly all their lives, it would be a work of fiction. Instead, it is filled with stories about real people who messed up a lot. There are stories of men who committed adultery, murdered, lied, stole, were jealous, prideful, deceitful, and unfaithful. It is filled with stories of people just like us. Not only does it tell us about their sin, but it also reveals what happened AFTER they messed up. If they repented and turned to God, He forgave them. They faced the consequences of their actions, but then He restored them and continued to use them. He wasn't done with them. We also see examples of men who did not repent and experienced God's wrath instead of His mercy. His work in our lives is not based at all on our virtue or ability, but on His mercy and grace and on our willingness to submit to Him.

I Kings 13-14
Psalm 72:1-7
Proverbs 15:29-30
Acts 10

June 14

Lord of All

> "Then Peter began to speak, 'Now I really understand that God doesn't show favoritism, but in every nation the person who fears Him and does righteousness is acceptable to Him. He sent the message to the Israelites, proclaiming the good news of peace through Jesus Christ---He is Lord of all." Acts 10:34-36 HCSB

SATAN IS THE father of lies. He excels at twisting the truth just a little bit so that it sounds true, but it is a complete lie. One of the lies that I hear a lot that is extremely deceiving is that Christianity is exclusive. They believe that since the Bible tells us that there is only one way to get to God, that it is excluding people. While that sounds like it may be true, it is not true at all. Jesus tells us in John 14:6 that He is "the way, the truth and the life and no one comes to the Father, but by Him." (NIV) It is true that there is only one way to get to God. There are not lots of paths. All religions do not ultimately lead to God. Any religion that does not claim that Jesus is God's Son, the Messiah, who came to Earth as a baby, lived a perfect life, gave His life as a sacrifice for our sins, was resurrected and now sits at the right hand of God is a false religion created by Satan to deceive. However, this verse in Acts 10, proves that Christianity is not exclusive. It is available to everyone, Jew, and Gentile, male and female, every race, every ethnicity. It is available to people from every country, every tribe and nation. The good news of peace through Jesus Christ is available to anyone who believes. He is Lord of all. The invitation is open to anyone. Not only is the invitation open to anyone, 2 Peter 3:9 tells us "He is patient with you, not wanting anyone to perish, but everyone to come to repentance." (HCSB) Jesus wants everyone to come to Him. He is patient and loving and merciful. He loves us and pursues us because He wants each of us to accept Him.

Our world is filled with lots of exclusive organizations, places, and groups. There are groups only available to men, or women, organizations that are only open to people of a certain race, places that are only open to people who meet their criteria and events that will not admit you if you don't belong to a certain group of people. But Christianity is not like that. Anyone is welcome to come to Jesus. Unfortunately, there are some churches who do not exhibit this welcoming spirit and therefore do not reflect the message of Christ well, but that does not change the fact that Jesus does not turn any away who earnestly seek Him. The ground is level at the foot of the cross. No matter our gender, race, ethnic background, socioeconomic status, or any other criteria by which humans tend to divide themselves, Jesus' invitation is the same to all of us. We can choose to reject His invitation, but that does not make it exclusive. Merriam Webster's definition of exclusive is "excluding or not admitting other things, restricted or limited to the person, group or area concerned."[8] We must refute Satan's lie with the truth that Jesus is Lord of all.

I Kings 15-16
Psalm 72:8-11
Proverbs 15:31-33
Acts 11

June 15

Cool, Calm and Collected

> "Peter began to explain to them in an orderly sequence... When they heard this, they became silent. Then they glorified God, saying, 'So God has granted repentance resulting in life even to the Gentiles.'" Acts 11:4, 18 HCSB

PETER GIVES US an excellent example here of how to deal with conflict within the Body of Christ. This could have easily been one of those things that caused a church to split. Peter was changing how they did things. This was radical. It wasn't just changing the color of the women's restroom. Up until this time, the only people who could receive God's forgiveness and follow Jesus were the Jews. If someone who was not a Jew wanted to accept Christ, they had to follow the rules and be circumcised just like the Jews. There were rules that had to be followed and if they weren't followed exactly, salvation was not available to them. When the Jews in Jerusalem heard that Peter was baptizing Gentiles who had not been circumcised, they were furious. They thought that he was in biblical error. These were not the Pharisees and the Sadducees; these were Christian Jews who were responsible for starting the early church. They knew that they had to get it right. They had to follow God's plan for redemption. They had a great responsibility. Emotions were probably high. Opinions were set and it was Peter's responsibility to explain to them why he did what he did and to help them understand what God had revealed to him. He did not become defensive. He did not get cocky and tell them he was in charge, and they had to do what he said. Instead, he calmly explained to them in an orderly sequence what God had revealed to him in a vision and what it meant. Their reaction was equally appropriate. Instead of insisting on doing things the way they were used to, they listened to reason, and they were overjoyed that God had granted repentance to the Gentiles. This is how it should be done.

There are definite issues of major importance that churches must deal with. That is true today, just like it was true then. Thankfully, today we have God's Word to guide us. They did not have the benefit of the New Testament to guide their steps and had to rely on the leading of the Holy Spirit. When approaching matters of conflict, it is essential that we rely completely on biblical truth. Many areas of debate are dealt with directly in scripture. If the Bible addresses them, there should be no conflict. We cannot dismiss the truths found in scripture for personal preference or cultural norms. However, there are many issues that are not directly addressed in Scripture. In those instances, we cannot be dogmatic. There is room for variation in practice. Unfortunately, too often we find churches getting into huge conflict and splitting over matters that do not matter. People put personal preference and "how we've always done things" above biblical truth. They get caught up in making sure they get their way and forget to ask God what lines up with His plan. Situations of conflict must be approached calmly and in an orderly way with much prayer and humility.

I Kings 17-18
Psalm 72:12-16
Proverbs 16:1-3
Acts 12

June 16

Confidence

"So, she proceeded to do according to the word of Elijah. Then the woman, Elijah and her household ate for many days. The flour jar did not become empty, and the oil jug did not run dry, according to the word of the Lord He had spoken through Elijah." I Kings 17:15-16 HCSB

"At the time for offering the evening sacrifice, Elijah the prophet approached the altar and said, 'Yahweh, God of Abraham, Isaac, and Israel, today let it be known that You are God in Israel, and I am Your servant and that at Your Word I have done these things." I Kings 18:36 HCSB

ONE OF THE things that attracted me to Brian when we first met was his wit and that he is a bit of a smart aleck. I guess that is what I like about Elijah. I can just picture this event taking place on Mt. Carmel and it always makes me laugh. The reason that Elijah could be so calm and taunt the prophets of Baal was because he had complete confidence that God was the One and Only God and Baal could not do anything to him because he was not real. He knew that no matter how hard or loud they yelled and chanted, Baal could not hear them and answer because he did not exist. He also knew that God, his God, was real and He would answer. Elijah was able to stand alone against all the prophets of Baal because he had complete faith in God.

Elijah's interaction with the widow at Zarephath also shows his complete faith in God. It is one thing to put your faith completely in God to provide for you, but it is another level of faith to be so confident in God that you put a widow and her son's wellbeing on the line by asking them to provide food for you. He told the widow to make bread for him first and then she would have enough to make bread for her and her son as well. Taking the last bit of flour and oil that they had for himself revealed a confidence that God would continue to provide for them. Surprisingly, the widow did as he said and then the flour and oil jars never ran dry until the rain returned to the land.

Confidence in God in the face of insurmountable circumstances marked Elijah's life. We too can have that type of confidence. We can be assured that God is the One and Only God. We can place our trust in Him because He will never let us down. He will provide for His children. He will answer us when we call, and He will help us stand firm in the face of difficulty. We need not shrink back in fear. Taunting and responding with a smart aleck attitude might not be the best idea, but we can definitely respond with confidence and faith with no fear that our God can't or won't come through for us.

I Kings 19-20
Psalm 72:17-20
Proverbs 16:4-5
Acts 13

June 17

Confident

"Then Elijah became afraid and immediately ran for his life…he went on a day's journey into the wilderness. He sat down under a broom tree and prayed that he might die. 'I have had enough! Lord take my life, for I'm no better than my fathers.' At that moment the Lord passed by. A great and mighty wind was tearing at the mountains and was shattering cliffs before the Lord, but the Lord was not in the wind. After the wind there was an earthquake, but the Lord was not in the earthquake. After the earthquake there was a fire, but the Lord was not in the fire. And after the fire there was a voice, a soft whisper." I Kings 19:3-4, 11-12 HCSB

YESTERDAY, WE TALKED about Elijah's faith and confidence in the Lord. He stood up to the prophets of Baal. He taunted them and boldly called down fire from Heaven. Today we get a glimpse of Elijah that reveals he is just like us. There are moments in our lives when we are confident and bold, full of faith and ready to take on the enemy. Then something happens and we shrink back in fear and wonder if God will come through for us this time. A few years ago, Brian and I went to Israel, and we visited Mt. Carmel and the church that is built on the site where Elijah is believed to have had the encounter with the prophets of Baal. On top of the mountain, you can see for miles. Those mountaintop experiences are amazing, but they don't last. There are times in all our lives when we have huge spiritual victories, or when we feel the Lord's presence in a mighty way, when He answers a specific prayer we have been praying for a long time, or when we have a major spiritual breakthrough. Those are significant times, and their importance can't be minimized, but they are not the norm. Most of our days are spent further down the mountain. Some days we find ourselves in the valley, but most days we are just grazing on the plains. I think the secret to maintaining our confidence and remaining faithful when we are not on top of the mountain is found in this passage.

If we look at this passage, we find two things that are helpful. Elijah was at a low point. He was so scared that he asked God to take his life. He was not afraid of the prophets of Baal, but he was really scared of Jezebel, the queen. In verses 10 and 14, Elijah tells God, "I alone am left!" He feels all alone. His perception was not accurate: He was not really the only one left! In verse 18, God tells him that there are 7,000 in Israel who have not bowed to Baal and have remained faithful. Elijah just needed to be reminded that he was not alone. In difficult times, I think we tend to pull away and isolate ourselves. We say that we need "time alone to process." I'm not sure this is a good thing. The difficult times are when we need our fellow Christians the most. We need our people. We need them to pray with us and for us, to hold us accountable and to hold us up when we think we are going to fall. We are not intended to do this life alone. We are meant to be in community. Make sure you are a part of a community of believers. I don't just mean being in a church, although you do need to be in a church. I mean that you need to be in a group of people that you can be real with. That can come in lots of forms: a small group, a Bible study, a prayer group, an accountability group. You need people. If you don't have that, find it. Now! I'm serious. Do whatever you have to do to find a group of people to do life with. You need to know you aren't alone. You need them and they need you.

The other helpful thing in this passage is found in verses 12 and 13. It is important to recognize that God doesn't usually shout at us in an earthquake or fire. He usually speaks to us in a soft whisper. That means that we must listen carefully and pay attention, or we will miss it. Elijah was listening for God's voice. As soon as he heard the soft whisper, he got up and stood at the entrance to the cave to hear what God had to say to him. We are so busy and so easily distracted that we often don't slow down long enough to hear the soft whisper. We need to be in communication with God on a regular basis so that we recognize the sound of His voice. If we only call on Him when we are in trouble, it will be hard to distinguish His voice from all the other voices yelling in our ear. But if we are in the practice of meeting with Him every day, when trouble comes, our first instinct will be to go to Him, and we will know Him so well that we will not have difficulty discerning what He is telling us. And often, during our time with Him leading up to that crisis, He will be preparing us and giving us wisdom so that when it comes, we already know how we should react. Daily communication with God and staying connected with other believers are the secrets to remaining faithful and maintaining our confidence in God in all circumstances.

I Kings 21-22
Psalm 73:1-3
Proverbs 16:6-7
Acts 14

June 18

Atonement

> "By steadfast love and faithfulness iniquity is atoned for, and by the fear of the Lord one turns away from evil." Proverbs 16:6 ESV

God, in His infinite mercy and love has provided atonement for our iniquity, our sin. In this verse in Proverbs, years before Jesus' death on the cross, Solomon foretells of God's plan of atonement. The righteousness of God makes atonement for sin necessary, but His steadfast love and faithfulness prompted Him to provide the way of salvation for us. This passage has been misunderstood by many to mean that by showing love and mercy to others, we can somehow make atonement for our own sin. That is not what this verse means. We cannot do anything to atone for our sin. We are sinful creatures and our best attempts at righteousness fail. Isaiah 64:6 tells us, "All our righteous acts are like filthy rags; we all shrivel up like a leaf, and like the wind our sins sweep us away." (NIV) "All of us like sheep have gone astray, each of us has turned to his own way; But the Lord has caused the iniquity of us all to fall on Him." Isaiah 53:6 (NASB1995) "And He Himself bore our sins in His body on the cross, so that we might die to sin and live to righteousness; for by His wounds, you were healed." I Peter 2:24 (NASB1995) When we were unable to help ourselves, at the moment of our need, Christ died for us, although we were living against God. "Very rarely will anyone die for a righteous person, though for a good person someone might possibly dare to die. But God demonstrates His own love for us in this: While we were still sinners, Christ died for us." Romans 5:7-8 (NIV)

It is in recognizing our own sin and our need for atonement that we can come before a righteous, holy, merciful, and loving God. And the recognition of our condition should prompt in us a fear and reverence for the One who would be justified to leave us in our pitiful state but chose to sacrifice Himself instead to provide for our salvation. This respect and fear should compel us to turn away from evil. While we cannot be perfect, we should flee from sin whenever we are tempted and seek to please Him in all that we do. Appreciation for all He has done for us and recognition of His power and might should be incentive enough to cause us to stay away from sinful situations, and to spur us to confession and repentance whenever we stray.

June 19

2 Kings 1-2
Psalm 73:4-12
Proverbs 16:8-9
Acts 15

Passing on the Baton

"Elijah left there and found Elisha of Shaphat as he was plowing...Elijah walked by him and threw his mantle over him... Then he left, followed Elijah and served him." I Kings 19:19, 21 HCSB

"As they continued walking and talking, a chariot of fire with horses of fire suddenly appeared and separated the two of them. Then Elijah went up into Heaven in a whirlwind... Then he never saw Elijah again... Elisha picked up the mantle that had fallen off Elijah and went back and stood on the banks of the Jordan." 2 Kings 2:11-13 HCSB

Perhaps our greatest privilege and responsibility as believers is passing on our faith to the next generation. Since Jesus' death, burial and resurrection, each generation of believers has shared their faith with their children and grandchildren teaching and training them to then carry it on to the next generation. If any generation had failed to carry out their responsibility, it would not have been available to us. Their faithfulness has paved the way for our faith. And now it is our responsibility to pass on that faith to the next generation as well. I fear that our generation is not doing a very good job of passing the baton. While there are certainly faithful followers who are leading their children to faith, I see many who prefer to follow the crowd and submit to popular cultural norms instead of following biblical truth. Unfortunately, in doing this, they are teaching their children that biblical truth is relative and subjective. We can be assured that there will be a remnant of faithful believers until Jesus returns. We know that there will always be Christians. Christianity is not going to fade away as many false religions throughout history have done. But we do not want to be the generation that dropped the baton. We want to run the race with perseverance. We want to be found faithful.

We each have a responsibility to train our children and grandchildren, but like Elijah we also need to be training others in the faith. We can all do something to invest in the lives of the next generation. Maybe you could teach a children's Sunday School class or help with Vacation Bible School this summer. Maybe you can lead a high school small group, teach a Bible study for young adults or mentor someone younger in the faith than you. Perhaps the thing you are supposed to do is invite the kids who live next door to go to church with you. If you don't feel like you can teach others, you could rock babies in the nursery so that their parents can sit in the church service and hear God's Word preached. Or you could serve in a local ministry that shares Jesus' love with people through providing food, shelter, or other physical needs.

We can all do something to invest in the future. We have a race to run, and that race involves imparting the knowledge that we have been given to those who will come after us. Elijah left Elisha well prepared to take up the mantle and carry on. Are you preparing others to carry on the faith after you are gone?

June 20

2 Kings 3-4
Psalm 73:13-20
Proverbs 16:10-11
Acts 16:1-15

An Attitude of Praise

"About midnight Paul and Silas were praying and singing hymns to God and the prisoners were listening to them." Acts 16:25 HCSB

PAUL AND SILAS were doing everything right. They were evangelizing the lost throughout Europe, healing the sick, casting out demons, and following God's leading at every turn and yet they were beaten and thrown into prison. They might have expected that God would protect them because they were doing what He told them to do. How could God allow them to be mistreated and imprisoned? It seems logical that if you do the right things God will bless you and not allow anything bad to happen to you. Unfortunately, that isn't always how it works. Often, we can't see the big picture and we don't understand God's plans. "For as the heavens are higher than the Earth, so are My ways higher than your ways, and My thoughts than your thoughts." Isaiah 55:9 (NIV) Paul and Silas knew this, and they trusted God. That night sitting in prison, they could have been grumbling and complaining. They were probably in a lot of pain from their beating, and they were bound by chains which would be uncomfortable if you were not injured and must have been excruciating for them. Instead of sitting around feeling sorry for themselves, they were praying and singing hymns of praise. Ouch! That's convicting. I doubt I would have reacted that way. I probably would have been telling the other prisoners that I didn't deserve to be there and lamenting the unfairness of it all while sobbing about my cuts and bruises.

Verse 25 tells us that the other prisoners were listening to them. They were paying attention. The prisoners saw that despite their pain and horrible circumstances, Paul and Silas were praising God. God saw them, too, and He acted on their behalf in a powerful way. He sent an earthquake that opened the prison doors and loosed their chains. As a result, they had an opportunity to witness to the jailer and his family, and all of them were saved. If they had not been thrown in prison, this jailer and his family might have never come to know Jesus. Our comfort and ease are not God's number one priority for us. He wants to use us to accomplish His purposes. Sometimes that may mean that we will be put in uncomfortable or painful situations. We might be doing exactly what He wants us to do and find ourselves in difficulty. People are watching how we react to the problems we face. The challenge for us is to use that as an opportunity to praise Him and to testify about God's faithfulness. Our attitude makes all the difference. If our goal is ease and comfort, then whenever we face difficulty, we will be shaken and we will question God's faithfulness. If, however, our goal is to accomplish God's purpose in our lives, then we will look at every situation and evaluate how God might be using it to bring about His plans. I'm not suggesting that all the bad stuff in our lives is caused by God, but rather that sometimes He does allow bad things to happen to bring about a greater good and that He can use everything we face for our ultimate good or the good of others.

2 Kings 5-6
Psalm 73:21-28
Proverbs 16:12-13
Acts 16:16-40

My Feet Almost Slipped

"Yet I am always with You; You hold my right hand. You guide me with Your counsel, and afterward You will take me up to glory. Who do I have in Heaven but You? And I desire nothing on Earth but You. My flesh and my heart may fail, but God is the strength of my heart, my portion forever. Those far from You will certainly perish; You destroy all who are unfaithful to You. But as for me, God's presence is my good. I have made the Lord God my refuge, so I can tell about all You do." Psalm 73:23-28 HCSB

THIS PSALM WAS written by Asaph, who was a musician and singer during David and Solomon's reigns in Israel. Verse 2 would be an appropriate title for the psalm: "My Feet Almost Slipped." Asaph explains in the first few verses of the Psalm that he was almost led astray by envy. He looked around him at evil men and they seemed to prosper. They had easy lives, they were not afflicted, and they had plenty to eat. When he examined his own life, he feared that he had purified his heart and lived a good life for nothing. He felt afflicted and punished while the wicked seemed to be blessed. And then he entered God's sanctuary, God's presence. This gave him a totally new perspective. God's presence changed him. He was able to see that God was with him. He held his hand. He guided him with His wise counsel and one day would take him to glory. Asaph recognized that nothing was more valuable than that. He had an eternal perspective and recognized that nothing on Earth was of any value compared to what waited for him in Heaven. He saw that God was his strength and his portion. This phrase appears several times in scripture. David refers to God as his portion in Psalm 16:5 and 142:5. Solomon tells us in Lamentations 3:24, "'The Lord is my portion,' says my soul, therefore, I will hope in Him." (ESV) God is our source of all that we need. He is our portion in the life we live now and our hope for eternity. Relationships, riches, health, power, and all other things in our lives may fail, but we can say with confidence that "God is the strength of my heart and my portion forever." Asaph also recognizes that those who do not know God may have all the things this life can offer, but they are destined to destruction and face an eternity apart from God. Instead of slipping, Asaph acknowledges that God's presence is his good. He has made God his refuge and he will spend his days telling others about God's faithfulness.

This is a good lesson for us as well. If we look around, the wicked do often seem to prosper and have a much easier life. But the blessings we receive by virtue of God's presence in our lives surpass any difficulty we may face. His presence alone makes all the difference, but we also have the hope of eternity. This Psalm is a great reminder to us when we feel discouraged to enter God's presence for a change of perspective.

June 22

2 Kings 7-8
Psalm 74:1-4
Proverbs 16:14-15
Acts 17

An Unknown God

"For as I was passing through and observing the objects of your worship, I even found an altar on which was inscribed: TO AN UNKNOWN GOD. Therefore, what you worship in ignorance, this I proclaim to you. The God who made the world and everything in it—He is Lord of Heaven and Earth and does not live in shrines made by hands. Neither is He served by human hands, as though He needed anything, since He Himself gives everyone life and breath and all things."
Acts 17:23-25 HCSB

SEVERAL DAYS AGO, we looked at the account of Elijah and the prophets of Baal on Mt. Carmel. Today we see a very different approach by Paul. I think the key here is to know your audience. Elijah recognized that his job on Mt. Carmel was to display God's power and to prove that He is the one and only God. He accomplished that in a mighty way. Paul, however, is in a different situation. He was in Athens at the Areopagus. The Areopagus was a small hill covered in stone seats northwest of the city of Athens, Greece. It was once used as a forum for the rulers of Athens to hold trials, debate and discuss important matters. In Paul's day, groups of respected local men met there to discuss and investigate spiritual and philosophical ideas. Paul was called to speak to them when word of his teaching in Athens began to gain attention. The Greeks were known for their love of knowledge. The message Paul was preaching was "new", so they were intrigued. Paul used the opportunity to deliver one of the most dynamic evangelistic speeches in the New Testament.

When Paul came to Athens, he was very troubled because the city was full of idols. The Greeks were known for their worship of multiple gods. I have said before that Satan really doesn't have new tricks. He has used the same methods throughout the ages. He does not have to convince people to worship him; he only needs to convince people to worship anything other than the one true God. He provides options. In biblical times, he did that through multiple gods. There were gods for everything: the sun, love, wind, music, war, medicine, constellations, darkness, water, etc. Today he does that through various religions: Hinduism, Mormonism, Islam, Buddhism, being a good person, etc. His message is that there are many ways to get to God and that any way you choose to come is the same. That is a lie. There is only one way to God and that is through Jesus Christ, His one and only Son, who came to Earth to be a sacrifice and provide the way to bring us to God. There is no other way. Any religion that does not proclaim that Jesus is "the way, the truth, and the life" is a false religion.

Paul's approach at the Areopagus was very different than Elijah's approach on Mt. Carmel. Instead of ridiculing them for their belief in multiple gods which were nonexistent, he was not afraid to find some point of common ground with his audience. He quoted from several philosophers to show that God is indeed Lord over all. He did not water down biblical truth to reach his audience. Paul clearly outlined the claims of Christ and gave a concise and thorough presentation of the gospel. He was respectful and courteous. He did not insult them or do anything that would be considered offensive. As a result, some people decided they wanted to hear more about Jesus, and some people believed. There were not huge converts from the Areopagus, but they listened and had the opportunity to evaluate for themselves the truth. That is our goal. We do not determine the outcome. We cannot make people believe no matter how much we may want to. Our job is to present the gospel concisely so that they have the opportunity to believe. Paul gives us an excellent example of how to do this in a way that is respectful and yet does not compromise the truth. It is important that we spend time in prayer asking God to give us the right words and the right attitude as we witness to those He places in our path. It is important to know our audience and seek His wisdom to know what approach will reach their heart.

2 Kings 9-10
Psalm 74:5-11
Proverbs 16:16
Acts 18

June 23

Teachable

"This man had been instructed in the way of the Lord; and being fervent in spirit, he spoke and taught the things about Jesus accurately, although he knew only John's baptism. He began to speak boldly in the synagogue. After Priscilla and Aquilla heard him, they took him home and explained the way of God to him more accurately." Acts 18:25-26 HCSB

Apollos is an excellent example of a godly man. We aren't told a lot about him, but the details we are given provide insight into his character. Apollos was a Jew who was eloquent and powerful in the use of scriptures. As a Jew he probably grew up in the synagogue and was not only familiar with the scriptures, but he was able to use them in a powerfully effective way. We are told that he taught the things about Jesus accurately so at some point he had accepted that Jesus was the Messiah. He also was courageous and spoke boldly in the synagogue. While Apollos was not one of the apostles, God was using him in powerful ways to help spread the gospel and is one of the first evangelists. This is significant, but the best indicator of his character is found in his attitude toward correction. At some point when Apollos was speaking in the synagogue, Priscilla and Aquilla heard him. After he finished, Priscilla and Aquilla took him home with them and taught him the way of Jesus more accurately. Let's think about how this played out. Apollos is speaking in front of crowds of people. Instead of contradicting him in front of the crowd, they went to him after and pulled him aside. We aren't told what they said to him, but he went to their house and humbly listened to what they had to say. Instead of being offended or upset, he received their instruction.

Priscilla and Aquilla were just introduced to us earlier in chapter 18. They were not evangelists. They were tentmakers and had taken Paul in while he was in Corinth. Paul describes them in Romans 16 as being "fellow workers in Christ Jesus" and were very influential in the early church. They give us a perfect example of how to encourage one another and build each other up in faith. They did not call Apollos out or argue with him in the synagogue. They just gently took him aside and welcomed him into their home to teach him and help refine his message. We are told that his teaching was accurate, but apparently there were some points that needed clarification. Apollos was humble and able to be taught. He recognized that he didn't know everything he needed to know and was open to learning more about the ways of God. It is important for all of us to recognize that we don't have all the answers and we need to humbly accept instruction from others. We can also learn from Priscilla and Aquilla the proper way to build others up in their faith and the importance of coming alongside fellow believers helping them accurately understand the ways of God.

2 Kings 11-12
Psalm 74:12-17
Proverbs 16:17-19
Acts 19

June 24

Pride

"Pride comes before destruction, and an arrogant spirit before a fall. Better to be lowly of spirit with the humble than to divide plunder with the proud." Proverbs 16:18-19 HCSB

THIS VERSE IS very familiar to most people. It is one of those verses that even people who don't know anything about the Bible like to quote. Nobody likes an arrogant person, and we all get a little bit too much satisfaction when a prideful person falls. That is unless we happen to be the person who gets humbled. This principle can be found throughout Scripture. Jesus Himself taught about pride repeatedly during His ministry. He saw the religious pride of the Pharisees and rebuked them harshly. He also called His disciples out on several occasions when they exhibited prideful attitudes. It is difficult to overstate the destruction pride can cause. Pride is the main reason why people do not believe in and worship God. Fallen man tends to worship himself and elevate his desires and wants above anything else. We do not recognize who God is and therefore fail to humble ourselves before Him.

A sure path to destruction is found in exalting ourselves. Pride is so deceptive because it promises the world and cannot deliver. Matthew 23:12 tells us, "For those who exalt themselves will be humbled, and those who humble themselves will be exalted." (NIV) Pride can come in many forms and is encouraged in our culture. We are taught that we deserve to be exalted. Everybody gets a trophy. You can have whatever you want because you deserve it. You need to look out for number one. We are constantly bombarded with ideas of the importance of having a healthy self-esteem. This is pride disguised as "taking care of yourself." I'm not suggesting we should have low self-esteem. Thinking poorly of yourself is just as prideful as thinking too highly of yourself because the focus is on you. Our focus should never be on ourselves. Our focus should be on Christ. When our eyes are fixed on Him, we can see ourselves clearly. This inevitably leads to humility. It was pride that caused Satan who was once the most beautiful angel, to be jealous of God's position and the worship He received. He rebelled against God and fell from Heaven. Since that time, he has used pride as his favorite method to draw humanity away from God. He promises wealth, status, privilege, and honor. This path leads straight to destruction. When we think rightly about God, we can think rightly about ourselves. Focus on ourselves always leads to comparisons which leads to jealousy and discontentment. Keeping our eyes fixed on God creates a humble heart that is content and grateful.

2 Kings 13-14
Psalm 74:18-23
Proverbs 16:20-21
Acts 20

June 25

Personal Responsibility

"In the seventh year of Jehu, Joash became king and reigned forty years in Jerusalem. Throughout the time Jehoiada the priest instructed him, Joash did what was right in the Lord's sight." 2 Kings 12:1-2 HCSB

"In the twenty-third year of Judah's king Joash son of Ahaziah, Jehoahaz son of Jehu became king over Israel in Samaria and reigned seventeen years. He did what was evil in the Lord's sight and followed the sins that Jeroboam son of Nebat had caused Israel to commit. In the thirty-seventh year of Judah's King Joash, Jehoash son of Jehoahaz became king over Israel and reigned sixteen years. He did what was evil in the Lord's sight." 2 Kings 13:1-2, 10-11 HCSB

During the period of the kings during the divided kingdom in Israel there were twenty kings of Judah and nineteen Kings of Israel. Every one of the kings of Israel were described as doing evil in the Lord's sight. In Judah, eight of the kings were described as doing what was right in the Lord's sight and twelve did evil in the Lord's sight. We find the accounts of these kings in 1 and 2 Kings. The biblical accounts lay them out together chronologically, but it is interesting to see a list of them by kingdom. In Judah, the good and bad kings are dispersed throughout their history. Often the good kings had sons who followed them who were wicked and did not follow God. But there were also bad kings who were followed by sons that were good kings. This reinforces the idea of personal responsibility. While it is extremely important for Christian parents to teach their children about Jesus and to raise them in a home where God is exalted and Scripture is esteemed as truth, we cannot accept Jesus for them. Each of us must decide individually what place we will allow Jesus to have in our lives. Having godly parents and grandparents doesn't get you into Heaven. Having people praying for you every day doesn't get you a ticket to salvation. No matter how much we may want to force our children to believe, that isn't how it works. We have a responsibility to provide the right conditions for them to hear, but ultimately, they must make the decision for themselves. We can do all the right things and they may choose to do evil in the Lord's sight. Our job is to teach them consistently and diligently and then pray for them.

On the other hand, it is encouraging that we are not bound by our parents' choices. We may have been raised by parents who did not follow God and who did not lead us to Jesus. We can break the cycle of evil. We can choose to accept Jesus and follow Him in doing good in the Lord's sight. We each get to decide for ourselves the life we choose. We are not held accountable for our ancestor's bad choices, but we cannot rely on their good ones either.

June 26

2 Kings 15-16
Psalm 75:1-5
Proverbs 16:22-23
Acts 21

Life Purpose

"But I count my life of no value to myself, so that I may finish my course and the ministry I received from the Lord Jesus, to testify to the gospel of God's grace." Acts 20:24 HCSB

At the end of our lives, when we look back, I think most of us want to be able to say that we have finished our course and accomplished the ministry that God has given to us. We want to hear the words, "Well done, good and faithful servant." Matthew 25:23 (HCSB) We hope to be able to say, "I have fought the good fight. I have finished the race; I have kept the faith." 2 Timothy 4:7 (NIV) Unfortunately, I don't think this is the norm. I don't think many people finish the race and accomplish the ministry they have been given. To do that, we must be very intentional. We have to live our lives with a purpose. Most of us are just making it day to day with very little thought about God's purpose and plans.

I guess the first thing we need to settle is that God has a ministry plan and purpose for each of us. Romans 8:28 tells us, "And we know that in all things God works for the good of those who love Him, who have been called according to His purpose." (NIV) The Bible is very clear that ministry is not just for ministers. We are all a part of the Body of Christ, and we all fit together to accomplish His plans. We each have a unique role that He has equipped us to perform. It is not for our glory or benefit, but for the benefit of the body and to bring glory to Him. Paul summed up his purpose in verse 24, "to testify to the gospel of God's grace." Paul examined his life and activities consistently to determine if they fit God's purpose. Most of us probably don't have such a concisely defined purpose like Paul, and our purpose may change with different seasons of our lives. We should, however, do as Paul did and evaluate our lives and activities consistently to determine if we are allowing Him to accomplish His purposes in and through us. This will require time alone with God so He can reveal His plans to us. We don't decide what we want to do for Him, we allow Him to lead us and empower us to minister in an effective, meaningful way. You can't get to the end of your life and look back trying to figure out if you did what you were supposed to do. It is a lifelong process of seeking and serving God that leads to finishing the course and keeping the faith. We must be diligent and purposeful, seeking Him every step of the way.

June 27

2 Kings 17-18
Psalm 75:6-10
Proverbs 16:24-25
Acts 22

The Narrow Road

> "There is a way that seems right to a man, but its end is the way to death." Proverbs 16:25 HCSB

I HAVE THOUGHT of this verse often in the last year. The culture around us is changing so quickly. Things that ten years ago would have shocked the conscience are now, not only accepted, but praised. Tolerance is lauded as the ultimate goal, while right and truth are discounted as narrowminded and hateful. Let me be clear about my position. "Jesus Christ is the same yesterday and today and forever." Hebrews 13:8 (NIV) His standards do not change with cultural shifts. If the Bible speaks to an issue, it is definitive. We cannot pick and choose what we want to agree with and decide what we will follow and not follow. The Bible is the inerrant, perfect Word of God. It is God's instruction book to us. He hasn't changed His mind. Satan knows how to deceive. He is a master at making things seem like they are right, when in fact they are contrary to God's plans. He twists it just enough so that it seems like what God would say, but it is counterfeit. God tells us to love our neighbor as ourselves, so Satan convinces us that to love others we should be tolerant and accepting of them. In truth, the most loving thing we can do for them is to help them understand that their sin is not God's best for their life. Accepting their sin will only lead them to destruction. That is the least loving thing we can do for them. God is a loving God and does not wish for any to perish. Instead, He has provided the way, the one and only way, for us to come to Him and that is through His Son, Jesus. Satan has twisted that to say that God loves us too much to send anyone to Hell. He has created many false religions to convince people that there are many ways to get to God. He doesn't have to convince people to follow him. He only has to convince them to follow anything but the only true way, Jesus. Satan is a master manipulator. We must hold everything to the standard of God's Word. If it is not consistent with God's revealed Word, then it is not from God. He never contradicts Himself. There are lots of teachings that seem right to man, but in the end, they lead to death. We must be in the Word so that we will not be deceived. "Enter through the narrow gate. For wide is the gate and broad is the road that leads to destruction, and many enter through it. But small is the gate and narrow the road that leads to life, and only a few find it." Matthew 7:13-14 (NIV)

2 Kings 19-20
Psalm 76:1-6
Proverbs 16:26-27
Acts 23

June 28

When We Don't Understand

> "This is what the Lord God of your ancestor David says, 'I have heard your prayer; I have seen your tears. Look, I will heal you. On the third day from now you will go up to the Lord's temple. I will add fifteen years to your life. I will deliver you and this city from the hand of the king of Assyria. I will defend this city for My sake and for the sake of My servant David.'" 2 Kings 20:5-6 HCSB

THIS IS AN interesting passage of scripture that provides some lessons for us but can also be misused. In this passage Hezekiah has a terminal illness. We aren't told what it is, only that it is an "illness unto death." Isaiah tells him that he needs to put his affairs in order because he is going to die. Hezekiah's response is appropriate. He turns his face to the wall and prays to God privately. He wept bitterly and brought his concern before God. He didn't grumble and complain and rail about the unfairness of it all to those around him. He went to God sincerely and humbly. In the Old Testament blessings and curses were tied to behavior. He is asking God to remember that he has been faithful and has followed God wholeheartedly. We do not approach God this way now because we recognize that any faithfulness and goodness on our part is filthy rags. We approach God in Jesus' name recognizing that it is by his grace and mercy that we can bring our requests before God. His righteousness covers us and allows us to have access to God. Hezekiah's prayer may seem arrogant, but at that time it was appropriate. I love that God's response was, "I have heard your prayer." That is very comforting. God always hears our prayers. We do not always get an immediate answer like Hezekiah did, but He always hears us. We also may not always get the answer we want. God gave Hezekiah an additional fifteen years. Instead of just healing him, God told him he had fifteen more years and we see at the end of the chapter that at the end of that time, he died.

I can't explain why God chose to give Hezekiah fifteen more years of life when he prayed, and He doesn't do that when other people who have terminal illnesses pray. The only explanation is that God knows what is best. I admit that it is beyond my ability to understand how a child's death could be best or how it is best for a young mother to die instead of being healed by God. We know that He can heal them and yet sometimes He doesn't. Hezekiah's healing was also tied to the deliverance of Israel. He was not healed for his sake as much as for the sake of Israel. This fit into God's greater purpose. When God chooses to heal now it usually has a greater purpose than just preserving that person's life. When we do not get the answer we want, if we are seeking Him, He will give us the strength and courage to accept the answer we are given. Only in turning our face to Him can we hope to experience the peace that passes understanding when we don't have all the answers.

June 29

2 Kings 21-23
Psalm 76:7-12
Proverbs 16:28-29
Acts 24

Time for God

"After some days, when Felix came with his wife Drusilla, who was Jewish, he sent for Paul and listened to him on the subject of faith in Christ Jesus. Now as he spoke about righteousness, self-control, and the judgment to come, Felix became afraid and replied, 'Leave for now, but when I find time, I'll call for you.'" Acts 24:24-25 HCSB

Felix sent for Paul. He was seeking. He wanted to know about Jesus, but when Paul started talking about righteousness, self-control and judgment, Felix got scared and sent him away. "When I have time, I'll call for you." I think that is all too common. We want to know about Jesus. We want to hear about how much He loves us, takes care of us, and helps us, but then when the subject of righteousness, self-control and judgment comes up we don't really want to hear about all of that. Unfortunately, many churches have succumbed to the temptation to "tell them what they want to hear" to increase numbers. I don't think it is all vanity, although I suspect there is some measure of that involved. Rather, I think they believe that it is better to hear part of the truth than nothing at all, so they present only the parts that will keep people coming back. The problem with that thinking is that if you don't present all the truth, it is not really the truth at all. Jesus is loving and caring, but He is also righteous and just. We don't just need a helper; we need a Savior. If we do not recognize our own sin and our position before a holy and righteous God, we cannot understand our need for salvation. A watered-down gospel is not really the gospel at all. If we are not accepting Jesus for who He is, then we are not really accepting Him. We don't get to pick and choose the parts we want to hear and dismiss the rest. If we accept Jesus as our Savior and Lord, we are accepting that He is in control of our lives. We are His servants. He gets to call the shots. He isn't just someone we turn to when we need help.

It seems that Felix didn't really want to deal with the idea of judgment and personal responsibility and righteousness, so he decided to wait till later. He kicked the can down the road. We are just like that, aren't we? We hear a sermon or read a devotion that hits a little too close to home. Instead of addressing the issue and asking God to reveal to us what He wants to teach us, we dismiss it and choose to brush it aside, thinking, "I'll deal with it later when I have time." Unfortunately, we rarely ever find the time and the issue is left unresolved. When we accept Jesus into our hearts, He begins the process of shaping and refining us. It is a lifelong process of teaching, correcting, and training us in righteousness. We must deal with the hard stuff to grow. Let us allow God to show us areas where we need to grow and cooperate with Him so that we may become mature in our faith.

2 Kings 24-25
Psalm 77:1-6
Proverbs 16:30-31
Acts 25

June 30

Maturity

"Gray hair is a glorious crown; it is found in the way of righteousness." Proverbs 16:31 HCSB

REDHEADS DON'T REALLY turn gray, but my hair is getting lighter and lighter, especially around my face and someday I will probably be white headed. I would have thought this would bother me, but it really doesn't. I recognize that there are benefits to aging. My body may be feeling some wear and tear, but spiritually and emotionally I can rejoice with the freedom of maturity. There is a perspective that comes with age that is not possible to gain any other way. I'm not suggesting that younger people cannot be wise. There are certainly young people I know that are wise beyond their years. Sometimes that comes because of life experiences and sometimes they just have a unique wisdom from God at an early age. The opposite is also true. I know older people who are foolish that I would not consider mature at all. But generally, wisdom and maturity come with age. With more life experiences, good and bad, we have a broader range of knowledge and insight that allows us to make better decisions and see life from a wider perspective. And more importantly, years spent at the feet of Jesus allows Him time to shape, refine and mature us. As I get older, I recognize the importance of spending time with Jesus every day. I have always known it is important, but I have not always recognized how essential it is to my peace and emotional well-being. With maturity there is also a recognition that God's way really is the best thing for me. Righteousness produces benefits. Following His plan for my life and adhering to the principles He has provided in Scripture actually does produce blessings. I'm not suggesting that if you follow His ways, you will never have difficulty or heartache. Obviously, that is not accurate, but we are able to avoid many of the foolish decisions and pitfalls that come because of following our own path. God has the benefit of being able to see into the future. If we seek Him, He will guide us to make decisions that are good for us.

No matter what your age, there is tremendous benefit to seeking out older, more mature believers for wisdom and insight. We can all benefit from their years of knowledge and depth of experience. The elderly are often pushed aside in our culture to make room for new and "better" ways of doing things. Let us not make the mistake of failing to learn from the lessons of the past or thinking we are smarter than our elders.

I Chronicles 1-2
Psalm 77:7-15
Proverbs 16:32-33
Acts 26

July 1

Patience

"Patience is better than power, and controlling one's temper, than capturing a city."
  Proverbs 16:32 HCSB

I cannot say I am very good at the whole patience thing, but I am better than I used to be. Right now, we are remodeling our house and I must admit that I have not always shown patience during this process. We have been living in our basement for 3 months with no kitchen or laundry, which has been more than a little challenging. On days when I can see progress, I'm fine, but inevitably there are days when nothing gets done and, on those days, I struggle with the patience thing. If you had asked me a few months ago if I was a patient person, I would have told you that I was. Now, I can't honestly say that. Patience is like the other fruits of the Spirit. I don't think we can develop them. I think God has to develop them in us. Looking back, I can see that He has been developing patience in me. The process of developing character traits doesn't happen overnight. It happens little by little by little. It comes through being in situations where you have to exercise that trait. You can't develop character traits by reading about them in a book. Head knowledge can aid in the process, but the only way to develop that trait is through exercising it. It is kind of like physical exercise. You can read all about it, know the best techniques for getting fit, and subscribe to all the fitness blogs, but until you do the exercises consistently and diligently, you will not develop any muscle and the head knowledge will not do you any good.

   Love, joy, peace, patience, kindness, goodness, gentleness, faithfulness, and self-control don't come naturally. They are a work of the Holy Spirit in and through us. I think God puts us in a situation where we have to use that trait, we struggle at first and then slowly begin to do better at it. Then we get a break, and He works on something else. A while later He comes back to that trait and works on it again by putting us in a little more difficult situation where we need to use it. Slowly, but surely, we develop it. I'm not sure there will ever be a time when we can say we have complete patience, or complete gentleness, or complete self-control, but hopefully, when we examine our lives, we can see maturity in those areas. The verse above says that patience is better than power. I think that is equally true of all the other fruits of the Spirit. Self-control is better than power. Gentleness is better than power. Faithfulness is better than power. The work of the Holy Spirit in our lives gives us control over our mind, will and emotions. That is truly better than power because it enables us to deal with all the situations in our lives with purpose instead of being controlled by our whims and desires.

I Chronicles 3-5
Psalm 77:16-20
Proverbs 17:1-2
Acts 27

July 2

Through No Fault of Our Own

"But the centurion paid attention to the captain and the owner of the ship rather than to what Paul said... For many days neither sun nor stars appeared, and the severe storm kept raging. Finally, all hope that we would be saved was disappearing... For this night an angel of the God I belong to and serve stood before me, and said, 'Don't be afraid, Paul. You must stand before Caesar. And look! God has graciously given you all those who are sailing with you.' Therefore, take courage, men, because I believe God that it will be just the way it was told to me." Acts 27:11, 20, 23-25 HCSB

SOMETIMES WE FIND ourselves in difficult circumstances through no fault of our own. We can be doing everything right, following God's leading and doing what we are supposed to do, but someone close to us makes bad choices that result in very bad problems for us. Unfortunately, we often cannot control the actions of those around us. No matter how bad we want them to seek God and follow His leading, sometimes that does not happen, and we suffer the consequences. This happened to Paul. He was a prisoner taken on a ship to Rome. Paul told the officers on the ship that they should not go forward. He warned them of the consequences, but they chose not to listen to him. They proceeded on their route and a very bad storm came up that threatened all their lives. While the storms of life that we face often don't physically threaten our lives, it sure can feel that way. A spouse who has an affair and chooses to leave his family, a child who succumbs to drug addiction, an employee who embezzles money and causes the company to fail and many to lose their jobs, a father who decides he isn't "happy" and walks out on his family. These are just a few examples of many where our lives can be turned upside by the choices of others. In those situations, we may feel like the people on that ship who thought "all hope that we would be saved was disappearing." It is incredibly scary. There is nothing we can do to change the situation and we feel hopeless and helpless.

In those times, it is important that we recognize that while we cannot do anything to "fix" the situation, we know who can. The only One who can actually make a difference loves me and is taking care of me. Even during horrible situations, God has my back. God gives each of us free will and our choices inevitably affect those around us. We don't just suffer for our own bad choices. Thankfully, we can be assured that God will look out for us. We are not shielded from all difficult circumstances, but God never leaves us, and He is constantly working on our behalf to bring about good for us. God protected Paul and all of those on the ship with him because His plan was for Paul to go to Rome and stand before Caesar. We can know that God's plans will be carried out. In difficult times, it is so hard to see how God can possibly work good through it, but He is faithful, and He will bring us through to the other side. If we continue to seek Him and we remain faithful, He will not let us down.

1 Chronicles 6-7
Psalm 78:1-8
Proverbs 17:3-4
Acts 28

July 3

Future Generations

"I will speak mysteries from the past—things we have heard and known and that our fathers have passed down to us. We must not hide them from their children but must tell a future generation the praises of the Lord, His might, and the wonderful works He has performed. He established a testimony in Jacob and set up a law in Israel, which He commanded our fathers to teach their children so that a future generation—children yet to be born—might know. They were to rise and tell their children so that they might put their confidence in God and not forget God's works but keep His commands." Psalm 78:2-7 HCSB

My first grandbaby is due in September, and I am so excited I can't hardly stand it! Every night when Brian and I pray, we pray for Hadley. We don't pray that she will have an easy life or that everything will always go her way. Nor do we pray that she will have a trouble-free life because that is not realistic. In this fallen world, we all experience difficulties, heartache, and pain. Hadley will face all those things. What Brian and I pray for her every night is that she will come to know Jesus at an early life and that she will walk with Him all the days of her life. If He is by her side, she will be ok. He will give her the strength, peace, and wisdom to deal with anything that comes her way.

As I reflect on my life, I am so grateful that I had parents and grandparents that did exactly as those verses above instruct us. I do not remember a time when I did not know God loved me and when I was not confident in His presence in my life. I accepted Him as my personal savior when I was nine years old, but long before that I knew Him, and He was a consistent part of my life. I prayed to Him and read my Bible. I knew the Bible stories and believed in His power to work miracles and to take care of me. My parents took me to church, they prayed with me at night, and they taught me about Jesus. I saw my parents and grandparents praying and reading their Bibles. God was not just talked about on Sunday; He was a part of everything we did. They prayed for guidance about any decisions they made, for healing of the sick, for comfort for those who were grieving. They studied their Bibles for wisdom, and they taught me that God is the source of wisdom and strength to help me in my life. I have tried to model that for my children and to tell them about God "so that they might put their confidence in Him and not forget God's works but keep His commands." Our children watch everything we do. If they rarely see us reading our Bible, only hear about God on Sunday, and only see us turn to God when we are facing a crisis, that is likely the example they will follow. If, on the other hand, God is intimately involved in all aspects of our lives, they see us seek Him in all our decisions, and they witness our reliance on Him during good times and bad times, it will be natural for them to involve Him in their lives as they mature and grow. This is my prayer for Hadley and for those in her generation. I pray they will know Him intimately and learn to rely completely on Him.

I Chronicles 8-9
Psalm 78:9-16
Proverbs 17:5-6
Romans 1

July 4

The Foundation of our Faith

> "For I am not ashamed of the gospel, for it is the power of God for salvation to everyone who believes, to the Jew first and also to the Greek. For in it the righteousness of God is revealed from faith for faith; as it is written, 'The righteous shall live by faith.'" Romans 1:16-17 (ESV)

ROMANS IS BRIAN'S favorite book. We joked in our college Bible study that every week he referenced Romans in some way. He could even find something in Ruth and Jonah to point back to Romans. The more I study Romans, the more I realize how important this book is to our faith. God appointed Paul to spread the gospel to the Gentile world. In that day, Rome was the center of the Gentile world. There was a growing church in Rome and Paul knew the importance of giving them a solid foundation and a firm understanding of the doctrines of their faith. I think many Christians have the idea that foundational doctrines and theology are things that our pastors are supposed to learn in seminary, but they are too difficult for us to understand. We know the basics and just trust that our preachers and teachers will tell us what we need to know. That is not a biblical idea. As Christians we believe in the priesthood of the believer. That means that we have personal access to God. We do not have to go through a priest to receive forgiveness of our sins. We can go before God personally, confessing our sin and He relates to us individually. He is not a far-off God who speaks to us only through a priest or a preacher. It also means that we have access to God's Word. We have all the revelation that our pastors and teachers have. We have the Holy Spirit living in us to teach us, instruct us and help us understand God's Word. And thankfully, the internet gives us access to every study tool we could possibly need to help us know what we believe and why. We are without excuse for our biblical ignorance.

Romans gives a detailed summary of our Christian faith and explains the gospel in terms that we can understand and be able to relate to others. Over the next couple of weeks, we are going to study Romans more closely. I encourage you to continue reading your daily readings through the Bible, but our devotions will focus mostly on Romans. I will do an overview of each chapter and hopefully it will spark an interest in you to study the concepts more deeply. Write down your questions and do some research to figure out the answers. Got Questions.org is an excellent source. If you can't figure it out, ask your pastor or a trusted Bible teacher.

In Romans 1, Paul gives an introduction to the letter to Rome, and he lays out clearly and thoroughly the Gentile's need of salvation. In verse 16-17, he gives a concise overview of the gospel. He explains that there is no need to be ashamed of the gospel. We can boldly proclaim the gospel because it is true and reliable. The power of God provides salvation to everyone who believes. It is not based on anything we do but rather it is completely based on our faith in God and His ability. In verses 18-32, Paul introduces the wrath of God. It is impossible to understand the good news that the gospel provides unless we first grasp the bad news. The bad news is that we are sinful, and we stand before a holy, righteous God. His righteousness cannot overlook sin. His holiness will not tolerate our absolute depravity and we face His wrath which will result in death and Hell. Modern culture does not like to talk about the wrath of God. Many churches focus on God's love and mercy. They prefer to talk about His compassion and grace and skim over His holiness and wrath. If we do not understand our true state and the ugliness of our sin, we cannot possibly understand why we need a savior. Satan's most insidious deception is convincing us that we really aren't that bad, and that God loves us so much He will just overlook our sin. God loves us so much that He sent His Son to take the punishment for our sin and to provide a way for His righteousness to be imparted to us. If our sin was not that bad and He would just overlook it then there would have been no reason for His crucifixion. Jesus' death, burial and resurrection is the foundation of our faith. If there was no need for it, then it all falls apart and our faith is pointless. God's love and mercy cannot be separated from His righteousness and wrath. Our understanding of this is critical to our faith.

I Chronicles 10-12
Psalm 78:17-31
Proverbs 17:7-8
Romans 2

July 5

Circumcision of the Heart

> "For he is not a Jew who is one outwardly, nor is circumcision that which is outward in the flesh. But he is a Jew who is one inwardly; and circumcision is that which is of the heart, by the Spirit, not by the letter; and his praise is not from men but from God." Romans 2:28-29 (NASB1995)

In Romans 1, Paul described the progression of sin in humanity and concludes with a list of the different kinds of sin we indulge in after we choose to reject God. A self-righteous religious person is tempted to read that list and convince themselves that it is about other people who are "sinners" and does not apply to them. In chapter 2, Paul addresses those religious people and calls them hypocrites for judging others and failing to acknowledge their own sinfulness. All of us are guilty of the sin nature that leads to those sinful practices. Looking at that list, most people would agree that those who practice those things deserve God's judgment. He is pointing out to them that no one can follow the law completely and perfectly all the time. Since God's standard is perfection, we are all doomed to face His judgment. They were not protected because they were under the law or because they had been circumcised, just as we are not protected by going to church and trying to be a "good" person.

Circumcision in that day was an outward sign of their inner commitment to God. It set the Jews apart from the rest of the world. By choosing circumcision, they were entering into a covenant relationship with God in which they bore a physical mark on their body that symbolized a spiritual commitment to obeying God and following His will. Paul was stressing to them that it was not the physical, outward mark of circumcision that protected them, but rather the inward commitment of their heart. It can be compared to baptism. The act of baptism does not produce salvation. Baptism is an outward symbol of the inner commitment we have made to follow Jesus and submit to His will in our lives. The outward act is of no significance if there has not been an inner change in our hearts. There are those who believe that because they were baptized as a baby, they have experienced salvation. That is not how it works. There must first be a change in the heart that results in confession and repentance. This is then followed by baptism to acknowledge and celebrate before the world that inward commitment. Paul wanted the Jews to understand that God looks at the heart. He is more concerned with the motives and intentions of our heart than our attempts to follow rules to make others think we are holy. His desire is to remove or circumcise everything in our hearts that is evil so that we have pure hearts that are completely committed to Him.

I Chronicles 13-15
Psalm 78:32-39
Proverbs 17:9-11
Romans 3

July 6

All Have Sinned

"There is no one righteous, not even one. There is no one who understands; there is no one who seeks God. All have turned away; all alike have become useless. There is no one who does what is good, not even one." Romans 3:10-12 HCSB

"For all have sinned and fall short of the glory of God." Romans 3:23 HCSB

In Romans 3, Paul completes the accusation that both the Jews and the Gentiles are guilty before God. He dispels the idea that any man can stand before a holy God and be declared righteous on his own merits. He leaves no room for doubt that we are all sinners and that no one is righteous, not even one. After establishing his case for the sinfulness of man, Paul explains that the righteousness that the law was powerless to provide, God Himself provided by sending His Son, Jesus. This righteousness comes by faith to all who believe in Jesus. I John 1:8, 10 tells us, "If we say, 'We have no sin,' we are deceiving ourselves, and the truth is not in us... If we say, 'We don't have any sin,' we make Him a liar and His Word is not in us." (HCSB) We don't like to think of ourselves as sinners. If you asked most people if they think they are a good person, they would probably say that they do consider themselves to be good. We tend to think positively about ourselves and overlook areas in our lives where we know we are not living up to God's standards. We tend to compare ourselves to those around us.

The problem with comparisons is that we can always find someone who is worse than we are. If we compare ourselves to murderers, thieves, adulterers, rapists, and corrupt politicians we look pretty good. We can easily convince ourselves that if we don't do any of the big stuff then we are ok. The problem is that is not how it works. At the end of our lives, we will not stand before the judgment seat of God with a bunch of other people while He ranks us based on the severity of our sin letting the ones with the least sin in and casting out the ones with a lot of sin. There is also not some giant scale in Heaven that God uses to weigh our sins. The big sins weigh more so at the end of our life if our good deeds outweigh our bad ones, God lets us in. The standard is not other people. The standard is Jesus. We will not be compared to all the other people in the world and judged based on how we measure up to them. We are judged by how we measure up to Jesus. He is perfect, so no matter how good we are, no matter how many good deeds we do and how well we can follow the rules, we cannot possibly be perfect. If we stand before God based on our own merits, we are all doomed.

Thankfully, God recognized this, and He provided His Son to be the propitiation for our sins. That is a big word that simply means that He is our substitute. He assumed our obligation, took our punishment, and covered our sin by His sacrifice on the cross. We have two choices. If we have believed in Jesus and accept Him as our Savior and Lord, then at the end of our life when we stand before a holy and just God, the righteousness of Jesus is imparted to us, and we are judged based on His righteousness not based on our own merits. We are covered by His cleansing blood and accepted into glory. If, on the other hand, we have not believed in Jesus and have not accepted Him into our hearts, then we must stand before God based on our own merits and inevitably, we will be found guilty and be condemned to death and Hell. None of us deserve Heaven. We deserve death and Hell, but His love and mercy have provided a way for our redemption through faith in Jesus.

I Chronicles 16-17
Psalm 78:40-55
Proverbs 17:12-13
Romans 4

July 7

Justified by Faith

"He believed, hoping against hope, so that he became the father of many nations according to what had been spoken: So, will your descendants be. He considered His own body to be already dead (since he was about 100 years old) and also considered the deadness of Sarah's womb, without weakening in the faith. He did not waver in unbelief at God's promise but was strengthened in his faith and gave glory to God, because he was fully convinced that what He had promised He was fully able to perform. Therefore, it was credited to him as righteousness. Now it was credited to him was not written for Abraham alone, but also for us. It will be credited to us who believe in Him who raised Jesus our Lord from the dead. He was delivered up for our trespasses and raised for our justification." Romans 4:18-24 HCSB

ROMANS 4 IS the proof that faith has always been the means for justification. Paul uses Old Testament patriarchs to establish the fact that faith and not works is the means to salvation. The whole world was blessed through Abraham because he chose to believe God rather than looking at his circumstances. It would have been easy for Abraham to laugh at the idea that God could give him descendants more numerous than the stars when he was childless at the age of 100. His ability to father children and Sarah's ability to conceive had long passed. It must have seemed impossible and yet Abraham believed God. He chose to trust in God instead of trusting in his own reasoning and knowledge. Justification is a legal term with a meaning similar to acquittal. In religious terms, it points to the process whereby a person is declared to be right with God.

Since Jesus' death, burial, and resurrection, that justification takes place by faith in Jesus. In the Old Testament, God imputed righteousness to individuals based on their faith. Hebrews 11 recounts the faith of the Old Testament saints. We are not told that they were justified by their mighty works or their great accomplishments for God. Moses was not praised for leading the children of Israel out of Egypt. He was praised for his faith in trusting God and obeying Him. We are told that Rahab, Samson, David, Enoch, Samuel, and the prophets by faith were able to carry out God's purposes. They did not do great things for God and then God imputed righteousness to them because of their actions. Their righteousness was based completely on their faith. God was able to accomplish great things in and through them because they trusted in Him. In the same way, God does not need us to do great things for Him. He doesn't credit righteousness to us based on our abilities and deeds. What He desires is for us to completely trust Him to work in and through us. Our best efforts are worth nothing, but our total surrender allows Him to accomplish more than we can even imagine.

July 8

I Chronicles 18-19
Psalm 78:56-64
Proverbs 17:14-15
Romans 5

Reconciled

"Therefore, since we have been declared righteous by faith, we have peace with God through our Lord Jesus Christ. We have also obtained access through Him by faith into this grace in which we stand, and we rejoice in the hope of the glory of God. For while we were still helpless, at the appointed moment, Christ died for the ungodly. For rarely will someone die for a just person—though for a good person perhaps someone might even dare to die. But God proves His own love for us in that while we were still sinners, Christ died for us! Much more then since we have now been declared righteous by His blood, we will be saved through Him from wrath." Romans 5:1-2, 6-9 HCSB

IN ROMANS 5, Paul explains how we are reconciled to God through Jesus Christ. This reconciliation is not something we are waiting for, but in every way, we are already righteous, holy, and acceptable to God. We have obtained access to God through Jesus by faith. I once heard an illustration that explains this very well. You are sitting in your house with your family watching TV when the doorbell rings. You open the door, and a young boy is standing at your door asking to come in. Before you let him in you would ask him some questions. You would want to know his name, where he lives, who his parents are and what he wants. It would be unsafe for you to allow him into your house with your family if you didn't know who he was or what he wanted. You would not give access to your home to a stranger. However, if you are sitting at home watching tv with your family and your son comes home with a young boy you don't know your reaction would be very different. Your son would bring him in, introduce him to you and tell you a little about him. You would welcome him with open arms and offer him something to eat. He would be treated as a guest and given access to your home. Before we know Christ, we are strangers. We do not have access to God, but once we know the Son, we have access to the Father. Jesus brings us home and welcomes us as an honored guest. It is not based on who we are or what we have done, but rather, we are given access because we are with the Son.

"While we were still sinners, Christ died for us." This verse refutes the idea that we need to clean ourselves up before we can come to God. Some people have the idea that we can't come to God when we are at our worst, but that we have to clean up our lives and make ourselves more presentable to get to God. I've heard people say that they would not be allowed in the church doors because of all the bad things they have done. Unfortunately, there are churches where this may be true, but it could not be further from the truth of the gospel. Jesus welcomes us just as we are. It is impossible to "clean" up enough to be presentable to Him. Thankfully, that is not what He requires. We are told that a humble and contrite spirit pleases Him more than anything else.

I Chronicles 20-22
Psalm 78:65-72
Proverbs 17:16-17
Romans 6

July 9

Freedom from Sin

"Therefore, do not let sin reign in your mortal body, that you should obey its desires. And do not offer any parts of it to sin as weapons for unrighteousness. But as those who are alive from the dead, offer yourselves to God, and all the parts of yourselves to God as weapons for righteousness. For sin will not rule over you, because you are not under law but under grace. For the wages of sin is death, but the gift of God is eternal life through Jesus Christ our Lord." Romans 6:12-14, 23 HCSB

When we are born again, sin's power is broken in our lives. We are freed from sin and made alive to God through Jesus. Our sinful nature was crucified with Him, and we are no longer bound by that sinful nature. Through Jesus, we have received the gift of God which is eternal life. We have the power of the Holy Spirit living within us to overcome the power of sin in our lives. On our own power and strength, we cannot overcome the power of sin, but we are not on our own. We do not face temptation alone. I Corinthians 10:13 tells us, "No temptation has overtaken you except what is common to mankind. And God is faithful; He will not let you be tempted beyond what you can bear. But when you are tempted, He will also provide a way out so that you can endure it." (NIV) James 4:7 assures us, "Submit yourselves, then, to God. Resist the devil, and he will flee from you." (NIV) Romans 6:6 tells us, "We know that our old self was crucified with Him in order that sin's dominion over the body may be abolished, so that we may no longer be enslaved to sin, since a person who has died is freed from sin's claims." (HCSB) If we died with Christ, we also live with Him. He has given us the power to live lives free from sin and the entanglements it creates. While living in this fallen world, we are never free from the temptation and allure of sin. Our human nature is drawn to sinful desires, but it is empowering to know that we can overcome those desires and to choose life and freedom instead of sin and bondage.

Romans 6:23 is a very effective verse to use when explaining the gospel. Wages are the price we earn as a result of our labor. It is the amount we deserve based on what we have done. When we work, we expect to be paid. This verse tells us that the wage we earn for sin is death. What we deserve and should expect to receive for our sin is death. But through faith in Jesus, we are given the free gift of eternal life. There is nothing we can do to earn it; we can only receive it.

I Chronicles 23-24
Psalm 79:1-4
Proverbs 17:18-20
Romans 7

July 10

The Problem of Sin

"For I do not understand what I am doing, because I do not practice what I want to do, but I do what I hate... For the desire to do what is good is with me, but there is no ability to do it. For I do not do the good that I want to do, but I practice the evil that I do not want to do. What a wretched man I am! Who will rescue me from this dying body? I thank God through Jesus Christ our Lord!" Romans 7:15, 18-19, 24-25 HCSB

IN ROMANS 7, Paul deals with the relationship between the law and human sinfulness. He begins by making it clear that those who are in Christ are not bound by the law of Moses. We are also free from our slavery to sin. When we come to faith in Christ we are so closely associated with His death and resurrection that we experience a spiritual death and are resurrected into a new spiritual life. He uses the illustration of marriage to explain this. A woman whose husband has died is no longer obligated to remain faithful to him. She is free to marry another man. Our death with Christ has freed us from any obligation to the law. Paul makes it clear that the law itself is not bad. It is holy and good and reveals to us how sinful we are. We would not recognize that coveting is sinful if the law did not warn us of the dangers of coveting our neighbors' possessions. He describes how his failed attempts to keep the law convince him of his need to be delivered from sin by faith in Christ.

In verses 13-23, Paul describes the experience of wanting to do what is good and finding himself doing what is sinful instead. Bible scholars disagree about whether Paul is describing himself before he was a Christian, when he was trying desperately to follow the law, or whether he is describing a current experience of trying to do good in his own power as a Christian. I tend to believe that he is describing the ongoing struggle of a believer against sin. The book of Romans centers around the idea that non-Christians are unable to keep the law. The law is not able to make us righteous before God. Christians are freed from the power of sin, but often still find the temptation of sin difficult to overcome. Becoming a Christian gives us the power to overcome sin, but it does not make us sinless. We can have the best intentions to do good and still find it difficult to always live that out in our everyday lives. Paul cries out in frustration that he is a wretched man who needs to be delivered. He recognizes that we can find deliverance only through faith in Jesus.

I Chronicles 25-26
Psalm 79:5-8
Proverbs 17:21-22
Romans 8:1-17

July 11

Life in the Spirit

> "Therefore, there is now no condemnation for those who are in Christ Jesus, because through Christ Jesus the law of the Spirit who gives life has set you free from the law of sin and death. The Spirit Himself testifies with our spirit that we are God's children. Now if we are children, then we are heirs—heirs of God and co-heirs with Christ, if indeed we share in His sufferings in order that we may also share in His glory." Romans 8:1-2, 16-17 NIV

ROMANS 8 IS one of the most loved chapters in the Bible by biblical scholars and Christians in general. It helps us understand the doctrine of eternal security and explains how to live by the Spirit and let peace rule in our hearts. The Holy Spirit living within us gives us constant assurance that we are God's children, heirs of God and co-heirs with Christ. He does not want us to live in doubt and fear because we do not face condemnation if we are in Christ. It is comforting that Paul placed this chapter filled with assurance and hope immediately following chapter 7 that dealt with the struggle of sin in the life of the believer. He went from saying he is a wretched sinful man to claiming that there is no condemnation for those who are in Christ Jesus. It is difficult to grasp how we can struggle with sin and at the same time not be subject to condemnation. Paul wants us to understand that our eternal security is not based on our ability to be good. Just like we could not do anything to deserve salvation, we cannot do anything to keep ourselves saved. In John 10: 27-29, Jesus Himself tells us that we cannot lose our salvation. "My sheep listen to My voice; I know them, and they follow Me. I give them eternal life and they shall never perish; no one will snatch them out of My hand. My Father who has given them to Me is greater than all; no one can snatch them out of My Father's hand." (NIV)

Paul does an extensive comparison between those who live according to the flesh and those who live according to the Spirit. Their lives are completely different. They have a different focus, different passions and desires, and a different destiny. In verse 16 Paul tells us that we are God's children. "So, you are no longer a slave, but God's child; and since you are His child, God has made you also an heir." Galatians 4:7 (NIV) That is an amazing truth. We deserve death and Hell, but instead He chose to willingly sacrifice Himself to pay the penalty for our sin. We are indebted to Him for our very lives, and we should expect to become His servants, but instead He loves us so much that He has adopted us as His children. We have all the rights and responsibilities that come with being an heir. We have been adopted into His family. The adoption papers have been signed and sealed and we can rest in the knowledge that we belong to Him, and He will not let anyone take us away from Him. If you struggle with this truth, please examine these verses for yourself and ask God to give you peace and confidence that your eternity is secure.

July 12

I Chronicles 27-29
Psalm 79:9-13
Proverbs 17:23-24
Romans 8:18-39

More than Conquerors

"And we know that in all things God works for the good of those who love Him, who have been called according to His purpose. What, then, shall we say in response to these things? If God is for us who can be against us? No, in all these things we are more than conquerors through Him who loved us. For I am convinced that neither death nor life, neither angels nor demons, neither the present or the future, nor any powers, neither height nor depth, nor anything else in all creation, will be able to separate us from the love of God that is in Christ Jesus our Lord." Romans 8:28, 31, 37-39 NIV

THERE ARE SO many amazing verses in this chapter I had a hard time deciding which ones to focus on. These verses are some of the most encouraging in all scripture. Verse 28 explains to us that in all things God is working on our behalf to bring about good. It does not say that we will never experience anything bad and that we will always only face good things in our lives. What it says is that no matter what we face, good and bad, God is always working on our behalf to bring about good. Sometimes He allows us to face difficulties to prepare us for things to come or to bring about a greater purpose. His goal for us is not to give us an easy life. His goal is to conform us into the image of Christ. Growth rarely happens during times of ease and comfort. But we can be assured that He is always at work on our behalf. When I am going through difficulty, somehow it is easier to deal with if I know there is a purpose. Knowing God is working through my pain makes it more bearable.

"If God is for us, who can be against us?" We have nothing to fear. The Creator of the universe is taking care of us. The One who made everything is on our side. No matter what we face, we can know that we are not just conquerors, we are more than conquerors. Nothing can separate us from the love of God. The beginning of chapter 8 discusses our eternal security. Since we know that our future is secure, we can be confident that no matter what happens to us in this life, nothing can separate us from God. "Do not be afraid of those who kill the body and cannot kill the soul. Rather, be afraid of the One who can destroy both soul and body in Hell." Matthew 10:28 (NIV)

I am a huge football fan and I love to watch any football game, especially Auburn football. I love the thrill of the game, the tense moments when you aren't sure if they will pull out a win, and the feeling of exhilaration when they do. As an Auburn fan, I am also well acquainted with the taste of defeat. I think that is what makes the victories sweeter. Having been through the games that were so close when they didn't pull out a win makes you appreciate even more the ones when they do. My son-in-law loves to watch football, too. He is a huge Vanderbilt fan, but he is a little different from me. I like to watch games to find out the ending. I'm not into watching games that are being replayed. If I know the ending, it just isn't as much fun. I like the suspense, anxiety, and uncertainty. He likes to study the game. He will watch games over and over to figure out the plays and study the players, their tendencies, what makes them good, and their weaknesses. I don't care about all of that. I just want the thrill of the game. That suspense and excitement is great for football, but I am grateful I don't have to experience that about my eternal destiny. I don't have to worry that it will be a close call and if I mess up, I might not make it into Heaven. I don't have the anxiety and fear that if I don't do everything just right and execute the last play well that I am going to blow it and not make it in. I know the ending. I know my eternal destiny. Romans 8 gives me great peace that no matter what this life holds for me, one day I will be with my Savior in Heaven. He has gone to prepare a place for me, and He is waiting there for me to join Him. Knowing the end gives me the confidence and hope to face life now with peace.

July 13

2 Chronicles 1-2
Psalm 80:1-3
Proverbs 17:25-26
Romans 9

Children of the Promise

"That is, it is not the children by physical descent who are God's children, but the children of the promise are considered to be the offspring. What should we say then? Is there injustice with God? Absolutely not! For He tells Moses, 'I will show mercy to whom I will show mercy, and I will have compassion on whom I will have compassion.' So, then it does not depend on human will or effort but on God who shows mercy." Romans 9:8, 14-16 HCSB

CHAPTER 9 TEACHES us that it is not natural children that are God's children, but rather children of the promise. The promise comes through faith in Jesus, not by works of the Law. The Israelites pursued righteousness by the law and did not obtain it. The Gentiles pursued it by faith and obtained righteousness through faith in Jesus. This chapter is a stark reminder that faith in Christ is the only thing that saves us. Paul is saddened by Israel's rejection of the Messiah because God has given her so many opportunities as His chosen people. He entered covenant with them, He gave them the Law, the promises, the temple, and the prophets. He also gave them the privilege of having the Messiah come from among them. God kept all His promises to Israel and yet they were not faithful, and they rejected Him.

Paul then examines the question of God's mercy. In Western culture, we have a deep sense of personal responsibility. We believe that we should work for what we get, everyone should get what they deserve. It is a matter of pride to not accept something that you haven't earned. Paul is addressing that idea here. He is insisting that no one can claim that God is unjust because He shows mercy to some and not to others because none of us deserve mercy in the first place. In our minds, we would give mercy to the ones who seem the most deserving of the mercy. So, the ones that look like they are trying the hardest would get the mercy. But then that would still make it about works. Paul is trying to hammer home the fact that God is sovereign. He gets to decide who He gives mercy to and who He doesn't. He is the one who makes the rules. We don't get a say. Again, the Western culture in us pushes back at this because we are used to living in a democracy where we get a vote, we get to help determine the outcome, our voice is heard, our opinion matters. That works well when we are dealing with humans because we are not infallible. No one of us really knows best in every situation. We are better as a group when we can all have input, voice our opinions, and come up with the best solution. But God does know what is best, every single time. He can see the end and He knows the best solution to every problem. His will and His plans are perfect. We may not understand them or like them, but we can be confident that whatever He chooses to do is right.

July 14

2 Chronicles 3-5
Psalm 80:4-7
Proverbs 17:27-28
Romans 10

Everyone who Calls

"If you confess with your mouth, 'Jesus is Lord,' and believe in your heart that God raised Him from the dead, you will be saved. One believes with the heart, resulting in righteousness, and one confesses with the mouth, resulting in salvation. For everyone who calls on the name of the Lord will be saved. So, faith comes from hearing and hearing by the Word of God." Romans 10:9-10, 13, 17 HCSB

By confessing with our mouth that Jesus is Lord and believing in our hearts, we are saved. Nothing more and nothing less. Paul is very clear. This is the gospel message. All who call on the name of the Lord believing He is who He said He is, will be saved. From Paul's time till today, men have tried to add more to it. Like the Pharisees added to the Law that God gave Moses, religious leaders throughout the ages have tried to add to the gospel message with lists of rules and standards of how to get saved and what you must do once you are saved. Unfortunately, most of those things are not biblical. The Pharisees in Jesus' day created an elaborate system of rules and regulations that everyone must follow to control them. They were in charge, and the rules gave them more power. We are quick to condemn them and yet we are guilty of the same thing. We welcome sinners in to be saved, but once they are saved, we have a long list of rules and expectations. There is a fine line, because we are told to hold each other accountable, we cannot overlook sin in a fellow believer, and we have a responsibility to help others live lives that are pleasing to God. The problem is that we must be careful that the rules we expect them to follow are God's rules and not our rules.

If God's Word speaks to an issue, then we must obey whatever it says. If it is not found in scripture or is unclear, then we cannot be dogmatic about it. God has given us each the Holy Spirit living in us to guide and convict. Something that may be sinful for me, may not be sinful for someone else. If I have an issue with self-control, having a glass of wine might be sinful for me, but for someone who does not struggle with this, one glass might be totally fine. If I have an issue with lusting, going to a beach with bikini clad women might be sinful for me, but if this is not something that I struggle with, then I am free to go to the beach. However, drunkenness and pornography are not acceptable behaviors for anyone. When someone gets saved, God does not expect them to immediately be perfect. He begins the long, slow process of sanctification. He works on different areas of our lives at different times. We have to be sensitive to His leading in addressing sin in our own lives and even more careful in confronting sin in others. We must guard our hearts from being judgmental and let Him lead us regarding addressing sin in the life of another. Sometimes He will call us to do that, but when He does it will be with gentle humility and love, never piety. Most often our response should be sincere prayer for the person.

July 15

2 Chronicles 6-7
Psalm 80:8-11
Proverbs 18:1-2
Romans 11

Grafted In

"Now if some of the branches were broken off, and you, though a wild olive branch, were grafted in among them and have come to share in the rich root of the cultivated olive tree. Oh, the depth of the riches both of the wisdom and the knowledge of God! How unsearchable His judgments and untraceable His ways! For from Him and through Him and to Him are all things. To Him be the glory forever. Amen."
Romans 11:17, 33, 36 HCSB

ALTHOUGH ISRAEL, AS a whole, rejected Jesus as the Messiah, there is still a remnant chosen by grace. Their rejection of the Messiah opened the door for the Gentiles. This chapter explains that even though the Jews were God's chosen people, when they rejected Him, He then offered salvation to the Gentiles. One day, after all of those who have believed and accepted Him are raptured, God will return His focus to the Jews and many of them will believe and be saved. While we are not of physical descent, we have been grafted into the branch. The Jews who rejected Him were cut off and we were joined to the vine in their place. This is a beautiful picture of adoption. We are not a separate tree growing apart from the vine, but we are part of the vine, joined to it. All believers, Jew and Gentile alike, who accept Christ are part of the same vine. We are one body of believers. On a tree, you do not look at the individual branches and marvel at their beauty. You see the tree as a whole. Jew and Gentile, men and women, different races, different ethnicities, different cultures, are all one in Christ.

Brian and I have a new friend from South Africa. He came to visit right before the pandemic hit. He is a pastor and found Brian through his Healthy Church Initiative website. (Brian does a lot of legal work for churches helping them prepare and update their church documents.) When we met TK, we had an instant bond with him, and he has become a dear friend. We have not seen him since then, but He and Brian meet on Zoom often and have become very close. He is a different race, his life experience has been very different from ours, we do not share the same hobbies or interests. Basically, we have very little in common, except that we are brothers and sisters in Christ. I have had this same experience with many other people over the years. The common bond we have in Christ produces a love that does not happen naturally. We are part of the same vine. Our differences are not as important as what we have in common. Satan seeks to divide people based on their differences. God brings people together in unity and love. I am not suggesting we compromise scriptural truth, but as a body of believers we need to be more focused on what binds us than on our differences. Focusing on the differences creates division and dissension. If we keep our focus on Jesus, He will unite us together in love.

2 Chronicles 8-9
Psalm 80:12-19
Proverbs 18:3-5
Romans 12

July 16

Gifted

"Now as we have many parts in one body, and all the parts do not have the same function, in the same way we who are many are one body in Christ and individually members of one another. According to the grace given to us, we have different gifts: If prophecy, use it according to the standard of one's faith; if service, in service; if teaching, in teaching; if exhorting, in exhortation; giving, with generosity; leading, with diligence; showing mercy, with cheerfulness." Romans 12:4-8 HCSB

IF YOU HAVE ever been in a Bible study I taught, you know that I am very passionate about spiritual gifts. I believe that God has designed each of us to work within the body of believers. We each have talents and personality traits given to us by God that make us unique and special. In addition, when we are saved God gives us spiritual gifts. Those gifts are given to us to prepare and enable us to carry out His purposes. They are not given to us for our benefit or to bring glory to us, but rather they are for the benefit of the body of Christ. We each have a calling within the body. We each serve different functions and when we are all working within our giftedness and using the gifts we have been given, then everything is accomplished. If we are not serving the body, then something is left undone. And if we are not doing the thing we are supposed to be doing, what we are doing is not being done in the best way. Unfortunately, I think in many churches people are doing things they are not designed to do, are getting burned out and quit serving. When we are filling the role that we are designed to fill, it gives us energy and excitement, not anxiety and frustration.

In Romans 12 and I Corinthians 12, Paul gives a list of the spiritual gifts. Each of the gifts has a purpose and is equally important. As a part of the body, we do not all serve the same purpose. We cannot all function as an eye, or as a foot or a heart. If everyone was an eye, we could see, but we couldn't do anything else. If everyone was a foot, we could walk, but we couldn't see. In the body of believers, we each have our function. Some of us are designed to teach, some to serve, some to encourage, some to give, some to preach, and some to show mercy. One illustration of how this works within the body of believers is as follows. You are at a potluck supper at church. You are walking to your seat with your plate piled high with food in one hand and your drink in the other, with a big piece of chocolate cake in a dessert plate propped on top of your food when you step in some water on the floor. Your feet fly out from under you, both plates splatter on the floor and your drink lands on top of you. For a second no one moves, and then suddenly everyone springs into action. Someone with the gift of mercy immediately comes over and begins to tell you that it is fine, they have done that before, and it is no big deal. Someone with the gift of administration begins to organize everyone to clean up the mess. They send someone to get a mop, someone to get paper towels, someone to get you a new plate of food, etc. Someone with the gift of service will immediately begin to clean up the mess. Someone with the gift of teaching will tell you how you probably should not have been carrying so much stuff in your hands at one time and that next time it would be a better idea to take your plate to the table and then go back and get your drink. Someone with the gift of encouragement would pick you up, take you to the bathroom and help you get cleaned up and then tell you that you need to hold your head up high and get back out there and not be embarrassed. Someone with the gift of prophecy would try to find out who spilled the water and did not clean it up. Someone with the gift of intercession will immediately start praying that you aren't hurt and that you aren't embarrassed. Obviously, this is a simplistic example, but you can see that all the parts are important. Everyone serves a different purpose, but combined the mess gets cleaned up and you feel better. When approaching any situation, we respond based on how God has gifted us. Your initial reaction is a good indicator of your spiritual gift. I have the gift of administration. My first response is to step in and organize the situation. That is an important function, but it is just as important that someone cleans up the mess and someone makes sure you aren't embarrassed, and you are ok. It is important that we each know our role.

There are lots of spiritual gift tests that help you figure out what your gifts are. I recommend one from Lifeway that can be found online. You can find the link in the endnotes.[9] For those who have never done a spiritual gifts inventory or may want to do it again I highly recommend that you do. Being aware of how God has gifted you can help you understand how He wants you to serve others. As I mentioned above, I have the gift of administration. Over the years I have used this gift in lots of different ways. I have organized events for women's ministry, VBS, children's ministry, events at my girl's schools, college ministry, youth ministry, etc. At different times in my life, I have been involved in different things, but God has always used my gift of administration in some way. I also score high in faith and intercession. When you take the assessment, you will probably score high in one area and then pretty high in a couple of other ones. God can use your gifts in different areas within the body of Christ at different times, but your gifts remain constant.

2 Chronicles 10-12
Psalm 81:1-5
Proverbs 18:6-8
Romans 13

July 17

Authority

> "Let everyone be subject to the governing authorities, for there is no authority except that which God has established. Give to everyone what you owe them: if you owe taxes, pay taxes; if revenue, then revenue; if respect then respect; if honor, then honor. So let us put aside the deeds of darkness and put on the armor of light. Rather, clothe yourselves with the Lord Jesus Christ, and do not think about how to gratify the desires of the flesh." Romans 13:1, 7, 12, 14 NIV

It is tempting when we do not like or agree with those who are in authority over us to be rebellious. If they are not good, we think we are justified in not obeying them. Romans 13 disputes this. Verse 1 tells us that all authority is established by God. We may not like who won the election. We may not like our parents, our boss or our coach, but if they are in a position of authority over us, Paul is telling us that we have an obligation to honor and respect them. Unless they are instructing us to do things that are directly against God's Word, then we should obey them. We don't have to agree with them, but we cannot act in a way that is disrespectful and rebellious. Jesus Himself tells us in Luke 20:25, "Give back to Caesar what is Caesar's, and to God what is God's." (NIV) Authority is good and necessary. We cannot function in society without a system of laws and regulations. As Christians, we should be the best citizens of any group we are involved in. We should always conduct ourselves in a manner that is worthy of the gospel of Christ. (Philippians 1:27) We should be above reproach. If they are not worthy of our respect, then we are to respect them since God has placed them in their position over us. In respect to God, we treat them with honor and respect. This is very difficult at times, especially when we are being treated badly, but keeping in mind that we are submitting to God's authority, helps us to submit to the earthly authorities over us.

Verse 14 also helps us deal with the authorities in our lives. If we keep our focus on Jesus, He helps us to put aside our own agenda and desires. If we focus on our rights and what we think we deserve, it is much more difficult to submit to someone who is acting in a way that is contrary to what we want. I'm not suggesting that we should not voice opposition to things that are ungodly and go against scripture. But we must do it in a way that is lawful and respectful. Thankfully, we live in a country where we can give our opinions and speak our minds, but we must remain humble and respectful. God will honor our submission to authority.

July 18

2 Chronicles 13-15
Psalm 81:6-10
Proverbs 18:9-10
Romans 14

Stumbling Block

> "Therefore, let us stop passing judgment on one another. Instead, make up your mind not to put any stumbling block or obstacle in the way of a brother or sister. I am convinced, being fully persuaded in the Lord Jesus, that nothing is unclean in itself. But if anyone regards something as unclean, then for that person it is unclean. If your brother or sister is distressed because of what you eat, you are no longer acting in love. Do not by your eating destroy someone for whom Christ died." Romans 14:13-14 NIV

THIS IS A difficult passage. We are not bound by the same dietary practices that were part of the Law. God was very specific with the Israelites about the foods they were able to eat, and which ones were banned. Reading it from our cultural perspective, this seems arbitrary, but I'm sure God had important reasons to ban those foods. They did not have the sanitation and refrigeration capabilities that we have today. God was protecting them from illness and disease resulting from many food-borne bacteria. But I think these verses can apply to many other areas of liberty. Growing up in the Baptist church there were things considered taboo that are not necessarily supported biblically. Drinking alcohol, dancing, playing cards, and even Bingo were frowned upon. Obviously, drunkenness, gambling, and dancing in inappropriate ways are sinful and should be avoided, but drinking in moderation, playing cards and dancing are not prohibited in the Bible. Adding rules and regulations that are not in the Bible makes us no different from the Pharisees. However, this passage encourages us to be sensitive to those around us in using our liberty. If we are with someone who is weaker in the faith, we should consider whether participating in any activity would be a stumbling block for them. If drinking in front of them will cause them to sin, then we should forego drinking when they are present. We should not encourage them to participate in any activity that would be detrimental to their faith.

We also need to be very careful not to judge others with rules and regulations that are based on tradition and not scripture. Looking down on others is strictly prohibited in scripture. Jesus tells us very plainly, "Do not judge, and you will not be judged. Do not condemn, and you will not be condemned." Luke 6:37 (NIV) We should prayerfully consider our actions and ask God to lead us in making wise choices regarding our own behaviors. We are not allowed to judge others based on their behaviors. Thinking we are more holy because we do not drink alcohol or have a tattoo or say bad words is prideful and more sinful than those behaviors. We are accountable to God for our actions, and they are accountable for theirs.

2 Chronicles 16-18
Psalm 81:11-16
Proverbs 18:11-12
Romans 15

July 19

Harmony

"Now may the God who gives endurance and encouragement allow you to live in harmony with one another according to the command of Christ Jesus, so that you may glorify the God and Father of our Lord Jesus Christ with a united mind and voice." Romans 15:5-6 HCSB

Unfortunately, I do not think that the word harmony is very descriptive of the body of Christ today. We are marked by division and dissension. There is division between denominations, between churches in the same denomination and within local church bodies. Churches and denominations are splitting over issues that are not significant and there is major dissension over issues that are matters of biblical truth. I am afraid that when the world looks at the church today, it does not see Romans 15:5-6 being lived out. Satan knows that when the body of believers is united in love and purpose, he is powerless to stop us, but if he can create disagreements, fighting and hurt feelings, he can render us ineffective. If he can get us focused on the ways that we are different, he is able to make us distrust each other and be suspicious and then resentment and fear arise. This should not be.

Within the Body of Christ there are many denominations. Some differences are based on theological issues of biblical truth and are very significant, and some differences are based on tradition and culture. I am certain that no one denomination has it all figured out. We will not get to Heaven and be told that the Baptists were right about everything or the Methodists or the Church of Christ. Instead of being dogmatic and arrogant, we need to be humble and teachable. There are issues that the Bible is very clear about. On those issues, there is no room for discussion. If the Bible addresses an issue, we should be united on that issue. However, there are issues that are not addressed directly where there is room for personal preference and debate. Styles of worship are a matter of preference, but the fundamental message of the gospel is not. If Satan can get us focused on things that are not of primary importance, he can take our attention off spreading the gospel and reaching people who need Jesus. Any issue that distracts from the gospel is of less importance and should not be a focus within the church. I'm not saying that those issues aren't important, but if they are taking our attention off the most important thing, we need to examine our priorities. Issues of social justice, racial discrimination, poverty, abortion, and religious freedom are all significant. We should address them within the church, but if they become our primary focus and distract from our most important calling, bringing people to Jesus and discipling them, we have failed.

Unity and peace are common themes throughout the New Testament. God knew that this would be an issue for the church, and He made it very clear that we should seek unity and avoid division. We would do well to listen.

> "Finally, brothers and sisters, rejoice! Strive for full restoration, encourage one another, be of one mind, live in peace. And the God of love and peace will be with you." 2 Corinthians 13:11 (NIV)

> "And over all these virtues put on love, which binds them all together in perfect unity." Colossians 3:14 (NIV)

> "Let us therefore make every effort to do what leads to peace and mutual edification." Romans 14:19 (NIV)

> "Make every effort to keep the unity of the Spirit through the bond of peace. There is one body and one Spirit, just as you were called to one hope when you were called; one Lord, one faith, one baptism, one God and Father of all, who is over all and through all and in all." Ephesians 4:3-6 (NIV)

> "Whatever happens, conduct yourselves in a manner worthy of the gospel of Christ. Then, whether I come and see you or only hear about you in my absence, I will know that you stand firm in one Spirit, striving together as one for the faith of the gospel." Philippians 1:27 (NIV)

> "There is neither Jew nor Gentile, neither slave not free, nor is there male and female, for you are all one in Christ Jesus." Galatians 3:28 (NIV)

July 20

2 Chronicles 19-20
Psalm 82:1-4
Proverbs 18:13-14
Romans 16

Deception

"I urge you, brothers and sisters, to watch out for those who cause divisions and put obstacles in your way that are contrary to the teaching you have learned. Keep away from them. For such people are not serving our Lord Christ, but their own appetites. By smooth talk and flattery they deceive the minds of naïve people." Romans 16:17-18 NIV

Yesterday we discussed division among the body of believers. In Romans 16, Paul addresses dealing with individuals who seek to cause division and dissension. This topic is much more personal and affects each of us. We all know people who just like to stir up trouble. It seems that whatever situation they are in, they are not happy, and they try to make everyone else unhappy, too. They grumble and complain and go behind the scenes to sow seeds of discontent. They elevate their own opinions above biblical truth. If they are in a Bible study, they may seek to draw attention to themselves by contradicting the teacher or getting the discussion off track. If they don't like something the pastor said, they will call people during the week and try to get them upset, too. They twist the truth just enough to make it sound right when it is very wrong. Smooth talk and flattery can lead many astray. Paul is very clear on how we should deal with people like this. We should keep away from them. This passage is referring to people within the body of Christ who are believers, but instead of seeking peace and unity, they are constantly stirring up division. Paul has no tolerance for people like this, and we shouldn't either.

It is very difficult to deal with people like this because they are usually influential and can persuade others to take their side. It is uncomfortable to confront people who are causing division. Sometimes it is best to just distance yourself from them and make sure that you do not fall prey to their persuasion. But often, they must be dealt with. This should be done prayerfully and with humility. Matthew 18 gives us the pattern we should take in confronting fellow believers. We should confront him and if he refuses to listen, we should take one or two others with us to talk to him. If he still refuses to listen, we should bring him before the church for discipline, and if he persists in the behavior, he should be removed from the church. Obviously, we should be very careful how this is done and who does this. If it is a major issue in the church, the leaders of the church should be involved in this process. Unfortunately, too often, people like this are left unchecked because no one wants to confront the issue and it results in division and dissension in the church. We cannot allow them to lead those that are not as mature in their faith astray. We have an obligation to the body of believers to deal with them decisively.

July 21

2 Chronicles 21-23
Psalm 82:5-8
Proverbs 18:15-16

Romans Road

THE ROMANS ROAD to salvation is a way of explaining the good news of salvation using verses from the Book of Romans. It is a simple yet effective method of explaining why we need salvation, how God provided salvation, how we receive salvation and the results of salvation.

1. *"For all have sinned and fall short of the glory of God." Romans 3:23 (NIV)*
2. *"For the wages of sin is death but the gift of God is eternal life in Christ Jesus our Lord." Romans 6:23 (NIV)*

We have all sinned. We have all done things that are displeasing to God. Romans 3:10-18 gives a detailed picture of what sin looks like in our lives. The punishment that we have earned for our sins is death. Not just physical death, but eternal death and separation from God.

3. *"But God demonstrated His own love for us in this: While we were still sinners, Christ died for us." Romans 5:8 (NIV)*

Jesus Christ died for us! Jesus' death paid the price for our sins. Jesus' resurrection proves that God accepted Jesus' death as the payment for our sins.

4. *"If you declare with your mouth 'Jesus is Lord,' and believe in your heart that God raised Him from the dead, you will be saved. For it is with your heart that you believe and are justified, and it is with your mouth that you profess your faith and are saved." Romans 10:9-10 (NIV)*
5. *"For everyone who calls on the name of the Lord will be saved." Romans 10:13 (NIV)*

Because of Jesus' death on our behalf, all we must do is believe in Him, trusting His death as payment for our sins and we will be saved! Jesus died to pay the penalty for our sins and rescue us from eternal death. Salvation, the forgiveness of sins, is available to anyone who will trust in Jesus Christ as their Lord and Savior.

6. *"Therefore, since we have been justified through faith, we have peace with God through our Lord Jesus Christ." Romans 5:1 (NIV)*
7. *"Therefore, there is now no condemnation for those who are in Christ Jesus." Romans 8:1 (NIV)*
8. *"For I am convinced that neither death nor life, neither angels nor demons, neither the present or the future, nor any powers, neither height nor depth, nor*

anything else in all creation, will be able to separate us from the love of God that is in Christ Jesus our Lord." Romans 8:38-39 (NIV)

These verses give us the results of salvation. Through Jesus we can have a relationship with God. We are not condemned for our sins because Jesus has been punished in our place. And nothing can ever separate us from the love of God.

If you google Romans Road, you will find several variations of this plan of salvation, but they are all similar. I would suggest putting these verses on index cards stapled or joined on a ring with the verses on one side and the explanation on the other. Keep them in your Bible, your purse, your car or somewhere that is readily available to you so that if the opportunity arises for you to tell someone about Jesus, you will be able to pull it out and explain it to them without having to memorize anything or stress about where to find the verses. You can expound on it from your personal experience, but this gives you the basic points that are important for them to grasp.

I hope you have benefitted from our overview of Romans over the past couple of weeks. In Romans, Paul provides us with the systematic theology of the New Testament. It is critical to understanding the foundation of our faith.

2 Chronicles 24-25
Psalm 83:1-8
Proverbs 18:17-18
I Corinthians 1

July 22

Foolishness or Power?

> "For the message of the cross is foolishness to those who are perishing, but it is God's power to us who are being saved. For it is written: I will destroy the wisdom of the wise, and I will set aside the understanding of the experts." I Corinthians 1:18-19 HCSB

IN VERSE 17, Paul explains that God did not send him to give eloquent words of wisdom, but rather to preach the gospel so that the cross of Christ would not be emptied of its power. He divides the world into two categories of people: those who are perishing and those being saved. For those who are perishing the cross seems foolish. Ungodly people think that believers and their faith are either stupid or weak. In Paul's day, the cross was still used by the Romans as a means of public execution. It was a symbol of shameful crimes and powerlessness. The Greeks and Romans believed in all kinds of gods, and they ranked them based on their perceived power over nature and humanity. The cross of Christ was seen as foolish by the pagan culture because Jesus was rejected by His own people and crucified like a common criminal. They did not understand why anyone would worship a god who was powerless to stop his own execution. Any god who would die on a Roman cross, especially as a sacrifice for human sin, seemed weak and foolish. Today, those who are perishing do not believe that Jesus was raised from the dead. They do not believe in miracles and think that those who believe in those things are foolish. Many think that to believe in miracles and a god who performs miracles is a sign of weakness and only for people who need a crutch to get through life.

For those who are being saved, the cross is understood to be God's most powerful act. Jesus did not lose a battle with the Jewish leaders or the Roman government. He wasn't overpowered or outmatched. God the Father sent His Only Son to be a sacrifice for the sins of the world. Jesus, with complete power and authority, willingly gave His life as a ransom to pay the penalty for the sins of those who were perishing. The Romans did not take His life. Jesus gave His life. Only through immense power and self-control was Jesus able to endure the cross, experience death, and then raise Himself from the dead to defeat death and Hell once for all. I imagine the angels were standing ready to come down if He had spoken the word, but He loved us so much that He chose to remain on the cross so that He could secure our redemption. This is true power.

2 Chronicles 26-28
Psalm 83:9-12
Proverbs 18:19-21
I Corinthians 2

July 23

The Mind of Christ

> "Now we have received not the spirit of the world, but the Spirit who is from God, that we might understand the things freely given us by God. And we impart this in words not taught by human wisdom but taught by the Spirit, interpreting spiritual truths to those who are spiritual. The natural person does not accept the things of the Spirit of God, for they are folly to him, and he is not able to understand them because they are spiritually discerned… 'For who has understood the mind of the Lord so as to instruct Him?' But we have the mind of Christ." I Corinthians 2:12-16 ESV

Have you ever wondered how spiritual truths that seem so clear to you are completely baffling to those who do not know Jesus? These verses explain why this is the case. When we receive Christ into our hearts, we receive the Holy Spirit to indwell us. This is not just a warm feeling of God's presence or peace. The Holy Spirit Himself dwells within us, so we have the benefit of all of the fullness of who He is working in and through us all the time. That means we have His power, His wisdom, His knowledge, and His mind. He gives us the ability to comprehend things that we previously could not comprehend. He gives us understanding and discernment to make wise decisions. He gives us the power to stand firm on biblical principles instead of caving to the pressures of the world around us. He gives us self-control and patience when it would be easier to indulge our own desires and lusts.

The ability to understand biblical truths is not natural. There are many very intelligent people who have studied the Bible thoroughly who do not understand the truths it contains. They can give you detailed explanations about the definitions of the Latin and Greek words and how they were translated. They can give you information about cultural norms and customs when it was written, but they have no idea how it applies to their own life or why they need Jesus to save them. There are also many people who are not considered to be intelligent by the world's standards who grasp deep spiritual truths and rely on God's Word to make wise decisions and live productive and fruitful lives. Intellectual capacity is not the prerequisite for understanding and applying biblical truth. Accepting Jesus as our Savior gives us redemption and eternal life. If that was the only benefit, it would certainly be worth it, but we are also given the benefit of His help in this life. He promises hope for the future and His presence and power here and now.

2 Chronicles 29-30
Psalm 83:13-18
Proverbs 18:22-24
I Corinthians 3

July 24

Milk or Meat

"But I, brothers, could not address you as spiritual people, but as people of the flesh, as infants in Christ. I fed you with milk, not solid food, for you were not ready for it. And even now you are not ready, for you are still of the flesh." I Corinthians 3:1-3 ESV

NEW CHRISTIANS ARE often referred to as "baby Christians." It has very little to do with the age of the person or the length of time that one has been a believer, but rather it refers to their maturity. There are people who have been Christians for a very long time who have not matured in their faith and would still be considered "baby Christians." There are also people who have not walked with the Lord very long who have grown a lot in their faith and are able to handle more difficult spiritual truths. When a baby is born, it does not have teeth and cannot chew up solid food, so it has to get all its nutrition from milk. As it gets older, it can eat soft baby food and eventually it can chew and swallow enough that it is able to eat solid foods. As believers we must go through this same process. When we first become a Christian, we need to learn the basics so that we have a good foundation to build on. As we grow in our faith, we can learn more and more. Yesterday we discussed how we receive the Holy Spirit when we accept Jesus into our hearts. Because He is living in us, He can lead and guide us, teach us, and give us discernment. He also helps us comprehend deep spiritual truths, but this does not happen automatically. We have a responsibility as believers to seek Him and to study His Word so that we can grow.

This happens in a lot of different ways. Being a part of a solid church where we hear biblically based sermons each week is a good place to start, but that cannot be all we do. We need to participate in Bible studies, small groups, Sunday School, and other organized programs that allow us to ask questions and be involved in discussions that will challenge us and make us want to delve deeper into God's Word. And we need to spend time studying the Bible on our own asking the Holy Spirit to help us understand what we are learning. There are countless resources online where we can find sermons, podcasts and videos that help us grow and learn. While we will never reach complete spiritual maturity in this life, there should be steady growth. We should see a difference year to year. If we are content to continue being spoon fed baby food instead of eating a nice thick steak, there is a problem, and it is time to evaluate where we are spiritually and figure out what we need to do to develop and mature. Growth doesn't happen accidentally. It happens when we are intentional and persistent in our pursuit of Him. Hebrew 5:14 says, "But solid food is for the mature, for those who have their powers of discernment trained by constant practice to distinguish good from evil." (ESV) Jeremiah 29:13 tells us, "You will seek Me and find Me, when you seek Me with all your heart." (ESV)

2 Chronicles 31-32
Psalm 84:1-7
Proverbs 19:1-2
I Corinthians 4

July 25

Integrity

"Better is a poor person who walks in his integrity than one who is crooked in speech and is a fool." Proverbs 19:1 ESV

MERRIAM WEBSTER DICTIONARY defines Integrity as "a firm adherence to a code of moral values, an unimpaired condition, and the quality or state of being complete or undivided."[10] The word integrity comes from the Latin word integer which means whole or complete. A person with integrity is "whole and complete" because they act according to the values, beliefs, and principles that they hold to. They are "unimpaired" because they do not compromise their values and beliefs for personal gain or convenience. They are "undivided" because they do not think one way and act another. Having strongly held beliefs and convictions is of no good if we are not willing to act on them. As believers we have the benefit of ultimate truth found in the Bible. God has given us very clear principles that we can use to form our beliefs. On most issues there are absolutes. The world wants us to believe that truth is relative, and that experience should determine our beliefs. That is a clever tactic by Satan to undermine God's Word and cause us to doubt. When the Bible speaks on an issue, we must not compromise to go along with cultural norms and traditions. We cannot say we believe in the sanctity of life and yet support a person's "right to choose." We cannot say that we personally believe in God's principles regarding sexual relationships, but then support homosexuality or sex outside of marriage. We must act in love to individuals but stand firmly against the public policies that go against biblical truth.

In the verse above, the phrase "crooked in speech" is easy to skim over. I have a picture in my head of a snake with a forked tongue spewing lies. I think this verse is referring to something far more subtle. Unfortunately, most of us are guilty of being crooked in speech more that we want to admit. Around our church friends we are firm in our beliefs and stand uncompromisingly on them, but at work or with our neighbors we don't want to appear judgmental or unloving, so we just don't talk about those difficult issues, or we water down what we say to avoid a conflict. In a world filled with compromise and tolerance, Christians must be different. We must be people of integrity. Those around us are longing to find someone they can trust. They may not like what we say, but they must know they can trust us to speak truth and to act accordingly. It is not loving to go along with things that are harmful and evil. Failing to speak truth when we have an opportunity to do so in a loving way is cowardly and sinful. Speaking truth in love may be messy and inconvenient. It may require us to help them find an alternative solution to their problems. It may require us to pray for them and love them even if they choose a path we don't agree with. We don't turn our backs on them, but they need to know they can count on us to tell them the truth. There are plenty of people who will tell them what they want to hear. They need someone willing to tell them what they need to hear.

2 Chronicles 33-34
Psalm 84:8-12
Proverbs 19:3-4
I Corinthians 5

July 26

In Our Midst

"I wrote to you in my letter not to associate with sexually immoral people—not at all meaning the sexually immoral people of this world, or the greedy or swindlers, or idolators, since then you would need to go out of the world. But now I am writing to you not to associate with anyone who bears the name of brother if he is guilty of sexual immorality or greed, or is an idolator, reviler, drunkard, or swindler—not even to eat with such a one. For what have I to do with judging outsiders? Is it not those inside the church whom you are to judge? God judges those outside. Purge the evil person from among you." I Corinthians 5:9-13 ESV

In these verses, Paul gives us very clear instructions about how to deal with people within the church who are living in sin. To avoid confusion, let's just say up front that we all sin. We all have sinful thoughts and act in ways that are less than perfect. That is not what Paul is referring to here. Paul is referring to willful, intentional sin. He is referring to a pattern of behavior that is contrary to God's Word. He is talking about someone who knows better and yet chooses to act in ways that are not pleasing to God. As Christians, when we are saved, we are freed from the consequences of our sins. Jesus took our punishment on the cross so that we do not face eternal damnation. This, however, does not give us license to continue in sin. We are not only freed from the consequences of sin, but we are also freed from the bondage of sin. We have the Holy Spirit living in us giving us the ability to resist temptation and flee from sin. The Holy Spirit gives us power over sin, and He convicts us when we do sin so that we can immediately confess that sin and turn from it. But He does not take away our free will. We are not robots or puppets being controlled by a higher force. We can choose to ignore His leading and continue in a pattern of sin. This is the person Paul is referring to in these verses.

The list Paul chooses to include is interesting. Sexual immorality and drunkenness seem obvious, but Paul also chooses to include greed, idolatry, reviling, and swindling. A reviler is a person who uses words to damage, control, or insult someone's character or reputation. That includes gossip, slander, angry outbursts, and foul language. Paul tells us not to have anything to do with fellow believers who do these things and to purge them from among us. Paul does not want us to become complacent about sin. When we see unbelievers doing these things, we do not have the right to judge them. God is their judge. We are to welcome them and love them. But when believers behave in these ways, Jesus Himself tells us how to deal with them in Matthew 18. We lovingly confront them. If they refuse to listen, we bring one or two others to talk to them and if they still refuse to listen, we bring them before the church for discipline. This is extremely uncomfortable, but if we do not deal with sin in our midst, we cannot expect a holy, righteous God to dwell among us. We should examine our own lives first and ask God to reveal to us any sin that we need to repent and turn from. Then we have a responsibility to hold our fellow believers accountable. We are to come alongside and help our brothers and sisters, encouraging them to seek God and to turn from their sins. We cannot have the attitude that we don't want to get involved, or it's none of our business. We need each other. This must be done with much prayer and humility allowing God to lead us in the best approach and above all it must be done in love. If I am confronted by someone who I know loves me and has my best interest in mind, I am going to listen to what they have to say. God will give us the right words if He leads us to be the one to confront. God takes sin seriously and so must we.

2 Chronicles 35-36
Psalm 85:1-7
Proverbs 19:5-6
I Corinthians 6

July 27

Temples

> "Do you not know that your body is a temple of the Holy Spirit within you, whom you have from God? You are not your own, for you were bought with a price. So, glorify God in your body." I Corinthians 6: 19-20 ESV

We often hear that our bodies are our own and we have a right to do with them what we choose. This is most said when talking about abortion, but we also hear it in reference to sexual assault and sexual activity. If we have accepted Jesus into our hearts, then that statement is not true. When we became a Christian, we accepted Him not only as our Savior, but as our Lord. He bought us at a very high price. He paid His own life to purchase our redemption. We no longer own our bodies, our minds, our hearts, or our souls. We belong to Him. We don't have the right to do whatever we choose. Our every move and actions are subject to His leading and direction. "I have been crucified with Christ. It is no longer I who live, but Christ who lives in me. And the life I now live in the flesh I live by faith in the Son of God, who loved me and gave Himself up for me." Galatians 2:20 (ESV) Our bodies are a temple of the Holy Spirit. Knowing that the Holy Spirit is dwelling in us should give us the desire to glorify God in all we say and do. In Old Testament times, God's presence dwelt in the temple. To come before God, the priest had to enter the temple with sacrifices and burnt offerings. Jesus' death, burial and resurrection put an end to the need to offer a sacrifice for sins. Jesus offered Himself as the sacrifice once for all. And then He sent the Holy Spirit to dwell in our hearts so that we no longer have to go to the temple to enter His presence. We are the temple where He dwells. We have access to Him at any time.

We would never dream of doing anything sinful at church because we consider it to be holy and special. In the same way, we should not do things in our bodies that are evil. Wherever we go, the Holy Spirit goes with us. Whatever we do, we are doing in His presence. We often think of this verse in reference to sexual activity. But this verse applies to every part of our lives. We should treat our bodies with respect and reverence. We should eat foods that are healthy, exercise and take care of our bodies, be careful not to take needless risks that put us in danger, dress in a way that is modest and not revealing, and not harm our bodies with dangerous substances like drugs, tobacco, or excessive alcohol. We have a responsibility to treat our bodies in a way that recognizes that it is the dwelling place of the Most High God. We cannot carry this too far and worship our bodies making them an idol, but also, we cannot allow our bodies to be defiled by gluttony, unhealthy living, or sexual immorality. Our bodies are precious gifts from God that deserve our protection.

Ezra 1-2
Psalm 85:8-13
Proverbs 19:7
I Corinthians 7:1-16

July 28

Used By God

"In the first year of Cyrus king of Persia, that the word of the Lord by the mouth of Jeremiah might be fulfilled, the Lord stirred up the spirit of Cyrus king of Persia, so that he made a proclamation throughout all his kingdom and also put it in writing: 'Thus says Cyrus king of Persia: the Lord, God of Heaven, has given me all the kingdoms of the Earth, and He has charged me to build Him a house in Jerusalem, which is in Judah." Ezra 1:1-2 ESV

IN JEREMIAH 25:11-12 we find the prophecy Jeremiah made that, because of the wickedness of Israel and their persistence in worshipping other gods, God was going to turn them over to Babylon and they would be in captivity for seventy years. After that time, God would rescue them from captivity, and He would bring them back to the land and fulfill His promise to them again. Jeremiah 29:10-14 explains that God has plans for the people of Israel and after seventy years in Babylon, they will call on Him and pray to Him and He will hear them, restore them, and bring them back from exile. In the first year of Cyrus king of Persia (Babylon), the seventy years had come to an end. God could have fulfilled this prophecy any way He chose. He could have raised someone up from among the Israelites to lead them to freedom, as He did with Moses. Or He could have caused a great uprising among the people. Instead, He chose to use a pagan king to accomplish His purposes. He stirred up the spirit of Cyrus to allow the people to leave Babylon, return to Jerusalem and build a house of worship. Perhaps Cyrus had heard of the prophecy of Jeremiah from Daniel, but we are not told that. All we are told in these verses is that God stirred up his spirit. This is a comforting passage because it is proof that God is in control of everything that is going on and He will accomplish His purposes. He will use whoever He chooses and do whatever He wills. No one can thwart His plans or hinder Him.

The world around us often feels very out of control. Evil men seem to be in control, and they seem to accomplish whatever they want. They can lie, steal, and cheat and it seems that they never get caught. But that is not really what is going on. God is in control of everything. He uses the actions of godly men to bring about His will, but He also uses the actions of evil men. He puts kings and presidents in power at the exact time to do what He has planned. He makes all things happen to bring about His purposes. Many people, including those in Israel, have compared Trump to King Cyrus. They believed that he was the one that God chose to rescue Israel and bring about a peace plan with its neighbors. There is even a coin minted in Jerusalem with Trump on one side and Cyrus on the other. I don't know how Trump fit into God's plans, but I take comfort in this passage because I believe that God is in control.

Trump accomplished God's plans and now Biden is furthering those plans. Things are not falling apart; they are falling into place. On days when I am discouraged by what is going on in the world around me, I remember King Cyrus and find peace in God's sovereignty and power.

Ezra 3-4
Psalm 86:1-4
Proverbs 19:8-9
I Corinthians 7:17-40

July 29

LIAR, LIAR!

"A false witness shall not go unpunished, and he who breathes out lies will perish."
Proverbs 19:9 ESV

LYING IS ONE of the surest ways to bring about failure. The book of Proverbs was written by Solomon under the inspiration of God to give us wisdom to live a successful life. Throughout Proverbs, we find verses encouraging us to live honestly and always tell the truth. As Christians, we know that from a moral standpoint we should be honest and truthful. But this admonition is not just for believers. If anyone wants to be successful and prosperous, the best way to do that is to be honest. In business dealings, if you are honest and trustworthy, you are more likely to gain the respect and loyalty of others. People who are dishonest, lie to get ahead and cheat may prosper for a little while, but their reputation will get out and they will eventually get caught in their lies. People will not want to do business with someone that they can't trust.

Some people lie to get ahead thinking that they can deceive others and progress faster in life. This may work for a time, but they will always be found out. Proverbs 21:6 tells us, "The getting of treasures by a lying tongue is a fleeting vapor and a snare of death." (ESV) Some lie to avoid punishment. They may deny wrongdoing or put the blame on others, but eventually they will face the consequences of what they did, and their lies will be revealed. Some exaggerate and embellish to make themselves look good and they end up looking foolish instead. Whatever the reason for lying, it never turns out well. Often, we get caught in a web of lies. We tell one lie and then must tell another to cover up for it and before we know it, we can't even remember which lies we told to whom. If we always tell the truth we don't have to remember what we have told different people to keep up the lie.

As believers, we must be trustworthy. People might not like what we have to say, but they should be able to rely on us to always be honest and tell them the truth. In Proverbs 6, Solomon tells us six things the Lord hates. Two of those six things are related to lying: a lying tongue and a false witness. Proverbs 12:22 says, "Lying lips are an abomination to the Lord." (ESV) John 8:44 explains that Satan is the father of lies. Satan's power is in the lie. He has no power over us except what we give him by believing his lies. We can break his power by exposing his lies. His primary weapon is lies and our defense against him is the truth. He hates truth and his goal is to get everyone to live in the bondage of lies. Jesus Himself tells us in John 8:32 that, "You will know the truth, and the truth will set you free." (HCSB) Lies lead to bondage, but the truth sets us free. May we seek to be people who live in the freedom of honesty.

Ezra 5-6
Psalm 86:5-10
Proverbs 19:10-11
I Corinthians 8

July 30

Good Sense

> "Good sense makes one slow to anger, and it is his glory to overlook an offense."
> Proverbs 19:11 ESV

I HAVE THOUGHT and repeated this verse many times in the last couple of years. We live in a time when everyone is easily offended, and we have to walk around on eggshells for fear of hurting someone's feelings or making someone mad. As believer's we should not be this way. If you are looking for something to be upset about, you can surely find it. You can be a person who always assumes the worst from others. You can pick apart everything people say to you and assume they meant it negatively. You can be easily offended and easily angered. Or you can choose a different path. You can do what Proverbs 19:11 instructs us to do. This verse explains that good sense makes one slow to anger. Instead of making assumptions, we should take time to figure out the situation. Certainly, there are situations where the worst is true, the person did mean what they said negatively, or you are being treated badly because the person is racist or sexist or just a terrible person. But that is not always the case. If we make assumptions about what other people are thinking, we may be very wrong. And even if your assumption is true, this verse tells us that it is to our glory to overlook an offense. As Christians we are told to forgive others when they wrong us seven times seventy times. It does not say to forgive if they ask for forgiveness, to forgive if they deserve our forgiveness, or to forgive if they apologize. We are just told to forgive them, over and over and over. Whatever they do to us, we are to forgive them. We do not have to continually put ourselves in the situation to be hurt by them, but we do not have the luxury of holding a grudge or staying angry with them. We are to assume the best in people. We are to love people, even if they treat us bad. We are to treat others respectfully even if they don't treat us that way. We live by a different standard than the world around us. We recognize that we have been forgiven much by our Heavenly Father. We do not deserve His love and mercy, but He freely gives it to us. Out of a grateful heart for all we have been given, we extend that grace and love to others. We can overlook the offenses done to us because God overlooks our offenses toward Him.

Being a person who is easily offended and angered also just makes you a miserable person. If you are always looking for something to be upset about, you are going to spend most of your time upset and unhappy. God knows that if we are focused on ourselves, we will always be discontented. Keeping our focus on Him allows us to rise above daily injustices and trust that He has our back and will take care of us. We don't have to defend ourselves or avenge ourselves because we trust His sovereignty.

Ezra 7-8
Psalm 86:11-17
Proverbs 19:12-14
I Corinthians 9

July 31

Self-Control

"Do you not know that in a race all the runners run, but only one receives the prize? So run that you may obtain it. Every athlete exercises self-control in all things. They do it to receive a perishable wreath, but we an unperishable. So, I do not run aimlessly; I do not box as one beating the air. But I discipline my body and keep it under control, lest after preaching to others I myself should be disqualified." I Corinthians 9:24-27 ESV

I AM ONE of the least athletic people on the planet. I did not grow up in the time when everyone gets a trophy and children's feelings were taken into consideration at all in sports. The process in PE or at summer camp recreation was that the two most athletic people were made team captains and they got to pick their teams. Back and forth they got to pick until everyone was on a team. I wasn't usually the very last person picked, but I was really close to the bottom. I remember praying on many occasions that I would not be the last because that was the most embarrassing position to be in as the one the last team "had" to take. I am, however, a huge sports fan. I love competition. I love the thrill of the game. Both my daughters are athletic (no idea where they get it) so I have seen the discipline it takes to excel in athletics. Getting up early for practice, eating healthy, running, working out, and going to bed early to get plenty of rest are all necessary to train your body to perform at its highest level. It takes a tremendous amount of self-control to excel in athletics, but it takes even more self-control to excel spiritually. Just as we need to train our bodies through exercise and eating healthy, it takes training to develop the disciplines to mature in our faith.

It takes tremendous self-control and discipline to get up early to spend time with God instead of hitting the snooze button 3 times. It takes self-control to go to bed early instead of staying up late looking through social media or playing games on your phone. It takes self-control to choose to not get angry at your friend who said something hurtful to you and to be patient and loving and gentle and kind when people treat you badly. It is much easier to just do what feels good at the time. But we are running a race. We are not working to obtain a trophy that will collect dust in our parent's attic, but rather we are disciplining ourselves to please our Father in Heaven. Our reward is eternal life, and our goal is to hear, "well done My good and faithful servant." "For the Spirit God gave us does not make us timid, but gives us power, love and self-discipline." 2 Timothy 1:7 (NIV)

August 1

Ezra 9-10
Psalm 87
Proverbs 19:15-16
I Corinthians 10

Temptation

> "So, if you think you are standing firm, be careful that you don't fall. No temptation has overtaken you except what is common to mankind. And God is faithful; He will not let you be tempted beyond what you can bear. But when you are tempted, He will also provide a way out so that you can endure it." I Corinthians 10:12-13 NIV

As Christians we must recognize that temptations are a very real and persistent threat in the life of the believer. The most dangerous thing a Christian can ever do is to believe that they are somehow immune to temptation. As a matter of fact, the more faithful we are in our service to the Lord and the more we are allowing Him to use us, the more likely we are to get Satan's attention. If we are not a threat to Satan, he has us where he wants us and will probably leave us alone. But if he sees us being effective in ministry, telling others about Jesus and having an impact on the world around us, he decides that he needs to stop us and he draws a huge target on our backs. Unfortunately, he knows us very well and he knows what to use to tempt us. Overestimating our own spiritual ability and underestimating our need for God's grace and deliverance will often result in moral failure and humiliation.

Jesus Himself taught us to pray for strength against temptation. "And lead us not into temptation but deliver us from evil." Matthew 6:13 (ESV) We are not able to resist temptation by our own power. Most of us know by experience that our willpower is not as strong as we might like to believe it is. We may do fine for a while, but there comes a point when it just gets hard to will more willpower. Thankfully, we do not have to do it on our own. We do not have to come up with some inner power to overcome temptation. The Holy Spirit who is living inside of us does it for us. We don't even have to come halfway and then He meets us there to help us. He does it all. He will deliver us from evil. He will provide the way out. But we have to take it. We have to let Him deliver us. Like a drowning person who often fights the person who is trying to rescue them, we often resist the deliverance and reject His help. "Deliver us" suggests desperation and powerlessness, not self-sufficiency. It is only by recognizing our own weaknesses and our need for His deliverance that we can overcome the temptations of the world, the desires of our sinful nature and Satan's evil schemes. This is a constant struggle. We cannot become complacent. Jesus included this in His model prayer because He knows that it isn't something we pull out on an as needed basis. It has to be a part of our daily prayer life. Acknowledging our propensity to sin and asking for His deliverance from temptation is a daily need. If we allow this to become a habit in our lives, we are more likely to recognize His methods of deliverance and take His way out.

Nehemiah 1-3
Psalm 88:1-5
Proverbs 19:17-18
I Corinthians 11

Receptive Hearts

> "When I heard these things, I sat down and wept. For some days I mourned and fasted and prayed before the God of Heaven." Nehemiah 1:4 NIV

THE BOOK OF Nehemiah is a beautiful picture of God accomplishing His will using ordinary people. Like Esther, God placed Nehemiah in the right place at the right time to carry out His plan. When Nehemiah heard what was happening in Jerusalem, he was heartbroken. The remnant who had survived the exile were in great trouble and disgrace and Jerusalem itself lay in ruins. Nehemiah was born in exile. His family had been carried away by King Nebuchadnezzar to Babylon. During that time many of the Jews assimilated into the culture there and Nehemiah's family was among them. Nehemiah grew up in Babylon and rose to the position of cupbearer for the king. This was an important role and very unusual for a Jewish young man to be given this honor with such close access to the king. It is important to recognize that Nehemiah did not grow up in Jerusalem. When he heard about the trouble in Jerusalem, he was not lamenting something happening in his hometown. He had possibly never even been to Jerusalem personally. Perhaps his mama talked about Jerusalem, or his dad had told him stories of growing up there. Maybe His grandma told him about going to the temple and about worshipping the Lord there. His reaction to hearing the news about Jerusalem is noteworthy. He wept, mourned, fasted, and prayed for a city and people he did not personally know. Nehemiah was an exceptional man. He had a tender and receptive heart. He knew that Jerusalem was important to God and to the Jewish people and it broke his heart. He didn't just hear about it and feel a little prick of sadness and then go on with his life. Nehemiah fasted and prayed for days, and he pleaded with God to help.

In His sovereignty, God had placed Nehemiah in exactly the place he needed to be, and Nehemiah took advantage of the opportunity. When the king asked why he was sad, Nehemiah had the courage to tell him why he was upset and to ask the king to allow him to go to Jerusalem and rebuild the walls. He even asked for letters so that he could get all the supplies he needed for free. And God softened the king's heart to grant all his requests. It is easy to just skim over this story without realizing the significance. At just the right time, God provided everything needed to bring about His plan. Nehemiah was receptive and obeyed God, and he was used by God to rebuild Jerusalem. This is challenging to me. When is the last time I wept for someone or something that didn't affect me personally? Am I concerned about the things that concern God? Do I take the opportunities He gives me so that I can be in the position to accomplish His purposes? My prayer today is to be more like Nehemiah.

Nehemiah 4-5
Psalm 88:6-12
Proverbs 19:19-20
I Corinthians 12

August 3

Prepared

> "There are different kinds of gifts, but the same Spirit distributes them. There are different kinds of service, but the same Lord. There are different kinds of working, but in all of them and in everyone it is the same God at work. Now to each one the manifestation of the Spirit is given for the common good. All these are the work of one and the same Spirit, and He distributes them to each one, just as He determines."
> I Corinthians 12:4-7, 11 NIV

There is a book by Max Lucado that I highly recommend to you, Cure for the Common Life. I like his simple way of explaining biblical truths that I can understand and relate to. He describes spiritual gifts this way, "You were born prepackaged. God looked at your entire life, determined your assignment and gave you the tools to do the job."[11] When we go on a trip, we pack our bags based on what we are going to need on the trip. If we are going to the beach, we pack a bathing suit and sunscreen. If we are going to a wedding, we pack a dress or a suit. If we are going to the mountains, we pack hiking boots and a jacket. We want to be prepared. When God made us, He did the same thing. Before we were formed in our mother's womb, He knew every day that we would ever face. He knew the day we would be born, the family we would have, the heartaches we would experience, the jobs we would have and the ministry that He had planned for us to do. He knew the people that He planned to bring into our lives to impact us and for us to have an impact on. He knew all our good days and our really bad days, and He prepared for those. He planned the course of our lives so that we would either come equipped with the tools we needed to face them, or He would allow events to happen so that before we needed them, we would develop them. He is sovereign. We never have to worry that we can't handle anything or that we won't be prepared to deal with whatever this life throws at us.

Not only are we prepared for the things that we are going to face, but we are also prepared to help others along the way. The unique abilities and gifts God gives us allow us to live lives that are purposeful and meaningful. We were not formed on an assembly line. Each of us was created by an artisan. David explains it this way in Psalm 139:15-16, "My frame was not hidden from You when I was made in the secret place. When I was woven together in the depths of the Earth. Your eyes saw my unformed body. All the days ordained for me were written in Your book before one of them came to be." (NIV) My friend Gloria is an artist. She makes beautiful pieces of art out of yarn, pottery, paper, fabric, or any other medium she decides to work with at the time. She will tell you that no two pieces of art are the same. She may use the same materials, but each one turns out just a little different. Each one is designed with purpose and meaning. Gloria cannot possibly know who will be touched by her artwork, or how it will ultimately be used. Thankfully, our Creator saw everything before He made us and designed us with the unique specifications that our lives required. Our task is to unpack our bags so that we understand where we fit into His plan and the purpose He has for our lives.

August 4

Nehemiah 6-7
Psalm 88:13-18
Proverbs 19:21-23
I Corinthians 13

Opposition

> "So, the wall was completed on the twenty-fifth day of Elul, in fifty-two days. When all our enemies heard about this, all the surrounding nations were afraid and lost their self-confidence, because they realized that this work had been done with the help of our God." Nehemiah 6:15-16 NIV

IN OUR READINGS for the last few days, we have seen that Nehemiah has faced opposition to rebuilding the wall in Jerusalem. Sandballot and Tobiah started causing trouble from the first day that he got to Jerusalem. Unfortunately, this is not unique to Nehemiah's situation. When we are doing God's will and are accomplishing His purposes, opposition is inevitable. Satan cannot sit idly by while we carry out God's plans. Opposition can be disheartening. It can make us question what we are doing and wonder if we are following God's plan. In those times, it is imperative that we are in constant communication with God. Throughout the whole process of building the wall, Nehemiah prayed. He sought God every step of the way. He was not fooled by their intimidation because he was listening to God instead of listening to his fears and anxiety.

Sanballot and Tobiah requested a meeting with Nehemiah, but he refused. He had a job to do and would not be distracted. One of Satan's most effective tactics against us is distraction. When he knows we have a job to accomplish for God, He tries to distract us to take our attention away from what we are supposed to be doing and onto something less important. Nehemiah recognized that they were attempting to take his attention off rebuilding the wall and he refused to meet with them. He also recognized that Shemaiah was a false prophet because he was trying to convince him to hide in the temple. Nehemiah knew that God would never ask him to do something that is contrary to His Word, so he refused. Our only defense against Satan's lies and distractions is staying grounded in the Word and staying in constant communication with God so He can give us wisdom and discernment. Opposition is inevitable, but how we deal with it determines whether Satan will be able to distract us from our mission.

August 5

Nehemiah 8-9
Psalm 89:1-7
Proverbs 19:24-25
I Corinthians 14:1-25
They Listened Attentively

> "They told Ezra the teacher of the Law to bring out the Book of the Law of Moses, which the Lord had commanded for Israel. He read it aloud from daybreak till noon as he faced the square before the Water Gate in the presence of the men, women and others who could understand. And all the people listened attentively to the Book of the Law. Day after day, from the first day to the last, Ezra read from the Book of the Law of God." Nehemiah 8: 1,3,18 NIV

THESE PEOPLE WERE so hungry for the Word of God that they listened for hours and hours on end as it was read to them. They didn't require humorous stories or creative explanations. They were not seeking to be entertained. Ezra opened God's Word and read it. That's it! He read the Bible and they listened attentively. We have a hard time reading a few passages without being distracted or interrupted. I wonder what would happen if our pastors Sunday morning just opened God's Word and read it for an hour. How would we respond? Would we be attentive? Or would we be annoyed? Would we listen to the words, or would we be thinking about where we want to go for lunch? The Bible is filled with drama and intrigue. There is murder, betrayal, adultery, manhunts, romance, war, family breakups and reconciliation, rape, vengeance, forgiveness, and any other literary plot you can come up with and yet somehow, we think it is boring and doesn't hold our attention.

I hope that in this journey to read through the Bible in a year you have found a new appreciation for God's Word and have become convinced that it is our source of hope and strength. It is our instruction book and our guide when we don't know what to do and our help pointing the way when we are lost. It is our source of comfort and peace when we are grieving and our encouragement when we are feeling down. It is our defense against temptation, and the means God uses to teach us and train us in righteousness. God's Word is also a source of rebuke and correction when we stray. "For the Word of God is alive and active. Sharper than any two-edged sword, it penetrates even to dividing soul and spirit, joints and marrow; it judges the thoughts and attitudes of the heart." Hebrews 4:12 (NIV) "All Scripture is God-breathed and is useful for teaching, rebuking, correcting and training in righteousness, so that the servant of God may be thoroughly equipped for every good work." 2 Timothy 3:16-17 (NIV) The verse in 2 Timothy tells us that God's Word thoroughly equips us for every good work. That means if we are not reading His Word and studying it then we are not thoroughly prepared for the work He has for us. God speaks to us through His Word. If we are not in the Word, we are missing what He wants to tell us. He reveals Himself through His Word. The more we get to know His Word, the better we know Him. The children of Israel understood the importance of God's Word and were attentive listeners. Are we?

August 6

Nehemiah 10-11
Psalm 89:8-18
Proverbs 19:26-27
I Corinthians 14:26-40

Who is Like You?

"Who is like You, Lord God Almighty? You, Lord, are mighty, and Your faithfulness surrounds You. The heavens are Yours, and Yours also the Earth; You founded the world and all that is in it. You created the north and the south; Righteousness and justice are the foundation of Your throne; love and faithfulness go before You. Blessed are those who have learned to acclaim You, to walk in the light of Your presence, Lord. They rejoice in Your name all day long; they celebrate Your righteousness. For You are their glory and strength." Psalm 89:8, 11, 12, 14-17 NIV

Psalm 89 is a wonderful reminder for us of the majesty and glory of God. It is easy to take these things for granted. In the world of technological advancements and indulgent consumerism it is important to recognize that it is God who founded the world and ALL that is in it. He created everything from nothing. He set it all in motion and it is Him who sustains it. The heavens belong to Him, and the Earth is His as well. It is comforting to know that He did not just set it all in motion and leave it alone. He is not just watching from Heaven to see how things go. Thankfully, our loving Heavenly Father is intimately involved in His creation. His love and faithfulness compel Him to intervene in our lives, to help us, to deliver us, and to be our constant companion. Throughout the Bible we find God's promise to never leave us or forsake us. No matter how far we stray from Him, He is always waiting to take us back. He is always there.

Verses 15-17 highlight the benefits of a life that recognizes these truths. "Blessed are those who have learned to acclaim You, to walk in the light of Your presence." The use of the word "acclaim" is interesting. We tend to think of a movie star, politician, or athletic champion when we think of this word. The Free Dictionary defines it as "to praise enthusiastically and publicly, with applause and cheering."[12] This verse tells us that those who praise God enthusiastically and publicly with applause and cheering are blessed. Do I take advantage of all the opportunities I have to praise Him publicly or am I afraid that people will mock me or laugh at me? Do I give Him the glory for the things He does for me? We had this discussion in my prayer group this week. We decided that we need to be more deliberate about acknowledging God's faithfulness and His intervention. It is easy to overlook the opportunities to point out God's work to our kids, our coworkers, family members and friends. We can choose to disregard His presence in our lives or just acknowledge Him when we need something. There is something very different about people who walk in the light of His presence all the time. Their countenance is different. No matter what is happening around them, or whatever circumstances they may be facing, they have a peace and strength that is noticeable. They can rejoice in His name and celebrate His righteousness during difficulty and heartache. He is their glory and strength. I am writing this passage on an index card to keep on my desk as a reminder to acclaim Him every opportunity I get.

Nehemiah 12-13
Psalm 89:19-26
Proverbs 19:28-29
I Corinthians 15:1-19

August 7

Resurrection of the Dead

> "But if it is preached that Christ has been raised from the dead, how can some of you say there is no resurrection of the dead? If there is no resurrection of the dead, then not even Christ has been raised. And if Christ has not been raised, our preaching is useless and so is your faith. And if Christ has not been raised, your faith is futile; you are still in your sins. Then those also who have fallen asleep in Christ are lost. If only for this life we have hope in Christ, we are of all people most to be pitied." I Corinthians 15:12-14, 17-19 NIV

SHORTLY AFTER JESUS' death, burial and resurrection, people started spreading the lie that Jesus had not been resurrected from the dead. They said that He had not really died, but was instead unconscious and woke up, or that the disciples stole His body. Both lies were proved to be false. A spear was jabbed into His side by the soldiers to prove that He was in fact dead, and He was seen alive by numerous witnesses following His resurrection. But many chose to believe the lie then and the lie is still being told to this day. Many people who claim to be Christians do not believe in His resurrection. They claim that it doesn't matter whether He really raised Himself from the dead or not. In these verses, Paul refutes this idea. Paul explains that Jesus' death, burial, and resurrection is the foundation of our faith and if it is not true then our faith is worthless. If Jesus was not able to raise Himself from the dead, then He did not conquer death and Hell and we are still dead in our sins. Paul is arguing that if it is not true, then we have been deceived. If it is not true, we are all fools and should be pitied because our hope is meaningless. If we do not have the hope of resurrection into eternal life, then Jesus is no different from any other prophet or religious leader. He can give us advice on how to live a good life, get along with people and deal with difficulties, but ultimately it is no better than self-help books and pop psychology that also offer those things.

No other world religion claims that their god came to Earth, lived a perfect life, took the punishment for our sins by dying in our place and then resurrected Himself from the dead. Moses, as great of a prophet as he was, is dead. Muhammad is dead. Buddha is dead. Confucius is dead. Baha'u'llah is dead. Joseph Smith is dead. All the founders of the world's religions are dead. Only Jesus overcame death by resurrecting and proving that He is in fact God. If it is not true, then He is no different from all the rest and He does not deserve our honor and devotion. He claimed to be God. If that is not true, He was either crazy and believed it, or He knew it wasn't true and was a liar. Either way, He is not someone we should follow. If He was in fact God, then He of course could raise Himself from the dead because He has ultimate power and control. We either believe it all or there is no reason to believe any of it.

Esther 1-2
Psalm 89:27-37
Proverbs 20:1-2
I Corinthians 15:20-34

Bad Company

"Do not be misled: Bad company corrupts good character." I Corinthians 15:33 NIV

There is an old Assyrian proverb that says, "Tell me who your friends are, and I will tell you who you are." The people who we hang out with really do affect us. If we hang out with gossipers, we are going to become gossipers. If we hang out with drunkards, we will more than likely become drunkards. If we hang out with cheaters and liars, we will become liars and cheats. If we hang out with people who are constantly grumbling and complaining, we will fall into their negativity. It usually doesn't happen suddenly. It begins with a little compromise here and then an indulgence there. Before we know it, we are doing things that we would not have thought we would do, and we find ourselves making excuses and believing it is ok. At first our conscience kicks in and we feel guilty, but the more we ignore it, the less guilt we feel, and we can convince ourselves that what we are doing is fine. And then, eventually, we believe we are justified and what we are doing is good. Peer pressure is a powerful influence. We want to believe that we will be able to influence them for good, but that is rarely the case. If you are in a hole and someone tries to help you out, it is lot easier for you to pull them down into the hole with you than it is for them to pull you up and out of the hole. This principle is multiplied if you are hanging out with a group of people who are doing things that you know you shouldn't. It is much easier for all of them to convince you to do bad, than for you to convince them to stop.

Proverbs 13:20-21 says, "Walk with the wise and become wise, for a companion of fools suffers harm." (NIV) Proverbs 24:1-2 tells us, "Do not envy the wicked, do not desire their company; for their hearts plot violence, and their lips talk about making trouble." (NIV) Psalm 26:4-5 encourages us, "Do not spend time with liars, nor make friends with those who hide their sin. Hate the company of evil people and do not sit with the wicked." (ICB) The argument we often hear is that Jesus spent time with sinners, and we cannot stay in our holy huddles if we want to reach the lost. I totally agree with this. I am not suggesting that we do not associate with people who don't have the same moral beliefs that we have. What I am saying is that they cannot be the people you hang out with all the time. They should not be your best friends. Jesus had his twelve disciples that He spent most of His time with. We need a group of people who love us, want what is best for us, and who will hold us accountable in our Christian walk. They should be the ones we spend most of our time with. They should be the ones who influence us and who we do life with. It is important to evaluate periodically who our friends are. Even our Christian friends may be having a negative influence on us if they are encouraging us to do things that do not glorify God. If we find ourselves struggling with some area of sin, we may need to look at our friends. If they are having a negative impact on us, we may need to distance ourselves from their influence and instead spend time with people who lift us up and encourage us spiritually.

Esther 3-5
Psalm 89:38-45
Proverbs 20:3-4
I Corinthians 15:35-58

August 9

PRAYpared

"Then Esther sent this reply to Mordecai: Go, gather together all the Jews who are in Susa, and fast for me. Do not eat or drink for three days, night or day. I and my attendants will fast as you do. When this is done, I will go to the king, even though it is against the law. And if I perish, I perish." Esther 4:15-16 NIV

ESTHER WAS A young girl who was humble and wise beyond her years. When she was taken to the palace, she had to complete a year of beauty treatments to prepare her to go before the king. When it was her turn, she was allowed to take anything with her that she wanted. Instead of assuming she knew how to best attract the king, she wisely consulted the king's eunuch, who oversaw the harem. He had known the king for some time and knew what he liked. Esther did exactly what he said. As a result, the king was attracted to her more than any of the other women and made her queen. In today's scripture, we read about Haman's plot to kill all the Jews because of his hatred of Mordecai. When Esther found out about the edict, Mordecai asked her to go to the king and beg for mercy and plead with him for her people. Esther was understandably scared because she knew the consequences of going before the king without being summoned. The memory of what the king did to Queen Vashti was still fresh in her mind. Mordecai told her that if she remained silent, deliverance for the Jews would come from another place, but she and her family would perish. And he told her that the reason she became queen may have been for that very moment so that God could use her to deliver His chosen people from destruction.

Again, Esther exhibited incredible wisdom. Instead of rushing in immediately to see the king, she took time to prepare. She spent three days fasting and praying asking God to help her. She also recognized that she needed the prayers of others, so she asked Mordecai to have all the Jews fast and pray for her during those three days as well. We aren't told what she prayed during that time, but I think we can assume she prayed that God would soften the King's heart and that he would allow her to come before him. And then she probably prayed for a plan to tell him. Instead of just rushing right in and tattling on Haman she invited the King and Haman to a dinner party. During that time God was at work reminding the king of the time Mordecai had saved his life and making him favorable to Mordecai. Esther did not know what God was doing behind the scenes, but she trusted Him. She had been raised in a faithful Jewish family and becoming queen did not make her forget her heritage. She is an excellent example for us to follow. Instead of reacting immediately to circumstances, we need to take time to pray and seek God for wisdom, direction, and a plan to proceed. We get ourselves in trouble when we react quickly out of emotion instead of preparation. It is also important to ask others to pray for us as we seek God. Esther was prepared because she was PRAYpared.

Esther 6-7
Psalm 89:46-52
Proverbs 20:5-6
I Corinthians 16

August 10

Amen and Amen

"Praise be to the Lord forever! Amen and Amen!" Psalm 89:52 NIV

Have you ever wondered why we say "amen" at the end of our prayers? It has become almost like a period at the end of a sentence or like saying, "bye, see ya later," at the end of a telephone call. It is just what you do to finish the conversation you are having with God. It really has much more meaning than that. Amen is an ancient Hebrew word that is a pronouncement, "So be it! Let this be done!" It is a firm and authoritative declaration. Amen implies an acceptance of the statement being made and a belief that it will be accomplished. Sometimes we say amen when we hear others praising God or giving testimony about His faithfulness. Amen is our affirmation that we agree with what they are saying. At the end of a prayer, it is affirming that we believe that God has heard our prayer and we know that He will answer us. It is an expression of faith and trust, not just a way to end the conversation. As we discussed a few days ago, Psalm 89 is a reminder to us of the majesty and power of God. The Psalmist tells of God's faithfulness and love and acknowledges that He is Creator and Sustainer of everything in Heaven and on Earth. He concludes the Psalm with "Amen and Amen." This is not just an ending to the Psalm. It is a declaration that he believes what he has said, and he is declaring, 'So be it!"

Amen is one of the few words that is pronounced almost the same way in every language in the world. It is also the same word that has been uttered as a confirmation of belief for thousands of years. We are speaking the same word spoken by the priests, prophets, and Jesus Himself. The word amen is used throughout the Bible in many different situations signifying affirmation and belief. Jesus uses the word a little differently. Instead of speaking it at the end of what He is saying, He uses it at the beginning. There are numerous times where Jesus says, "Amen, I say to you." It is often translated as, "Truly I say to you," but it is the same Hebrew word as "amen." Jesus is saying that what He is about to tell them is truth and they need to listen. In Revelation 3:14, Jesus refers to Himself as "Amen." So, He is saying that He is truth. He is the author and finisher of truth. When we speak "amen" we are affirming belief and faith in what we have said. Jesus however is affirming that it is true. He can verify that it is true because He is the source of all truth. Instead of mindlessly repeating "amen" at the end of our prayers, let's try to consciously mean that we know God hears our prayers and we trust that He will answer them. It will force us to be more purposeful and think about what we are saying when we talk to Him.

August 11

Esther 8-10
Psalm 90:1-6
Proverbs 20:7-9
2 Corinthians 1:1-14

It's Not All About You

"Praise be to the God and Father of our Lord Jesus Christ, the Father of compassion and the God of all comfort, who comforts us in all our troubles, so that we can comfort those in any trouble with the comfort we ourselves receive from God." 2 Corinthians 1:3-4 NIV

GOD USES EVERYTHING that happens to us, good and bad, to bring about good. He does not let our pain go to waste. He can take even the most horrible situations we go through to bring us closer to Him and then He can use us to help others. This life is filled with tragedy and heartache. Bad stuff happens all the time: a cancer diagnosis, a job loss, physical or sexual abuse, divorce, death of a loved one, an accident that causes permanent injury. I have heard it said that you are either just coming out of a difficulty, in the middle of one, or about to enter one. I am not suggesting that God makes the bad things happen or even that He allows them to happen so that at some time in the future we can help someone else going through the same thing, but rather that no matter what happens to us, God can use it. We live in a fallen world that is unpredictable and confusing. Thankfully we have a Father who never leaves us and never forsakes us. He is with us every step of the way. He loves us and can comfort and care for us no matter what we face.

When we are going through the shock and pain of any difficult situation, the person we want to talk to is someone who understands because they have been there before. Someone who is trying to break free from alcohol or drug addiction needs help from an alcoholic or drug addict who has been sober for a while. Someone who is reeling from the pain of divorce needs others who have been divorced to help them process how to move forward. Someone who has lost a spouse needs other widows to help them grieve and learn to keep living without their partner. Someone who has experienced a job loss or career failure can help someone who is experiencing a similar situation. We need each other. We don't have to walk through tragedy and pain alone. Our loving Heavenly Father is with us every step of the way and He provides people who can help us with whatever we need. He gives us what we need, and then He graciously uses us to help others. I think this is not just for their benefit, but also for ours, because the process of helping others aids in our healing as well. Processing through the pain with someone else helps us process our own pain. We are never fully healed from pain and tragedy in our lives. We may be functioning fine and able to move forward, but a memory can trigger the pain all over again. It is a process. Little by little, God helps us heal and continue living. Helping others is part of that healing process. Taking our eyes off our own pain to help someone else with their journey is beneficial and fulfilling. If we allow Him to use us, He will provide lots of opportunities for meaningful involvement with others.

August 12

Job 1-3
Psalm 90:7-12
Proverbs 20:10-11
2 Corinthians 1:15-2:17

The Gift of Presence

"When they saw him from a distance, they could hardly recognize him; they began to weep aloud, and they tore their robes and sprinkled dust on their heads. Then they sat on the ground with him for seven days and seven nights. No one said a word to him because they saw how great his suffering was." Job 2:12-13 NIV

THESE VERSES GIVE us an excellent example to follow when we are ministering to people who are going through difficult times. Job's friends started out doing all the right things. When they did open their mouths, they said all the wrong things and blew it, but there are several lessons we can learn from them. Their reaction when they saw Job tells us that they were good friends who loved him and cared deeply for him. They had no doubt heard about all the difficulty he had been through. They knew about his children's deaths and the loss of his possessions and how he was suffering from a terrible physical condition. Any one of those things would have been horrible, but all of them in such a short amount of time was unbearable. They wept. Then this passage tells us that they sat on the ground with him. That seems to be a detail that could have been omitted, but it wasn't. This is a beautiful picture of friendship. Job was on the ground in torment. Instead of standing over him giving him advice or judgement, they got down on the ground with him. They joined him in his pain. They didn't tell him to get up off the ground and shake it off. They got down there and wallowed in the pain with him and they stayed there for seven days and nights. That's a long time. If I stayed on the ground for an hour, I think I might have a hard time getting up, but they stayed there with him for a whole week. And during that week no one said a word. They just wept and joined him in his sorrow.

When we are going through unbearable pain the last thing we need is someone telling us what they would do or about a time when something similar happened to them. We don't need advice and we don't want to hear cliché phrases telling us things will get better. There will be a time for all of that later, but in the early days of facing tragedy, the best thing we can do is give them the gift of our presence. We need to get down on the floor with them, cry with them and let them grieve. All that really matters is that they know we love them, and we are grieving with them. They need to know that we are hurting with them and that because they are in pain, we are in pain too. Sometimes we feel like we should be strong for them, and we shouldn't cry, but I don't think that is the best approach. We should not fake emotion, but we should feel free to express the emotions we are feeling and give them the freedom to express theirs. We have discussed spiritual gifts several times lately. Those with the gift of mercy are much better at this than the rest of us. Mercy is definitely not one of my gifts, but I don't get to use that as an excuse. The Holy Spirit will provide me with everything I need to minister to anyone He places in my path. Knowing I don't have to worry about saying exactly the right thing makes it a little easier to face.

August 13

Job 4-5
Psalm 90:13-17
Proverbs 20:12-13
2 Corinthians 3

Tablets of Human Hearts

> "You yourselves are our letter, written on our hearts, known and read by everyone. You show that you are a letter from Christ, the result of our ministry, written not with ink but with the Spirit of the Living God, not on tablets of stone but on tablets of human hearts. Such confidence we have through Christ before God. Not that we are competent in ourselves to claim anything for ourselves, but our competence comes from God." 2 Corinthians 3:2-5 NIV

Our lives are our testimony to the world. Our words, actions, lifestyle, and countenance all reflect who we are. They are known and read by everyone. Whether we realize it or not, we are being watched. It is really creepy to me when I have a conversation with someone about something random and a little while later an ad for that very thing pops up on my phone. Siri is definitely watching everything I do and listening to what I say. It is a little scary when Siri does it, but it is sobering to realize that we are being watched by people as well. Our nonbelieving friends are watching us to see if our lives really are different from theirs. They want to know if this Jesus we keep talking about has any effect on our lives. Our Christian friends are watching us, too, because they want an example to follow. Our kids are watching us, even though they would vehemently deny that they are. Our coworkers are watching to see how we respond to our unreasonable boss or that annoying client. The waitress at the restaurant and the clerk at the grocery store are watching to see if we are impatient and rude like most of their other customers. What are we reflecting? Is Jesus evident in what we say and do? Does our countenance exude joy and peace or something else entirely?

Thankfully, Paul didn't just stop at telling us that we are being watched by everyone. I don't know about you, but that is intimidating. Verse 5 tells us that the confidence we have is not in our own competence, but rather our competence comes from God. We cannot possibly hope to have a testimony that is worthy of Christ. Our actions and words are not going to be perfect, and they don't have to be. But when people look at our lives, if we are allowing the Holy Spirit to lead us, they will see the difference Jesus makes. He is in the process of writing His story on the tablets of our hearts. He is working in our lives to mold us and make us into His image. It is important that we be mindful of the fact that our lives are on display. We all have bad days here and there, but we need to periodically examine our lives to see if the testimony we are giving reflects a consistent relationship with Christ. Prayerful reflection can allow God to gently prompt us to make necessary changes.

Job 6-7
Psalm 91:1-8
Proverbs 20:14-15
2 Corinthians 4

August 14

Shelter

"Whoever dwells in the shelter of the Most High will rest in the shadow of the Almighty. I will say of the Lord, 'He is my refuge and my fortress, my God, in whom I trust. Surely, He will save you from the fowler's snare and from the deadly pestilence. He will cover you with His feathers, and under His wings you will find refuge; His faithfulness will be your shield and rampart. You will not fear the terror of night, nor the arrow that flies by day, nor the pestilence that stalks in the darkness, nor the plague that destroys at midday. A thousand may fall at your side, ten thousand at your right hand, but it will not come near you." Psalm 91: 1-7 NIV

IN THE AFTERMATH of 2020, these verses may seem unrealistic at best and a lie at worst. Before the global pandemic, we could read these verses and feel comforted and even a bit arrogant. Pestilence, plague, and death may affect other people, but surely it won't come near me. Christians are protected from bad things, right? I know this is a bit simplistic, but that seems to be what this passage suggests. It sounds like a nice sentiment, but it just doesn't work that way in real life. Covid didn't discriminate based on religious affiliation. We all know Christians and non-Christians who died because of complications from Covid. So, what exactly do these verses mean? We believe that every verse in the Bible is true, so this verse must be true, but experience tells us that death is an inevitable part of life. At some point, unless the rapture happens first, we are all going to die.

This passage is a powerful antidote to fear. Yesterday we talked about how our lives reflect our testimony. The life of the believer should not be characterized by fear. 2020 revealed a lot about us. Some of it was good, but a lot of what it revealed was disturbing. I watched many believers and unbelievers paralyzed by fear. I'm not talking about a reasonable, healthy caution that led to taking appropriate steps to protect themselves and others. I am talking about a fear that resulted in complete isolation, anxiety, and paranoia. Please do not take this as a political statement. It is not intended to be that at all. As believers we are not protected from every illness, injury, disease, or tragedy. We live in a fallen world that has pestilence and plague and we are not immune. But we do not approach the tragedies and difficulties in this life in the same way that someone who does not know our Savior does. We do not have to fear pestilence and plague, not because we are immune to them, but because we know that nothing has the power to destroy us. We may contract a plague and we may die as a result, but even if that happens, we know our destiny. We know that we have a secure future. Verse 4 makes me think of an eagle protecting its baby birds. Its nest is high up in a tree. When the storm comes, the mama eagle can't take her babies inside to protect them. So, she gets them snuggled down in the safety of the nest she has built for them. And then she spreads her wings over them. The storm rages and the winds blow. The rain is pelting her back, but her babies are dry and safe under her. They are not worried or afraid because they know that their mama is going to take care of them. We can experience that same protection and peace because we know that we are secure. God is going to take care of us. He will not leave us. He will not remove His wings from over us until the storm is over. We are not promised a life with no difficulty, pain, or death, but we are promised the security of God's presence and protection as we face the difficulties this life holds.

Job 8-10
Psalm 91:9-16
Proverbs 20:16-18
2 Corinthians 5:1-15

Earthly Tent or Eternal House

"For we know that if the earthly tent we live in is destroyed, we have a building from God, an eternal house in Heaven, not built by human hands. Meanwhile we groan, longing to be clothed instead with our heavenly dwelling, because when we are clothed, we will not be found naked. For while we are in this tent, we groan and are burdened, because we do not wish to be unclothed but to be clothed instead with our heavenly dwelling, so that what is mortal may be swallowed up by life. Now the One who has fashioned us for this purpose is God, who has given us the Spirit as a deposit, guaranteeing what is to come." 2 Corinthians 5:1-5 NIV

THIS IS A great follow-up to the reading yesterday in Psalm 91. When I was younger, I don't think I really understood this passage. I did not long for my heavenly dwelling. I remember very vividly a time right after Brian and I got married when we were living in Louisville. The Gulf War broke out and I watched as fighting took place in the Middle East. At the time, I was afraid that it was the end. The news reports looked very apocalyptic. I remember crying and telling Brian that I wasn't ready for it to all be over because I wanted to have kids and live longer. I don't feel that way anymore. There have been numerous times over the last few years when it has felt like we are living in the end times. I don't know when Jesus will come back, but it certainly feels like it will be soon. I'm not scared of that now. I am ready. I can honestly say I long for my heavenly dwelling. Maybe that comes with age. As our earthly bodies begin to wear out, we long for our eternal bodies that are perfect and never age. The longer we live on this Earth, we realize that it isn't that great. It is filled with heartache, pain, sorrow, and difficulty. Our earthly tents groan and we are burdened down with the cares of this fallen world. There are good times and joyful seasons as well, but this life is far from perfect. The prospect of going to a place where there are no more tears, no more sorrow, no more pain, and no more difficulty is appealing.

But there is more to it than that. It isn't just about leaving the pain and sorrow of this life. It is also the anticipation of getting to Heaven. It is the excitement of finally getting to see our Savior face to face. "For now we see in a mirror dimly, but then face to face. Now I know in part, then I shall know fully, even as I have been fully known." I Corinthians 13:12 (ESV) We will not have to deal with our fallen nature. The struggle of the temptation of sin will be gone. We will be in the presence of Jesus. The Holy Spirit living in us places a longing in us for a place that we have never seen. There are numerous old hymns about this longing: "When We All Get to Heaven," "When the Role is Called Up Yonder," "I'll Fly Away," "Oh Happy Day," and "Beulah Land" are just a few. There are also many contemporary songs with this theme: "I Can

Only Imagine," "There Will Be a Day," "You Hold Me Now," "Soon and Very Soon," "Peace in the Valley." I would encourage you today to pull up some of those songs and spend some time worshipping your Savior and longing to see Him face to face.

Job 11-12
Psalm 92:1-7
Proverbs 20:19
2 Corinthians 5:16-21

Blabbermouth

"A gossip betrays a confidence; so, avoid anyone who talks too much."
Proverbs 20:19 NIV

THERE ARE 126 Bible verses about the tongue or the mouth. I don't think there is any other specific topic in the Bible that has more verses. Obviously, God thinks it is important. There are verses in the Old Testament and the New Testament, and they are found in 34 different books. Controlling the tongue was an issue in biblical times and it is still an issue today. Our tongues can get us in a whole lot of trouble. Gossiping, lying, deception, slander, bragging, angry outbursts, cussing, taking the Lord's name in vain, grumbling and complaining are all ways that our tongues can cause us to sin. The ability to tame our tongue is a sign of spiritual maturity and the inability to do that is an indication of immaturity. I decided I would keep my own words to a minimum today and let God's Word speak for itself on this issue.

"May the words of my mouth and the meditation of my heart be acceptable to You, Lord, my rock and my Redeemer." Psalm 19:14 (HCSB)

"Keep your tongue from evil and your lips from deceitful speech." Psalm 34:13 (HCSB)

"Lord, set a guard over my mouth; keep watch at the door of my lips." Psalm 141:3 (HCSB)

"When there are many words, sin is unavoidable, but the one who controls his lips is wise." Proverbs 10:19 (HCSB)

"The one who guards his mouth protects his life; the one who open his lips invites his own ruin." Proverbs 13:3 (HCSB)

"Even a fool is considered wise when he keeps silent, discerning when he seals his lips." Proverbs 17:28 (HCSB)

"A fool does not delight in understanding, but only wants to show off his opinions." Proverbs 18:2 (HCSB)

"The one who guards his mouth and tongue keeps himself out of trouble." Proverbs 21:23 (HCSB)

"Without wood, fire goes out; without a gossip, conflict dies down. As charcoal for embers and word for fire, so is a quarrelsome man for kindling strife. A gossip's words are like choice food that goes down to one's innermost being. Smooth lips with an evil heart are like glaze on an earthen vessel." Proverbs 26:20-23 (HCSB)

"Do you see a man who speaks too soon? There is more hope for a fool than for him." Proverbs 29:20 (HCSB)

"She speaks with wisdom, and faithful instruction is on her tongue." Proverbs 31:26 (NIV)

"I tell you that on the day of judgment people will have to account for every careless word they speak. For by your words you will be acquitted, and by your words you will be condemned." Matthew 12:36-37 (HCSB)

"What goes into someone's mouth does not defile them, but what comes out of their mouth, that is what defiles them." Matthew 15:11 (NIV)

"A good man produces good out of the good storeroom of his heart. An evil man produces evil out of the evil storeroom, for his mouth speaks from the overflow of the heart." Luke 6:45 (HCSB)

"Do not let any unwholesome talk come out of your mouths, but only what is helpful for building others up according to their needs, that it may benefit those who listen." Ephesians 4:29 (NIV)

"But avoid irreverent babble, for it will lead people into more and more ungodliness." 2 Timothy 2:16 (ESV)

"If anyone thinks he is religious without controlling his tongue, then his religion is useless, and he deceives himself." James 1:26 (HCSB)

"Though the tongue is a small part of the body, it boasts great things. Consider how large a forest a small fire ignites. And the tongue is a fire. The tongue, a world of unrighteousness, is placed among the parts of our bodies. It pollutes the whole body, sets the course of life on fire, and is set on fire by Hell. Every sea creature, reptile, bird, or animal is tamed and has been tamed by man, but no man can tame the tongue. It is a restless evil, full of deadly poison." James 3:5-8 (HCSB)

Job 13-14
Psalm 92:8-15
Proverbs 20:20-21
2 Corinthians 6:1-13

Shut up!

"If only you would shut up and let that be your wisdom! Hear now my argument and listen to my defense. Would you testify unjustly on God's behalf or speak deceitfully for Him? Be quiet and I will speak. Let whatever comes happen to me. Why do I put myself at risk and take my life in my hands? Even if He kills me, I will hope in Him. I will still defend my ways before Him." Job 13: 5-7, 13-15 HCSB

A FEW DAYS ago, we looked at Job's friends' interactions with him when they first came to visit him. They did all the right things. They got down on the ground with him and grieved with him. They cried with him, and they didn't say a word. The last couple of days we have read what they said when they decided to open their mouths. Today we see Job's response to them. When Hannah was five or six, one Sunday on the way home from church she said, "Gregg said the "S" word in church today." Gregg is our pastor and a close friend. She seemed very disturbed by the fact that he had used a "bad word" in church. I didn't know how I missed what she was talking about, so I probed further and asked her what she meant. She did not want to repeat this "bad word," but I promised her she wouldn't get in trouble for telling me what it was, and she said that he said, 'shut up." That was definitely a "bad word" in our house, and she had heard her sister get in trouble for saying it. I don't remember the context now that Gregg used it, but it certainly struck a chord with Hannah. While that is a phrase that is used far more often than it should be, it seems very appropriate for Job to say it here to his friends. Proverbs 17:28 tells us, "Even a fool is considered wise when he keeps silent, discerning when he seals his lips." (HCSB)

We have the advantage of reading in the book of Job about God's conversations with Satan. His friends did not have this insight. When they looked at all the things that were happening to Job, they were not unreasonable to think that Job was being punished for some unknown sin. But that was not what was going on. I think his response to them is proof of a personal meaningful relationship with God. Job knew his God. He was the real deal. He was undeterred in his faith. His response to them is that he will defend his ways before his God and even if God kills him, he will still hope in Him. This is the reaction of someone who is secure in their faith and in their relationship with God. He trusted God. He was experiencing unfathomable pain, physically and emotionally, and yet He still trusted God. No matter what our well-meaning friends may say to us when we are facing difficulty, we can remain faithful if we have an intimate personal relationship with our Savior. The closer we are to God; the less influence people have on our thoughts and opinions and the more we are influenced by His Word and the Holy Spirit living in us. We are able, like Job, to stand firm and resolute and hope in Him no matter what we face.

Job 15-17
Psalm 93
Proverbs 20:22-23
2 Corinthians 6:14-18

August 18

Unequally Yoked

"Do not be unequally yoked with unbelievers. For what partnership has righteousness with lawlessness? Or what fellowship has light with darkness? What accord has Christ with Belial? Or what portion does a believer share with an unbeliever?"
2 Corinthians 6:14-15 ESV

This is a difficult passage, but it cannot be dismissed. I think ignoring this passage leads to much heartache, difficulty, and pain. I believe this refers to many different areas of our lives. The one where it is used most often is in reference to dating and marital relationships. It is not intended to make it more difficult for us, but rather it is God's protection for us. The most important thing in our lives should be our relationship with Jesus. If that is our number one priority, then it will affect every aspect of our lives. Our lives cannot be compartmentalized into spiritual matters and nonspiritual matters. Everything is affected by our relationship with Jesus. Our work, our leisure activities, our financial priorities, our family time, our parenting styles, etc. Marriage is difficult. Two lives are joined as one, so there are bound to be conflicts. When both of you are seeking to follow Jesus and are living according to biblical principles, your ultimate priorities are the same and you can compromise and prayerfully resolve those issues. If your spouse is not committed to Jesus, their priorities are different, and it is very difficult to reach a resolution. There will be major differences about childrearing, how to spend your money, what to do in your free time, etc. When your ultimate goals are different, conflict is inevitable.

This also applies to business relationships. Entering partnerships with people who do not share your biblical values will lead to conflict. Differences in financial priorities, ethical responsibilities and personal relationships can cause difficulties that are hard to overcome. God has graciously included this warning to us in His Word to protect us from some of these issues. Marrying a Christian or entering partnerships with a Christian does not guarantee that we will not experience conflict, but it does at least give you a good foundation. If you are both seeking God, He can help you resolve any issues that arise. It is very important that before you enter any relationship, you prayerfully seek God to determine if that is His will for you. If the person is not a believer, it is clear from God's Word that it is not His best for you, and you should not pursue it any further. It is best not to even date anyone who is not a believer because once you are in the relationship, emotions get involved, and then it is very difficult to walk away. I know this sounds harsh, but it is God's way of protecting us from the difficulties that relationship will inevitably bring. It is easy to convince ourselves that we can change them, but it is very unlikely. If you already recognize things you want to change about them during the early stages of the relationship when you are enamored with them, that is a huge red flag. Don't settle for anything less than God's best for you and that is always someone who loves Jesus and will encourage you in your faith.

Job 18-19
Psalm 94:1-7
Proverbs 20:24-25
2 Corinthians 7

Providence

"A man's steps are determined by the Lord, so how can anyone understand his own way?" Proverbs 20:24 HCSB

GOD IS OMNISCIENT, which means that He knows all things past, present, and future and He is sovereign which means that He has complete power and authority over everything. Romans 8:28 tells us that "God is working all things together for the good of those who love Him and are called according to His purpose." (NIV) This verse in Proverbs explains that God determines our steps. He guides our way. God is at work in our lives whether we acknowledge Him or not. He has an ultimate will and purpose and it will be accomplished. In our finite minds it is difficult to reconcile the fact that we have free will and that God is ultimately in control and will bring about His purposes. The tension can be resolved in two different ways. For some people, they walk with God closely, He reveals His plans to them through prayer and His Word and they obey. They give glory to God and their steps align with His plan. For others, it is not such an easy path. They are not walking closely with God, and they react to His leading with rebellion and selfishness. For them the process of guidance often happens through discipline. In the end, God's will is accomplished either way, but for some it takes a lot longer and the process is filled with heartache and pain. Seeking Him and obeying His leading is a much easier road forward.

The second part of this verse asks how anyone can understand his own way. As we have been reading the last few days in Job, it is sometimes difficult to understand what is happening in our lives at a particular moment. We can look at our circumstance and the difficulties we are facing and completely misunderstand what is happening because we cannot see the whole picture. We are only seeing a small piece of the puzzle. It is necessary to examine our lives over a period of time and with the perspective of trying to see how God has been working to gain insight. We need His wisdom to show us what He is doing at the right time and help us grasp how we fit into His plans. It is not something we can understand in our limited ability, but through the power of the Holy Spirit He can guide us to understand enough that we are able to obey Him. The more we submit to His guidance, the easier it becomes to trust that His will is best and that His plans bring about good for us, and glory to Him.

August 20

Job 20-21
Psalm 94:8-15
Proverbs 20:26-28
2 Corinthians 8

Generosity

"During a severe testing by affliction, their abundance of joy and their deep poverty overflowed into the wealth of their generosity. I testify that, on their own, according to their ability and beyond their ability, they begged us consistently for the privilege of sharing in the ministry to the saints." 2 Corinthians 8:2-4 HCSB

THIS IS A really important lesson to learn. Generosity has nothing to do with wealth. In Mark 12:41-44, Jesus makes this very clear. Jesus and His disciples were at the temple and Jesus was people watching. He watched as many people came and put their money into the treasury. Many rich people put in large sums of money. Instead of telling His disciples how great they were for giving so much money to the Lord, He instead pointed out a poor widow who gave what would have been less than two pennies. That small amount of money couldn't do anything and yet Jesus said she gave more than all the people who gave a lot of money. They gave out of their wealth, but she gave all she had. They did not sacrifice anything to give their offering and she sacrificed greatly. Jesus is trying to make the point that He can do more with 2 pennies that are given in love and sacrifice than a large amount of money given out of guilt or in hopes of recognition. The motive of our hearts matters when we give. Paul is telling us in these verses about the church in Macedonia. They were experiencing a time of extreme poverty and persecution. Typically, when we are going through seasons of financial hardship, we tighten our belts. We limit any nonessential expenses, and we discipline ourselves to get by on less. These seasons are not typically characterized by generosity to others. We are in hunker-down mode, so we are barely getting by and have nothing to spare. That was not the case with the church in Macedonia. They begged Paul to let them give to his ministry. They were so committed to his work and to the Lord that even though they barely had enough money for their own expenses, they gave all they could to help Paul.

This is a powerful example for us. Unfortunately, I think that some people have the idea that the rich should give a lot and the poor don't need to give anything. The problem with that is that we can always find someone who has more financial resources so if we are trying to get out of having to give generously, we can easily find an excuse. We can tell ourselves that when we have more money, we will give more and until then we just aren't able. Then when we have more money, we also increase our expenses so there never seems to be any left over to give. Many churches are barely making ends meet because the people of God do not give generously to His kingdom work. Brian and I made a commitment early in our marriage to tithe. There have been seasons when this was very difficult because we weren't sure how we were going to pay all our bills, but God has never failed to meet all our needs. There have been a few times when our bills were late, but we have always had the money we needed when we needed it. I believe that God has been faithful to us financially because we have been faithful to give generously to Him. We have been blessed so much by the opportunity to give to ministries all around the world that are making a kingdom difference. There is a deep abiding joy that comes from knowing that our resources are being used for eternal purposes. I am blessed to have a husband who is committed to giving. I struggled with writing this devotion because I do not want to seem like I am bragging about tithing. Please understand that I am telling you this to testify to God's faithfulness. He has been so generous with us over the years when we absolutely did not deserve it. We have certainly not done everything right, even in tithing, but we have been consistent. I would strongly encourage you to give generously to the work of your church and to other ministries as you are able. Prayerfully ask God to show you needs that He can meet through you. Ask Him to show you how He wants to use your money and resources for eternal purposes. May we be so committed to His work that we beg for opportunities to participate as those in the church in Macedonia did.

August 21

Job 22-24
Psalm 94:16-23
Proverbs 20:29-30
2 Corinthians 9

Sowing and Reaping

"Remember this: The person who sows sparingly will also reap sparingly and the person who sows generously will also reap generously. Each person should do as he has decided in his heart—not reluctantly or out of necessity, for God loves a cheerful giver. And God is able to make every grace overflow to you, so that in every way, always having everything you need, you may excel in every good work."
2 Corinthians 9:6-8 HCSB

This is a great follow-up to yesterday's devotion. In the Old Testament, there were very specific instructions laid out about how much you had to give. A tenth of your harvest, flock, livestock, etc. was required. There were specific offerings that were given at specific times and for different purposes. It was part of the law. Jesus' death, burial, and resurrection did away with the sacrificial system and therefore we are not bound by the ten percent rule. These verses explain that we are now instructed to give according to what we have decided in our hearts. I don't think that means that we can just give one or two percent and be totally fine if that's what we have decided we were going to do. I think ten percent is pretty much the baseline and He may want us to give even more than that. I think the key is that we ask Him what He wants us to give. This may also be different in different seasons of your life. When you are young and starting out it may be difficult to give ten percent. If you seek God and ask Him to show you how much He wants you to give, He will reveal it to you. There may be times when five percent is what you need to give and other times when He wants you to give much more. He may reveal a specific amount to you, or He may tell you to give of your time and energy. The key is that we need to allow Him to lead us.

There have been many times over the years when Brian and I both felt compelled to give to a ministry. We have decided to take a few days to pray and ask God to show us how much we should give, and He has revealed the same amount to both of us. When He does reveal to you how much you should give, it is extremely important to stick to it faithfully. There will be times when it is hard to give, but it is important to trust Him to provide for your needs even when you can't see how He can. He is faithful. He will not let you down. God is able to make His grace overflow to you in every way. There is perhaps no area that reveals our faith and trust in Him better than our finances. If we sow sparingly, we will reap sparingly. But if we sow generously, we will reap generously.

Job 25-27
Psalm 95:1-5
Proverbs 21:1-2
2 Corinthians 10

August 22

Taking Every Thought Captive

> "We demolish arguments and every pretension that sets itself up against the knowledge of God, and we take every thought captive to make it obedient to Christ." 2 Corinthians 10:4-5 NIV

A FEW DAYS ago, we looked at the power of the tongue and the destructive influence it can have over our lives. Today we will examine another part of our body that gets us in a lot of trouble. Like our tongue, our minds are difficult to tame. This verse admonishes us to take every thought captive and make it obedient to Christ. So, what does that mean? How do we do that? I must admit that I struggle with this. I am a planner. I like to be prepared so I tend to go over things in my head thinking of all the problems that can occur and how I will respond if they do. This most often leads to worry and anxiety about things that usually never happen. This is not taking every thought captive. I call this tendency chasing rabbits. I chase them around and around and down dark holes until I work myself into a frenzy needlessly. Instead of trusting that God will take care of me and that He will prepare me for anything that does happen, I let my mind wander down dark paths of fear and anxiety. The things that we fill our mind with will have an impact on our thought patterns and will determine how well we are able to make our minds obedient to Christ. Filling our minds with evil and sinful things will inevitably lead to evil and sinful things coming out. If we allow foul language in, foul language will eventually come out. If we allow grumbling and complaining in, grumbling, and complaining will come out. If we fill our minds with negative thoughts and ideas, we will be discontented and unhappy.

If filling our minds with negative things leads to negative thinking, then filling our minds with positive, encouraging things will help us control our minds. Spending time reading and studying God's Word, reading Christian books, spending time with godly friends who encourage and uplift us in our faith, fellowshipping with believers, and listening to podcasts and sermons that point us to God are all excellent ways to fill your minds. If we are filling our minds with God's Word then whenever we encounter arguments and pretensions that are contrary to the knowledge of God, we recognize them immediately and can demolish them completely. When a negative or wrong thought comes into our minds, we can dismiss it right away as being false and it does not have control over us. The best time to demolish an argument is right when it begins to form so that it does not have time to take root. This is difficult to do, and we need the help of the Holy Spirit to recognize when we are allowing our minds to stray down paths that are not pleasing to God. It is often subtle at first and we don't even realize it until we are way down the rabbit hole. I would encourage you to pray today and ask God to reveal areas in your thought life where you need to take your thoughts captive to make them obedient to Christ.

Job 28-29
Psalm 95:6-11
Proverbs 21:3-4
2 Corinthians 11

August 23

Wisdom and Understanding

"Where then does wisdom come from? Where does understanding dwell? God understands the way to it, and He alone knows where it dwells, for He views the ends of the Earth and sees everything under the heavens. When He established the force of the wind and measured out the waters, when He made a decree for the rain, and a path for the thunderstorm, then He looked at wisdom and appraised it; He confirmed it and tested it. And He said to the human race, 'The fear of the Lord--- that is wisdom, and to shun evil is understanding.'" Job 28:20, 23-28 NIV

THE FEAR OF the Lord is difficult for us to grasp because we have grown up in a culture where God's love and mercy are highlighted, and His holiness and justice are downplayed. Many modern churches never discuss His wrath and the image in our heads is of a gentle, meek God who gives us a hug when we mess up and overlooks our sin. In that context, it is difficult to imagine why we would have any reason to fear God. His wrath is reserved for really bad people and His vengeance is only delivered to our enemies. Many people have the idea that the fear of the Lord is talking about respect and awe, which I think are certainly important, but I think that the fear of the Lord is actual fear. It is not figurative, misleading, or overstated. He knows everything about us, our thoughts, our actions, our intentions, and our deepest darkest secrets. One day we will stand before Him in judgment. God is to be feared, not just because of what He might do to us, but because of who He is. The reality of a holy, almighty, all powerful, eternal God who is above all, beyond all and sovereign over all should make us tremble in His presence. He is not "the man upstairs," or "the big guy." He is the Lord Almighty, Creator of Heaven and Earth, Savior, Redeemer, Yahweh. He is our Heavenly Father, and He loves us, but we must approach Him with respect and reverence.

Most of us would be horrified if our friends and family knew everything we thought, desired, spoke and did because we care what they think of us, and we don't want them to know all the bad stuff about us. Are we that concerned about God knowing all those things? The knowledge that He is fully aware of everything should fill us with humility and appreciation that He knows all our secrets and He still loves us so much that He died to save us from the punishment His justice requires. It should also give us the desire to shun evil and live lives that are pleasing to Him. Sin is abhorrent to Him, and we should not treat it lightly. In a sermon recently, the pastor said, "Where sin isn't serious, Jesus isn't precious." Our sin cost Him His life so we cannot treat it lightly. Job grasped these spiritual truths that the fear of the Lord is wisdom and to shun evil is understanding. Several other scripture verses instructing us to fear the Lord are found in Proverbs 1:7, 3:7, 8:13, 14:26-27, Psalm 33:8, 86:11, 111:10, and Philippians 2:12-13.

Job 30-31
Psalm 96:1-6
Proverbs 21:5-6
2 Corinthians 12

Weakness

"But He said to me, 'My grace is sufficient for you, for power is perfected in weakness.' Therefore, I will most gladly boast all the more about my weaknesses, so that Christ's power may reside in me. So, I take pleasure in weaknesses, insults, catastrophes, persecutions, and in pressures, because of Christ. For when I am weak, then I am strong." 2 Corinthians 12:9-10 HCSB

WE DON'T LIKE to think about our weaknesses. We all have them; areas in our lives where we know we struggle. Those are the areas we like to keep hidden from other people, from God and even from ourselves. We don't talk about them and hope no one will notice them. The funny thing is that often these are the areas God wants to use to bring Himself glory. He wants to bring them to light so that He can shine through them. If a clay pot has a crack in it and you put a light down in it, you can't see the light through the perfect part of the clay, but you can see the light peeking out through the crack. He can make even the ugly parts of our lives beautiful when we allow His glory to shine through them. Our weaknesses produce humility in us which is always pleasing to God. Our strengths tend to create pride and it is very difficult for God to work through our pride. Weaknesses also produce the recognition that we need God's help. We know in those areas we cannot succeed without Him, and we are drawn to Him. In the things we perceive as our strengths, we aren't as likely to turn to Him for help. We tend to think we can handle those things on our own and we save Him for when we need Him.

We also have the idea that Satan uses our weaknesses to tempt us, but then he surprises us and uses the areas of our greatest strength to cause our greatest failures. Because we are not relying fully on God in those areas, Satan sees that as an opportunity to intervene. In our weaknesses, God's presence provides our strength and protection. Paul says that he takes pleasure in weaknesses, insults, catastrophes, persecutions, and pressures because of Christ. I can't say that I take pleasure in those things, but I can see that they are beneficial in bringing glory to God. It is easier to see that after the fact than during the struggle. Instead of attempting to hide my weaknesses, I need to acknowledge them and ask God to use them in whatever way He can. And I need to be cautious in the areas where I think I am strong not to become prideful and fail to seek His help. There is no area of my life where I don't need His constant help and guidance.

Job 32-33
Psalm 96:7-13
Proverbs 21:7-8
2 Corinthians 13

August 25

He is Coming

"Say among the nations: 'The Lord reigns. The world is firmly established; it cannot be shaken. He judges the peoples fairly.' Let the heavens be glad and the Earth rejoice; let the sea and all that fills it resound. Let the fields and everything in them exult. Then all the trees of the forest will shout for joy before the Lord, for He is coming—He is coming to judge the Earth. He will judge the world with righteousness and the peoples with faithfulness." Psalm 96:10-13 HCSB

THE LORD REIGNS! God has established the Earth and everything in it is under His power and authority. It cannot be shaken. It is fixed and immovable. His sovereignty and power are not temporary and changing like the powers of this world. Governments and leaders come and go. World powers rise and fall, but God's reign is eternal and firm. Nothing can remove Him from power and control. I love the imagery of the next verses. I imagine the sea and all its creatures shouting praises to God, the grass of the fields standing tall in praise, all the woodland animals joining in songs and the trees of the forests shouting for joy at the glory of God. Isaiah 55:12 tells us, "You will indeed go out with joy and be peacefully guided; the mountains and the hills will break into singing before You and all the trees of the field will clap their hands." (HCSB) In Luke 19:40 Jesus says, "I tell you, if they were to keep silent, the stones would cry out." (HCSB) Creation stands ready to praise its Creator. "The heavens declare the glory of God, and the sky proclaims the work of His hands. Day after day they pour forth speech; night after night they communicate knowledge." Psalm 19:1 (HCSB) If we fail to proclaim the praises of our God, all of nature will declare it for us. As I am sitting here on my back porch writing this devotional, 2 deer wandered through my yard into the woods and I am listening to a crow, a woodpecker and a few other random birds singing. The trees are swaying in the wind, and I hear the sound of distant thunder. Creation is praising its Creator all around me. It would be easy to overlook and dismiss the sounds of nature instead of recognizing that all of nature is exulting God. If I fail to declare His glory, the deer and the birds will certainly proclaim His praises!

The next verse gives us a stark reminder that He is coming. We don't know the day and hour, but He is coming back to judge the living and the dead. He will judge all the Earth with righteousness and faithfulness. He is the only One who is worthy to judge. He is the only One who is completely righteous and holy. He has the authority and the integrity to judge because He alone is holy and just. Not only is He righteous, but He is also faithful. He has never let us down. Even if we are faithless, He is always faithful. No matter how many times we let Him down by our sin and selfishness, He remains ever faithful.

Job 34-35
Psalm 97:1-5
Proverbs 21:9-10
Galatians 1

August 26

A Nagging Wife

"Better to live on the corner of a roof than to share a house with a nagging wife."
Proverbs 21:9 HCSB

OUCH! I THINK most of us need to be reminded of this verse periodically. I try hard not to be a nagging wife. I'm not sure why, but when I think of a nagging wife, the image of Gladys Kravitz from Bewitched comes to mind. She was always nagging her husband and everyone else. Her voice was so annoying like fingernails on a chalk board. I DO NOT want to be like her! But I am a list maker. I get a strange pleasure out of checking things off my to-do list. Unfortunately, that lends itself to nagging when the list is undone for longer than I want. Brian hates it when I ask him to do something and then something else and one more thing. After thirty-one years of marriage, we have a system. He wants a list. He does the things on the list but hates it when I keep adding to the list. He would rather I just give him the full list to start. This can be complicated when I remember something after I have made the list. Since we moved into our new house, every weekend I have a to-do list for him, and he works the list without complaint unless I try to add to it and then he is not so compliant.

I can't tell you the number of times I have said to the girls that it is not so much what they say as how they say it that is the problem. If you ask someone nicely and humbly to do something they are much more likely to do it than if you demand it. Brian hates when I say, "I need you to..." I'm not sure exactly what about this pushes his buttons, but I have learned that is not a good way to start a request to him. If, however, I say, "could you please help me with..." he is always willing to help me in any way he can. I think most of our husbands love us and want to help us but nagging and complaining never gets the result we want. Pride leads to demanding our rights and expecting them to meet our expectations without considering their feelings and plans. In biblical times, houses had flat roofs and so a man could escape his nagging wife by going up on the roof to be alone. It was the biblical equivalent of a man cave. I pray that my husband doesn't have to escape to his man cave to get away from my nagging.

August 27

Job 36-37
Psalm 97:6-12
Proverbs 21:11-12
Galatians 2

Christ in Me

> "I have been crucified with Christ and I no longer live but Christ lives in me. The life I now live in the body, I live by faith in the Son of God, who loved me and gave Himself for me." Galatians 2:19-20 HCSB

CHRIST WAS CRUCIFIED for our sin. By faith, we trust that His death paid for our sin. We are crucified with Him, our sin died with Him on the cross. Our sinful self dies and is replaced by the resurrected Christ in us. We continue to live in our mortal bodies, but our lives are no longer controlled by our sinful selves but are now directed by our faith in Christ. While our sinful nature is still present and at work within us, we have the power of the Holy Spirit living within us as well to help us overcome the power of temptation and the pull of our sinful nature. The life we now live in the body is bound by the pull of this fallen world, but we live by faith in Jesus. Paul explains in this verse Jesus' motive for dying for us. The law was meant to bind and restrict, but Jesus died to set us free. His love for us motivated Him to die a cruel death in order that we might live. We do not face this life alone. He is with us. Whatever we encounter, good or bad, He has gone before us and is beside us and is our rear guard. He surrounds us with His presence.

We are no longer in control of our lives. Christ has bought us. He has paid a very high price for us, and we belong to Him. He has saved us from death and Hell, and we owe our very lives to Him. He is Lord and we submit to His dominion and authority over every aspect of our lives. What areas do you need to submit to Him? Are there any areas you have been holding out control over? Ask Him to reveal to you if there is anything you need to relinquish to His authority. He is Lord!

Job 38-39
Psalm 98:1-3
Proverbs 21:13-15
Galatians 3

The Lord Speaks

"Where were you when I established the Earth? Tell Me if you have understanding." Who fixed its dimensions? Certainly, you know! Who stretched a measuring line across it? Who supports its foundations?

Who enclosed the sea behind doors when it burst from the womb, when I made the clouds its garment and thick darkness its blanket, when I determined its boundaries and put its bars in place, when I declared: 'You may come this far, but no farther; your proud waves stop here.'?

Have you ever in your life commanded the morning or assigned the dawn its place so it may seize the edges of the Earth and shake the wicked out of it?

Have you traveled to the sources of the sea or walked in the depths of the oceans?

Have the gates of death been revealed to you? Have you seen the gates of deep darkness? Have you comprehended the extent of the Earth? Tell Me if you know all this.

Where is the road to the home of light? Do you know where darkness lives, so you can lead it back to its border?

Have you entered the place where the snow is stored? Or have you seen the storehouses of hail, which I hold in reserve for times of trouble, for the day of warfare and battle?

Where is the source of the east wind that spreads across the Earth? Who cuts a channel for the flooding rain or clears the way for the lightning, to bring rain on an uninhabited land, on a desert with no human life, to satisfy the parched wasteland and cause the grass to sprout?

Can you bring out the constellations in their season and lead the Bear and her cubs?

Do you know the laws of Heaven? Can you impose its authority on Earth? Can you command the clouds so that a flood water covers you? Can you send out lightning bolts, and they go?

Who put wisdom in the heart or gave the mind understanding? Job 38 (HCSB)

QUESTIONING GOD IS utterly pointless. He is sovereign. He is almighty. He is Lord. In every situation He knows best, and we are foolish to doubt. It is good to read Job 38 periodically to humble us and remind us that He is God, and we are not!

Job 40-42
Psalm 98:4-9
Proverbs 21:16-17
Galatians 4

August 29

Restoration and Hope

> "After Job had prayed for his friends, the Lord restored his prosperity and doubled his previous possessions. So, the Lord blessed the last part of Job's life more than the first. Job lived 140 years after this and saw his children and their children to the fourth generation. Then Job died, old and full of days." Job 42:10, 12, 16 HCSB

LIFE IS UNPREDICTABLE. Job's life was going along just fine and then he was blindsided by pain and heartache. Sometimes our pain and suffering are a consequence of our poor choices or sin. Sometimes it is a result of the sin and bad choices of someone else. But sometimes, it is no one's fault. A tragic accident kills someone you love, a bad economy causes you financial problems, an illness strikes out of the blue, or you lose your job because your company had to downsize. In those times, it is very difficult to see God's hand at work. Like Job, we may be tempted to wallow in our pain and grief and even question why God would allow these things to happen to us. I'm so glad the Bible is not full of stories about how the people of God were perfect and always did everything they were supposed to do. I'm glad we get to see how they reacted to life. We get to see that they are real people just like us with real emotions, real fears, real joys, and real weaknesses. Job did not react to losing everything he had and then becoming very sick by rejoicing and praising God for his troubles. That would be ridiculous. Job reacted in just the way that is reasonable and expected. He cried and mourned and asked God why. But Job did not cross the line. He knew who God was and he feared God. He remained faithful even in his suffering. His wife suggested that he curse God and die, but he did not do that. When God confronted Job, he was humble and repented. And then God restored him completely.

God responds to humble and grateful hearts. Restoration might not always be immediate. Depending on the circumstance, restoration may take a long time. A financial failure, a marriage infidelity resulting in divorce, an addiction that leads to public humiliation, a wayward child, or a broken relationship all can leave us in the pit of despair like Job. At the time, it is hard to imagine a time when we will ever feel good again. Whether we caused the pain or are just suffering the consequences, it is hard to feel hopeful. And yet, our God is the God of hope. He brings beauty out of ashes and joy out of sorrow. If we turn to Him in our darkest moments instead of becoming cynical and bitter, He will restore us. He has good plans for us. He desires good for us. He is our loving Father who wants us to be happy and to live in peace. He may discipline us for a season, but His plan is always to bring about complete restoration. During the seasons of pain and sorrow, we can experience a depth of intimacy with Him that is not possible any other way. Like Job, we will be able to say,

"My ears had heard of You, but now my eyes have seen You." Job 42:5 (NIV) We may have head knowledge about God, but it is in seasons of difficulty and sorrow that we can experience the depth of His love and mercy.

Ecclesiastes 1-2
Psalm 99:1-5
Proverbs 21:18-19
Galatians 5

Love Your Neighbor as Yourself

> "For you were called to be free, brothers; only don't use this freedom as an opportunity for the flesh but serve one another in love. For the entire law is fulfilled in one statement: Love your neighbor as yourself. But if you bite and devour one another, watch out, or you will be consumed by another. I say then, walk by the Spirit and you will not carry out the desire of the flesh. But the fruit of the Spirit is love, joy, peace, patience, kindness, goodness, faith, gentleness, self-control. Against such things there is no law." Galatians 5:13-16, 22-23 HCSB

"The entire law is fulfilled in one statement: Love your neighbor as yourself." The law filled scrolls and scrolls! There were rules and regulations for everything including religious festivals, food, sacrifices, work, leisure time, money, illnesses, debts, etc. They even had specific laws about a woman's period. Paul says in these verses that the whole purpose of the law is loving our neighbor as ourselves. God knew from the very beginning that we are selfish, sinful beings, and we would not treat each other with love all the time. He gave us a system of rules and regulations that would teach us how to treat others. Unfortunately, the law didn't really work because we still tended to treat others in ways that were not loving. We bite and devour others, and, in the end, we are the ones who are consumed. So, in His love for us, He provided a better way. On our own, we are incapable of truly loving others and treating them like we would want to be treated. He gave us a helper to assist us. When we come to Jesus as our Savior, He provides the Holy Spirit who comes and lives in us. He fills us with His presence, and we no longer have to walk on our own strength and power, but we have access to His strength and power. Verses 22-23 tell us that the fruit or benefit of having the Spirit indwelling us are love, joy, peace, patience, kindness, goodness, faith, gentleness, and self-control.

We are not capable of manufacturing those things ourselves. We are not loving, patient, gentle, good, etc. They do not come naturally to us, and they aren't supposed to. We are sinful, flawed humans who are selfish, mean, bad, and have very little self-control. But through the power of the Holy Spirit, we can exhibit all those traits in increasing measure as we grow and mature in our faith. We cannot be patient with difficult people, but the Holy Spirit who lives in us can. We can't exhibit self-control when tempted, but the Holy Spirit in us can. We can't have joy when we are facing trials, but He can. We can't be kind to people who are mean and rude, but the Holy Spirit can do that through us. As we grow in our faith, He begins the slow process of developing those things in us. Just like a body builder must develop muscles by using them, we develop these fruits by being forced to apply them. We develop patience by being in situations where we need patience. We develop self-control by making wise choices over and over. And we learn to love others by developing relationships where we have to consider others' needs above our own. As we cooperate with His leading, we ae able to experience the fruit in our lives.

August 31

Ecclesiastes 3-5
Psalm 99:6-9
Proverbs 21:20-21
Galatians 6

Time and Seasons

"There is an occasion for everything, and a time for every activity under Heaven; a time to give birth and a time to die; a time to plant and a time to uproot; a time to kill and a time to heal; a time to tear down and a time to build; a time to weep and a time to laugh; a time to mourn and a time to dance; a time to throw stones and a time to gather stones; a time to embrace and a time to avoid embracing; a time to search and a time to count as lost; a time to keep and a time to throw away; a time to tear and a time to sew; a time to be silent and a time to speak; a time to love and a time to hate; a time for war and a time for peace." Ecclesiastes 3:1-8 HCSB

ECCLESIASTES IS A depressing book. Solomon had everything anyone could possibly want. He had money, fame, women, possessions, wisdom, power, basically everything and he realized that none of it really mattered. None of it was the secret to contentment and happiness. People chase after the same things today and come to the same conclusion. When you climb to the top of the ladder, whatever ladder that might be, you realize it is just propped against a blank wall. Fame is fleeting, the richest people in the world are some of the most miserable, power can be taken away or lost in an instant, and possessions don't provide love and intimacy. Solomon's wisdom made him realize that nothing this world can offer is worth anything. It is a good reminder for us of the dangers of relying on the security and pleasure of temporal things. Value and meaning in this life are found in the things that are eternal. Our relationship with God, loving and serving people, building others up in their faith, and telling people about Jesus bring a sense of fulfillment and purpose that possessions and money are incapable of giving.

While most of Ecclesiastes is anything but encouraging, chapter 3 is comforting to me. I've been thinking a lot about seasons lately. Looking back over my life, there have been many different seasons I can identify. Seasons of laughter and tears, mourning and dancing. I've given birth to two beautiful daughters, and I am about to have the joy of watching as one of them gives birth to my granddaughter. I have spent seasons in hospital rooms with loved ones as they battled illnesses that ended in death. I have had seasons of health scares myself where I have faced my own mortality followed by seasons of thanksgiving for healing. There have been times when I knew I needed to speak up and other times when I needed to keep my mouth shut. I have watched as war broke out in other countries and I've seen what looked like war zones on the streets of cities across this country. But they are just seasons. War is always followed by a time of peace. Tearing down is followed by building up. Plowing is followed by planting and that is followed by reaping what we have sown. No matter how bad things get, another season is around the corner. Seasons come and go, but God is always faithful. He is with us through every season we face, and He brings good out of bad. He is our strength for today and our hope for tomorrow.

September 1

Ecclesiastes 6-8
Psalm 100
Proverbs 21:22-24
Ephesians 1

Thanksgiving and Praise

> "Enter His gates with thanksgiving and His courts with praise. Give thanks to Him and praise His name. For Yahweh is good, and His love is eternal; His faithfulness endures through all generations." Psalm 100:4-5 HCSB

Living in an instant gratification culture, I'm afraid that thanksgiving is often not our default position. When we don't get exactly what we want when we want it, we tend to resort to grumbling and complaining instead of recognizing the many things that we have to be thankful for. We are bombarded with "have it your way" and "you deserve the best" and "don't settle for anything less than what you want" messages everywhere we turn. We also have been conditioned by social media to see the "perfect" lives everyone else has and think that ours just doesn't measure up. This leads to dissatisfaction and discontentment and does not foster thanksgiving and praise. I am convinced that to develop a grateful heart, we must be intentional. It does not come naturally. We have to train our minds to recognize our blessings and to look for the good in every situation. We can always find so much to be thankful for. We are abundantly blessed even during difficult seasons of our lives. We may be experiencing heartache and pain, but we have the love and protection of our faithful Heavenly Father who is good and never leaves us. He is always working on our behalf to bring about good for us.

There are lots of strategies to train our hearts to be thankful. Keeping a journal of blessings where you can regularly record things you are thankful for is a good place to start. Keep it somewhere that is easily accessible so you can enter things in it often and look back over it to remind yourself that you are abundantly blessed. I also write my prayer requests on small business cards and then record when it was answered. I keep them in a jar on my desk. Every Thanksgiving my family reads the answered prayers from the past year. We are always amazed at how many of the answered prayers we had forgotten about. God intervenes in our lives so often that it is easy to take it for granted and forget to thank Him for everything He does.

One of my favorite songs as a little girl was **"Count Your Blessings."**[13]

When upon life's billows you are tempest tossed,
When you are discouraged, thinking all is lost,
Count your many blessings, name them one by one,
And it will surprise you what the Lord has done.

Are you ever burdened with a load of care?
Does the cross seem heavy you are called to bear?
Count your many blessings, every doubt will fly,
And you will be singing as the days go by.

When you look at others with their lands and gold,
Think that Christ has promised you His wealth untold.
Count your many blessings, money cannot buy,
Your reward in Heaven, nor your home on high.

So, amid the conflict, whether great or small,
Do not be discouraged, God is over all.
Count your blessings, angels will attend,
Help and comfort give you to your journey's end.

September 2

Ecclesiastes 9-10
Psalm 101:1-4
Proverbs 21:25-26
Ephesians 2:1-10

Divine Appointments

"For we are His creation, created in Christ Jesus for good works, which God prepared ahead of time so that we should walk in them." Ephesians 2:10 HCSB

As you all know, I am a planner. If I am going on a trip, I plan the itinerary. I know where we will stay, where we will eat and what activities we will do. I even plan unstructured time because my family likes time to just chill. They make fun of me, but as a result, things go more smoothly because we are not scrambling to find a place to eat, and we don't waste time trying to figure out what we are going to do. I am almost that structured in my day-to-day life as well. I make lists every day and check off my list. Unfortunately, this can lead to frustration and irritation when things don't go the way I planned. This has always been a struggle for me, but I am beginning to recognize that often when things don't go as I plan, it is God setting up divine appointments for me. Thinking back over the last few months, I can think of several times when my plans got altered that resulted in me being able to minister to someone that I would not have been able to if I had been on my schedule. Instead of getting frustrated, I am learning that His schedule is always better than mine. Admittedly, I am still growing in this area and there are more times than not that I still get irritated in the moment. When I look back at it, I can see how God orchestrated my timing so that I would be at the right place at the right time, or He made me aware of a need that I was able to meet because I was not off doing something else I had planned to do. Proverbs 19:21 says, "Many are the plans in a person's heart, but it is the Lord's purpose that prevails." (NIV)

I sometimes miss these divine appointments because I am too fixated on my plans to take time to recognize the opportunities He puts in front of me. This verse in Ephesians may be referring to big things in our lives like our career path or ministry opportunities, but I also think it is referring to these everyday little things that may not seem like a big deal at the time but may be God intervening in someone's life for a specific purpose. He knows our hearts and minds and He knows the exact time to send someone to tell us what we need to hear. He can use us to bring that message if we are listening to His prompting. An encouraging word to someone who is really struggling, a smile when someone is having a bad day, a big hug to someone who is feeling unloved, a wise word of advice for someone who is struggling to make a decision, dropping what you are doing to help someone else with a task, or just providing a listening ear for someone who is hurting may alter your plans slightly, but may have a huge impact on someone else. The more we allow God to use us to be His hands and feet to the world around us, the more we will find ourselves in these divine appointments that only He could orchestrate.

Ecclesiastes 11-12
Psalm 101:5-8
Proverbs 21:27-28
Ephesians 2:11-22

Built Together

> "So, then you are no longer foreigners and strangers, but fellow citizens with the saints, and members of God's household, built on the foundation of the apostles and prophets, with Christ Jesus Himself as the cornerstone. The whole building, being put together by Him, grows into a holy sanctuary in the Lord. You also are being built together for God's dwelling in the Spirit." Ephesians 2:19-22 HCSB

THIS PASSAGE IS such a beautiful picture of God's plan of redemption in a nutshell. God did not have two plans. He didn't start out with the Jewish people and then decide that wasn't going to work so He turned to the Gentiles. It was one plan from the beginning. He built the foundation on Abraham, Isaac, and Jacob, and then the prophets. Then the apostles built on that faith. Now we are one faith, one body of believers. Everyone who calls on the name of the Lord are joined together as one. Jews, Gentiles, male and female, every race, every nationality are one body in Christ. We serve One God who is Creator, Lord, Savior, Redeemer of all. We are all members of God's household. There are differences in traditions, culture, temperament, gifts, talents, and rituals, but there should be no division. We all work together to function as a body, each with its purpose and each bringing an important piece of the puzzle to form a holy sanctuary in the Lord.

We are not foreigners or strangers. We are not intruding or invading God's plan. We were not an afterthought. He didn't just agree to let us in because the Jews were not faithful. God knew everything before it ever happened so He knew exactly how it would all play out. His plan was to bring redemption to the Jews first and then to the Gentiles. "Because it is God's power for salvation to everyone who believes, first to the Jew, and also to the Greek. For in it God's righteousness is revealed from faith to faith, just as it is written: The righteous will live by faith." Romans 1:16-17 (HCSB)

Jesus is the cornerstone. Since ancient times, builders have used cornerstones in their construction projects. A cornerstone was the most important stone, placed in the corner of the building to guide the workers in the construction. Once it was set, it was the basis for determining every measurement. Everything was aligned to it. As the cornerstone of the church, Jesus is our standard of measure and alignment. In Isaiah we find a reference to the cornerstone that is foretelling about the Messiah. "See, I lay a stone in Zion, a tested stone, a precious cornerstone for a sure foundation; the one who relies on it will never be put to shame." Isaiah 28:16-17 (NIV) This verse is affirmed in I Peter 2:6. The promised Messiah was the foundation of the faith of the Old Testament saints and Jesus is the fulfillment of that promise and the foundation of our faith. One faith, one body, one church built together in Christ.

September 4

Song of Solomon 1-2
Palm 102:1-11
Proverbs 21:29-31
Ephesians 3

The Love of Christ

"I pray that out of His glorious riches He may strengthen you with power through His Spirit in your inner being, so that Christ may dwell in your hearts through faith. And I pray that you, being rooted and established in love, may have power, together with all the Lord's holy people, to grasp how wide and long and high and deep is the love of Christ, and to know this love that surpasses knowledge—that you may be filled to the measure of all the fullness of God. Now to Him who is able to do immeasurably more than all we ask or imagine, according to His power that is at work within us, to Him be glory in the church and in Christ Jesus throughout all generations, forever and ever! Amen." Ephesians 3:16-21 NIV

This is one of the most encouraging scripture passages in the Bible. Paul is trying to express in the strongest possible words the extent of the love of Christ for us and the importance of our understanding that love. He believes that only by God's grace could someone as unworthy as him be entrusted with spreading the gospel to the Gentiles and only through the power of the Holy Spirit could he possibly be able to carry out his mission. Our imagination cannot even grasp the full extent of God's love. Its width, length, height, and depth are lost in their immensity. Its eternality and infinity are beyond our grasp and its intensity is well beyond our comprehension. Its width encompasses all the vast universe. Its length reaches back from the beginning of creation and stretches forward to the eternal reign of Christ. its depth touches the deepest depravity of the human heart from the fall of Adam to the evil of our own sin. And its height reaches to the heavenly throne of grace.

When we begin to understand how much He loves us, we are filled with such an appreciation that it compels us to live lives that are pleasing to Him, and it creates a love in us for Him which overflows in love and grace to others. This kind of love goes beyond mere information. It is so compelling that it overflows in action. It cannot be contained. His love gives us strength and power to accomplish everything He has intended for us to do. We are filled with all the fullness of His power and His love so that we are enabled to give that love to others. His love for us is not based on anything we do or don't do. It cannot be earned, and it cannot be lost. His love is part of His character. He is faithful and true. The only thing that can even give us a tiny picture of this love is the love of a mother for her child. The Mother loves her newborn baby even though the baby cannot return her love. She would do anything for this child, even die for it. As human mothers we are not perfect, so our love is not perfect and inevitably we fail to express that love completely all the time. God is perfect. His love is perfect, and He always acts in our best interest. He always does what is best for us and He always does immeasurably more that we ask or imagine. I pray that you feel the love of your Heavenly Father today.

September 5

Song of Solomon 3-4
Psalm 102:12-14
Proverbs 22:1-2
Ephesians 4:1-16

A Good Name

"A good name is to be chosen over great wealth; favor is better than silver and gold. The rich and the poor have this in common: the Lord made them both." Proverbs 22:1-2 HCSB

IN THIS PASSAGE in Proverbs, Solomon is encouraging us to do everything we can to pursue a good name and then keep it. Instead of pursuing gold and silver, riches, power, and fame, we should focus our attention on doing the things that will lead to a good reputation. Pursuing suggests chasing after or actively seeking it. It is not a passive thing that will just happen automatically. Let's examine a few of the qualities of someone with a good name and prayerfully seek to pursue them.

1. Honesty- A person with a good name is someone that can be trusted to be honest in all their dealings. They will not lie to you, and they will not cheat you. You know that you can rely on what they tell you. They will treat you fairly. You may not always like what they say to you, but you can rely on it being truthful. "Whoever desires to love life and see good days, let him keep his tongue from evil and his lips from speaking deceit; let him turn away from evil and do good." I Peter 3:10 (ESV)
2. Humility- A person with a good name is humble. "For all those who exalt themselves will be humbled, and those who humble themselves will be exalted." Luke 14:11 (NIV) "Pride goes before destruction, a haughty spirit before a fall." Proverbs 16:18 (NIV) "Pride brings a person low, but the lowly in spirit gain honor." Proverbs 29:23 (NIV) Arrogance and pride do not lead to having a good name. Thinking more highly of ourselves than we ought is the mark of a fool and not of someone who is highly respected.
3. Wisdom- A person with a good name is known for their wisdom. They make decisions based on careful contemplation and prayer. They do not engage in foolish activities and are not known for sinful habits. "Be very careful, then, how you live—not as unwise but as wise, making the most of every opportunity, because the days are evil." Ephesians 5:15-16 (NIV) "If any of you lacks wisdom, you should ask God, who gives generously to all without finding fault, and it will be given to you." James 1:5 (NIV)
4. Kindness- A person with a good name treats others with kindness and respect. They are caring and generous with their time and resources and they are known for treating others well. "Be kind to one another, tender-hearted, forgiving one another, as God in Christ forgave you." Ephesians 4:32 (ESV) "So, as those who have been chosen of God, holy and beloved, put on a heart of compassion, kindness, humility, gentleness and patience." Colossians 3:12 (NASB1995)

September 6

Song of Solomon 5-6
Psalm 102:15-22
Proverbs 22:3-4
Ephesians 4:17-32

Righteous Anger?

"You took off your former way of life, the old self that is corrupted by deceitful desires; you are being renewed in the spirit of your minds; you put on the new self, the one created according to God's likeness in righteousness and purity of the truth. Be angry and do not sin. Don't let the sun go down on your anger, and don't give the devil a foothold. All bitterness, anger, wrath, shouting and slander must be removed from you, along with malice." Ephesians 4:22-24, 26-27, 31 HCSB

Throughout scripture we are told that anger is bad. It never says it is ok to be angry, but rather that when we get angry, because we are human and we will inevitably get angry, we should not sin. It tells us to forgive and forgive over and over and over and over. It says to treat others as if they are better than we are and to always be concerned more about other people than we are about ourselves. It encourages us to forfeit our right to be offended and that we are not allowed to hold on to our anger. Actually, we are not forfeiting some right, because that right does not exist.

We somehow have the idea that it is virtuous to get angry. We use Jesus as an example and say that since Jesus got angry, we are justified to get angry when we see sin or injustice. The problem with that is that Jesus was God. He was perfect. His motives were always pure. He was completely justified. He knew all the facts and because He was completely wise and all knowing, His anger was exhibited in a perfectly just way. We are not God. We are not all wise and all knowing. We only see our side and that is skewed by our self-interest and selfish motives. My arguments are amazingly convincing to me. I am naturally going to side with me because I think I'm right. I tend to think that my righteous anger is justified, but other people are not justified in their anger. In the moment, everyone's anger always seems righteous. Anger sweeps over us and tells us that we are being denied something we deserve, and we must respond. The hard part is that sometimes we are justified. Sometimes we are being treated unfairly and the person is a jerk. Jesus tells us that in those times, especially in those times, we are to forgive. We don't get to be angry and treat them bad. We don't get to hold on to our anger and bitterness. The stuff that is understandably offensive, the thing that we think makes our anger righteous, is the very thing we are called to forgive. We are called to love our enemies and pray for those who persecute us.

There is a legitimate question we must ask ourselves. Is it ok to get angry at people who treat others badly? Can we be angry at racists and bigots and child molesters? I think the answer to this is complicated. Obviously, these things are wrong, and we should do everything we can to get rid of those things. But we do not have to get angry and emotional to do that. Police officers don't have to get angry to respond to abuse cases. They are much more effective if they respond with a cool, calm head than if they react in anger. Parents who respond to their children's bad behavior in anger do not get the best result. Anger does not enhance sound judgment. When we become angry, the best strategy is to step back, take a breath and pray, asking God to help us react appropriately and wisely. As Christians, we have put off our old self that is corrupted by deceitful desires and put on the new self that is created in Christ's likeness because His Holy Spirit lives in us. Let us strive to remove all anger from our lives and react in love and forgiveness.

September 7

Song of Solomon 7-8
Psalm 102:23-28
Proverbs 22:5-6
Ephesians 5:1-20

Light in the Darkness

"Let no one deceive you with empty arguments, for God's wrath is coming on the disobedient because of these things. Therefore, do not become their partners. For you were once darkness, but now you are light in the Lord. Walk as children of the light—for the fruit of the light results in goodness, righteousness, and truth—discerning what is pleasing to the Lord. Don't participate in the fruitless works of darkness, but instead expose them. For it is shameful to even mention what is done by them in secret. Everything exposed by the light is made clear, for what makes everything clear is light." Ephesians 5:6-14 HCSB

SATAN LOVES DARKNESS. He loves secrets and hidden things. He loves them because they entangle us in a web of deceit. Have you ever done something that you were so ashamed of that you had to keep it a secret from everyone? Shame brings bondage and fear. There is a knot in your stomach and a weight on your chest that feels like one of those blankets they lay over you when you get x-rays at the dentist. You feel paralyzed by the guilt, and it is hard to function because you are afraid everyone is going to find out what you did. This is just what Satan wants. He knows if he can get you into this position then he can convince you to lie to cover up the secret and maybe even sin more. It becomes a vicious cycle. The more secrets you keep hidden, the more lies you have to tell to cover them up. Satan will fill your head with lies to convince you that you are all alone and no one has ever done the things you have done, God could never forgive you, your friends and family could never forgive you, it would ruin your life if everyone found out, etc. He is the father of lies. He will say whatever he has to say to keep you in bondage.

There is freedom in truth and light. Everything exposed by the light is made clear. Our God wants you to be free. He is the God of restoration and hope. I John 1:9 tells us, "If we confess our sins, He is faithful and righteous to forgive us our sins and to cleanse us from all unrighteousness." (HCSB) It does not say that He will forgive our sins if they aren't too bad or that He might forgive them. It says that if we confess, He will forgive. Everything. All the stuff that is yucky and ugly and shameful. If we confess it to Him, He will forgive us and cleanse us from all that unrighteousness. Now if we confess it to Him, He may tell us to confess it to others that we have hurt by our sin. God loves the light because He knows that freedom comes from transparency. He does not want us to be bound by secrets and lies. That burden is so heavy, and He wants to lift it off us. It may be difficult to admit what we have done, but once we have, the healing and the restoration process can begin. If the secrets and lies are hanging over us, complete healing is not possible. If you are living with a burden of sin and shame, I pray that you would confess it to God and let Him begin to restore you. Don't believe Satan's lies. He does not love you and he does not want what is best for you, but your Heavenly Father does.

September 8

Isaiah 1-2
Psalm 103:1-5
Proverbs 22:7-8
Ephesians 5:21-33

Love and Respect

> "To sum up, each one of you is to love his wife as himself, and the wife is to respect her husband." Ephesians 5:33 HCSB

There is a book I give to every couple I know that is getting married because I think it is the best book available on marriage. It is called <u>Love and Respect</u> by Emerson Eggerichs. I encourage all of you to get this book if you are getting married or if you have been married a few years or 50 years. Read it now and then read it again every 5 years or so. I believe it holds the secret to a successful marriage and can have a profound impact on your relationship. I have never read a book that nails it like this one does. It basically says what the Bible has been saying for centuries, but in a way that is easy to understand and apply to our personal lives. The truths we find in the Bible are timeless. God's instructions for marriage are not culturally bound. They are as applicable today as they were when they were written because God created us, and He knows us better than we know ourselves. He made us male and female with innate qualities that enable us to function together in the bonds of marriage and as a family unit. Men have a God-given need to be respected. It is not narcissistic or prideful. It allows them to function in their role as husbands. It gives them the confidence and courage to lead their families in a godly, righteous way. As wives, the most important thing we can do is treat our husbands with respect and honor. Speaking to them in demeaning and condescending tones and treating them as though they are incompetent will kill their spirit.

Women have a God-given need to feel loved and secure. I am not in any way suggesting that women are weak and need to be taken care of. A lot of the strongest people I know are women. It has nothing to do with weakness, but it is important that we feel loved and cherished. This allows us to function in our roles as wives and mothers. When we feel secure and loved then we can fulfill our roles, but when we do not feel secure in our relationships, we feel vulnerable, and we react in ways that are unhealthy. It can lead to unhealthy cycles of communication and conflict that can destroy the marriage and family bonds. It does not always come naturally for men to make their wives feel loved or for women to show respect to their husbands. It takes conscious effort and awareness. This book gives insight into things we do that we aren't even aware of that undermine our relationships. Most of us want to give our spouses what they need. We want healthy marriages with good communication and intimacy. But if you have been married very long you know that it is easy to slip into patterns of busyness and complacency and neglect the most important relationship you have. At least 50% of marriages end in divorce. I pray that we will each be purposeful and prayerful so that we will not be in that statistic.

September 9

Isaiah 3-5
Psalm 103:6-10
Proverbs 22:9-11
Ephesians 6:1-9

Children and Parents

> "Children, obey your parents as you would the Lord, because this is right. Honor your father and mother, which is the first commandment with a promise, so that it may go well with you and that you may have a long life in the land. Fathers don't stir up anger in your children but bring them up in the training and instruction of the Lord." Ephesians 6:1-4 HCSB

Family relationships are complicated. None of us are perfect, so none of us get it right all the time. Sometimes we just completely blow it as moms, dads, and children. We love the people in our family, but sometimes we say things we shouldn't or do things that are not very loving. Our families know us better than anyone. They see the good, the bad and the ugly. We can let down our guard with them because we know they love us, and we can be ourselves with them. Unfortunately, sometimes that leads to hurt feelings and misunderstandings. Family relationships always require mercy and grace. No family is perfect. No mom or dad is perfect. No kids are perfect. We all have regrets, and we can look back over our lives with a lot of what ifs and if onlys. At this point we cannot change the past. We can't undo and redo anything, but we can move forward in a healthier way. These verses give us a good place to start. Children, obey your parents because this is good. God gave you the parents He gave you for a reason. He picked them for you. You may not like everything about your parents, but they are the ones God chose. Our responsibility as children is to obey them and as adults, we are to honor them. Sometimes this is difficult to do and will require a lot of prayer and patience from God to help us do this in a way that is pleasing to Him. This may look different for different people depending on your circumstances, but God expects us to honor our parents.

The second instruction is for fathers not to stir up anger in their children. Other translations use the word exasperate or frustrate. We all cause our children to be angry when they don't get their way. That is not what this verse is talking about. It is referring to being arbitrary and controlling. It is the "because I said so" mindset. Don't get me wrong, children should obey their parents because they said so, but parents have a responsibility to make sure their instructions are reasonable and wise. We must train our children in the instruction of the Lord. This may cause them to not be happy with us sometimes because they want their way and not what is best. Prayer and seeking the Lord will help us to make wise decisions and not arbitrary or inconsistent ones.

We all have relationships that are more difficult than others. Some people are hard to get along with. It may be a parent, a child, or a sibling. Old hurts and unresolved issues can complicate relationships. "If it is possible, as far as it depends on you, live at peace with everyone." Romans 12:18 (NIV) Sometimes it is not possible to live at peace because the other person refuses to restore the relationship. We are not responsible for their actions, but we are responsible for ours. We must do our part. We must do everything we can to bring about peace and then we pray and leave it in God's hands. In a sermon recently, my pastor was talking about reconciliation and restoration. He said that reconciliation may never happen. Old hurts and problems can't always be fixed in a satisfactory way. But reconciliation is not necessary to bring about a restoration of the relationship. Sometimes it is best to choose to move on and restore the relationship and just leave the past in the past. This is hard. It requires choosing to forgive, setting aside your own interests, and putting others above yourself. It involves deciding that the relationship is more important than being vindicated or getting your way. Being right isn't always as important as being at peace. Prayerfully ask God for guidance in restoring any relationships that are strained.

September 10

Isaiah 6-8
Psalm 103:11-14
Proverbs 22:12-13
Ephesians 6:10-23

Spiritual Armor

"Finally, be strong in the Lord and in His mighty power. Put on the full armor of God, so that you can take your stand against the devil's schemes. For our struggle is not against flesh and blood, but against the rulers, against the authorities, against the powers of this dark world and against the spiritual forces of evil in the Heavenly realms. Therefore, put on the full armor of God, so that when the day of evil comes, you may be able to stand your ground, and after you have done everything, to stand. Stand firm then, with the belt of truth buckled around your waist, with the breastplate of righteousness in place, and with your feet fitted with the readiness that comes from the gospel of peace. In addition to all this, take up the shield of faith, with which you can extinguish all the flaming arrows of the evil one. Take up the helmet of salvation and the Sword of the Spirit, which is the Word of God." Ephesians 6:10-17 NIV

MANY YEARS AGO, I was in a Sunday School class with a dear friend, Dr. Bill Daniel, who has since gone to be with the Lord. He was talking about this passage of scripture and told us that most mornings when he woke up, before he ever got out of bed, he recited this passage in his head and mentally put on the armor of God before he started his day. He explained that he had no idea what his day might hold, but he knew that he needed spiritual protection for whatever he might face. Whenever I read this passage, I can't help but think of Bill. When I was in college, I participated in a Bible study called Masterlife. It was a discipleship program that led you through the basics of the Christian faith. One of the assignments was to memorize this passage. I am not great at memorizing scripture now, but the verses that I memorized when I was younger, I can usually still recall. I don't do it every day, but I often will go through this verse in my head in the mornings as Bill suggested, especially when I know my day is going to be stressful or I am facing a difficult situation. Each piece of the armor has a certain function to protect us from Satanic attack and it is important to equip ourselves so that we are prepared for battle.

1. Belt of Truth- The belt is used to keep the rest of the armor in place. Satan is the father of lies and he will tell you clever and convincing lies about God and yourself. The only way to protect yourself is to know and trust the truth God has given us in His Word. When we know the truth, we will recognize Satan's lies and we will not believe them.
2. Breastplate of Righteousness- The breastplate protected the soldier's chest and heart and was tucked into the belt. We put on the breastplate of righteousness by claiming for ourselves the righteousness that comes through faith in Jesus.

Jesus' death means we no longer have to strive to be righteous by our own actions, but by faith the righteous character of Jesus is made available to us. We are then able to grow in our own obedience as the Holy Spirit changes us and makes us more like Him.

3. Shoes for Your Feet- Shoes are necessary for a soldier. They needed to be able to move quickly across various terrains and they needed shoes that would protect them. The shoes in the spiritual armor are "the readiness that comes from the gospel of peace." We have to be prepared to share the gospel whenever we have the opportunity. What are we doing to stay prepared and alert?
4. The Shield of Faith- The shield is the soldier's greatest defensive weapon. It was made of leather, wood and metal and would have been large enough to cover his vital organs. With it, he was able to extinguish the flaming arrows of the enemy. Faith is our shield against all the lies and attacks Satan throws at us.
5. The Helmet of Salvation- The helmet protected the soldiers head from attack. Salvation is the greatest gift we have. In I Thessalonians 5:8 Paul describes the helmet of the hope of salvation. Our hope is based on our salvation. The certainty of our salvation gives us the confidence to enter battle knowing we are protected against anything Satan can throw at us.
6. The Sword of the Spirit- The sword is the only offensive weapon in the armor. The Sword of the Spirit is the Word of God. The Bible is our offensive weapon against Satan. Just as Jesus used scripture against Satan's attacks when He was in the wilderness for 40 days, we have scripture available to us when we are under attack.

Paul finishes this passage describing the spiritual armor with encouragement to pray on all occasions with all kinds of prayers and requests. He knows that we need to be in constant communication with Jesus to stand firm against Satan's schemes. Our struggle is not against flesh and blood, but against the rulers, authorities, powers, and spiritual forces of evil in the Heavenly realm. We cannot hope to fight Satan on our own power so we must rely on Him to protect us and help us be victorious.

September 11

Isaiah 9-10
Psalm 103:15-22
Proverbs 22:14-16
Philippians 1:1-20

CONFIDENT

"Being confident of this, that He who began a good work in you will carry it on to completion until the day of Christ Jesus." Philippians 1:6 NIV

BEING CONFIDENT OF something is to be fully and firmly persuaded or convinced that something will occur. Paul was not just wishing or hoping that it would happen. He was not speaking positively about it so that he could will it to be. He was confident because he knew that it was God that would make it happen and not men. Anything that men are responsible for is subject to changing circumstances and faltering abilities. We may have good intentions, but we cannot guarantee something will happen because we do not know what tomorrow holds that might change the outcome. That is not the case with God. He can see all the things that will happen in the future. He can plan for those, and we can be confident that anything that He starts, He will finish. He is perfectly able to do whatever He plans to do and does not begin anything that He does not intend to see to completion.

The good work He begins in us is our salvation, the work of grace and faith in our hearts. It is God's work and not a work of our will or ability. The transforming of our hearts from dead in our sin to alive in Christ requires almighty power. He calls us, convicts us, and draws us to Himself. He knows what circumstances are necessary to make us willing to accept Him. Once we come to Him, He begins the process of regeneration, sanctification and faith that conforms us into the image of His Son. This process continues until we breathe our last breath here and come into His presence in eternity. It is His work in us from the beginning. We do not have to worry that we will mess up and lose our salvation. He will not give up on us. He knows every step of the process He will have to go through to get us "completed." "For we are His workmanship, created in Christ Jesus for good works, which God prepared beforehand, that we should walk in them." Ephesians 2:10 (ESV) We are His masterpiece. He is molding us, shaping us, and chiseling away at us to form us into a beautiful piece of art that is pleasing to Him and serves His purposes. He will continue His work until the day of Christ Jesus. It is a continual process. He does not complete His work in us and put us in a museum on display. He is constantly changing, renewing, and remodeling us. There is not some point in this life when He finishes His work. Until we die or He returns to take us all to Heaven, He is continuing to perfect and complete us. We can rest in the confidence of knowing He is doing a good work in us, and He always finishes His work.

Isaiah 11-13
Psalm 104:1-9
Proverbs 22:17-21
Philippians 1:21-30

To Live is Christ and to Die is Gain

"For to me, to live is Christ and to die is gain. If I am to go on living in the body, this will mean fruitful labor for me. Yet what shall I choose? I do not know! I am torn between the two: I desire to depart and be with Christ, which is better by far; but it is more necessary for you that I remain in the body." Philippians 1:21-24 NIV

God knows the number of our days. He has plans for each of us and His plans continue as long as we are here. He can use us to bring glory to Him until our last breath. His purpose is different for us in different seasons, but we can be effective for Him in every season. Whether you are young and starting out in your career, chasing young children, and building a family, or middle-aged dealing with a business, teen-aged children, and aging parents. You may be retired and dealing with health issues, adult children, and grandchildren, or nearing the end of your life spending your days in a nursing home with serious health problems. God still has plans for you. He can use you every day. Until He takes you home, you have a purpose.

"For we are His workmanship, created in Christ Jesus for good works, which God prepared beforehand, that we should walk in them." Ephesians 2:10 (ESV) I know we looked at this verse yesterday, but it bears repeating. Our lives are a testimony to Him. We can give glory to Him all the days of our lives and He can use us in mighty ways at every stage of life. It is never out of our own ability or strength that we can do anything for Him, but rather our availability allows Him to accomplish much through us. When I was in college, I worked summers at a nursing home. There was a dear sweet lady there who spent her days praying. She was in very poor health; her eyesight was very limited, and she was bound to a wheelchair. She couldn't do much of anything, but she could pray and so she did. Any time you went in her room, you would find her in prayer. She had visitors all during the week because people came by to share their prayer requests with her so she could pray for them. Her pastor brought all the church's prayer needs to her each week and the residents and staff at the home came to her room often whenever they had a prayer need. Looking at her life, you might think she didn't have much purpose. But you would be wrong. She had a ministry until the day Jesus called her home. As a young stay-at-home mom, you might feel like you are not accomplishing much because you spend your days changing diapers, playing blocks, and rocking babies to sleep. God is at work in and through you. Our job is to remain faithful and available. His job is to accomplish His purposes. So, for me to live is Christ and someday when I have accomplished everything He intends for me to do, it will be for my gain that I depart and go to be with Christ.

September 13

Isaiah 14-16
Psalm 104:10-15
Proverbs 22:22-23
Philippians 2:1-11

Humble Yourselves

"Do nothing out of selfish ambition or vain conceit. Rather, in humility value others above yourselves, not looking to your own interests but each of you to the interests of others. In your relationships with one another, have the same mindset as Christ Jesus: Who being in very nature God, did not consider equality with God something to be used to His own advantage; rather He made Himself nothing by taking the very nature of a servant, being made in human likeness. And being found in appearance as a man, He humbled Himself by becoming obedient to death—even death on a cross!" Philippians 2:3-8 NIV

I realize I refer to humility a lot. That probably means that God is working on me in this area. My process when I write these devotions is that I read all the passages for the day, and I pray about them and ask God to show me which one He wants me to focus on for the devotional. It seems that whenever there is a passage about humility, that is the one that screams out at me. This one is definitely an ouch! Do NOTHING out of selfish ambition or vain conceit. NOTHING. Ouch! Value others more than I value myself. Ouch! Look out for the interests of others instead of looking out for my own interests! Ouch! I want to think I do that, but do I really? This gets at not only my actions, but my motives behind my actions. So, when I do things for others am I doing it so they will like me or think highly of me? What is my motive? Am I doing it because I want to exalt them and value them and honor them? Or am I doing it to bring honor to me? Ouch! Ouch! Ouch!

In my relationships with others, I am instructed to have the mindset of Christ. Jesus was God. He was equal to God. He could have come to Earth, announced He was the Messiah, and taken over. He could have made Himself King and ruled over everyone. But that is not what He chose to do. His love for us was more important than getting what He deserved. He humbled Himself willingly, coming as a servant and offered Himself as a sacrifice in my place. His motive was love. So, in my relationships, I am to have that same mindset. My motive must be love. Instead of thinking about what I want or think I "deserve," I need to focus on my love for them and what I can do to show that love to them. If I am focused on others, God will take care of me. I don't have to worry about myself because God loves me more than anyone else possibly could and He is looking out for me. I can trust His love for me and so that frees me up to love others humbly and lavishly. Oh, how I want to follow His example in this. I fear that I fall very short of the mark. My prayer is that Christ would do this work in me. I pray that I would humble myself so that He does not have to humble me.

September 14

Isaiah 17-19
Psalm 104:16-26
Proverbs 22:24-25
Philippians 2:12-30
Discontented

> "Do everything without grumbling or complaining so that you may become blameless and pure, children of God without fault in a warped and crooked generation."
> Philippians 2:14-15 NIV

THIS IS ANOTHER one that hits a little too close to home. Negativity is a bad habit and one that is easy to slip into. It is very easy to focus on the negative instead of the positive. Grumbling and complaining is a verbal expression of our dissatisfaction with our circumstances. We live in a world that is prone to complaining. Whenever we don't get exactly what we want, how we want it, and when we want it, we are discontented. Grumbling and complaining is not unique to our culture. When God delivered the Israelites from slavery in Egypt, they complained about a lack of water. They complained about the lack of food and then about the kind of food God gave them. They complained about their trials in the wilderness, and they complained when they got to the promised land. It is easy to be critical of them, but let's be realistic. If we went three days without water, we would definitely be complaining. If we had the same thing to eat every day, who of us would not complain about that. If we got to the promised land and saw the giants in the land, it is highly likely that we would be grumbling and murmuring among ourselves. People living in glass houses should not throw stones. God reacted very strongly to their complaints. They were saved from slavery in Egypt and God thought it was unreasonable for them to complain after their deliverance. Their complaining was a lack of faith because after experiencing such a miraculous deliverance they did not trust that God could provide for them in the desert and bring them into the promised land.

We have been delivered from slavery to sin. We have been given eternal life and adopted as children of God. How can we doubt that He will provide everything we need? Grumbling and complaining about our circumstances is a lack of faith in His provision. It is a lack of faith that He loves us and knows what is best for us. When we are grumbling and complaining we are saying that we do not think He is providing for us adequately. It comes naturally to be negative, but we can choose to see the good and believe the best. Being around negative people is exhausting and I'm sure none of us wants to be one of those people who is unpleasant to be around because we are always unhappy about something. If you are looking for something to be unhappy about, you can surely find it, but you can also easily find blessings if you are looking for them.

September 15

Isaiah 20-22
Psalm 104:27-35
Proverbs 22:26-27
Philippians 3:1-11

P & L

"But everything that was a gain to me, I have considered to be a loss because of Christ. More than that, I also consider everything to be a loss in view of the surpassing value of knowing Christ Jesus my Lord. Because of Him I have suffered the loss of all things and consider them filth, so that I may gain Christ and be found in Him, not having a righteousness of my own from the law, but one that is through faith in Christ—the righteousness from God based on faith." Philippians 3:7-9 HCSB

OUR DAUGHTER, HANNAH, just graduated from college with her degree in accounting. She is currently in school getting her masters and studying for the CPA exam. Profit and Loss Statements (P&L) have been a topic of conversation in our house recently. The terms used here are accounting terms referring to business dealings. Paul is doing the math. The losses are the kind that would occur when goods were lost at sea. They signify a total loss. In the verses preceding these, he examines all the things in his life that he had accomplished. When he became acquainted with the truth of the gospel found in Jesus, he realized that none of the things that he believed gave himself value and which he had relied on to give him acceptance by God were of any value at all. He is saying that when presented with salvation in Jesus through faith alone, he chose to toss all those other things overboard because they were of no value in purchasing salvation. He was no longer relying on the advantages of his birth, his education, or conformity to the law. Not only were those things not sufficient in providing salvation, but they were also a disadvantage or hindrance because they gave him a false sense of security.

The profit and loss statement (P&L) summarizes the revenues, costs, and expenses of a company. The purpose is to help you evaluate how you can end up with more money or profit than you are spending. When you set up a spreadsheet comparing a life lived in the righteousness from God based on faith compared to the life lived based on the law or a life lived to fulfill the desires of the flesh, there is no comparison. The joy, peace, freedom, and security found in Christ are eternal and far surpass the temporary satisfaction of material possessions, power, and indulgence in sinful behavior. Whatever we may desire that is contrary to the life we have in Christ can never satisfy us and will fail to meet our needs. Paul figured this out by counting the cost. We would do well to do a P&L of our lives and determine if we are relying on things that have no lasting value or if the things we are pursuing are based on the truth of God's Word.

September 16

Isaiah 23-25
Psalm 105:1-6
Proverbs 22:28-29
Philippians 3:12-21

Leaving the Past in the Past

> "Not that I have already reached the goal or am already fully mature, but I make every effort to take hold of it because I also have been taken hold of by Christ Jesus. Brothers, I do not consider myself to have taken hold of it. But one thing I do: Forgetting what is behind and reaching forward to what is ahead, I pursue as my goal the prize promised by God's heavenly call in Christ Jesus." Philippians 3:12-14 HCSB

THIS IS SUCH a freeing passage of scripture. I use it often in mentoring relationships. You cannot undo the past. You cannot change the things you did in the past and you cannot change the things in the past that were done to you. I am convinced that one of Satan's favorite schemes against Christians is to convince them that they cannot be effective for Christ now because of all the stuff they did in the past. That is a lie. I believe that one of the reasons this passage is included in scripture is because God wants us to know that He can redeem us, restore us, and use us regardless of all the evil, ugly things we may have done. Paul persecuted and killed Christians. It doesn't get much worse than that. He was responsible for the deaths of God's children. Paul could easily have decided that it would be best for Him to just live a quiet life in the background supporting others in ministry because God couldn't use someone who had done the things he had done. If he had chosen that, it is likely we would not have most of the New Testament, the gospel might have never been spread to the Gentiles, and we would have never heard about Jesus. Instead, to move forward and allow God to use him, he had to make a conscious choice to forget what was in his past and keep his eyes focused ahead. No doubt, Satan tried to torment him with the things he had done. Paul was not insulated from Satan's attacks and I'm sure Satan took every opportunity he could to fill his mind with lies and doubt, but Paul refused to listen. He chose to keep his eyes focused on Jesus and the goal of his calling. In humility, he recognized that God was at work in him to bring him into full maturity. He knew he had not reached the level of perfection, but that he needed to keep striving toward the goal. That is the secret for us. We cannot allow Satan to paralyze us with guilt. If we have confessed our sins and asked for forgiveness, then we need to move on. We cannot keep living in the past. Embrace the forgiveness He provides and focus on Jesus, allowing Him to work in you to bring you to full maturity in faith.

It is also important that we do not dwell on the past things that were done to us. We cannot change what someone did to us. Whether they have asked for forgiveness or not, it is important that we forgive them and move on. We may not be able to resolve the issues, but we can choose to leave the past in the past and move forward.

Bitterness and anger will cause more damage in our lives than the hurt inflicted on us by others. We can choose to lay the hurt and anger at the feet of Jesus and leave it with Him to deal with. No good comes from living in the past.

September 17

Isaiah 26-27
Psalm 105:7-11
Proverbs 23:1-3
Philippians 4

The Secrets

"Don't worry about anything, but in everything, through prayer and petition with thanksgiving, let your requests be made known to God. And the peace of God, which surpasses every thought, will guard your hearts and minds in Christ Jesus. Finally, brothers, whatever is true, whatever is honorable, whatever is just, whatever is pure, whatever is lovely, whatever is commendable—if there is any moral excellence and if there is any praise—dwell on these things. I am able to do all these things through Him who strengthens me. And my God will supply all of your needs according to His riches in glory in Christ Jesus." Philippians 4:6-8, 13, 19 HCSB

I AM CONVINCED that Philippians 4 holds the secrets to joy, peace, and contentment. If we do the things in this chapter our lives will be radically different. These four principles will transform our hearts and our minds if we apply them daily.

1. Don't worry, pray! Most of the stuff we spend our time worrying about either does not happen or does not turn out to be as bad as we thought it would. We have very little control over any of it and worrying about it does not change one thing. But we know the One who does have control and can do something about it. The best thing we can do is pray. And after we pray, we need to leave it at His feet. If we pick it back up and keep worrying about it, we are exhibiting a lack of faith in His willingness and ability to take care of our concerns.
2. Dwell on the positive instead of the negative. We just dealt with this a few days ago, so I'm not going to spend much time on it. Instead of seeing the negative in every situation, choose to see what is true, honorable, just, pure, lovely, commendable and of moral excellence. Changing your focus can change your situation.
3. He is the One who strengthens me. I do not have to come up with internal strength and power. I don't have it in me to deal with a lot of the stuff I am faced with, but I have the Holy Spirit living in me who is Almighty. He can do whatever needs to be done in my life.
4. He will meet all my needs. I don't have to worry about anything. He's got this. Whatever this is, He can handle it. I am His precious child. He loves me and He will take care of me. I can rest in His provision.

That's it! Do these things and your life will be characterized by joy, peace, and contentment.

September 18

Isaiah 28-29
Psalm 105:12-22
Proverbs 23:4-5
Colossians 1:1-14

Process and Procedure

"Does the plowman plow every day to plant seed? Does he continuously break up and cultivate the soil? When he has leveled its surface, does he not then scatter black cumin and sow cumin? He plants wheat in rows and barley in plots, with spelt as their border. His God teaches him order; He instructs him. Certainly, black cumin is not threshed with a threshing board, and a cart wheel is not rolled over the cumin. But black cumin is beaten out with a stick, and cumin with a rod. Bread grain is crushed but is not threshed endlessly. Though the wheel of the farmer's cart rumbles, his horses do not crush it. This also comes from the Lord of Hosts. He gives wonderful advice; He gives great wisdom." Isaiah 28:24-29 HCSB

IN THIS PASSAGE, Isaiah uses agricultural principles that the people of his day would have been very familiar with to make the point that God is a God of order. There are processes and procedures that must be followed in any endeavor to be successful. There is a correct order to follow to produce a crop. There is a time of plowing, digging, tilling, cultivating, planting, harvesting, threshing, etc. You would not plant before you had plowed. You cannot harvest before you cultivate. God, in His infinite wisdom, has placed seasons in their proper order and given man the wisdom to know what we need to do when. He has also created regional variations so that weather patterns help to determine what crops grow best in what areas. If you stop and ponder the intricacies and delicate balance of just our planet and consider how minute that is in the vastness of the universe, it will blow your mind. God has set in motion and continues to maintain the perfect environment to meet all our needs. The oxygen and carbon dioxide levels are balanced perfectly. Seasons come and go year after year predictably so that farmers can provide the food we need to survive. Unfortunately, the Garden of Eden that God created was tainted by the introduction of sin into our world. Famine, plague, natural disasters, and drought are evidence of the presence of Satan and his demons. And yet God faithfully maintains order and provides for our needs.

God also provides order in our individual lives. He is growing us and maturing us into the people He wants us to be. He has a plan and a purpose, and He is following that plan. He will not give us a task to accomplish before He develops the qualities in us that we need to be successful. He may place a dream in our hearts that will take years to bring about. We cannot get ahead of Him. His timing is perfect just like His plans are perfect. Many of the men and women in the Bible waited years for God to fulfill the promises He gave them. During that time, He was preparing and maturing them, so they were ready when it happened. Joseph spent a lot of years in a jail cell learning to trust God. David spent years as a fugitive in the wilderness. The children of Israel wandered around in the desert for forty years. Just as God was at work in their lives, He is at work in ours. He is in all the intricate details, and we can trust His plan because He loves us and knows exactly what is best for us.

Isaiah 30-31
Psalm 105:23-36
Proverbs 23:6-8
Colossians 1:15-29

September 19

The Great Mystery

"I have become its servant, according to God's administration that was given to me for you, to make God's message fully known, the mystery hidden for ages and generations, but now revealed to His saints. God wanted to make known among the Gentiles the glorious wealth of this mystery, which is Christ in you, the hope of glory. We proclaim Him, warning and teaching everyone with all wisdom, so that we may present everyone mature in Christ." Colossians 1:25-28 HCSB

WE KNOW THE secret, the one that all humanity has been trying to figure out since the beginning of creation. The meaning and purpose of all existence and the secret to being able to live lives that glorify God and are transcendent to time and place. I know that sounds arrogant and presumptuous, but it isn't. We know the secret because God has revealed it to us. We are in the know. All of history from the beginning of creation led up to God's Son leaving Heaven, coming to Earth as a baby, living a perfect, sinless life, dying on a cross as the sacrifice for our sins, being buried and raising Himself back to life, defeating sin and death, and then ascending to Heaven. All of that is amazing and our belief in that is what saves our souls and gives us eternal life, but that isn't the mystery. For centuries the Old Testament saints followed God. They had an elaborate system of rules and regulations they had to follow to live a good life and please God. They had prescribed sacrifices to offer when they messed up and even sacrifices just in case they messed up and didn't know it. But their lives were still characterized more by sin and evil than by holiness. God's chosen people failed Him time and again. God knew before He ever created humans that we were going to be sinful and selfish and rebellious. And He still created us. He knew that no matter how hard we tried, we were going to mess up. So, He provided the sacrifice, His Only Son, that would allow for our salvation.

God knew that even that would not be enough. His Son came to Earth and walked among us. In His human body, He could not be with everyone everywhere all at once, so He had another plan. He knows how weak we are and that we each need constant attention and guidance. When He ascended to Heaven, He sent His Holy Spirit to indwell us. That is the secret! That is the mystery! As soon as we accept Jesus as our Savior and Lord, we receive the Holy Spirit! He not only saves us, but He also gives us the assurance of His constant presence. He comes to live in us to help us. He is our guide, comforter, encourager, companion, protector, mediator, and friend. We are never alone, and we have access to His wisdom, foreknowledge, strength, peace, and love. We don't have to figure this all out ourselves. We have Him to do it for us. The secret to living a life of meaning and purpose is "Christ in us." He created us and placed us on Earth at this time on purpose. He indwells us to carry out His plans at this time in history. We fit into His grand plan. We are a piece of the puzzle, and the picture will not be complete without our contribution. Apart from Him, this life does not have purpose: it is here today and gone tomorrow. But in Him and through Him we find meaning in life. No other world religion or philosophy offers a god who indwells you and helps you day by day because their gods are not real. We alone know the Great Mystery. Let us be bold to proclaim it to anyone who will listen.

September 20

Isaiah 32-33
Psalm 105:37-45
Proverbs 23:9-11
Colossians 2

Dead → Alive

"When you were dead in your sins and in the uncircumcision of your flesh, God made you alive with Christ. He forgave us all our sins, having canceled the charge of our legal indebtedness, which stood against us and condemned us; He has taken it away, nailing it to the cross." Colossians 2:13-14 NIV

THERE IS A misconception about Christianity that many nonbelievers have and unfortunately, I think many Christians have the same idea. It is the idea that it is all about being a good person vs. being a bad person. The problem is that no one thinks they are a bad person. There is always someone that you can think of that is worse than you and you can always come up with excuses for why you do all the things you do. Everyone looks pretty good in their own eyes. So, by that standard, no one thinks they need to be saved. The truth is that all of us are bad people. "There is no one righteous, not even one. All have turned away, there is no one who does good, not even one." Romans 3:10-12 (NIV) It isn't about being good or bad. It isn't about following a list of rules so that our good deeds outweigh our bad deeds. At the end of our life, we are not going to get to Heaven and have God look over our life and see if overall we did more good stuff than bad stuff and let us in. He isn't comparing us to other people to see if we get to come in. I think we will all be shocked to see some of the people that are there. Ted Bundy, the serial killer, claims to have accepted Jesus as his personal Savior in prison. If he did, he is in Heaven now. We would all agree that he was a bad person. I'm convinced that the idea of good vs. bad was devised by Satan to confuse us. From the world's perspective, I'm sure there are a lot of "good" people that will end up in Hell and a lot of "bad" people in Heaven.

This verse is very clear that it is not about good verses bad. It is about dead verses alive. We are all condemned to death. We are living on death row because we willfully choose sin, selfishness, and rebellion. No one is righteous. No one is perfect. When we come to the realization that we are dead in our sins and ask Jesus to forgive us and save us, our sins are nailed to the cross, and buried with Him. We are raised to life through His resurrection. We go from being dead in our sins to being alive in Christ. Instead of Christianity being about being good or bad, it is about being dead or alive. It is a totally different discussion. Once we are made alive in Christ, He begins the work of sanctification, the process of making us more like Him. He begins to work in our hearts to take away the sinful attitudes and behaviors. This takes time. This side of Heaven none of us will ever be perfectly righteous. We will not always be good. Some bad stuff still shows up in our actions, but thankfully our salvation is not dependent on our goodness. We are no longer dead. We have been made alive in Christ. This is the gospel message.

September 21

Isaiah 34-36
Psalm 106:1-5
Proverbs 23:12-14
Colossians 3:1-17

Chosen and Loved

> "Therefore, as God's chosen people, holy and dearly loved, clothe yourselves with compassion, kindness, humility, gentleness, and patience. Bear with each other and forgive one another if any of you has a grievance against someone. Forgive as the Lord forgave you. And over all these virtues put on love, which binds them all together in perfect unity. Let the peace of Christ rule in your hearts, since as members of one body you were called to peace. And be thankful." Colossians 3:12-15 NIV

COLOSSIANS 3 STARTS out with a long list of the things that were part of our lives before we met Christ: sexual immorality, impurity, lust, evil desires, greed, idolatry, anger, rage, malice, slander, filthy language, and lying. Paul tells us that we have taken off our old selves with its practices and have put on a new self that is being renewed by Christ. Paul knows that when we get rid of our old practices, we need to replace the void that is left behind, so he gives us a list of things to fill our hearts and minds. He encourages us to clothe ourselves with compassion, kindness, humility, gentleness, patience, forgiveness, love, peace, and gratitude. He tells us that we are chosen. The Creator and Lord of the Universe chose us to be His children. We are holy not because of our own righteousness, but because we are covered by the righteousness of Christ. And we are dearly loved. That is not some blanket statement that God loves everyone and all of humanity. It is personal and individual. He loves me! And He loves you! He knows us each individually and personally and He loves us each dearly. I don't know about you, but that brings tears to my eyes. It is very humbling. He knows everything about me: the good, the bad and the ugly and He loves me dearly. He has forgiven all the stuff in my life that I don't even want anyone to know about. I can't hide it from Him. He has seen all the bad stuff I've done and even the stuff I've thought about and wanted to do. He knows how selfish I am down deep and yet He sacrificed Himself to save me.

When I recognize the depth of my own depravity, I am filled with an overwhelming sense of appreciation for what He has done for me. This recognition enables me to see those around me differently. Instead of being annoyed by their neediness or irritated by their behaviors, I can look past their actions and see a hurting person who needs the love of Jesus as much as I do. The only way that I can exhibit kindness, gentleness and patience toward people who do not treat me that way is by allowing the Holy Spirit who is living in me to love them through me. I can forgive much because I have been forgiven much. I can put on love and live at peace with others because I am loved, and I am at peace with God. Sometimes we all need a change of perspective. Instead of looking at the world from the lens of my personal rights and what I think I deserve, we need to be reminded that what we really deserve is death and Hell, but we have been mercifully spared that by our Savior who loves us. How can we not then extend that love and mercy to others?

Isaiah 37-38
Psalm 106:6-12
Proverbs 23:15-16
Colossians 3:18-4:1

September 22

Motivation

> "Whatever you do, work at it with all your heart, as working for the Lord, not for human masters, since you know that you will receive an inheritance from the Lord as a reward. It is the Lord Christ you are serving." Colossians 3:23-24 NIV

MY PARENTS AND grandparents taught me by words and example to work hard and always do my very best. They taught me that no matter what I am doing I have a responsibility to give it my all. I may not like my boss and I may find myself doing something I don't enjoy, but if I have made a commitment to do it, I need to do it well. Brian and I tried to instill this in our children as well. You finish what you start, and you do your best to do it well. I am afraid that this is something that is not being taught in our world today. It is evident all around us. Most people get by with doing as little as they possibly can, when they don't like what they are doing they just quit, and they are not being held accountable for sloppy work. As Christians this should not be said of us. We must be different. In a world of complacency, laziness, and half-hearted effort, we need to stand out. We should be the ones who are always on time, work hard, stay late to finish the job, always keep our word, and don't grumble and complain. We should be reliable, loyal, dependable, and trustworthy. If we promise to do something, we better do it. If we bear the name of Christ, everything we do reflects on Him.

Sometimes it is difficult to find the motivation to work with excellence. It is much easier to just do what we must do to get by. It is easier to be like everyone else. Why should we put in the extra effort when no one else does and when it often isn't appreciated? This verse provides us with the motivation we need. Even when no one else notices what we are doing, God does. He sees everything we do. He sees when we honor our commitments. He sees when we work hard and always do our best. He appreciates when we are reliable and dependable and trustworthy. We may not like our earthly masters: our bosses, parents, teachers, government officials, etc. We may not agree with them. They may not be worthy of our respect and loyalty. But if God has placed them over us in any capacity, we have a responsibility to honor them. Realizing that ultimately, we aren't serving them, but we are serving God makes it a lot easier to submit to their authority and do our work with excellence and integrity. God will reward our efforts. He is the source of our provision, and we can depend on His faithfulness.

Isaiah 39-41
Psalm 106:13-18
Proverbs 23:17-18
Colossians 4:2-18

September 23

STRENGTH FOR THE WEARY

"Do you not know? Have you not heard? The Lord is the everlasting God, the Creator of the ends of the Earth, He will not grow tired or weary, and His understanding no one can fathom. He gives strength to the weary and increases the power of the weak. Even youths grow tired and weary, and young men stumble and fall; but those who hope in the Lord will renew their strength. They will soar on wings like eagles; they will run and not grow weary; they will walk and not be faint." Isaiah 40:28-31 NIV

"So do not fear, for I am with you; do not be dismayed, for I am your God. I will strengthen you and help you; I will uphold you with My righteous right hand. All who rage against you will surely be ashamed and disgraced; those who oppose you will be as nothing and perish. For I am the Lord your God who takes hold of your right hand and says to you, 'Do not fear; I will help you.'" Isaiah 41:10, 11, 13 NIV

THESE VERSES ARE a great source of hope and comfort to believers. The last two years have made us all weary. A worldwide pandemic, racial unrest, political divisions, unemployment, financial difficulties, natural disasters, wars, etc. have blindsided us all. It seems that we are in the middle of one problem when another one sneaks up behind us that is worse than the first. We are all living with a sense of dread wondering what is going to happen next and waiting for the other shoe to drop. As I write this I have several friends in ICU on ventilators with Covid pneumonia, my uncle who has significant heart issues was just diagnosed with Covid, a friend's three year old child was diagnosed with leukemia, my sister (not by blood but by choice) had brain surgery and is in rehab, a dear friend's husband has prostate cancer, 2 young men that I am very close to and another that I am close to his wife's family are undergoing treatment for testicular cancer, and several women I know are in the midst of breast cancer treatment. Hospitals are full, goods and services are becoming scarce, schools are contemplating shutting down again because so many students and teachers are either sick or in quarantine. Just when we thought things were getting back to normal, Delta raised its ugly head and seems to be even worse than the original virus and there seem to be more variants ahead. And if that isn't enough, the news is filled with heartbreaking stories about the horrors in Afghanistan, Lebanon, Syria, and Iran. We can hardly catch our breath.

There are difficulties in life that overwhelm even the strongest of people and fears that plague the hearts of even the most courageous. Young men grow tired and weary, and they stumble and fall because they are relying on their own inner strength and human resources. Only God's power is sufficient to sustain us during the storms of life. If we place our hope in our own power and ability, our weaknesses will quickly become evident. If we place our hope in government and leaders, we will be disappointed. If we place our hope in money and resources, they will prove to be inadequate. But these verses assure us that those who place their hope in the Lord will renew their strength. We will be able to soar above our difficulties. We will run and not grow weary and walk and not faint. It does not mean that we will not face difficulties because we certainly will. Relying on God does not protect us from problems, but we can be confident that when we place our faith and trust in Him, He will take care of us. His grace is sufficient for us. His peace sustains us, and His strength enables us to face whatever this life holds. "I have told you these things, so that in Me you may have peace. In this world you will have trouble. But take heart! I have overcome the world." John 16:33 (NIV) In these passages, Isaiah promises us that we have no need to fear because He is always with us, and He will help us. No matter what we are facing, we can trust that He will not let us down. He is the Creator of the ends of the Earth, and He never grows tired or weary. We cannot even fathom the depth of His understanding. In His wisdom and knowledge, He always knows what is best for us and is working tirelessly on our behalf to bring it about.

Isaiah 42-43
Psalm 106:19-27
Proverbs 23:19-21
I Thessalonians 1

September 24

"You are Mine"

"But now, this is what the Lord says— 'Do not fear, for I have redeemed you; I have summoned you by name; you are Mine. When you pass through the waters, I will be with you; and when you pass through the rivers, they will not sweep over you. When you walk through the fire, you will not be burned; the flames will not set you ablaze. For I am the Lord your God, the Holy One of Israel, your Savior; Since you are precious and honored in My sight, and because I love you, I will give people in exchange for you, nations in exchange for your life. Do not be afraid, for I am with you; I will bring your children from the east and gather you from the west." Isaiah 43:1-5 NIV

ISRAEL IS GOD'S chosen people. Out of all the people of the world, He picked them. It was not because of anything they did to deserve His blessing. Throughout history they failed Him over and over and over. He protected them, rescued them, provided for them, and loved them and they repeatedly turned to other gods and forsook Him. They were faithless and yet He remained faithful. They even rejected His Son and still refuse to believe that Jesus is their promised Messiah. These verses explain to us that God has not turned His back on Israel even though they have been disobedient. Because He loves them, He promises to always be with them. He has redeemed them and called them by name. They belong to Him. When they rejected Him, God turned His attention to the Gentiles, but there will come a day when He again focusses His attention on Israel. They are His children, and He has not forgotten them. He will gather them all again in Israel and at that point they will turn to Him and trust Him.

God's faithfulness to Israel as displayed time and time again in the Bible is a source of great comfort to me. Just as He chose Israel, He has chosen me. He has redeemed me and called me by name. I am His. It is not based on my efforts or faithfulness. Faithfulness is part of His character. He cannot be unfaithful. His faithfulness to Israel gives me complete confidence in His faithfulness to me. I am precious and honored in His sight and He loves me. Psalm 100:3 says, "Know that the Lord, He is God! It is He who made us, and we are His; we are His people, and the sheep of His pasture." (NIV) I John 3:1 tells us, "See what kind of love the Father has given to us, that we should be called children of God; and so, we are." (ESV) John 1:12 says, "But to all who did receive Him, who believed in His name, He gave the right to become children of God." (ESV) I belong to Him. I am His precious child. Nothing can change that. I can rest in the assurance that He will never leave me or forsake me, and He will protect and provide for me.

September 25

Isaiah 44-46
Psalm 106:28-39
Proverbs 23:22-23
I Thessalonians 2

The Absurdity of Idols

"I am the First and the Last; apart from Me there is no God. Who then is like Me? No, there is no other Rock; I know not one. All who make idols are nothing, and the things they treasure are worthless. He fashions a god and worships it; he makes an idol and bows down to it. They know nothing, they understand nothing; no one stops to think, no one has the knowledge or understanding to say, 'Half of it I used for fuel; I even baked bread over its coals, I roasted meat and I ate. Shall I make a detestable thing from what is left? Shall I bow down to a block of wood?' Such a person feeds on ashes; a deluded heart misleads him; he cannot save himself, or say, 'Is not this thing in my right hand a lie?'" Isaiah 44:6-8, 9, 15, 18, 19, 20 NIV

I LOVE THESE two chapters in Isaiah. They lay out the absolute absurdity of bowing down and worshipping idols. Isaiah lays out the case that a blacksmith or goldsmith formed the idol, shaped it, and cast it in gold. Chapter 46 tells us that they take it out of the fire and put it up on a shelf and then bow down to it. They cry out to it expecting an answer to their pleas, but they get none because it is a worthless object made by human hands. It has no power and cannot do anything but sit on a shelf. This does seem utterly ridiculous. It does not make any logical sense. We know that an inanimate object has no power to do anything to help us. The idea of bowing down to an idol seems foreign to us now. Most of us do not have gold statues or altars in our homes that we worship. However, I think this passage is still applicable to our lives. Isaiah is referring to worshipping anything other than the One True God. While we may not bow down to statues, we all need to evaluate our lives to examine our priorities. Are we worshipping anything in our lives instead of or in addition to God? Are we allowing anything to take precedence over God? Even good things can become idols if we let them become more important than our relationship with God. Material possessions, our reputation, power, careers, family, relationships, children, leisure activities, health and fitness, alcohol, drugs, are just a few of the things that can take over our time and attention in such a way that they become an idol to us.

This is difficult to evaluate because obviously we have responsibilities. We must take care of our children, we must give time and attention to our jobs to support our family and fulfill God's purposes for our lives, we need to engage in activities to stay fit and take care of the bodies God entrusted to us, and it is important to nurture and care for our family and friends. All those things are necessary and take our time and attention. The problem comes when those things consume us and become too important. Balance is the key. We each need to periodically do some self-evaluation and prayerfully ask God to show us if our priorities are not where they need to be.

Different seasons bring different responsibilities and priorities, so it is important to seek God and allow Him to show you if you need to make any changes. Stress, anxiety, and feeling overwhelmed are good indicators that something is out of balance and that it is time to ask Him for wisdom and help. Let us not be guilty of bowing to things that are worthless and cannot give meaning and purpose. "Jesus said, 'Worship the Lord your God and serve Him only." Luke 4:8 (NIV)

September 26

Isaiah 47-48
Psalm 106:40-48
Proverbs 23:24-25
I Thessalonians 3

The Evil of Magic

"Keep on, then, with your magic spells and with your many sorceries, which you have labored at since childhood. Let your astrologers come forward, those stargazers who make predictions month by month, let them save you from what is coming upon you. They cannot even save themselves from the power of the flame. All of them go on in their error; there is not one that can save you." Isaiah 47:12-15 NIV

YESTERDAY WE DISCUSSED the absurdity of worshipping man-made idols and giving our time and attention to things that cannot satisfy. Today Isaiah warns us of another danger that is just as prevalent today as it was in biblical times. Astrologers, sorcery, and magic are all around us. Satan has used the entertainment industry to desensitize us to the evil it represents. It has happened so slowly that we didn't even realize it. When I was a kid, I loved watching *Bewitched*. It was pretty harmless. Samantha was a "good witch" and just wanted to live a normal life married to a human. *Sabrina the Teenage Witch, Wizards of Waverly Place, and The Good Witch* were all used to slowly introduce witchcraft to us in a way that seemed harmless and intriguing. Harry Potter introduced a more exciting element to sorcery and witchcraft and targeted impressionable preteen and teenaged kids. It is nothing new. Ouija boards have been around since the late 1800's. Astrologers, fortune tellers, and Tarot cards have been around for centuries. Magic has been used by Satan since the beginning of time to entice people to participate in activities that do not glorify God. We all have an innate desire to want to know our future and control the world around us. I know Christians who read their horoscopes every day. They think it is just harmless fun, but there is an element to which they believe it.

Satan is very powerful, and he is very smart. He has been around for centuries. He cannot tell the future because He is not omniscient. Only God, the One True God, Creator of the Universe knows what the future holds. He knows everything that has happened in the past and everything that will happen for all of eternity. Satan does not have that power. However, he can see things happening in the present that we cannot see that affect future events. A fortune teller could tell you that your boyfriend is going to propose to you, and it come true because Satan saw him buy you a ring. A medium could tell you something they claim to have "received" from your dead grandmother that only she could know because Satan saw when it happened years ago. Satan is very good at deception. He knows you and he knows how to entice you. He looks at what is happening now and what has happened in the past and makes an educated guess as to what is likely to happen in the future. Magic and fortune telling are schemes by Satan to tempt us with knowledge we are not intended to have and power that does not belong to us. We are not supposed to know the future. God holds our future. We have the idea that if we know what is going to happen in the future, we can prepare for it, good or bad. But the thing is, we don't have to worry about it. God can see the future and He is already at work preparing us for whatever will happen. He is giving us the life experiences we will need to deal with whatever comes to us. He is developing and maturing us so that we are ready for what He can see is in our future. Our loving Father is taking care of all of it. Satan is not tempting us to find out the future for our good. His motive is to get us to trust in ourselves and not to place our faith in God. As believers we need to recognize his schemes and flee from them. We do not need to allow Satan to get a foothold in our lives by participating in any of these activities. Horoscopes, astrology, tarot cards, witchcraft, Ouija boards, and fortune tellers are evil. There is no place in the life of a believer for any of these things. And it is even more important that we protect our children from these things. They may seem harmless, but they are not. Even allowing them to watch movies and read books about witchcraft and sorcery desensitizes them to the evil in the world that is very real and powerful.

September 27

Isaiah 49-50
Psalm 107:1-9
Proverbs 23:26-28
I Thessalonians 4

The Dead in Christ

"Brothers and sisters, we do not want you to be uninformed about those who sleep in death, so that you do not grieve like the rest of mankind, who have no hope. For we believe that Jesus died and rose again, and so we believe that God will bring with Jesus those who have fallen asleep in Him." I Thessalonians 4:13-14 NIV

Covid, cancer and death are all around us. It seems that every few days I find out about someone else who has been diagnosed with cancer or who is hospitalized with Covid. Disease and viruses do not discriminate. They strike men and women, black and white, the elderly and the young, Christians and nonChristians, rich and poor. None of us are immune. Unless Jesus comes back first, every one of us will have to face death. In the last year, I can't even count the number of funerals that I have either been to or been unable to attend due to Covid restrictions. Most of those funerals were for people that I believe were Christians. Some of them, however, were for people who I know did not believe in Jesus or who did not live lives that would suggest that they did. A funeral for a believer is very different than one for a non-believer. While there is grieving, sadness and crying at both, there is just a different atmosphere. When someone who loves Jesus dies, we grieve for ourselves. We miss them and we grieve our loss. We grieve going on with our lives knowing that they are gone, but we do not grieve for them. We have an assurance that they are in a better place. When they take their last breath here, they are ushered into Heaven where they are greeted by their Lord and Savior, Jesus Christ. They get to see Him face to face and experience the reality of the hope of our salvation. If they have experienced a period of illness, we know that they have been freed from their suffering and are no longer experiencing pain, disability, and weakness. This gives us comfort and hope in the midst of our grief. And we know that, while we may be apart for a while, we will see them again when we make it to Heaven.

There is no such hope at the funeral of someone who does not have a relationship with Jesus. We grieve for them because we know that they are not in Heaven. There is a very real place called Hell that is the eternal resting place of all those who do not accept Jesus as their Savior. It is a place of torment, pain, and horror. Satan would like for us to believe that it is not a real place and that ultimately everyone either goes to Heaven or just dies and ceases to exist. The Bible is very clear that is not the case. Hell is described as "eternal fire," "weeping and gnashing of teeth," "a pit of darkness," "Lake of Fire," "fire and brimstone," "unquenchable fire," and "tormented day and night forever and ever." The sobering reality of Hell should make us passionate about sharing the hope we have in Jesus with everyone we know.

Isaiah 51-53
Psalm 107:10-16
Proverbs 23:29-35
I Thessalonians 5:1-11

September 28

The Gospel According to Isaiah

"But He was pierced for our transgressions, He was crushed for our iniquities; the punishment that brought us peace was on Him, and by His wounds we are healed. We all, like sheep, have gone astray, each of us has turned to our own way; and the Lord has laid on Him the iniquity of us all. He was oppressed and afflicted, yet He did not open His mouth; He was led like a lamb to the slaughter and as a sheep before its shearers is silent, so He did not open His mouth." Isaiah 53:5-7 NIV

Isaiah lived 700 years before Jesus. In chapter 53, Isaiah describes the life and ministry of Jesus in great detail. He describes His early life, His appearance, and His rejection by the people of Israel. He then goes on to foretell the events leading up to His death and lays out the gospel message in a clear and understandable way. The book of Isaiah was available before Jesus ever took His first breath on Earth. Looking back on it now, it seems like this chapter could have been written by Luke or John to tell us about Jesus' ministry and sacrifice. Or it could have been written by Paul to explain the meaning of His death and resurrection. But that is not the case. This chapter was written at least 700 years before Jesus was born. God inspired Isaiah to put these details in his book to tell us what to expect and as proof that Jesus was indeed the long-awaited Messiah. We can clearly see that this chapter is talking about Jesus, but at the time I doubt that even Isaiah understood what he was writing. The Jews expected the Messiah to come as a conquering hero, not as a suffering servant. Only God could have inspired him to write this description. Isaiah could not have guessed the events that were to transpire with such accurate detail.

Not only does chapter 53 describe the events of Jesus' life accurately, but it also lays out God's redemptive plan and explains the purpose behind the plan. We all, individually and collectively, have gone astray. We have each chosen to follow our own path and wandered away from His perfect plan. Instead of following our loving, protective Shepherd, we have chosen our sin and selfish desires. Jesus humbly and willingly accepted the punishment for our sins. He remained silent before His accusers to pay the price for our redemption. He was pierced for our transgressions and crushed for our iniquities. We can have peace with God because He took the punishment that we deserved. He was spotless and pure like a sacrificial lamb, but He chose to be numbered with the guilty. He not only suffered the physical pain of death, but He also willingly accepted the humiliation and emotional agony of crucifixion. Jesus knew that this was the plan from the beginning. He was motivated to follow through with the plan by His love for us and His commitment to obeying His Father's will.

September 29

Isaiah 54-55
Psalm 107:17-22
Proverbs 24:1-2
I Thessalonians 5:12-28

The Picture

"'For My thoughts are not your thoughts neither are your ways My ways,' declares the Lord. 'As the heavens are higher than the Earth, so are My ways higher than your ways and My thoughts than your thoughts. As the rain and the snow come down from Heaven, and do not return to it without watering the Earth and making it bud and flourish, so that it yields seed for the sower and bread for the eater, so is My Word that goes out from My mouth: It will not return to Me empty but will accomplish what I desire and achieve the purpose for which I sent it." Isaiah 55:8-11 NIV

THE OLDER I get the more I recognize how much I don't know. When I was younger, I thought I was pretty smart. I thought I had it all figured out or at least had a good grasp of what was right and good. I am beginning to realize how little I understand. What I can see and perceive is only a small portion of the whole picture. I once heard a story of a little girl watching her grandmother embroidering a picture. Day after day she saw her grandmother tirelessly sewing, weaving her needle in and out of the material and tying knots while she played on the floor below. Her grandmother talked about the beautiful picture she was making and seemed very happy with her progress. As the days passed, the little girl became more and more confused because all she could see was random seams of thread dotted by ugly knots with dangling string. From her perspective on the ground, it was not a beautiful picture at all. She loved her grandmother and did not want to hurt her feelings, but she was afraid that her grandmother was wasting her time making something that no one would like. One day her grandmother took the picture out of the embroidery hoop and placed it on the kitchen table. She picked up the little girl, held her up, and showed her the finished product. The little girl was shocked. In front of her was the most beautiful picture she had ever seen. It was a garden with all different kinds of brightly colored flowers. In the middle was a large tree with a swing and a puppy and kitten playing below. It made her happy just to look at the beautiful scene. Her grandmother saw that she was confused and asked why. The girl explained that she had been watching her work on this picture for days and it just looked like a jumbled mess with strings and knots, so she didn't understand how it had become this beautiful picture. Her grandmother turned the picture over and she realized that what she had been seeing was the bottom of the picture.

We are like this little girl. We are watching what God is doing from below. What we see often just looks like a big mess. We see random events that don't make sense and sometimes everything just feels like it is all tied up in knots. We are only seeing a tiny piece of the big picture and our perspective doesn't allow us to understand everything that is really going on. When we can't understand, we have to just trust. We can place our faith in our Heavenly Father and have confidence that His ways are higher than our ways and His thoughts are higher than our thoughts. He knows what He is doing. His purposes will be accomplished, and He will do what He says He will do. I believe that one day He will pick us up in His arms and show us the big picture and reveal to us the beauty of His plan. That may not happen this side of Heaven, but in the meantime, we can rest in the knowledge of His sovereignty and love for us.

September 30

Isaiah 56-57
Psalm 107:23-32
Proverbs 24:3-4
2 Thessalonians 1

Interceding Prayers

"With this in mind, we constantly pray for you, that God may make you worthy of His calling, and that by His power He may bring to fruition your every deed prompted by faith. We pray this so that the name of our Lord Jesus may be glorified in you and you in Him, according to the grace of our God and the Lord Jesus Christ." 2 Thessalonians 1:11-12 NIV

Throughout Paul's letters to the churches, he repeatedly tells them that he is praying for them. He prays for strength when they are being persecuted, boldness to share their faith, hope when they are suffering, and peace during times of difficulty. This is a common theme in his interactions with the believers in the early church. Paul knew that they could not serve the Lord and be successful in ministry on their own strength and power. He knew that they needed God's help. Paul could not be in each of these churches all the time and even if he was present, he recognized that he does not have the power to help them. But what he could do for them was pray for God to indwell them and empower them to accomplish His purposes. His prayers were the best and most effective help he could give them.

I don't think we do a very good job of praying for our fellow believers. We pray for them when they are sick or when they are hurting. We pray in times of crisis and difficulty, but do we pray for each other daily? Do we pray for the ministry of our fellow believers? Do we pray that God will embolden them and give them opportunities to share the gospel? Do we pray for their spiritual growth? Do we pray that God would use them to accomplish His purposes and that God would be glorified through their lives? This is what Paul is teaching us to do. He is leading by example and encouraging us to go before the throne of God on behalf of others. We need each other. This should be a part of our daily prayers for each other. How much more effective could each of us be if we had others praying for us daily that God would work mightily in our lives and that He would be glorified and exalted by our actions? Our prayers on their behalf might be the very thing that keeps them from falling to temptation or that gives them the boldness to share their faith with someone. It might be the thing that gives them the strength to keep pressing on even when life is hard. Prayer is the most effective tool we have to help each other. We do not have the power to help anyone, but we know the One who does, and we have access to the throne room of Heaven so we can boldly take our requests to God pleading with Him on their behalf. Instead of just praying in a crisis, let's set aside time to pray for others the way Paul prayed for them and make this a part of our daily routine.

October 1

Isaiah 58-59
Psalm 107:33-43
Proverbs 24:5-6
2 Thessalonians 2

The Man of Lawlessness

"And now you know what is holding him back, so that he may be revealed at the proper time. For the secret power of lawlessness is already at work; but the One who now holds it back will continue to do so till He is taken out of the way. And then the lawless one will be revealed, whom the Lord Jesus will overthrow with the breath of His mouth and destroy by the splendor of His coming." 2 Thessalonians 2:6-8 NIV

SATAN IS CLEARLY at work in our world today. We see evil and darkness everywhere we look. We only have to turn on the news to see the horrors that Satan and his demons have unleashed on our world. There are times when it appears that evil is winning. Persecution, oppression, and injustice seem to be unchecked. Bad people go unpunished and good people suffer. But then we hear about people helping their neighbors during a hurricane, putting their own lives at risk to rescue people stranded on a roof, and providing food, water and supplies to those whose houses have been flooded. We see pictures of soldiers comforting scared children and risking their lives to get as many people out of Afghanistan as possible. We hear about healthcare workers who tirelessly care for the sick and dying day in and day out with no end in sight. Right now, there is a restrainer who is preventing Satan from doing all that he wants to do. That restrainer is the Holy Spirit. The Holy Spirit is living in the hearts of millions of Christians all over the world. Evil is present, but good and light are also present. Light overcomes darkness. As long as there are Christians in the world, the Holy Spirit is present because He is alive and active in each of us. Goodness, love, peace, and joy are all very evident. Darkness cannot defeat the light. Light shines the brightest in the darkness.

One day, every Christian on Earth will be removed in the rapture. At that point, the Holy Spirit will be gone, and the goodness we see now, will not be found. Evil will prevail. This passage supports the pretribulation rapture of the church. It explains that the Restrainer, the One now holding back the power of lawlessness, will be taken away and then the Man of Lawlessness, the Antichrist, will be revealed. For seven years, he will rule and reign on Earth and God's wrath will be poured out on the Earth and those who are left behind. At the end of that time, Jesus will return and overthrow Satan with the breath of His mouth. He will throw him into the Lake of Fire and Jesus will establish the millennial kingdom. We do not know when these events will take place, but we can be certain that when God decides it is time, the trumpet will sound and everyone on Earth who has accepted Jesus as their Lord and Savior will be taken to Heaven. The evil we see now is nothing compared to the evil that will dominate the world after the Holy Spirit is taken out. Let us be bold in sharing Jesus with everyone who will listen so that no one is left behind when the Restrainer is removed. We do not want anyone to experience the evil Satan and the Antichrist have planned for the world when we are gone.

October 2

Isaiah 60-61
Psalm 108:1-6
Proverbs 24:7
2 Thessalonians 3

The Value of Work

"For when we were with you, we gave you this rule: 'The one who is unwilling to work shall not eat.' We hear that some among you are idle and disruptive. They are not busy; they are busybodies." 2 Thessalonians 3:10-11 NIV

THIS PRINCIPLE IS one that we seem to have forgotten in our politically correct culture. Now, before you get angry with me and send me hateful comments, this is not talking about those who are truly disabled and those who cannot work. It says, "the one who is unwilling to work." But this principle does apply to those who can't find a job that they like or that they think they deserve or a job that matches their education. As a society we have raised a generation of kids who were awarded for participation and told how special they are. In an attempt to give them healthy self-esteem we have created kids who do not know the satisfaction of hard work and the thrill of earned accomplishments. They don't understand how good it feels to work really hard for something and then get it instead of it being given to them because they "tried." Instead of creating healthy self-esteem, this generation of young adults suffers from more depression and higher incidences of suicide than any previous generation. I do not believe it is because we are more aware of it and so it just seems higher. If you look at society as a whole and at young adults you know, it is painfully evident that there is a problem. I know there are exceptions to this. I know many young adults who are hardworking and diligent. But if you drive down the road you can see dozens of help-wanted signs and every business I know is trying to find more people to work. Showing up on time, working hard all day, doing whatever needs to be done, staying late until the job is done, not complaining about being asked to do something that isn't in your "job description," actually working instead of staying on your phone or on social media all day, and being happy that you have a job that is paying you so that you can pay your bills have all become rarities.

We were designed by our Creator to work. Adam and Eve were given a garden to tend and animals to care for. We are not meant to be idle. Idleness leads to boredom, which leads to sin. God knows that we need to keep busy. He has designed each of us for a purpose. He has work for each of us to do. As parents our job is to help our children figure out what God has designed them to do and prepare them for it. Our job is not to make their lives easy. An easy life is not the ultimate goal. The goal is that we train them to be the productive, godly, diligent, hardworking adults that God needs them to be so that they can accomplish what He has planned for them. We are all uniquely made by our Creator for a purpose. Our self-esteem should be founded in who we are in Christ. A hard day's work is good for all of us. Paul explains in this passage that if we are not busy, we will become busybodies. If we are not working hard at the things we are supposed to be doing, we will have time to get into things we have no business being involved in. If you find yourself with idle time, do not spend it on social media, go volunteer at a local ministry. There are plenty of opportunities all around you to help others. You only need to look around to see hurting people in need of someone to take the time to love them. Be that person. I feel like I need to make a disclaimer here. I am not saying we don't need times of rest. God's perfect plan is for us to work hard, be productive and accomplish His purposes for six days a week and then on the seventh we are supposed to rest and worship. We all need to have the proper balance. Rest time is good and profitable. Idle time is unproductive and leads to destruction.

October 3

Isaiah 62-64
Psalm 108:7-13
Proverbs 24:8-9
I Timothy 1

The Worst Sinner

"Here is a trustworthy saying that deserves full acceptance: Christ Jesus came into the world to save sinners---of whom I am the worst. But for that very reason I was shown mercy so that in me, the worst of sinners, Christ Jesus might display His immense patience as an example for those who would believe in Him and receive eternal life. Now to the King eternal, immortal, invisible, the Only God, be honor and glory forever and ever. Amen." I Timothy 1:15-17 NIV

PAUL HAS GIVEN us an excellent example to follow. He is not telling us that he is the worst sinner so that we can be at ease because we are not as bad as him. Unfortunately, I think most of us think that we aren't really that bad. We compare ourselves to others and we usually come out looking pretty good. We tend to look at the sins of others and think they are terrible, but when we evaluate our own sin, we justify and rationalize and make excuses. We blame others or our circumstances. Often, we don't even understand why we do the things we do or why we make the choices that we make, so we conclude that it isn't our fault, and we can't help ourselves. Paul did not do that. Paul honestly examined his heart and his life. He did not compare himself to others. He realistically viewed himself in relation to a holy and just God. He compared himself to the perfect, sinless Son of God and concluded that Jesus Christ came into the world to save sinners and he was the worst of them all. He admitted that he was a wretched sinner that needed to be saved and asked God to forgive him. Then he gratefully accepted Jesus' offer of mercy and grace that gave him eternal life. He recognized that he had nothing to offer Jesus that could earn His favor. He came humbly and meekly begging for mercy. And then he spent the rest of his life telling others how they can receive this free gift for themselves.

Paul could have become arrogant because Jesus revealed Himself to Paul on the road to Damascus. He could have thought he was special because God chose him to take the gospel to the Gentiles. He could have been prideful that God used him to write most of the New Testament. Instead, he was humbled that God would use someone who was the worst of sinners to display His patience as an example for others. He never lost sight of who he was and that all the glory belonged to God and not to him. This is a powerful reminder to us when we begin to think more highly of ourselves than we ought. A realistic examination of our hearts in comparison to a holy and just God will fill us with humility and appreciation. Like Paul, we will want to tell everyone who will listen what He has done for us and what He can do for them. Viewing ourselves realistically will also help us view others differently. Gratitude for the mercy and grace we have been given will overflow from our hearts so that we can extend that mercy and grace to others. Can we, like Paul, say with full acceptance, "Jesus Christ came into the world to save sinners—of whom I am the worst"?

Isaiah 65-66
Psalm 109:1-8
Proverbs 24:10-12
I Timothy 2

Those in Authority

"I urge, then, first of all, that petitions, prayers, intercession and thanksgiving by made for all people—for kings and all those in authority, that we may live peaceful and quiet lives in all godliness and holiness. This is good, and pleases God our Savior, who wants all people to be saved and to come to a knowledge of the truth."
1 Timothy 2:1-4 NIV

This is a challenging passage. Over the last year, we have witnessed more division in our country than we have seen since the Civil War. Hatred and anger are evident on social media, in the workplace and at family gatherings. For almost 250 years we have been a diverse nation. The thing that has made us work for so long is that we have the freedom to express different opinions. Sometimes one side is right and sometimes the other side is right, but most of the time both sides get some of the things right and some of them wrong. None of us have all the answers. Life is complicated and none of us have it all figured out. We can have very strong opinions and believe that we are right, and the other side is wrong. Our forefathers were just as strident in their beliefs and did not waver in expressing them. But what is different now is that we have lost our respect and civility. This country works because we respect our diversity. We know that we function better in community. We work best when we come together and discuss our opinions. When we listen to the other side, we can understand where they are coming from and why they believe what they believe. We may not change our mind and we may still think they are totally wrong, but if we look at an issue from someone else's perspective, instead of getting angry and hating them, we can empathize with them. It is not necessary to hate someone who has a different opinion than we do. We don't have to "pick sides." If you are an Auburn football fan, it is required that you hate everyone who is an Alabama fan (at least during football season). In real life, we don't have to do that. We can love people who have completely opposite opinions than we have. We can love people who voted for the person we think is horrible.

Both sides of the political aisle are equally guilty of this. We have made it personal. Instead of listening to the other side and trying to understand where they are coming from, we have vilified them and called them all evil. If you voted for _____, you are a bad person. Or if you didn't vote for _____, then you can't be a Christian. Don't get me wrong. I know there are very important issues at stake. I have very strong opinions about most of those issues myself. I am preaching to myself here. This passage in I Timothy tells us what we need to be doing instead of getting on social media spewing hatred. Paul urges us to pray for each other. He tells us to intercede for our leaders and to live a peaceful, quiet life of godliness and holiness. God wants all people to be saved and to come to a knowledge of the truth. That means that those leaders that we are bashing and vilifying, God wants to save. The ones we are calling evil and terrible, God loves and more than anything He wants them to turn to Him. Instead of hating them, we need to be praying for them. Instead of saying terrible things about them, we need to pray for their souls. We need to be quick to listen and slow to speak. Paul is telling us that we not only can live peacefully with those we disagree with, but we should. As believers we must be different from the world. We should stand up for what we believe. We should fight for godliness and holiness in our culture. We should be concerned about the things that concern God. But we should do it in a way that is loving, respectful and godly with much prayer and seeking God for wisdom and clarity.

October 5

Jeremiah 1-2
Psalm 109:9-20
Proverbs 24:13-14
I Timothy 3

As Sweet as Honey

> "Eat honey, my son, for it is good; honey from the comb is sweet to your taste. Know also that wisdom is like honey for you: If you find it, there is a future hope for you, and your hope will not be cut off." Proverbs 24:13-14 NIV

WISDOM IS AN interesting thing. We often equate wisdom with intelligence, but that is inaccurate. There are a lot of very smart people who have no wisdom and a lot of people who would not be considered very smart, who are very wise. Wisdom has very little to do with intelligence. The Cambridge Dictionary defines wisdom as "the ability to use knowledge and experience to make good decisions and judgements."[14] The Free Dictionary defines it as "the ability to discern or judge what is true, right or lasting; insight."[15] The Bible tells us a lot about wisdom. It explains that wisdom is not something that we can study and learn. It isn't a course we can take with homework and tests and then a grade when we complete the course. Wisdom is from God. Wisdom is something to be sought after like precious treasure. Proverbs is filled with promises for those who seek after wisdom. Let's look at a few of those promises:

1. Divine Guidance-

   "Trust in the Lord with all your heart and lean not on your own understanding. In all your ways submit to Him, and He will make your paths straight." Proverbs 3:5-6 (NIV)

   "For the Lord gives wisdom, from His mouth come knowledge and understanding." Proverbs 2:6 (NIV)

2. Divine Protection-

   "Don't abandon wisdom, and she will watch over you; love her and she will guard you." Proverbs 4:6 (HCSB)

   a. Wisdom can protect us from the evil of dangerous situations, harmful substances, and destructive circumstances. "The wise fear the Lord and shun evil, but a fool is hotheaded and yet feels secure." Proverbs 14:16 (NIV)
   b. Wisdom can protect us from people who entice us to do evil. "Wisdom will save you from the ways of wicked men, from men whose words are perverse, who have left the straight paths to walk in dark ways, who delight in doing wrong and rejoice in the perverseness of evil, whose paths are crooked and who are devious in their ways." Proverbs 2:12-15 (NIV)
   c. Wisdom protects us from our own emotions, feelings, and desires. "The one who trusts in himself is a fool, but the one who walks in wisdom will be safe." Proverbs 28:26 (HCSB)

3. Divine Peace-

   "Maintain your wisdom and discretion. My son don't lose sight of them. They will be life for you and adornment for your neck. Then you will go safely on your way; your foot will not stumble. When you lie down, you will not be afraid; you will lie down, and your sleep will be pleasant. Don't fear sudden danger or the ruin of the wicked when it comes, for the Lord will be your confidence and will keep your foot from a snare." Proverbs 2:21-26 (CSB)

4. Divine Health- This includes physical, mental, and spiritual health.

   "Don't consider yourself to be wise; fear the Lord and turn away from evil. This will be healing for your body, strengthening for your bones." Proverbs 3:7-8 (HCSB)

   "The fear of the Lord prolongs life, but the years of the wicked will be short." Proverbs 10:27 (ESV)

5. Divine Provision- Wisdom brings riches and wealth. This is not only speaking of material possessions, but more importantly the riches of personal relationships, peace, joy, and love.

   "Blessed is the one who finds wisdom, and the one who gets understanding, for the gain from her is better than gain from silver or profit better than gold. She is more precious than jewels, and nothing you desire can compare with her. Long life is in her right hand; in her left hand are riches and honor. Her ways are ways of pleasantness, and all her paths are peace." Proverbs 3:13-18 (ESV)

   Solomon compares wisdom to the sweetness of honey because the one who is wise is spared many of the heartaches of life that are a consequence of poor choices and foolish living. The wise also have the benefit of God's guidance, presence, and protection to help them deal with any difficulty they experience. They have hope for the future because they understand that they do not face the future alone. God is already there making provision for their every need.

October 6

Jeremiah 3-4
Psalm 109:21-31
Proverbs 24:15-16
I Timothy 4

Youthful Leaders

"Don't let anyone look down on you because you are young, but set an example for the believers in speech, in conduct, in love, in faith and in purity. Be diligent in these matters; give yourself wholly to them, so that everyone may see your progress. Watch your life and doctrine closely. Persevere in them, because if you do, you will save both yourself and your hearers." I Timothy 4:12, 15-16 NIV

PAUL WROTE THIS letter to Timothy. Timothy was probably around forty years old when this letter was written. He was younger than many of the other apostles and apparently there were some who were questioning his authority because of his age. Paul is encouraging Timothy that he does not need to get all upset about it. He just needs to keep doing the things he is doing, and everyone will see his maturity and will follow his leading. This is a good reminder to all of us. For those of us who are a little older, it is a good reminder that we don't know everything. While it is true that age and experience do bring wisdom and understanding, it is also true that wisdom and knowledge come from God, and He imparts that as He chooses. Just as God chose to use Timothy, He is using many godly young men and women today to reach a lost and dying world. We should not dismiss the teaching of anyone simply because of their age. Thankfully, there are many younger men and women who read these devotions every day. Seeing their zeal and commitment to the Lord is encouraging to me and gives me hope for the future. I want to encourage you as Paul encouraged Timothy. Do not let anyone look down on you because of your age. Please keep doing the things you are doing. The next generation is depending on you. Set an example for believers and be diligent. Give yourself wholly to the Lord, watch your life and persevere. Paul told Timothy several things to keep an eye on and I think these are applicable to each of us:

1. Speech- This includes gossip, cursing, angry outbursts, lying, slander, taking the Lord's name in vain, idle chatter, vulgar jokes, grumbling and complaining, etc.

   "Do not let any unwholesome talk come out of your mouths, but only what is helpful for building others up according to their needs, that it may benefit those who listen." Ephesians 4:29 (NIV)

2. Conduct- This includes everything we do.

"Whatever happens, conduct yourselves in a manner worthy of the gospel of Christ." Philippians 1:27 (NIV)

"Whatever you do, whether in word or deed, do it all in the name of the Lord Jesus." Colossians 3:17 (NIV)

3. Love- Everything we do should be an expression of our love for God and others.

"Jesus replied, 'Love the Lord your God with all your heart and with all your soul and with all your mind.' This is the first and greatest commandment. And the second is like it: 'Love your neighbor as yourself.'" Matthew 22:37-39 (NIV)

4. Faith- Paul is most likely referring to faithfulness here and is telling Timothy to be faithful to carry out His responsibilities, the things that have been entrusted to him. It is a powerful testimony to others when we work hard and are diligent to fulfill our commitments.

"His master replied, 'Well done, good and faithful servant! You have been faithful with a few things; I will put you in charge of many things. Come and share your master's happiness.'" Matthew 25:21 (NIV)

5. Purity-This is referring to purity of mind and body.

"Finally, brothers and sisters, whatever is true, whatever is noble, whatever is right, whatever is pure, whatever is lovely, whatever is admirable, if anything is excellent or praiseworthy, think about such things." Philippians 4:8 (NIV)

"Create in me a pure heart, O God, and renew a steadfast spirit within me." Psalm 51:10 (NIV)

6. Doctrine- It is essential that our doctrine be accurate. We must not be guilty of false teaching. If you are unsure about a principle, go to your pastor or teacher who can help you make sure your teaching is doctrinally sound.

"He must hold firmly to the trustworthy message as it has been taught, so that he can encourage others by sound doctrine and refute those who oppose it." Titus 1:9 (NIV)

October 7

Jeremiah 5-6
Psalm 110
Proverbs 24:17-18
I Timothy 5

Conspicuous

"The sins of some people are conspicuous, going before them to judgment, but the sins of others appear later. So also, good works are conspicuous, and even those that are not cannot remain hidden." I Timothy 5:24-25 ESV

I USUALLY USE the Holman Christian Standard Bible or the New International Version, but I like the translation of this verse in the English Standard Version. This version uses the word "conspicuous." The NIV and HCSB use the word "obvious." I think the word conspicuous gives us a better image of the meaning Paul is trying to convey. We all know about conspicuous sins, those sins that are out there for everybody to see. To be clear, a sin is a sin. Sin is rebellion against God in any form or fashion. The specific act is not as important as the condition of the heart in doing it. Humanly speaking we have put sins on a scale with murder and rape measuring a 10 and having bad thoughts about people and jealousy at a 1. Somewhere in between we put in premarital sex, lying and all the other things on the list. Each of our lists may vary in the middle, but the top and bottom are probably pretty consistent. That scale cannot be found anywhere in the Bible. It is completely human made. That isn't how God measures sins. To God all sin is a 10. Anything we do that we know we shouldn't do is rebellion against Him. The good news is that God loves us so much that He knows we are going to mess us. He knows we are sinful, and He provided the way for us to be forgiven for all our sins. This verse is not telling us that there are some sins that are worse than other sins. Paul is making the point that there are sins that are more conspicuous than others, but that all sins will be revealed, and be judged. Certainly, some sins hold much more significant earthly consequences. Imprisonment, public humiliation, financial ruin, loss of relationships, and embarrassment are the inevitable consequences of some sins while others are more easily hidden. We may be able to hide our thoughts and actions from other people, but we cannot hide from God. He knows our thoughts and the intentions of our hearts. He knows us better than we know ourselves, but thankfully, He loves us more than we can even imagine. He won't let us get away with sin because He knows that it is not what is best for us. Like a loving Father, He loves us too much to ignore something that is detrimental to us. He will bring it out in the open so we can be free from the bondage it brings.

In the same way, some good works are conspicuous. Some of the good things we do are more public than others. I don't think Paul is talking about purposefully doing things to be seen. Our motives matter. If we are doing things with the motive of having others see us and be impressed, Paul probably would not be calling those "good deeds." He is referring to those good things we do that happen to be more conspicuous. There are other good deeds that are behind the scenes. Paul is assuring us that God sees what we are doing even if no one else does. Our good deeds are not hidden from Him.

October 8

Jeremiah 7-8
Psalm 111
Proverbs 24:19-20
I Timothy 6:1-10

A Root of Evil

> "But godliness with contentment is a great gain. For we brought nothing into the world, and we can take nothing out. But those who want to be rich fall into temptation, a trap, and many foolish and harmful desires which plunge people into ruin and destruction. For the love of money is a root of all kinds of evil, and by craving it, some have wandered away from the faith and pierced themselves with many pains."
> I Timothy 6:6-10 HCSB

MANY PEOPLE HAVE twisted this verse to say that money is the root of all kinds of evil. That is not what it says. It says that the love of money is the root of all kinds of evil. Money itself is not evil. It isn't even bad. Money can be used for a lot of good things. David was very wealthy. Abraham was wealthy. Job was wealthy. The Bible never tells us that having money is a bad thing or even that it is a problem. Our attitude toward money is the thing that makes it good or bad. A proper attitude toward money results in a generous person who holds onto earthly possessions lightly. He recognizes that anything he has been given is a blessing from God and he willingly shares from his bounty with others. God can use him to meet the needs of the church and fellow believers as needs arise. He is content because he knows that God will provide for his needs. He trusts that God knows what he needs before he does and believes that God will do whatever is necessary to meet those needs. He finds his purpose and meaning in his relationship with the Lord and not in his earthly possessions. His eye is on eternity, so he recognizes that money and the things it can buy have no lasting value.

On the other hand, a problematic attitude toward money results in greediness and can lead to "foolish and harmful desires which plunge people into ruin and destruction." The desire to make money can lead people to do things that they never thought they would do. They do not trust that God will meet their needs and they are not content with what they have been given by God. They want more and when they get more, they want even more than that. They find their meaning and purpose in what they have and the status it affords them. Instead of investing in things that have eternal significance, they invest their time and energy in earthly pursuits. They are not able to enjoy the blessings they have because they are consumed with the desire for more. The amount of money one has is not as important as their attitude toward it. There are people with a lot of money and people who don't have much money who manage their money well and have a healthy attitude toward money. There are also people in every financial situation who have unhealthy money habits. It is good to periodically evaluate our attitude toward money asking God to reveal any areas where we need to improve. Financial issues can cause a lot of worry and fear. We need to be purposeful in trusting God and giving Him control of this area of our lives.

October 9

Jeremiah 9-10
Psalm 112:1-5
Proverbs 24:21-22
I Timothy 6:11-21

Boasting in the Lord

"This is what the Lord says: The wise man must not boast in his wisdom; the strong man must not boast in his strength; the wealthy man must not boast in his wealth. But the one who boasts should boast in this, that he understands and knows Me—that I am Yahweh, showing faithful love, justice, and righteousness on the Earth, for I delight in these things." Jeremiah 9:23-24 HCSB

Nobody likes a braggart. We all know those people who brag about themselves and their accomplishments all the time. Social media has made that even easier. We can brag on Facebook and Instagram about things that we wouldn't tell people in person. Tooting our own horns has become an acceptable sign of a "healthy self-esteem." I'm not suggesting we shouldn't post things on social media. There is nothing wrong with being proud of our kids and their achievements or posting pictures to let people know what is going on in our lives. The motive behind the post is the important thing. If we are posting to impress people or to "keep up with the Jones'" there is a problem. Or if we are posting selfies all the time and are worried about how many likes we get, we may need to evaluate our motives. God gives this reminder to Jeremiah because He knows that we tend to think more highly of ourselves than we ought. We need to remember that the only thing we have a right to boast about is our relationship with God. Anything else we may think we have to boast about is something that we received from God. It is not anything that we did so that we should deserve the praise for it. Wealth is a blessing from God. Wisdom is from God. Strength is from God. Any talents and accomplishments that we have are from God, so we have no right to boast about them. The only thing that we can boast about is that we understand and know God, that He is Yahweh, the One, True God. We can boast about all the things He has done for us. We can boast about His faithfulness. We can boast about His love, and we can boast about His presence in our lives. Boasting about God reflects a grateful, humble heart. We are encouraged throughout scripture to boast in the Lord. Instead of being known as someone who brags about themselves all the time, may we be known as someone who won't stop bragging on God.

"Just as it is written, 'Let him who boasts, boast in the Lord.'" I Corinthians 1:31 (NASB1995)

"My soul will make its boast in the Lord; the humble will hear it and rejoice." Psalm 34:2 (NASB1995)

"In God we have boasted all day long. And we will give thanks to Your name forever. Selah." Psalm 44:8 (NASB1995)

"Some boast in chariots and some in horses, but we boast in the name of the Lord our God." Psalm 20:7 (NASB1995)

"But may it never be that I would boast, except in the cross of our Lord Jesus Christ, through which the world has been crucified to me, and I to the world." Galatians 6:14 (NASB1995)

October 10

Jeremiah 11-12
Psalm 112:6-10
Proverbs 24:23-25
2 Timothy 1

Persuaded

"But I am not ashamed, because I know the One I have believed in and am persuaded that He is able to guard what has been entrusted to me until that day." 2 Timothy 1:12 HCSB

I LOVE THIS passage. When I was a little girl, we sang this verse in a hymn and it has stuck with me all these years. It is not talking about knowing facts about God or about knowing all the Bible stories and being able to quote verses about Him. This verse is talking about knowing God in a personal, intimate way. Paul was in prison when he wrote this letter. He had suffered beatings, starvation, shipwreck, and chains for the sake of the gospel. He boldly continued to preach Christ everywhere he went. He was not ashamed of the message because he knew it was the truth. He was completely persuaded because he knew the One that he believed in. He didn't just have head knowledge about Him; he had heart knowledge of Him. He had spent time getting to know Jesus through prayer and studying scripture. Jesus had been with him during those beatings, when he was shipwrecked, and in chains in prison. Paul knew he could trust Jesus with whatever might happen in his future, because He had never let him down before. He had never left his side and had given him the strength to deal with everything that had happened to him. Jesus had proven Himself to be faithful. The more we know Jesus and His character, the easier it is to trust His Word. Whenever we find ourselves doubting and afraid, the best thing we can do is spend more time getting to know Him better. He will prove Himself faithful to us as well.

This old hymn expresses it well. **"I Know Whom I Have Believed."**[16]

I know not why God's wondrous grace to me He hath made known,
Nor why unworthy, Christ in love redeemed me for His own.
But I know whom I have believed, and am persuaded that He is able
To keep that which I've committed unto Him against that day.

I know not how this saving faith to me He did impart,
Nor how believing in His Word wrought peace within my heart
But I know whom I have believed and am persuaded that He is able
To keep that which I've committed unto Him against that day.

I know not how the Spirit moves, convincing us of sin,
Revealing Jesus through the Word, creating faith in Him.
But I know whom I have believed, and am persuaded that He is able

To keep that which I've committed unto Him against that day.

I know not when my Lord may come, at night or noonday fair,
Nor if I walk the vale with Him, or meet Him in the air,
But I know whom I have believed, and am persuaded that He is able
To keep that which I've committed unto Him against that day.

Jeremiah 13-14
Psalm 113:1-3
Proverbs 24:26-27
2 Timothy 2

October 11

Disciple Making

> "And what you have heard from me in the presence of many witnesses, commit to faithful men who will be able to teach others also." 2 Timothy 2:2 HCSB

As a college student, I was involved in the Baptist Student Union. (It is now called Baptist Campus Ministries.) This organization had a profound impact on my life. I made a lot of great friends and grew in my faith. I served in local missions, went on several mission trips, and had a lot of fun. But looking back, there was one thing that had the most lasting impact on me. My campus minister, Clete Sipes, was passionately committed to discipleship and he instilled that passion and commitment in me. He drilled in our heads the principle that Jesus taught His followers. When Jesus died, He only had 3,000 followers. The Son of God came to Earth and reached only 3,000 people. He spent some of His time preaching to huge crowds, but He spent most of His time with a group of twelve guys. He invested in them. He taught the multitudes, but He discipled the twelve. He committed to faithful men who would be able to teach others what they had heard. He prepared them to be disciple makers. He discipled twelve who would then go on to disciple others who would go on to each disciple others. These disciples are responsible for spreading the gospel to the whole world. The message didn't stop when all of those who had heard Jesus' preaching died; it continued to spread because those who heard were equipped to pass it on to others.

Sharing the gospel with others so that they can commit their lives to Christ is essential, but we can't stop there. It is vitally important that we come alongside new Christians and grow them up in their faith. Salvation is only the beginning, not the ultimate goal. The goal is to disciple them so that they are mature believers who can then disciple others. Jesus knew that the way to reach a lost and dying world across generations was discipleship. Jesus trained twelve men. If those 12 men each trained 12, that is 144. If those 144 each trained 12, that is 1,728. If those 1,728 trained 12, that is 20,736. If those 20,736 trained 12, that is 248,832. If those 248,832 trained 12, that is 2,985,984. Almost 3 million people discipled in just six steps. Instead of trying to reach multitudes, our time is better spent doing as Jesus did investing in a few faithful people who will be able to teach others. This principle is not just for church leaders. It applies to all of us. We are not all called to be preachers and teachers. But we are all called to be disciple-makers. Our children, grandchildren, a Bible study group, a Sunday School class, friends, family members, whoever God has placed in our lives, we can build them up and encourage them in their faith. We can invest in their lives and help prepare them to pass on their faith to others. It isn't necessary to be a biblical scholar to be a disciple-maker. Wherever you are in your faith, you can encourage others. Clete went to be with the Lord several years ago, but his legacy of discipleship lives on in me and in many others that he discipled. Are you passing on your faith? Are you making disciples?

October 12

Jeremiah 15-16
Psalm 113:4-9
Proverbs 24:28-29
2 Timothy 3

GOD-BREATHED

"All Scripture is God-breathed and is useful for teaching, rebuking, correcting and training in righteousness, so that the servant of God may be thoroughly equipped for every good work." 2 Timothy 3:16-17 NIV

This verse clears up any doubt about the authorship of the Bible. Every book, every chapter, every verse, and every word came out of the mouth of God. God inspired forty writers over a period of 1500 years to write down His words. Historians and archaeologists have repeatedly confirmed its authenticity. The Bible is filled with historical detail. Not everything in the Bible has been confirmed archaeologically, but not one archeological find has conflicted with biblical accounts. Some people have the idea that the Bible has been translated so many times that it has been corrupted over the years. If translations of the Bible were made from other translations that might be true, but most of todays' translations were made by looking at the Greek, Hebrew and Aramaic texts based on ancient manuscripts. In 1947, archaeologists found the "Dead Sea Scrolls" in Israel. They contained the New Testament scriptures that dated back 1,000 years older than anything that had been uncovered before. Comparing these manuscripts with what we already had, there was 99.5% agreement between the texts with the .5% being spelling variances and sentence structure that did not alter the meaning of the sentence. Because printing presses were not available in ancient times, scribes hand wrote manuscripts on papyrus. There are over 5,000 handwritten copies of the New Testament. The monks who copied them were meticulous in checking and rechecking to make sure the copies were exact. The New Testament is regarded by scholars as being the most reliable ancient document available.

There is also confusion about how the books of the Bible were determined and which ones were included. The first five books of the Bible were called the Pentateuch and were the first to be accepted probably during the fifth century before Christ. The prophets' writings were not brought together until around 200 BC. By this time the Jewish people were widely scattered, and they needed to know which books were the authoritative Word of God because a lot of other books were floating around. Before the birth of Christ, Jewish leaders established the Old Testament canon. The writers of the New Testament were well known to the early church. Matthew, John, and Peter were disciples. Mark and Luke were friends of the disciples. James and Jude were Jesus' brothers. And Paul met Jesus on the rode to Damascus and then became a follower of Jesus and a companion to the disciples. They all had personal access to Jesus and His life. The accounts they gave were confirmed by thousands of eyewitnesses. If their words had not been accurate, it would have been immediately apparent. When other books began to show up that were written by other people, it was obvious that they were fake. The Gospel of Thomas was written in 140 AD long after the apostle Thomas had died and was rejected immediately. The Gospel of Judas was written after Judas was dead and was also rejected. In 367 AD, Athanasius, a respected church historian formally listed the twenty-seven New Testament books, along with the thirty-nine Old Testament books as the only ones that were universally accepted by the church as the books that were inspired by God and authoritative to faith. Jerome and Augustine then confirmed this list soon after. This same list of books is the canon of scripture we have today. These are the books that God Himself chose to give us. The Bible is the most widely distributed book in the world. More copies of the Bible are sold every year than any other book in all human history. The Bible has lasted for centuries because it is God's Words given to us to teach, rebuke, correct and train us in righteousness. No other book has the power to change lives and hearts like the Bible. It is not an ordinary book. It is God's message to His people. We can base our lives on what it says because we know it is from God Himself.

October 13

Jeremiah 17-18
Psalm 114
Proverbs 24:30-34
2 Timothy 4

Crown of Righteousness

"I have fought the good fight, I have finished the race, I have kept the faith. Now there is in store for me the crown of righteousness, which the Lord, the righteous Judge, will award to me on that day—and not only to me, but also to all who have longed for His appearing." 2 Timothy 4:7-8 NIV

A CROWN OF righteousness is being stored up for us that we will receive on "that day." "That day" is referring to the day of judgment when all Christians will stand before the judgement seat of Christ to be judged and receive rewards based on the life we have lived. Thankfully, the crown of righteousness is not a crown based on our works or our righteousness. It is based on the righteousness of Christ and His work on our behalf. The crown of righteousness will be given to everyone who has accepted Jesus as their Savior and Lord and has been credited with His righteousness. "The words 'it was credited to him' were written not for him alone, but also for us, to whom God will credit righteousness— for us who believe in Him who raised Jesus our Lord from the dead. He was delivered over to death for our sins and was raised to life for our justification." Romans 4:23-25 (NIV) We will all get a crown of righteousness on that day, but we will also be judged for what we did here on Earth.

We all hope at the end of our lives we will be able to look back and say the words, "I have fought the good fight, I have finished the race, I have kept the faith." 2 Timothy 4:7-8 (NIV) We want to enter our Father's presence and hear the words, "Well done My good and faithful servant." Matthew 25:23 (NIV) Throughout the New Testament, Paul uses the imagery of an athlete running a race. He is not giving us a picture of an easy, leisurely life. The life of an athlete is strict and disciplined. They are in constant training. They don't let up. From a spiritual perspective, Paul is stressing that God has a race marked out for each one of us. He has things we are supposed to be accomplishing and that should be our mindset. I am a very goal-oriented person, so I hope when I get to Heaven, I can see that I accomplished the things that God put me here to do. I don't want to have wasted the life He gave me on things that had no eternal value. I want to finish the race and finish it well. I don't want to come huffing and puffing across the finish line in last place. Runners know that you have to pace yourself. Many people start out on fire, but then when life gets tough, they lose their passion, and their discipline. They don't finish well. They don't do the things they need to do to continue to grow in their faith. I don't want that to happen to me. I don't just want a participation trophy; I want a gold medal. How about you?

October 14

Jeremiah 19-21
Psalm 115:1-8
Proverbs 25:1-3
Titus 1

Not To Us

"Not to us, Lord, not to us, but to Your name be the glory, because of Your love and faithfulness." Psalm 115:1 NIV

Me! Me! Me! Me! Me! Our culture revolves around me! We hear it all day, every day, wherever we turn. My rights! My body! My choice! Have it your way! Do what you want! If it feels good, do it! You can't make me do anything I don't want to do! Commercials and ads sell selfishness! News stories encourage it! Social Media thrives on it! Churches even cater to this mindset. It is Satan's biggest achievement. I can imagine a meeting in some dark room in Hell with Satan and a group of his demons where they devised a scheme to convince everyone that they are the center of the universe, and everything revolved around them. It wasn't very difficult. It didn't take a lot of enticing. We fell right into his ugly web of deceit. He started out by convincing us that there was an epidemic of low self-esteem and that the solution was to make everyone feel good about themselves. We began giving everyone participation trophies and downplayed competition, working hard, and achieving success. Then he convinced us that saying no to children and punishing them for bad behavior was damaging their self-esteem. Before long entitlement and selfishness replaced loving your neighbor as yourself, considering others as more important than yourself, and laying down your life for your friends. Self-esteem does not come by getting everything you want. It doesn't come from demanding your rights and getting what you think you deserve. That is not what it is about at all. Having a healthy self-esteem comes from viewing yourself the way God views you. We are made in His image. We are special and we are unique. He created us for a specific purpose to glorify Him with our lives. Our self-worth is found in that and that alone.

We listened to Satan's lies and we are now reaping the consequences. Apart from God we cannot think rightly about ourselves. We were created to be in relationship with Him. If we don't have that right, we will never have a healthy self-image. When we think rightly about ourselves, we also recognize our sinfulness before a holy and just God. We can accept what He has done for us and our gratitude overflows in love for Him. Instead of worrying about our rights and getting what we want, we focus on glorifying Him with our lives. When we stop focusing on ourselves and focus our attention on the needs of others, it is amazing how much more content we are with our own lives. An other-centered life gives us a deep sense of meaning and purpose that brings joy and peace to our lives that is far better than anything the "me" culture can provide. As we take our eyes off the mirror, we can turn our eyes toward Jesus. The things of this world pale in comparison. We will gladly proclaim with David, "not to us, Lord, not to us, but to Your name be the glory, because of Your love and faithfulness."

Jeremiah 22-23
Psalm 115:9-18
Proverbs 25:4-5
Titus 2

October 15

Self-Control

"It teaches us to say 'no' to ungodliness and worldly passions, and to live self-controlled, upright and godly lives in this present age, while we wait for the blessed hope—the appearing of our great God and Savior, Jesus Christ, who gave Himself for us to redeem us from all wickedness and to purify for Himself a people that are His very own, eager to do good." Titus 2:12-14 NIV

PAUL IS ENCOURAGING Titus in this chapter to teach the older men to be temperate and self-controlled. He says to teach the older women to control their mouths and not to drink too much. He tells him to urge the younger women to be self-controlled and pure, and the young men to be self-controlled. That pretty much covers everyone: older men, older women, younger women, and younger men. So, everyone needs to be self-controlled. None of us get to escape this instruction. I guess you could argue that he isn't talking to children, but we need to teach children when they are younger to use self-control, or when they get older, they won't know how. This is such a broad topic that covers so many areas. I think we all can think of some area where we really need to improve our self-control. Maybe you struggle with eating too much or eating foods that are bad for you and you need to use self-control to improve your diet. Maybe you struggle with self-control in your finances, and you need to establish and stick to a budget to get that under control. You may drink too much alcohol or take drugs that you shouldn't. Perhaps you struggle with self-control in some sexual area like pornography or extra-marital sex. Maybe your mouth gets you in trouble too much and you need to use self-control to stop cussing, gossiping, or lying. Do you spend too much time on social media or playing video games? It could be that you don't need to stop doing something, but instead you need to use self-control to start doing something. You know you need to exercise to take care of the body God has given you. You have been meaning to get up earlier to spend time with God every day but instead of using self-control, you keep hitting the snooze button over and over. You want to tithe, but you never seem to have enough money to do it (budgeting might help with this).

Self-control is a fruit of the Spirit. That means that it isn't something we can just will ourselves to do. We need the help of the Holy Spirit who is living in us. He wants to help us live self-controlled lives and He is ready and willing to help us. We just have to cooperate with Him. He will give us the strength we need if we ask Him. He will even give us the desire to do it. But He won't make us do it. The more time we spend with Him and the more we involve Him in the process, no matter what area it is in, the more likely we are to be successful. Pray and ask Him to show you any areas that you need to work on. Develop a game plan and get started. It won't happen overnight but stick to it. Set measurable goals so you can see your progress and seek Him so that we can be called "a people that are His very own, eager to do good."

Jeremiah 24-26
Psalm 116:1-11
Proverbs 25:6-7
Titus 3

October 16

Different

"Remind the people to be subject to rulers and authorities, to be obedient, to be ready to do whatever is good, to slander no one, to be peaceable and considerate, and always be gentle toward everyone. At one time we too were foolish, disobedient, deceived and enslaved by all kinds of passions and pleasures. We lived in malice and envy, being hated, and hating one another. But when the kindness and love of God our Savior appeared, He saved us, not because of righteous things we had done, but because of His mercy. And I want to stress these things, so that those who have trusted in God may be careful to devote themselves to doing what is good. These things are excellent and profitable for everyone." Titus 3: 1-5, 8 NIV

PAUL IS REMINDING us that Christians should be different. Our interactions with people, our actions, what we say, our very countenance should be radically different from that of someone who does not know Jesus. Nothing about our lives should be the same as it was before we met Jesus. We are different because He is different, and He resides in us. He does not come into our lives to save us and then leave us as we were. That is not how it works. We come to Him as we are, but then He begins the process of transforming us into what He wants us to be. When people get married, they often have the idea that they are going to change their mate to be what they want them to be. That never works. I have advised many young people who are dating that if there are already things about the other person they can't stand and want to change, they need to think long and hard about whether this is the right person. You should love them for who they are, all of who they are. It is unlikely you will be able to change them. That is not true for our relationship with Jesus. We go into it knowing that He is going to change us. He is a holy, righteous, perfect God and wants to transform us into the image of His Son. He comes to live in us and begins the sanctification process as soon as He enters our lives. It is part of the deal. It does not happen all at once, but He takes away our sinful desires and recreates a clean heart in us. When a spouse, parent or friend wants to change us, they are trying to make us into what they want us to be. It may or may not be what is truly best for us. But God created us. He knows us better than we know ourselves, and He knows what is truly best for us. He can shape us into the person that we are intended to be. We can trust Him.

Obedient, ready to do whatever is good, peaceable, considerate, and gentle towards everyone are not the words I would use to describe a lot of Christians I know. I can't even say that those words describe me all the time. We somehow have the idea that we must fight for what we believe in. I agree with this, but it matters how we do it. We don't get to be obnoxious and rude with people who disagree with us, even if they are wrong. We don't get to call them names and say horrible things about them even if the things we want to say may be true. We don't get to treat them like the enemy. Paul describes those things as foolish, disobedient and being enslaved by all kinds of passions and desires. Being hated and hating one another is never the way Jesus would want us to interact with others. Kindness and love should always be our goal.

October 17

Jeremiah 27-29
Psalm 116:12-19
Proverbs 25:8-10
Philemon 1

God's Plan or Our Agenda

> "'For I know the plans I have for you,' declares the Lord, 'plans to prosper you and not to harm you, plans to give you hope and a future. Then you will call on Me and come and pray to Me, and I will listen to you. You will seek Me and find Me when you seek Me with all your heart.'" Jeremiah 29:11-13 NIV

THIS IS ONE of the most known and quoted verses in the Bible. I'm afraid that it is often claimed by people who do not understand it. This was a promise given to the children of Israel when they were in captivity in Babylon. This is not a promise given to everyone in the world. However, it does contain a principle that we can all rely on and follow. The problem is that many people stop with verse 11. The Lord does have plans for each of us. He created us each with a specific and unique purpose. They are plans to prosper us and not to harm us. They are plans to give us hope and a future. Unfortunately, many people do not want to follow His plans for their life. They want Him to follow their plans. They want God to rubber stamp all the things that they want and make it go smoothly. They want Him to prosper them and make their lives easy. God's plans are rarely easy. His goal is not to give us a leisurely life with no difficulty or pain. As we saw yesterday, God's plan is to transform us into the person that He wants us to be. His goal is to sanctify us. Often, that is painful. Shaping us, molding us, and purifying us usually does not involve giving us everything we want. In fact, it usually involves teaching us, training us, and disciplining us. That may not seem pleasant at the time. While it is happening, it may not feel like He is prospering us or blessing us. When we look back on it later, hopefully we can see the benefit of not getting what we asked for, but sometimes this side of Heaven we can't understand.

Verses 12 and 13 explain the process. We call on God, come to Him, pray to Him, and He listens to us. We seek Him with all our hearts and when we do that, we find Him. When we seek Him and His plan, then He reveals His plan to us. If we are not seeking Him, we will not find His plan. If our hearts are not humble and teachable, we will likely miss His plans all together. If we have the idea that we have it all figured out, take our plans to Him, and expect Him to make them work, we are likely to be disappointed. That is not how it works. He already has it all figured out. He knows what is best for us. He knows all the things He has planned for us to accomplish. He knows how we fit into His big picture. His plans are far better than any that we could come up with, but we must be willing to submit to Him. These verses require humility. They require that we set aside our own agenda and seek His agenda. They require obedience.

October 18

Jeremiah 30-31
Psalm 117
Proverbs 25:11-12
Hebrews 1

Angels

"So, He became as much superior to the angels as the name He has inherited is superior to theirs. Are not all angels ministering spirits sent to serve those who will inherit salvation?" Hebrews 1:4, 14 NIV

There is a lot of misinformation about angels. I often hear people talk about their grandmother who has passed away that they think is now their guardian angel. A lot of people believe that when we die, we become angels. That is not accurate. Nothing in the Bible supports that idea. Angels are a separate entity of beings. There are no scriptures that indicate that when we die, we become angels. Angels have a specific function and are created for a specific purpose that is distinct from that of humans. The Bible speaks about a Heavenly realm in which the angels operate that is distinct and separate from the physical realm that we live in. There are battles going on that we are not aware of that are nonetheless very real and impact our lives greatly. Angels and demons fight daily battles to gain ground in the culture war and they battle in our individual lives as we fight off temptation and evil. God uses angels to protect us, to guide us, to deliver us from evil, to comfort us, and to encourage us. In biblical times, God used angels to deliver messages and to prophecy about coming events. They are real beings that exist in the Heavenly realm and have an impact on the physical realm. God created us in His image. We have a soul that was created in God's image and likeness. Angels are created beings that were made to serve and worship Him. Some people worship angels and exalt them. Angels are created beings. They are not worthy of worship or exaltation. God is the Only One worthy of our worship. Angels are not superior to us. They are created to serve us and help us. They are ministering spirits to us. We do not pray to angels or exalt them in any way. We pray to God, and He uses angels in whatever way He chooses to bring about His purposes in our lives.

This may seem like I am nitpicking about something that doesn't matter, but it is actually very important. Exalting anything, even angels, is idolatry. Our Heavenly Father, His Son Jesus and the Holy Spirit, the triune God, is the Only One worthy of any praise, worship, or exaltation. Worshipping anything or anyone else is an insult. No one or nothing else is worthy of our praise and worship. Angels, like humans, are created beings who were made to serve God and do His will.

October 19

Jeremiah 32-33
Psalm 118:1-4
Proverbs 25:13
Hebrews 2

Like Us

"For this reason, He had to be made like them, fully human in every way, in order that He might become a merciful and faithful high priest in service to God, and that He might make atonement for the sins of the people. Because He Himself suffered when He was tempted, He is able to help those who are tempted." Hebrews 2:17-18 NIV

He became like us. God Himself became like us! He could have picked another way, but He chose to leave Heaven, come to Earth as a poor, insignificant human baby, and live a simple, ordinary life so that He could relate to us. He knew what it was like to be hungry. He knew what it was like to be cold and hot and sweaty. He experienced family difficulties, sibling rivalry, and the death of a parent. He knew what it felt like to have friends run away when the going got tough and even to be betrayed by someone who was supposed to be one of His best friends. He knew the frustration of trying to teach and prepare His followers when they did not understand what He was telling them. Any situation we face He can relate to because He chose to experience humanity. Instead of staying up in Heaven on His throne, He lowered Himself to our level. He wanted to fully understand what we were going through and what it was like to be human. Instead of exalting Himself, which would have been expected and completely right, He chose to identify with us. He made Himself one of us.

He knew what it was like to be tempted in every way, just like we are. "For we do not have a high priest who is unable to sympathize with our weaknesses, but One who in every respect has been tempted as we are, yet without sin." Hebrews 4:15 (ESV) When we think of Jesus being tempted in the desert, we may think it was easy for Him to overcome the temptation because He was God. It couldn't have been difficult for Him to turn away from sin because He was perfect. But we have to remember that He was also fully human. When Satan came to Him, Jesus had not eaten in forty days, and He was hungry. Satan didn't just hand Him a loaf of bread; He questioned His identity. He basically said that if Jesus was who He said He was, then why would He be hungry. If He was God, He could change the stone into bread to eat. Jesus later defied the natural laws by multiplying five loaves of bread into enough to feed 5,000 men so why would it be wrong to turn a stone into a loaf of bread for Himself? Jesus knew that His Father would provide everything He needed, and He did not need to use His powers in that way. Satan then appealed to His authority. He took Him to Jerusalem and set Him on the top of the temple. He challenged Him to throw Himself off and call on the angels to rescue Him proving that He could command the angels. Jesus did not need to prove He had authority over the angels and everything else. He knew His power and authority and did not need to prove it to anyone. Satan then appealed to His pride. Satan has been allowed to exercise his power in the world. He and his demons rule and reign over this dark world. One day he will be cast into a fiery pit and will no longer have any power, but until that day, he uses his evil influence to wreak havoc in the world around us. He offered the kingdoms of the world to Jesus to rule if Jesus would bow down and worship Him. He was telling Jesus that He didn't have to do it the way God wanted. He didn't have to go along with God's plan. Instead, He could rule the Earth. He could take over and establish an earthly kingdom. Just as Satan and his demons had gone against God's plan and been thrown out of Heaven, Jesus could go against God's plan and rule the Earth. Jesus knew exactly what God's plan was. He knew that it involved pain, difficulty, betrayal, a horrible, excruciating death, and then three days separated from God. Satan was offering an easier alternative. That had to have been tempting, even to Jesus. But Jesus knew that this authority was not Satan's to offer. Satan may think he is in control, but any control he has is only because God has allowed him that power. God is the only One who has ultimate power, authority, and dominion in this world and in the Heavenly realm. Jesus chose to follow His Father's plan. He did not succumb to the temptation.

When we face temptation, we not only have Jesus' example to follow, but we also have Him living inside of us giving us the power to overcome the temptation. We cannot overcome temptation on our own strength and power. We aren't supposed to. If we could overcome temptation on our own, there would not have been any reason for Jesus to die on the cross to pay the penalty for our sins. Jesus knows that we cannot do it, so He provided us with the power in the form of the Holy Spirit to reside in us and enable us to stand firm when tempted. We have access to all the power that Jesus had to overcome temptation, because we have personal access to Jesus. He wants us to utilize His power. He wants to help us. He loves us so much that He became human so He could identify with us and relate to us better. What areas do you need to let Him help you overcome temptation?

October 20

Jeremiah 34-36
Psalm 118:5-14
Proverbs 25:14-15
Hebrews 3

Refuge

"I called to the Lord in distress; the Lord answered me and put me in a spacious place. The Lord is for me; I will not be afraid. What can man do to me? The Lord is my helper; therefore, I will look in triumph on those who hate me. It is better to take refuge in the Lord than to trust in man. It is better to take refuge in the Lord than to trust in nobles. You pushed me hard to make me fall, but the Lord helped me. The Lord is my strength and my song; He has become my salvation." Psalm 118:5-9, 13-14 HCSB

There are many Bible verses about taking refuge in God. But what does that really mean and how do we do it? It sounds good, but from a practical standpoint what does that look like in our lives? Merriam-Webster defines refuge as "a shelter or protection from danger or distress, a place that provides shelter or protection, something to which one has recourse in difficulty."[17] So, taking refuge is finding a safe place to go during a storm or getting comfort in a time of distress. How can I take refuge in God when He is not physically with me? He cannot protect me physically when I'm in danger and He does not speak to me audibly to give me direction, so how can He be a refuge? When we are in distress or facing difficulty in our lives, we all seek refuge in something. Sometimes those things can be things that bring us comfort and not necessarily protection. What is the first thing you turn to when you are stressed and anxious? Do you turn on a movie, get on social media, or read a book to escape reality? Do you call a friend to vent? Do you eat your favorite comfort food? Do you go to the mall or Target or shop online? What is your go-to when you need to be comforted? Unfortunately, most of the things we turn to do not provide real solutions or help, but only temporarily make us feel better. The problem is still there, and the anxiety and stress inevitably come back. If we can identify those things that we turn to that don't work, then maybe we can learn to replace them with something that actually has the power to change our situation and give us real protection and comfort.

The Psalms link taking refuge in God with trusting Him. Psalm 56:1-2, Psalm 62: 7-8, Psalm 91:2, and Psalm 62:8 are just a few passages that draw a correlation between the two. Is trusting God a feeling? Or maybe it is a thought process? Is trust an action? I think it is all three. I think it begins as a thought process which leads to action and results in a feeling. Anxiety and stress usually are a result of a thought process. When a crisis or some sort of trouble happens, we begin by processing in our minds all the ramifications. We go to the what ifs and if onlys and end up down a dark hole thinking about all the things that may or may not happen. At this point, we have a choice. We can turn to the things that bring us temporary comfort or we can choose to turn to God instead. There are some actions that we can take that can help us to trust God and take refuge in Him.

1. **Turn to God's Word to remind us of His promises.** The more we get to know God, the easier it is to trust Him. The best way to get to know God is to read His Word. I keep a ring of Bible verses in my desk that I turn to when I need to remind myself of God's faithfulness and promises. They are verses that are comforting to me and give me strength and hope. If we are filling our minds with God's Word, we are less likely to believe the lies that Satan is whispering in our ears. When we go to God's Word, there are real answers to our problems. Sometimes He will give us clear direction about what we need to do next and sometimes it is a more general sense of comfort and peace, but either way it is pointing us in a positive direction.
2. **Fill our minds and hearts with praise and thanksgiving.** Turning on praise music, singing praises to God, reading praise scripture verses, and making a list of all the things we have to be thankful for are excellent ways to demonstrate trust. I am not suggesting that listening to praise music will make our problems go away, but rather that praising God can change things because it changes us. It changes our perspective. Instead of focusing our attention on our problem, we focus our attention on the One who can truly help us deal with whatever situation we face. We can replace our what ifs with even ifs.
3. **Talk to God about our problem.** When life feels overwhelming and we have no idea what to do, the best thing we can do is bring it to Him. Our most powerful weapon at our disposal is the power of prayer. When we call and talk to a friend, mom, or coworker about our problem, they can tell us what they would do, give us advice, or listen to us cry, but they don't usually have the ability to fix the problem. When we take our problem to God, we are presenting it to the Creator of the Universe, the One who sustains everything and holds it all together. He is almighty, all-knowing, all-powerful and Lord of all. He cares about us and our problems and He knows how to fix them. Prayer is always our best and most effective recourse.

When we take these actions to demonstrate our trust in our sovereign, loving God, the result is a feeling. Our anxiety and fear are replaced with peace and joy. The situation may not immediately change, but we are changed. We experience His protection and shelter even if the storm rages all around us because He is our refuge.

October 21

Jeremiah 37-38
Psalm 118:15-21
Proverbs 25:16-17
Hebrews 4:1-13

Penetrating

"For the Word of God is living and effective and sharper than any double-edged sword, penetrating as far as the separation of soul and spirit, joints and marrow. It is able to judge the ideas and thoughts of the heart. No creature is hidden from Him, but all things are naked and exposed to the eyes of Him to whom we must give an account." Hebrews 4:12-13 HCSB

THE WORD OF God is different from any other book that has ever been written. There are some amazing books out there. There are books that have been around for centuries, like the Bible, but none of them have the power the Bible has. Some books move us emotionally, some make us angry, some make us cry, some motivate us to change an area of our lives, and some teach us new things. There are millions of books in print today and millions more that line library shelves throughout the world. There are books that appeal to literary scholars, books written for teenage girls, and self-help books for every problem we could possibly face. There are children's books, romance novels, murder mysteries, classics, biographies, and sci-fi novels. Books can give us an escape from our problems or a nice distraction on a rainy day. There are a lot of gifted authors who can spark our imagination and fuel our deepest dreams with their stories. Books are powerful, but no book has the power the Bible has. This verse explains why.

The Bible is a living document. It is just as applicable to our lives today as it was when it was written hundreds of years ago. When we read the Bible, God speaks to us through its words. He can lead us to just the right scripture we need at the exact time we need it. Whether it is in our daily quiet time, through a song on the radio, in a sermon or in a Bible study, He communicates to us through the power of His Holy Spirit using His Word. Whatever our situation He can use a passage in scripture to speak to us giving us wisdom, insight, and guidance. When we are lonely or hurting, He uses it to assure us of His constant presence. When we are grieving, He uses it to give us comfort and hope. When we are confused and needing direction, He uses it to lead us and provide instruction. He uses His Word to train us and teach us in the way that we should go. No matter what we are going through, the Bible offers us help. It is effective in every situation we will ever find ourselves. It is also sharper than any two-edged sword penetrating to the deepest part of our hearts. It has the power to reveal our sin to us, to convict us of our sinful actions and judge even our motives and intentions. It can correct, chasten, and discipline us. God's Word is His instruction manual to help us navigate this life and it comes with internal tech support to assist us. The only catch is that we must utilize it. It does us no good sitting on our nightstand, in a drawer or on a bookshelf. If we don't open it, God can't use it to speak to us. If we don't read it, we are missing what He wants to tell us. It isn't meant to just be pulled out when we are in a crisis, it is intended for daily use.

Jeremiah 39-41
Psalm 118:22-29
Proverbs 25:18-19
Hebrews 4:14-16

The Throne of Grace

"Therefore, let us approach the throne of grace with boldness, so that we may receive mercy and find grace to help us in our time of need." Hebrews 4:16 CSB

The "throne of grace" is an oxymoron. A throne is a place of authority and judgment, not grace. In the throne room a king is exalted high on his throne. No one is allowed to enter that room unless they have been invited and they cannot approach the throne until the king extends his scepter allowing them to draw near. The throne separates the king from his subjects. He is superior and they are inferior. In the book of Esther, Esther asks Mordecai to have the Jewish people pray for her before she approaches the king because she knows that even the queen cannot approach the throne unless she is summoned, and she could be executed as punishment for daring to enter the throne room uninvited. The throne room is a place of fear and trepidation. Even if you are invited to come before the king, you do so reverently and timidly. The king had the power of life and death with no accountability. He could have you thrown in prison or executed if you said something wrong or for no reason at all. One would never dare to approach the king boldly and with confidence.

God is the King of the Universe. He is Lord of all, the Supreme Being. He is above all and beyond all. He is on His throne in Heaven and seated next to Him to His right, is Jesus, His One and Only Son. They rule and reign the world. If anyone deserves to be separated from His subjects, it is God. He is obviously superior, and we are inferior. He deserves our utmost reverence and awe. It bothers me greatly when people call God "the man upstairs" or "the big guy." He is not our buddy, and we absolutely should not treat Him as such. "Do not be afraid of those who kill the body but cannot kill the soul. Rather, be afraid of the One who can destroy both soul and body in Hell." Matthew 10:28 (NIV) God alone has the power to send us to eternal damnation. Unlike earthly kings, however, God is filled with love and compassion. Instead of giving us what we deserve, He offers us the opportunity to be adopted as sons and daughters. As children of the king, we can approach the throne because we have been invited. We are always welcome in His presence. He is never too busy to talk to us. No matter how many times we go to Him with the same problem, He never gets annoyed with us. We do not enter His presence arrogantly or demanding anything. We approach Him with respect and gratitude for accepting us and for allowing us the privilege of being His children. But this verse tells us that we can approach Him boldly presenting our concerns to Him and asking for His help. We can be confident that we will receive mercy and find grace to help us in our time of need because He loves us and wants what is best for us. Those who are not His children do not have this same privilege. All are invited to become His children, but not all choose to accept. Those who do not accept His invitation face the throne for judgment and do not receive His mercy and grace.

October 23

Jeremiah 42-43
Psalm 119:1-8
Proverbs 25:20-22
Hebrews 5

Solid Food

"In fact, though by this time you ought to be teachers, you need someone to teach you the elementary truths of God's Word all over again. You need milk, not solid food! Anyone who lives on milk, being still an infant is not acquainted with the teaching about righteousness. But solid food is for the mature, who by constant use have trained themselves to distinguish good from evil." Hebrews 5:12-14 NIV

As a new grandmother, I am having to relearn a lot of things about babies. I need to brush up on developmental milestones so I can remember what they are supposed to do at what age. Right now, Hadley drinks breastmilk, but I'm sure in the next few months she will begin eating soft foods and cereal and then eventually more solid foods. The same thing will happen with mobility. She will roll over and then crawl, and then she will begin to pull up and eventually walk. Communication will follow a similar progression. Right now, she cries to tell us she is hungry, something is hurting, or she just wants to be held. Then she will learn a few simple words and eventually she will be able to talk and communicate in complete sentences. The development of each child is a little different. Some learn to walk sooner than others. Some talk earlier and some children get potty trained earlier, but by four or five most children can eat solid food, walk unassisted, communicate effectively with their words, and are potty trained. There is a natural progression that takes place unless there are specific developmental problems. Paul is telling us that there should be the same natural progression of development in our spiritual lives.

When we accept Jesus into our hearts, we are like spiritual babies. We have much to learn and God begins the process of developing us into mature believers. We begin by learning the basics of the Christian faith. We learn what we believe and why. We develop the disciplines of the faith like reading our Bibles, praying, and worshipping. Our faith grows and we begin to exhibit the fruits of the Spirit in our daily lives. There is a natural progression in our development. As we mature in our faith, we gain understanding and wisdom. We can grasp concepts that previously we could not understand. If this development does not occur, there is a problem. Paul told the believers in the church in Corinth, "Brothers and sisters, I could not address you as people who live by the Spirit but as people who are still worldly, mere infants in Christ. I gave you milk, not solid food, for you were not ready for it. Indeed, you are still not ready. You are still worldly." I Corinthians 3:1-2 (NIV) Many believers never progress in their faith. They remain as spiritual infants. They go to church, but they don't do anything else to grow spiritually. As a child gets older, any areas where they are not developing properly become evident. In our spiritual lives, we should experience noticeable progression in our development as well. If we are not growing from year to year, we need to evaluate our lives to determine if we are doing the things we need to do to build our faith so that we can digest deep spiritual truths and not have to be retaught the basics.

Jeremiah 44-45
Psalm 119:9-16
Proverbs 25:23-24
Hebrews 6:1-12

October 24

God's Word or Self-Help Book?

"How can a young man keep his way pure? By keeping Your Word. I have sought You with all my heart; don't let me wander from Your commands. I have treasured Your Word in my heart that I may not sin against You. Lord, may You be praised; teach me your statutes. With my lips I proclaim all the judgments from your mouth. I rejoice in the way revealed by Your decrees as much as in all riches. I meditate on Your precepts and think about Your ways. I delight in Your statutes; I will not forget Your Word." Psalm 119:9-16 HCSB

THE AUTHOR OF Psalm 119 is not named, but most scholars believe that David wrote it because it fits his writing style and is consistent with the themes of most of his psalms. The beginning of the Psalm seems to have been written by a young man, but the latter verses come from a place of age and wisdom. It is possible that this is a compilation of several of his writings concerning the treasure of scripture. He begins this section of the Psalm by asking how a young man can remain pure. He concludes that there is only one way: by keeping God's Word. He is fully convinced that God's Word contains the statutes, precepts and decrees that will lead us to a holy life and so he has dedicated himself to it. He has treasured God's Word in his heart so that he would not fall into a life of sin. Something we treasure is something we believe has great value. We do not treasure things that are disposable. David treasures God's Word as much as great riches. He meditates on it and delights in it. Verse 16 in the NIV says "I will not neglect Your Word." He commits to paying careful attention to apply it to his life and obey what it says so that he will not be guilty of neglecting it.

Our view of scripture is of utmost importance. Many people think of the Bible as a book that has a lot of good information and principles to follow to help us live a good life. They believe it was inspired by God in a general sense, but do not necessarily believe that it is God's Word to us specifically. They believe it contains general guidance, but not direct revelation. The problem with this view is that it makes it easy to take the parts you like and dismiss the parts that you don't like. If the words are just the words of a human author, then if you disagree with it or it doesn't fit your agenda, you can dismiss it as just someone's opinion or something that was historically relevant but does not apply to us today. This view of scripture also calls into question the definition of good and pure and right. If the Bible is not the definitive standard to give us the basis for determining right and wrong, and good and bad, then what is? God is the Creator of the Universe, so He is the One who determines those standards. If the Bible is not His way of giving us those standards, then we are each free to decide for ourselves what we think is right and wrong. This will ultimately lead to chaos and anarchy. There must be standards that define what is acceptable behavior and what is sin. God is the One who decides what those are, and His Word is the method He has chosen to use to deliver those standards. We either believe it, ALL of it, or we reject it. If we treasure it, then we believe it is of great value and we study it, meditate on it, memorize it, and obey it. It is either the standard by which we live our lives, or it is not.

October 25

Jeremiah 46-47
Psalm 119:17-24
Proverbs 25:25-26
Hebrews 6:13-20

THE ANCHOR FOR OUR LIVES

"For when God made a promise to Abraham, since He had no one greater to swear by, He swore by Himself. And so, after waiting patiently, Abraham obtained the promise. We have this hope as an anchor for our lives, safe and secure. It enters the inner sanctuary behind the curtain. Jesus has entered there on our behalf as a forerunner, because He has become a high priest forever in the order of Melchizedek." Hebrews 6:13, 15, 19-20 HCSB

IN THIS PASSAGE of scripture, Paul uses three different images to help us understand the concept of hope. Merriam-Webster defines hope as "to cherish a desire with anticipation, to desire with expectation of obtainment or fulfillment, to expect with confidence."[18] In I Timothy 1:1 Paul tells us that the object of our hope is Jesus Christ. He begins with giving us reason for our hope. Our confidence is based on evidence. God has given numerous promises in His Word. The example Paul uses is God's promise to Abraham and the fulfillment of that promise that can be proven historically. The Bible is filled with promises that have been fulfilled. The implication is that God can be taken at His Word. If He promises to do something, we can be confident that He will do it. Our hope is not wishful thinking. We know that if we place our faith in Jesus, we have eternal life. He has gone to prepare a place for us in Heaven and He will return and take us to be with Him. Those are promises that we can place confident hope in.

Then Paul explains what hope accomplishes for us. He gives us the practical result of hope. Our hope is an anchor for our lives. Anchors prevent a ship from being swept away by wind or waves. They also prevent the ship from being dashed against the rocks close to shore and torn apart. During a tempestuous storm, a ship can be tossed back and forth on the mighty waves until it is close enough to shore for the sailor to toss out the anchor. They are then able to ride out the storm in confidence knowing that the cable is strong, and the ground is firm. Though shaken, the ship holds firm. The wind and rain rages on, but she is secure. Eventually, the storm calms and she can reach the shore safely. Because we have Jesus as our hope, we can ride out whatever storms come into our lives. We may be shaken and tossed, but we hold firm. The wind and waves may rage all around us, but we are secure. We hold to the promises in God's Word, and we can come through the storm safely. If hope is the anchor, faith is the cable that attaches us to that hope. Without the cable, the anchor will not hold us steady. Once the anchor is thrown over the side of the ship, it cannot be seen. "Faith is the confidence in what we hope for and the assurance about what we do not see." Hebrews 11:1 (NIV) Faith tethers us to the anchor of hope. Finally, Paul explains that we have hope because Jesus has entered the inner sanctuary as our High Priest, and He has gone before us to His Father where He intercedes on our behalf. He has secured our place in Heaven and is waiting to take us there to be with Him. Our future is secure. We can rest in the assurance and confidence He provides.

October 26

Jeremiah 48-49
Psalm 119:25-32
Proverbs 25:27-28
Hebrews 7:1-10

Restraint

"It is not good to eat much honey, nor is it glorious to seek one's own glory. A man without self-control is like a city broken into and left without walls." Proverbs 25:27-28 ESV

SELF-CONTROL OR RESTRAINT provide protection for us. They protect us from ourselves and our own appetites. In ancient times, cities had walls for protection. If they had no walls, they had no means to protect themselves. There were watchmen on the walls who would warn of any danger coming. If they saw a raiding army, they would signal to the men in the city to prepare for battle. When the army arrived, they would be met with a defensive front. If they had no walls, they would have no warning and could be overtaken by surprise and destroyed. The walls also protected them from wild animals and bands of foreigners who could sneak in and steal from them. That is a great picture of the role of restraint in our lives. Restraint puts a wall of protection around us. This applies to every area of our lives. Proverbs is filled with verses about self-control. Verse 27 tells us that it is not good to eat too much honey. We all know that sweets taste good. They are delicious in fact. And in moderation they are ok. A cookie, a bowl of ice cream, a piece of cake or a brownie is perfectly fine. The problem is that too much of a good thing is bad. Too many sweets can lead to weight gain which leads to numerous health issues like diabetes and heart disease. The other problem with sweets is that the more you eat, the more you want. There is a physiological reason for this. When you eat sugar, your brain releases dopamine which gives you a pleasant feeling, a sugar high. The more you eat the more you want. Your brain actually craves sugar. That is one of the reasons it is so difficult to lose weight. We must train our bodies to be satisfied with other things like fruit and protein, things that are good for our bodies and not detrimental. We must use self-control. An occasional piece of cake is fine, but dessert after every meal is not good for anyone. Using restraint can protect us from having health problems later. This applies to other areas of our lives as well. Using self-control in our finances can keep us from racking up huge credit card bills. Living within our means is not only wise, but also protective. A lack of self-control in our sexual life can lead to relationship problems. Looking at porn, flirting with that cute coworker, or reading inappropriate books may seem harmless, but they can lead to desire for more sinful behaviors that destroy marriages and break up families.

Verse 27 also says that it is not glorious to seek out one's own glory. At first glance, this doesn't seem to fit in with the rest of the passage, but upon closer examination, it is very closely related. Seeking our own glory is, at its root, about getting our satisfaction from the approval of others. Ultimately, it is the constant need for the attention and positive affirmation from people in our lives. Instead of being motivated to please God, we are motivated by a desire to please people and have them tell us how great we are. This can be just as addictive as sugar. The more praise we get, the more we want. It takes a great deal of self-control to not be offended when our actions are not recognized, when someone else gets the credit for something we did, or when we don't feel appreciated. It takes restraint when your mom is talking about how smart your brother is, not to get jealous and point out something smart you did. When your boss suggests that your coworker should help you with your project because they have previous experience, it takes self-control to not get defensive and tell him you can handle it on your own. When your friend posts a picture of her daughter getting a trophy for sports, it takes restraint to not post a picture of your daughter doing something impressive. We don't like to think this verse could be talking about us, but I think we are all guilty of this at times. We all want people to think highly of us. We want others to like us and respect us. That is not a bad thing, but it becomes a problem when we crave the approval of others, and it becomes a motivating factor in our lives. Social media can feed into this. Posting pictures or comments seeking the likes and affirming comments of others is a form of seeking one's own glory. The constant need for the approval of men is not only unhealthy, but also sinful. "For am I now seeking the approval of man, or of God? Or am I trying to please man? If I were still trying to please man, I would not be a servant of Christ." Galatians 1:10 (ESV). The only thing that satisfies the cravings of our hearts is Jesus. Food, sex, material possessions, power, status, and popularity only provide temporary pleasure and leave us craving more. A deep abiding relationship with Jesus fills our soul and satisfies our heart. He can give us the strength to use self-control in all areas of our lives so that we have protection against our own desires and the temptations Satan uses to entice us.

October 27

Jeremiah 50
Psalm 119:33-40
Proverbs 26:1-2
Hebrews 7:11-28

Our Intercessor

"Consequently, He is able to save to the uttermost those who draw near to God through Him, since He always lives to make intercessions for them. For it was indeed fitting that we should have a high priest, holy, innocent, unstained, separated from sinners, and exalted above the heavens." Hebrews 7:25-26 ESV

JESUS CAN SAVE to the uttermost. Whatever it takes until our salvation is complete, He is able to do for us. He has the power to save us and to keep us saved until He presents us to His Father in Heaven. He does not save us and then leave us to work everything out on our own. If we come to God, depending on Jesus, we can rest secure in the knowledge of our redemption. He will secure to completion all those who entrust their salvation to Him. Jewish high priests were appointed for life, but when they died, they were replaced by other priests. Jesus conquered death and therefore, He lives forever and does not need to be replaced as our High Priest. The Levitical priests presented sacrifices continually to atone for their own sins and the sins of the people. Those sacrifices secured forgiveness for their sins, but they could not make them perfect. They continued to commit sins so that more sacrifices were necessary. Jesus provided atonement once and for all so that those who draw near to God through Him are made perfect. Not that we are perfect on our own, but that we are covered with His perfection so that when He presents us to His Father we appear as white as snow. He is innocent, pure, unstained, and holy and He imputes that perfection to us. It seems too good to be true, but that is what the Bible promises us.

It is comforting to know that our eternal destiny is secure and if that was the only thing we were promised, that would be enough. But faith in Jesus gives us so much more. The added bonus is that we also get His constant help now. He has given us the Holy Spirit to live in us and help us. He is our comforter, guide, mentor, and our constant companion. We are not alone. And this verse tells us that Jesus is in Heaven right now living to make intercession for us. Did you get that? He lives to make intercession for us. That is what He lives for! The thing we live for is our passion. Intercession is the action of intervening on behalf of another, appealing and pleading someone else's case. So, Jesus' passion is to intervene on my behalf. He is up in Heaven now appealing to God and pleading my case. He is my advocate. He knows I cannot do it on my own. He knows how much I need help and because of His great love for me, He is doing everything He needs to do to help me. Notice I said everything He needs to do, not everything He can do. If someone does everything they can do to help me, it might not be enough. Jesus does everything that needs to be done because He is able to complete everything He starts. He has no limitations. Having Jesus as my advocate allows me to rest and trust Him even when I don't understand what is happening. I do not need to fear because I know He is able to do whatever is best for me.

October 28

Jeremiah 51-52
Psalms 119:41-48
Proverbs 26:3
Hebrews 8:1-6

An Answer

"Let Your faithful love come to me, Lord, Your salvation as You promised. Then I can answer the one who taunts me, for I trust in Your Word." Psalm 119:41-42 HCSB

THE HEBREW WORD for faithful love found in this verse is hesed. There is no one English word that adequately translates its meaning. Hesed is used over 250 times in the Old Testament and most often describes the love God has for His people. Some descriptive adjectives that could be used for hesed are mercy, compassion, love, grace, and faithfulness, but none of them completely convey the depth of its meaning in Hebrew. GotQuestions.org gives a good explanation of this word and I would encourage you to go to their website to read it.[19] Hesed describes God's covenant relationship with His people that is loyal and faithful even if they are not faithful to Him. Our salvation is rooted in hesed. His love and affection compelled Him to sacrifice His Only Son to bring about our redemption and restore our relationship with Him. It not only prompted Him to forgive us, but to provide the means to reconcile us to Himself. David acknowledges the hesed of God and believes in the salvation He promised.

The assurance of the depth of God's love and faithfulness is sufficient to sustain David and give him confidence in the face of any attack. This is just as applicable to our lives as it was for David. Attacks can come from many directions. No matter what taunts are hurled at us, our best defense is always God's Word. We can trust His Word and His promises. The attack may come from an unbelieving neighbor or coworker. It may come from family members who disagree with us about an issue. The attack could even come from a fellow Christian who has different beliefs. It can also come in our own head from Satan who makes us question what we believe or is telling us lies to make us doubt. When He was tempted in the desert, Jesus Himself gave us the best example to fight off attacks. He certainly could have answered Satan with His own argument about why He was right, and Satan was wrong, but as an example to us, He chose to respond to all the attacks with scripture. Our best answer to any attack is always God's Word. Whether they are coming from Satan or other people, the main purpose behind the attack is usually to sway us, make us doubt, or change our mind. Relying on God's Word will allow us to remain steady and firm. The person may choose to ignore what we say or not to believe it, but we must be firm in our belief so that they cannot cause us to doubt. If we don't know the answer to the questions they pose or we don't know why we believe what we do about the issue, then we need to find the answer. We can go to God's Word, ask a trusted friend or pastor, and do the research until we figure out what God's Word says about it. We must settle the issue in our own minds based on the truth we find in God's Word. Then we can answer others. They don't need to know our opinion. They need to know what God says about it. Confidence in His hesed helps us trust and rely on the authority of His Word.

October 29

Lamentations 1-2
Psalm 119:49-56
Proverbs 26:4-7
Hebrews 8:7-13

Answering a Fool

"Don't answer a fool according to his foolishness or you'll be like him yourself. Answer a fool according to his foolishness or he'll become wise in his own eyes." Proverbs 26:4-5 HCSB

THESE TWO VERSES seem to contradict each other, but an examination of related scriptures in Proverbs can help us understand the message Solomon is trying to convey. There are times when it is best to just ignore a fool. He does not know what he is talking about and if you try to argue with him, it will do no good. Arguing with someone about things that don't matter is futile. He will not listen to wise reason and will try to draw you into an argument to prove his point. If you stoop to his level, you will end up looking like a fool yourself. However, there are times when a fool needs to be challenged. There are matters of importance that cannot be ignored. In those cases, it is important to confront the fool and point out his foolishness. A foolish person will most likely reject your argument, but he may recognize the wisdom of your words and change his mind and those listening will benefit from seeing the sharp contrast between wisdom and foolishness. If we do not speak up regarding important issues, he will think he is wise and continue in his own ignorance. It requires wisdom to know when to respond by ignoring the fool and when it is necessary to speak up. There are some principles we can follow when dealing with people who are foolish.

1. We need to recognize that fools despise wisdom. They are not interested in truth. (Proverbs 1:5-7, 22, 12:15, 23:9)
2. Fools are not honest. They will lie, deceive, and say anything to prove their point. You cannot trust them. (Proverbs 10:18-19, 12:22-23, 29:20, 18:6-7)
3. Fools enjoy arguing for the sake of arguing. Their convictions are often not as strong as their desire to win the argument. (Proverbs 18:2-3, 29:8-9, 20:3)
4. It is unwise to become friends with a fool. (Proverbs 13:20, 14:7, 29:9)
5. A fool is reckless and careless in his actions and words. (Proverbs 14:16, 18:13, 16:22, 22:3, 29:11)

Prayer and a humble heart are necessary to discern the best way to deal with a foolish person. God will give you wisdom and the right words to say to bring peace instead of fueling the fire.

October 30

Lamentations 3-5
Psalm 119:57-64
Proverbs 26:8-10
Hebrews 9:1-10

My Portion

"Because of the Lord's great love, we are not consumed, for His compassions never fail. They are new every morning; great is Your faithfulness. I say to myself, 'The Lord is my portion; therefore, I will wait for Him.' The Lord is good to those whose hope is in Him, to the one who seeks Him; it is good to wait quietly for the salvation of the Lord." Lamentations 3:22-26 NIV

"You are my portion, Lord; I have promised to obey Your words." Psalm 119:57 NIV

JEREMIAH IS USING the same word in verse 22 that David used in Psalm 119:41 for faithful love that we saw a couple of days ago. Because of the Lord's hesed, Jeremiah is convinced that he and the Jewish remnant will be ok. Because he knows God is faithful and loyal, he is secure in the knowledge that they will be saved. Jeremiah wrote Lamentations after Jerusalem had been destroyed and most of the children of Israel were either killed or taken off to Babylon into captivity. God had warned him what was going to happen because of their unfaithfulness, and it happened just as God told him it would. Jeremiah had seen with his own eyes the punishment God had inflicted on the wicked. He knew the extent of God's wrath and yet he was able to say, "The Lord is good to those whose hope is in Him, to the one who seeks Him; it is good to wait quietly for the salvation of the Lord." This faith comes from a place of an intimate, personal relationship with God. He not only knows about God and His love, but He also knows God and has experienced the depth of His hesed.

Two of the verses in our reading today say the Lord is "my portion." Jeremiah and David both use this term referring to God. This is an interesting choice of words. We think of God being our strength, our hope. our savior, our deliverer, our shelter, our refuge, and our peace. But what does it mean that He is our portion? When God gave the children of Israel the promised land, it was divided among the 11 tribes (the Levites were priests and did not get a section). Each tribe was allotted a portion based on the number of people in their tribe. The land was to remain in that tribe and was not to be sold or passed to anyone outside of the tribe through marriage. Family inheritance was very important and signified God's provision for His people. The Levites were not given a portion because God promised to be their portion and would take care of all their needs. Jeremiah and David both recognized that God is the One who meets their needs and they do not have to rely on their family inheritance. He is the source of their provision. They recognized that nothing is as valuable as the promises of God. Nothing else could satisfy their needs and bring peace and joy to their lives. As believers we have been given the same promises. He is all we need. A lot of the fear and anxiety we experience can be avoided if we recognize that God is our portion. Because of His hesed, we can trust that He will take care of us and meet all our needs.

October 31

Ezekiel 1-3
Psalm 119:65-72
Proverbs 26:11-12
Hebrews 9:11-28

Judgment

"But He has appeared once for all at the culmination of the ages to do away with sin by sacrifice of Himself. Just as people are destined to die once, and after that to face judgment, so Christ was sacrificed once to take away the sins of many; and He will appear a second time, not to bear sin, but to bring salvation to those who are waiting for Him." Hebrews 9:26-28 NIV

VERSE 27 IS a good reminder for us that one day we are all going to face judgment. The Bible is very clear. "For we must all appear before the judgment seat of Christ, so that each one may receive what is due for what he has done in the body whether good or evil." 2 Corinthians 5:10 (ESV) One day we must all stand before the Judgment Seat of Christ. Matthew 25:31-46 and Revelation 10:11-15 give more detailed descriptions of what the judgment will be like. Our destiny for eternity is determined by what we do here on Earth. It is not determined by whether we are good or bad. We are all bad. If that is the criteria, none of us will get to Heaven. The one and only criteria is whether we accepted Jesus Christ, the Messiah, the Son of God, as our Savior. Every person who has ever lived, will stand before God and at that time, judgment will be pronounced. If they accepted Jesus as their Lord and Savior while they were alive, then His righteousness covers them, and they are ushered into Heaven for eternity. If they rejected Christ while they were alive, they will be judged by their deeds and everyone is guilty of sin, so they will be thrown into the Lake of Fire for eternity. There is no opportunity to change their mind after they die. Philippians 2:10-11 declares that at the end of time, "at the name of Jesus every knee will bow, and every tongue confess that Jesus Christ is Lord, to the glory of God the Father." (ESV) There will come a time when everyone will acknowledge that He is Lord. The truth will be revealed. Satan's lies will be exposed, but it will be too late. Those who rejected Jesus while they were alive are destined to Hell.

There are several popular ideas that Satan has devised to deceive people into believing that they don't have to choose Christ now. The idea of reincarnation is refuted by Hebrews 9:27. It clearly says that people are appointed to die once and then face judgment. We do not come back to life repeatedly until we get it right. There is nothing in the Bible that suggests that is the case. Annihilation is the idea that those who do not make it to Heaven simply have their souls annihilated and they disappear. They cease to exist. This may be comforting to some, but it is not biblical. Another idea that is popular in Roman Catholicism is the idea of purgatory. It is based on the book of 2 Maccabees and church tradition that says there is a state of "limbo" in which souls that don't initially make it to Heaven stay for a while until they finally make it into Heaven. There is no biblical support for this. Luke 16:19-31 directly refutes this notion. There is another lie that has become popular in Christian churches that is perhaps more dangerous than any of the others. It is the idea that God loves us so much that He will not send anyone to Hell so that ultimately, we all make it to Heaven. This is a heretical lie. I cannot state this firmly enough. If no one was going to be sent to Hell, then there was no reason for Jesus to die on the cross and be resurrected. If there is no Hell, there was no reason for Jesus to come to Earth in the first place. This is an insidious lie. Satan does not want anyone to believe the truth that they are destined to spend eternity in Hell if they do not accept Jesus, so he has made up lots of lies about alternative versions of the afterlife. As believers, we must ground our beliefs in biblical truth, not popular ideas and trends. I know this is a sober topic, but perhaps fitting for Halloween. Haunted houses and horror movies provide temporary thrills, but the reality of an eternity in Hell is really scary. We do not want anyone to have to experience this, so we need to be bold in telling others the truth, so they do not believe Satan's lies.

Ezekiel 4-6
Psalm 119:73-80
Proverbs 26:13-15
Hebrew 10:1-18

November 1

Laziness

"A lazy one says, 'There is a lion on the road! A lion is in the public square!' As the door turns on its hinges, so does a lazy one on his bed. A lazy one buries his hand in the dish; he is weary of bringing it to his mouth again." Proverbs 26:13-15 NIV

PROVERBS HAS MUCH to say about laziness. God does not bless laziness. God expects His followers to be hard working and diligent. The Bible is very clear that laziness is sin.

1. Laziness leads to poverty and hunger-

    "A slack hand causes poverty, but the hand of the diligent makes rich. "He who gathers in summer is a prudent son; but he who sleeps in harvest is a son who brings shame." Proverbs 10:4-5 (ESV)

    "The sluggard does not plow in the autumn; he will seek at harvest and have nothing." Proverbs 20:4 (ESV)

    "Love not sleep, lest you come to poverty; open your eyes, and you will have plenty of bread." Proverbs 20:13 (ESV)

    "The hand of the diligent will rule, while the slothful will suffer hunger." Proverbs 12:24 (ESV)

    "For even when we were with you, we would give you this command, if anyone is not willing to work, let him not eat." 2 Thessalonians 3:10 (ESV)

    (Proverbs 24:30-34, 21:25, 19:15, 12:27, 15:19, 6:6-11, 12:11)

2. God created us to work, not to be idle.

    "The Lord God took the man and put him in the garden of Eden to work it and keep it." Genesis 2:15 (ESV)

    "Whatever your hand finds to do, do it with all your might." Ecclesiastes 9:10 (ESV)

    "And whatever you do, in word or deed do everything in the name of the Lord Jesus, giving thanks to God the Father through Him. Whatever you do, work heartily, as for the Lord and not for men." Colossians 3:17, 23 (ESV)

(I Corinthians 9:24-27, Hebrews 6:12, I Thessalonians 4:10-12, Ephesians 2:10, John 9:4)

How are you spending your time? When you are at work are you a good employee? Are you diligent and hard working? Are you putting in the 8 hours of work you are being paid for? Or are you spending a lot of time on social media, gossiping, doing personal business, or otherwise goofing off? What about your leisure time? Are you spending it wisely? Are you spending time serving God? Are you volunteering at church or with other worthwhile organizations? Are you exercising to take care of the body God gave you? Are you spending time growing in your relationship with the Lord through group Bible studies, podcasts, or personal time spent in God's Word? Or are you spending your free time watching TV, playing video games, or spending hours on social media? Those things are not bad in moderation, but if you are neglecting the things you should be doing and wasting time on things that have very little value, you need to reevaluate your priorities. One day we will each give an account for how we spent the time He gave us. Will He say we spent it wisely or that we wasted it?

November 2

Ezekiel 7-8
Psalm 119:81-88
Proverbs 26:16
Hebrews 10:19-39

Unwavering Hope

"Let us hold unswervingly to the hope we profess, for He who promised is faithful. And let us consider how we may spur one another on toward love and good deeds, not giving up meeting together, as some are in the habit of doing but encouraging one another—and all the more as you see the Day approaching." Hebrews 10:23-25 NIV

This morning at church, my pastor preached about patience and perseverance as we wait in unwavering hope for the second coming of our Lord Jesus. Hope is the only answer for despair. If we focus our attention on the world around us the natural reaction is despair. There are very serious problems that seem to have no solution and no end in sight. Our hope cannot be in a cure for Covid or in whoever is in the White House. Our hope cannot rest on the end of racism or human trafficking or war. Those things are not going to end until Jesus returns and establishes His millennial kingdom. At that time, there will be peace on Earth. There will be no racism or classism. There will be no slavery, child abuse, murder, or rape. Human leaders cannot bring an end to those things. They will exist as long as Satan is roaming around the world prowling like a lion seeking to steal, kill and destroy everything that is good. Our hope is in Jesus Christ. He is faithful. He will not let us down. I don't know when He is going to return, but I know that He is. And in the meantime, I know that He will take care of me. He will sustain me and help me deal with whatever comes my way. The passage gives us some pointers on how we can hold unswervingly to that hope.

We must remind ourselves repeatedly that He who promised is faithful. That requires that we focus our attention on Him. When Peter was walking on water to Jesus, when he kept his eyes on Jesus, he was able to stay above the waves, but as soon as he took his eyes off Jesus and looked around at the wind and waves, he began to sink. If our attention is focused on the state of the world, we will sink into despair and we will be overwhelmed by the waves. I have stopped watching the news all the time. Instead of keeping the TV on the news, I look at it on my phone once a day to catch the highlights and see what I need to know. I have taken my focus off it. I'm not putting my head in the sand and ignoring what is going on around me, but I am choosing to keep my eyes on the One who is ultimately in control instead of the ones who think they are in control. Next it says that we are to spur one another on toward love and good deeds. I am diligently trying to do this. I am trying to encourage and uplift instead of tearing down. I'm not always very good at it, but I am thinking about ways I can encourage others. Instead of focusing on my needs and wants, I'm trying to spend my time figuring out how I can help other people and encourage them to draw closer to God.

Finally, it tells us to not give up meeting together. While I am glad for the technology that allowed churches to deliver services every week during the pandemic, I think it was also a huge win for Satan. Watching a sermon online is not the same as gathering in the house of God for worship. Whatever we need to do to be able to meet together, we need to do. There is power in corporate worship. There is power in gathering together, opening God's Word, and learning together. I understand why it was necessary for a time to meet online, but we need to be back in church now. We need each other. We were not meant to live our lives in a bubble. That is not how God designed us. Satan hates for us to go to church. He knows that where two or more are gathered together, God is in their midst, and he hates it. He will do whatever he needs to do to convince us not to go to church. If you feel more comfortable wearing a mask, that is totally fine. If you choose to go to the 8 o'clock service because there are fewer people, or if you choose to sit in the back by yourself and slip out before the end so that you don't encounter a crowd, that's fine. But go. This passage tells us to not give up meeting together, as some are in the habit of doing. It encourages us to meet even more as we see the Day approaching. The Day is referring to the Day when He will come to take His children to be with Him, the rapture. When someone loses hope we are to come alongside them and lift them up. If we are together, we see when others are hurting, and we can recognize their needs. We realize when they are struggling, and we can help. It is difficult to be a community online. It is difficult to love each other from afar. There are a lot of hurting, lonely people who are in despair. They need us to see them and be willing to take the time to encourage and lift them up. Ask God to make you aware of those who need your encouragement and to protect you as you serve Him.

November 3

Ezekiel 9-11
Psalm 119:89-96
Proverbs 26:17
Hebrews 11:1-16

Unseen

"Now faith is the confidence in what we hope for and assurance about what we do not see." Hebrews 11:1 NIV

CHARLES SPURGEON, THE 19th century pastor and theologian said, "To trust God in the light is nothing, but trust Him in the dark—that is faith."[19] Oswald Chambers said, "Faith never knows where it is being led, but it loves and knows the One who is leading."[19] Corrie Ten Boom described faith as "the radar that sees through the fog—the reality of things at a distance that the human eye cannot see."[19] The assurance of what we do not see is not the assurance that something we want is going to happen. We do not place our faith in an event. Faith is not believing something is going to happen the way we want it to happen. We do not place our faith in the hope of good fortune and blessings. We place our faith in God. Our faith is based on the character and love of our Heavenly Father. Faith is placing our life in His hands because we believe that He will accomplish what is best for us. If we place our faith in a certain thing happening, we will likely be disappointed. Faith is trusting Him with the when, how, where and what.

Max Lucado said about faith, "Faith is not the belief that God will do what you want. Faith is the belief that God will do what is right."[19] Faith is knowing the character of God and trusting His absolute, undeniable ability and willingness to do what is best for us in every situation. We cannot firmly believe that a future event will happen unless it is specifically promised in the Bible. We know that if we accept Him as our Lord and Savior, we will go to Heaven and spend eternity with Him. We know that someday He will return and judge the living and the dead. Those things are specifically promised, and we can rely on them happening. We cannot have faith that we will get a certain job or that we will be healed of an illness or that tomorrow will be a perfect day. If we place our faith in those things, they may or may not happen. But if we place our faith in God, we can be assured that He will bring about His plan for us. We will get the job that He knows is best for us. We will be healed either here in this body or in Heaven with a restored body. Tomorrow may not be perfect, but we can be assured that He will walk through it with us no matter what we face. Elizabeth Eliot said, "Faith does not eliminate questions, but faith knows where to take them."[20] We may not understand everything that happens to us, but we are able to remain firm and steadfast because our faith is in His love and His sovereignty. The Old Testament saints that are listed in Hebrews 11 did not have all the evidence we have in His Word. They did not have the benefit of seeing the big picture and the unfolding of God's plan of redemption, but they trusted in God. We cannot see God, but we have an abundance of evidence of His faithfulness in our lives and in the lives of generations of believers that justifies our complete faith in Him.

November 4

Ezekiel 12-13
Psalm 119:97-104
Proverbs 26:18-19
Hebrews 11:17- 12:3

The Promise

"They were all commended for their faith, yet none of them received what had been promised, since God had planned something better for us so that only together with us would they be made perfect. Therefore, since we are surrounded by such a great cloud of witnesses, let us throw off everything that hinders and the sin that so easily entangles. And let us run with perseverance the race marked out for us, fixing our eyes on Jesus, the pioneer and perfecter of our faith. For the joy set before Him, He endured the cross, scorning its shame, and sat down at the right hand of the throne of God. Consider Him who endured such opposition from sinners so that you will not grow weary and lose heart." Hebrews 11:39-12:3 NIV

THE WRITER OF Hebrews finds that there are so many examples of persevering faith that he cannot list them all. He gives examples of incredible victories because of great faith, and he speaks of people who suffered terrible tragedies and extreme hardships and yet remained faithful. They were all commended for their faith and yet none of them received the fulfillment of the promise. The promise he speaks of is total and final redemption. They did not receive the promise because the plan had not been completed. There is a plan that God began with creation, carried on through Abraham, Isaac, and Jacob and continued through the judges, kings, and prophets of the Old Testament. Then Jesus, the Messiah, God's Son, came to Earth as a baby, lived a perfect life, died, buried, and rose again to purchase redemption once for all. Those of us who have accepted Him as our Savior and Lord have seen the partial fulfillment of the promise. Our sins have been forgiven, and we walk in the newness of life because we have the Holy Spirit living in us. But we have not seen the complete fulfillment of the promise because we still deal with sin and evil. The final fulfillment of the promise is yet to come.

Therefore, since we are surrounded by such a great cloud of witnesses, God's faithful people throughout the ages, we can run the race set before us. We each have our place in history. We each have a part to play in God's great redemptive plan. Because we have the examples of so many before us who have endured great hardship, and the example of Jesus Himself, we can overcome the temptations we face, and we can be victorious. By fixing our eyes on Jesus, we can persevere. I love that this verse says Jesus is the pioneer and perfecter of our faith. Pioneer means that He has gone before us and paved the way. And perfecter means that He is perfecting our faith. It is not up to us to be strong and hang in there. He is building our faith. He knows exactly what He needs to do to make us strong. He knows what obstacles we need in our lives to develop faith that will persevere through trials. God has promised that there will come a time when there will be no more sin, no more tears, no more pain, and no more death. When Jesus returns and establishes His millennial kingdom, the Old Testament saints will rise and experience the complete fulfillment of the promise along with all those who have accepted Jesus as their Savior. He will present us perfect and righteous to His Father and we will abide with Him forever.

November 5

Ezekiel 14-16
Psalm 119:105-112
Proverbs 26:20-22
Hebrews 12:4-13
The Lamp

"Your Word is a lamp for my feet, and a light on my path." Psalm 119:105 NIV

When I was a teenager, every summer my youth group went to church camp at Camp Chula Vista in Pell City, Alabama. I have so many wonderful memories from camp: canoeing on the lake, playing tetherball, singing worship songs in the pavilion, eating surprisingly good camp food, playing Take a Hike for hours after evening worship, and growing in my faith. One of the things I remember about the camp was the cabins. There was a girl's hill and a boy's hill which were separated by the lake, a pavilion, a dining hall, a swimming pool, and a long walk. They did everything they could to keep the teenage boys far away from the teenage girls. As an adult I now understand why that was so necessary. On each hill there were several cabins in the woods and a bath house in the middle with showers and bathrooms. The cabins did not have bathrooms. At 11:00pm the counselors turned the lights out in all the cabins. No exceptions. There were no lights on the hill except those lights in the cabins. As you can imagine, it was very dark in the woods. After 11, if you had to go to the bathroom, you had to walk in the dark. It was the woods, so there were sticks and rocks and limbs on the ground. One of the things on the packing list to take to camp was always a flashlight.

I remember Camp Chula Vista whenever I read this verse. I think of those summer nights making my way to the bathroom in the dark with my flashlight. God's Word provides us the light we need to find our way in the dark. If we follow its principles, we can avoid a lot of the obstacles in our path. Instead of tripping over the rocks, we see the dangers in front of us and we can walk around them. Many problems we face come from ignoring the guidelines God has provided for us. The other issue with walking to the bathroom in the dark was the danger of the creatures that occupied the woods. There were all sorts of creepy crawly things that came out at night. My greatest fear was stepping on a snake or getting attacked by some other wild animal. In 1980, Friday the 13th came out in theaters so that added a whole new level of fear about the dangers that lurked in the darkness. God's Word protects us from a lot of the evil and scary things we face in the world. God is our refuge and protection. He gives us the strength to face the evil around us and not be led astray by it. From the cabin I was not able to see the bathhouse. I knew the general direction I was supposed to go, but it was too dark to see the building. My flashlight did not provide enough light to see the whole way. It gave me the light I needed to take the next step and then the next step until I reached my destination. God's Word is like that, too. God rarely illuminates our whole way at once. We know the general direction we are supposed to go, but we can't see the ending. He gives us the light we need and the guidance to take the next step and then the next step until we reach the goal. His Word is a lamp and a light to illumine our path if we use it.

Ezekiel 17-18
Psalm 119:113-120
Proverbs 26:23-25
Hebrews 12:14-29

The Root of Bitterness

"Make sure that no one falls short of the grace of God and that no root of bitterness springs up, causing trouble and by it, defiling many." Hebrews 12:15 HCSB

THE ROOT OF a plant is something that grows below the surface. You don't see the roots unless you dig up the plant. The root fuels the plant. It gives it life and nutrients. Without the root system the plant will die. This is a very good description of bitterness. The root of bitterness is often hidden beneath the surface. It may not be discernable at first. Unfortunately, the root of bitterness is a poison that brings forth the deadly plants of unforgiveness, malice, anger, and resentment. Instead of fueling growth and health, it fuels destruction. Bitterness grows like a root under the surface and fuels rage, anger, and malice so that they grow and spread like weeds. Bitterness begins with hurt feelings that are not dealt with. Instead of addressing the issue, they are pushed down inside and begin to take root. Merriam-Webster defines bitterness as a "deep-seated ill will, animosity, antagonism, hostility, a harsh or sharp quality, biting sharpness of feeling or expression."[21] Ephesians 4:31 tells us to "get rid of all bitterness, rage and anger, brawling and slander, along with every form of malice." (NIV) Bitterness is a poison that eats away or corrodes from the inside.

My favorite TV shows are Criminal Minds, Bones, Rizzoli and Isles, NCIS, and Crossing Jordan. Do you see a theme? I love murder mysteries. When the person is murdered by a gun shot, suffocation, or stabbing, cause of death is easy to figure out, so they just need to figure out who did it. But poison is much more difficult to discern. It can be hidden or masked to look like a heart attack or other natural health issues. There are also a lot of different kinds of poison that cannot be discovered by a simple blood test and can go undetected. That is a perfect description of bitterness. It is a poison deep down in the soul that can slowly eat away at you and destroy you from the inside. It may be hidden for a while, but as the root of bitterness grows, it will eventually come to the surface. It results in holding on to angry feelings, being easily offended, angry outbursts, gossip, and slander. Eventually the person who is bitter comes across as cold, harsh, cynical, sarcastic, and unpleasant to be around. Left unchecked their bitterness and resentment will not only be directed at the person who originally hurt them but will manifest itself toward anyone in their lives. Ephesians 4:32 tells us how to deal with such bitterness by "being kind and compassionate to one another, forgiving one another, just as Christ God forgave you." (NIV) The best way to deal with bitterness is to appropriately handle the hurt and angry feelings when they happen instead of pushing them down inside and letting them consume us. The root must be dug up and thrown away to get rid of it. The first step is asking God to reveal any root of bitterness that we have toward anyone and giving those feelings of hurt and anger to Him. Asking Him to help us forgive and move on is the only way to get rid of bitterness.

November 7

Ezekiel 19-20
Psalm 119:121-128
Proverbs 26:26-28
Hebrews 13

Brotherly Love

"Keep on loving one another as brothers and sisters." Hebrews 13:1 NIV

THE WORD TRANSLATED for love here is the Greek word phileo. In the English language we have one word for love. The Greeks have 4 different words to describe the different kinds of love that we feel for others. Agape love is a perfect, selfless love. This is the love that God shows to us and the love that Jesus exhibited on the cross. It is not dependent on the behavior of the other person. It is unconditional. Phileo love is brotherly love. This is love between close friends or companions. It is based on mutual affection. Eros is a sexual love driven by desire. And storge love is the natural, unforced familial love. It is the love of a mother and child, or a grandfather to his grandchildren. It is based on a kindred connection. Agape and phileo are referred to often in the Bible. The word used in Hebrews 13:1 is phileo. As believers in Jesus, we are adopted into the family of God. We are His children and other Christians are our adopted brothers and sisters. Hebrews 13:1 is telling us how to treat other Christians. We are to treat each other with phileo love. There is a bond that exists between all believers that is unique and unmistakable. We may be different ages, a different race, a different gender, and from a different cultural background. We may be from different countries, different socioeconomic backgrounds, or different denominations. But if we have the Holy Spirit living in us, we have a common bond that ties us together that is stronger than any bond we can have with an unbeliever. This bond allows us to show phileo love to our brothers and sisters in Christ and results in mutual affection.

Phileo love is constant. It is not based on emotions or feelings. It is based on a commitment to each other and to the body of Christ. It seeks unity. We do not have to agree about everything to have unity within the body of believers. Phileo is not divisive. It goes out of its way to seek peace and show respect. This requires forgiveness and humility. Phileo love is compassionate and understanding. It walks alongside in good times and bad times sharing the joys and the sadness. It is available to help with whatever is needed. Sometimes that will be in the form of tangible resources like food and clothing. At other times it will come as encouragement or prayer. Sometimes it will be through serving a physical need or helping someone through a difficult time. Phileo is unselfish. "Do nothing out of selfish ambition or vain conceit. Rather, in humility value others above yourselves, not looking to your own interests but each of you to the interests of the others." Philippians 2:3-4 (NIV) Phileo love is expressed in action. It takes conscious effort to love in this way. It is not easy and often does not come naturally. It requires putting aside our own needs and desires to meet the needs of others. This verse reminds us to keep loving each other, even when it is hard. Don't give up.

November 8

Ezekiel 21-22
Psalm 119:129-136
Proverbs 27:1-2
James 1:1-18

Perseverance

"Consider it pure joy, my brothers and sisters, whenever you face trials of many kinds, because you know that the testing of your faith produces perseverance. Let perseverance finish its work so that you may be mature and complete, not lacking anything. Blessed is the one who perseveres under trial because, having stood the test, that person will receive the crown of life that the Lord has promised to those who love Him." James 1:2-4, 12 NIV

Mature and complete, not lacking anything! Doesn't that sound great! I want to sign up for that program. A marketing campaign focused on the end result would be an easy sell, until you read the fine print. It's kind of like a diet that promises to help you lose thirty lbs. in one day, but you have your legs cut off to do it. You will weigh less but... Being mature and complete and lacking nothing doesn't come easily. It comes as a result of persevering through all kinds of trials. We develop faith by having to exercise faith. We develop patience by being put in situations repeatedly where we need to exercise patience. We develop self-control by being in situations where we are tempted and must exercise self-control. We develop peace in our lives, not by being in peaceful circumstances all the time, but rather by being in stressful situations where we need to allow God to fill us with His peace. Notice the common theme here is exercise. I do not love exercise. I know people who love to work up a sweat and enjoy the burn from a good workout. That is not me. I do it because I know that the result is a healthier body. Exercise implies hard work. It requires diligence and consistency. Exercising one time does not do any good. It is only through a daily consistent routine that you see any meaningful improvement in your health. When you begin an exercise routine you do not start out running a marathon. You start out doing the Couch to 5K plan and then after months of daily running you can work up to a marathon. (At least that's how it's supposed to work. I can't speak to it from personal experience.) The same is true of faith. God develops our faith by giving us opportunities to trust Him in small things so that we are prepared to trust Him with bigger things when they come.

Notice verse 2 does not say, "if you face trials of many kinds." It says, "whenever you face trials of many kinds." Life is filled with trials and heartache. No one makes it through this life without any difficulty. Sin and death are present, and we cannot avoid their effects. The question is not whether life is going to be hard, but rather how are we going to deal with the hardships and difficulties we face. Will they make us bitter or better? Will they cause us to turn to God or turn away from Him. We avoid some difficulties by making wise choices and avoiding sin in our lives, but sometimes we have trouble because of the bad choices of others and sometimes bad things just happen like a natural disaster, a terminal illness, or an economic downturn. Faith develops perseverance and perseverance results in maturity and completion.

November 9

Ezekiel 23-24
Psalm 119:137-144
Proverbs 27:3-4
James 1:19-27

Listen and Do

"Everyone should be quick to listen, slow to speak, and slow to become angry, because human anger does not produce the righteousness that God desires. Do not merely listen to the Word, and so deceive yourselves. Do what it says." James 1:19-20, 22 NIV

LISTENING IS HARD. I must admit that I'm not very good at it. Listening is not a passive activity. Active listening requires attention and focus. I remember studying about active listening in my social work classes in college. I need to remind myself periodically of the suggestions they gave.

1. Make eye contact
2. Don't interrupt
3. Don't jump to conclusions before you hear them out
4. Listen to nonverbal cues such as facial expressions, posture, etc.
5. Don't start planning what to say next
6. Ask questions to clarify
7. Paraphrase and summarize to make sure you understand what they are saying

After we have done all those things, it is still best not to jump in with our opinions and solutions. The next step should be prayer. If we are in the middle of a conversation that might be hard, but while they are talking it is helpful to ask God to give you wisdom and the right words to say to them. I'm not suggesting that you stop and bow your head, but rather that you voice a quick prayer inviting God into the conversation and allowing Him to guide your mouth. This will also help with the next instruction: to be slow to become angry. Instead of immediately reacting to what they are saying in anger, a quick prayer can calm you down long enough to choose your words carefully and not add fuel to the fire. "Human anger does not produce the righteousness that God desires." That is an understatement. I don't think I have ever reacted in anger to anything and then later felt good about it. Even if I was right, I always regret how I dealt with it and wish I could take my words back. I have never regretted slowing down and thinking about how to respond appropriately.

Verse 22 gives us more advice about listening. It tells us not to just listen to God's Word but do what it says. It is possible to read our Bible every day and know exactly what it says and yet never apply it to our lives. Just like the Bible does us no good sitting on our nightstand or on a bookshelf, it also does us no good if we read it and then ignore what it says. God uses His Word to speak to us and tell us what we need to hear to grow spiritually and to live lives that please Him. We need to listen actively to what He is telling us and then do what it says.

November 10

Ezekiel 25-27
Psalm 119:145-152
Proverbs 27:5-6
James 2:1-13

Speaking the Truth in Love

> "Wounds from a friend can be trusted, but an enemy multiplies kisses."
> Proverbs 27:6 NIV

Ephesians 4:11-16 should be our guide when we are in a position where we need to give constructive criticism to someone. "So, Christ Himself gave the apostles, the prophets, the evangelists, the pastors, and teachers, to equip His people for works of service, so that the body of Christ may be built up until we all reach unity in the faith and in the knowledge of the Son of God and become mature, attaining to the whole measure of the fullness of Christ. Then we will no longer be infants, tossed back and forth by the waves, and blown here and there by every wind of teaching... Instead, speaking the truth in love, we will grow to become in every respect the mature body of Him who is the head, that is, Christ. From Him the whole body, joined and held together by every supporting ligament, grows and builds itself up in love, as each part does its work." (NIV) This is a picture of the body of Christ functioning together as one in love and support. The purpose of constructive criticism should always be to help the person become more mature in Christ. The motive should be a desire to seek the best for them and the means should be a humble and loving spirit.

Knowing when to speak up and when to keep our mouth shut is very difficult. We often find ourselves in situations where we must decide if something needs to be said to correct a friend or family member and whether we are the one that needs to say it. Prayerfully seeking God's guidance in examining our purpose, motive and means will help us answer that question. If it is an issue that affects their spiritual growth and will help them mature as a believer, then it most likely needs to be addressed. If it is just something that annoys you or that is a matter of personal preference, then it may be best to just ignore it. The motive behind your desire to confront the person is very important. If you feel the need to confront them because you truly want to help them and want what is best for them, then that is a good indicator that you should address the issue. If it is for your own personal benefit, then you need to pray and ask God for wisdom about how to proceed. All constructive criticism should come from a humble and loving spirit. If you go to the person in anger or with a demanding tone, they are likely to get defensive and you will not accomplish your purpose. Prayer and turning the situation over to God will allow you to go into the conversation with a gentle tone and loving heart that will help them see that you are not trying to hurt them, but that you want to help them.

It is important that we remember these things when we are the recipient of constructive criticism as well. It is easy to find people who will tell us what we want to hear, but true friends tell us what we need to hear. We need to surround ourselves with people who love us enough to tell us the truth in love.

November 11

Ezekiel 28-29
Psalm 119:153-160
Proverbs 27:7-8
James 2:14-26

Faith Without Works

"For just as the body without the Spirit is dead, so also faith without works is dead."
James 2:26 HCSB

THIS QUESTION IS the source of much debate in the church. It is the difference between denominations and is a point of division within the body of believers. Many scholars differ on this subject, and many believe that scripture contradicts itself on this topic. I do not believe that is the case. I believe that we are saved by faith and faith alone. "For you are saved by grace through faith, and this is not from yourselves; it is God's gift, not from works, so that no one can boast." Ephesians 2:8-9 (HCSB) If you believe that Jesus is the Son of God who was born of a virgin, lived a perfect life, died on a cross, was buried and raised Himself from the dead to pay the penalty for sin once for all and you ask Him to be your Lord and Savior, you are saved. Period. Nothing else is required. At that moment you were sealed by the Holy Spirit, and you are going to Heaven. We cannot earn salvation. Nothing we do, good or bad, can save us or keep us from being saved. We are sinners in need of a savior. We don't deserve it, but by His mercy and grace, He saves us if we put our faith and trust in Him. That's all He asks. Some people believe that faith is what saves you, but then after that you must be good to keep yourself saved. They believe that you can lose your salvation. I do not believe that is true. In John 10:28-29, Jesus says, "I give them eternal life, and they will never perish—ever! No one will snatch them out of My hand. My Father who has given them to Me, is greater than all, and no one is able to snatch them out of My Father's hand." (HCSB) We are not capable of being perfect before we are saved, and we cannot live a perfect, sinless life after we are saved. We are in constant need of His grace and mercy as we go through the process of sanctification. We grow and mature, but we must contend with our flesh and with the powers of darkness in this world until He takes us to Heaven to be with Him.

    I am equally convinced that if you are saved, your life will never be the same. You cannot believe and then go on with your life as before. It is impossible. If the Creator of the universe comes to live in your heart, you will be different. If you have been saved by faith, the evidence of that faith will be works. Works do not save you or keep you saved. Works are the evidence of true faith. The message that James is trying to convey in this passage is that, if you have faith, then you will also have works. The two are inseparable. A faith that saves is a faith that works. The life of a believer in Jesus Christ should be overflowing with evidence of that belief. If it is not, we should examine our hearts to determine if we truly believe what we say we believe. The moment we are saved, we go from being dead in our sins, to being alive in Christ.

James is saying that faith without words is still dead in sin and has not been made alive in Christ. The question is not whether we have lost our salvation, but whether we were ever saved to start with. There is no contradiction between what James is saying and Paul's teaching. True faith is evident in action.

November 12

Ezekiel 30-31
Psalm 119:161-168
Proverbs 27:9-10
James 3:1-12

Bits and Rudders

"Now when we put bits into the mouths of horses to make them obey us, we also guide the whole animal. And consider ships: Though very large and driven by fierce winds, they are guided by a very small rudder wherever the will of the pilot directs. So too, though the tongue is a small part of the body, it boasts great things." James 3:3-5 HCSB

OUR TONGUES CAN get us in a lot of trouble. They can also be used for good, but they must be controlled. If we don't have control of our tongue, we are destined to experience conflict, stress, pain, and regret. Letting our tongues run wild leads to sin. Gossiping, lying, slander, angry outbursts, cussing, inappropriate jokes, insincere flattery, inappropriate sexual speech, sarcasm, negativity, condescension, and boasting/bragging are all sins that are strongly admonished in the Bible. They flow out of the mouth, but they are the overflow of evil in the heart. The sins of the tongue usually lead to more sins. Lying leads to lying more to cover up the lie. Gossiping inevitably leads to the desire for even more juicy gossip that we can spread so that we can be the one in the know about what is going on. A little cussing desensitizes us to it so that we do it more and more frequently. Inappropriate jokes get a laugh, so we tell more. People like to hear good things about themselves, so we tell them what they want to hear. When we get the attention we are seeking from boasting and bragging about our success, we continue to do it to get more attention. Negativity breeds more negativity. Sarcasm and a tone of condescension usually reflect bitterness and an unforgiving spirit that becomes a pattern of negative speech.

Taming the tongue is a constant battle. It is not something that we can tame once and then is under control. We first need to recognize the devastation and destruction that a lack of self-control can cause. I suspect that we all have areas where we can do a better job of controlling our tongues and we need to ask God to reveal those areas to us. Then we need to be intentional. It is easy to run our mouths and say whatever comes into our heads. It is difficult to think before we speak. It is difficult to measure our words. It is difficult to stop and evaluate if what we want to say is edifying and encouraging or if it will make the situation worse. It is difficult to keep our mouths shut when we want to yell or scream or hurt someone as bad as they hurt us. Controlling our tongue can prevent a lot of the trouble and regret that we cause ourselves. I love the analogy of the bit in the mouth of a horse or the rudder that controls the ship. Allowing God to be the One who controls the bit in our mouth and letting Him be the pilot who steers our ship requires purposeful submission, but results in a life that is more peaceful and much less chaotic. Picturing the bit in our mouth before we speak can help us to stop, think and pray before we speak.

Ezekiel 32-33
Psalm 119:169-176
Proverbs 27:11-12
James 3:13-18

The Wisdom of Peace

> "But the wisdom that comes from Heaven is first of all pure; then peace-loving, considerate, submissive, full of mercy and good fruit, impartial and sincere. Peacemakers who sow in peace reap a harvest of righteousness." James 3:17-18 NIV

The description of wisdom in these verses is not necessarily how most people think of wisdom. We think of wise people as smart, resourceful, good decision makers, bright, and clever. But those things are not listed in James' description of wisdom. If you asked 100 people to describe wisdom, I doubt if the traits above would make the top ten list. And yet James says that wisdom from above, godly wisdom, is pure, peace-loving, considerate, submissive, full of mercy and good fruit, impartial and sincere. Those things seem to describe a loving person or a gentle, kind person, but they also characterize a wise person. There is wisdom in purity. There is wisdom in being a peace-lover and peacemaker. There is wisdom in being considerate and submissive. There is wisdom in being full of mercy and good fruit. And there is wisdom in being impartial and sincere. In examining these qualities, it seems that the common denominator is humility. A wise person is humble. They recognize their human condition in relation to a holy and just God. Their response is a grateful heart that overflows with love and compassion for others. Its motives are pure. Its actions are considerate toward the feelings of others. Instead of demanding its rights, it submits to the rights of others. It extends mercy and its judgments are impartial and sincere.

Wise people are peace-lovers. "Peacemakers who sow in peace reap a harvest of righteousness." If we sow seeds of peace, we reap righteousness? Interesting. If we sow corn seeds, we expect to get corn. If we sow pea seeds, we expect to get peas. If we sow sunflower seeds, we expect to get big, beautiful sunflowers. But this verse tells us that if we sow peace, we will reap righteousness. Righteousness is being in right standing with God. It is based on our covenant relationship with Him and not on our own actions and moral uprightness. So how does sowing peace lead to right standing with God? Again, I think this goes back to humility. Those who love and seek peace are demonstrating a humility that comes from recognizing what God has done for them and the desire to share that with others. Being at peace is more important than being right. I am not suggesting that being peace-loving means that we do not take a stand for what is right, just, and moral. We must not be afraid to speak truth. But a wise person does that in a peaceable, considerate, sincere way and not with a demanding, rude, and belligerent attitude. How you say something is usually more important that what you say. Sowing in peace is much more likely to result in a rightness in our heart that is pleasing to God and demonstrates a humble and wise attitude. It is also important to note that loving and seeking peace is not weakness. We are not talking about pacifism or a flowerchild hippie Woodstock kind of peace that is cowardly and timid. This peace comes from a place of self-control and restraint. It can evaluate the situation and determine the most appropriate response that will bring about the desired result. Instead of adding fuel to the fire, it is able to bring about resolution. In our contentious, competitive, and easily offended culture, being peaceable is rare. Choosing to seek peace instead of conflict takes effort and purpose. It is hard to overlook offenses and to submit to the desires of others. It is hard to be considerate toward inconsiderate people and to be merciful to difficult people. And yet our reward is right standing with God which is worth far more than any reward that vengeance and selfishness can provide.

November 14

Ezekiel 34-36
Psalm 120
Proverbs 27:13-14
James 4:1-12

Motives

"You do not have because you do not ask God. When you ask, you do not receive, because you ask with wrong motives, that you may spend what you get on your pleasures." James 4:2-3 NIV

Motives are tricky things. I think we don't even recognize our true motives most of the time. Our actions may be good, but the motive behind that action can be pride or jealousy or selfishness. It is difficult to sort through all the whys and hows of our actions. And it is even more difficult to sort through those things when it comes to our prayers. Why do we really want the thing that we are asking God for? Are we coming to God like Santa Claus with a list of things we want Him to do for us? Are we coming to God because we want a relationship with Him? Is our priority to get something from Him or to get to know Him? Do we only come to Him when we have a crisis or do we spend time with Him every day? Our view of God helps to answer those questions. Some people think of God as this Supreme Being who sits on a throne somewhere in the sky who has power to wave His hand and change things on Earth. They think that if we beg or plead with Him then maybe we can talk Him into intervening on our behalf or on behalf of those we love. They don't want to bother Him so they only go to Him when they can't handle something on their own. When they have run out of options, they pray and bargain and plead. That is not the God described in the Bible. And that is not how prayer works. Our God is not a disconnected dictator who rules from afar. He is not a king waiting in some throne room in Heaven for us to come to Him with a deal promising to serve Him or be good or stop being bad if He does what we ask. He isn't up in Heaven waiting to see if we can offer Him something good enough for it to be worth His while to give us what we want. That is a very misguided view of God, but I think it is all too common.

Our God loves us. He wants to be a part of everything we do. He wants to help us with every single decision. He wants to walk with us and talk with us and lead and guide us through every minute of our day. He isn't like Santa who is up in the North Pole all year making toys and waiting for us to send Him a list of the things we want most. He is with us 365 days a year. He doesn't just come down the chimney and leave our presents and then go back up to the North Pole. He wants to be our best friend, our mentor, and our confidante. The way that prayer works is that we have a personal intimate relationship with Him, talking to Him every day. We talk to Him about our hurts, our fears, our concerns, our anger, our dreams, and our desires. Most people go to God with an agenda. They have a problem, and they know how they want it to be fixed and they expect Him to do what they want. God rarely goes along with our plans. The purpose of prayer is not to get God to do what we want Him to do. The purpose of prayer is to take our concerns to Him and ask Him to do what is best. Submission to His agenda always brings about the best result even though it may not be the result we think we want. When we are seeking Him, then He can shape our desires so that they match His will for us. When we submit to His will, He changes our hearts so that our motives are pure, and our prayers go along with His desires for us. That happens in relationship. The better we get to know Him, the more we realize how much He loves us and that we can trust Him. The more we trust Him, the easier it is to submit to His plans and let go of our own.

November 15

Ezekiel 37-38
Psalm 121
Proverbs 27:15-16
James 4:13-17

Help

"I lift my eyes to the mountains. Where does my help come from? My help comes from the Lord, the Maker of Heaven and Earth. He will not let your foot slip—He who watches over you will not slumber; indeed, He who watches over Israel will neither slumber not sleep. The Lord watches over you—the Lord is your shade at your right hand; the sun will not harm you by day, nor the moon by night. The Lord will keep you from all harm—He will watch over your life; the Lord will watch over your coming and going both now and forevermore." Psalm 121 NIV

I think this is my favorite chapter in the whole Bible. Whenever I am stressed and anxious or when I am feeling helpless, I turn to this passage. I have to remind myself that God is the source of my help. When I turn to other people for help, they often disappoint. When I rely on my own resources and strength, their limitations become quickly apparent. Any earthly source I turn to cannot ultimately be sufficient to help me in every situation. But there is a source that is available to me that is always faithful and always sufficient to meet every need I will ever face. My God made all of Heaven and Earth. He set it all in motion and He keeps it all going. And even better than that, He watches over me! He never sleeps. He never needs to take a break. He is always by my side helping me. He watches over my life. He watches over my coming and going now and forever. Sometimes it does not feel like He is here with me, and I feel alone. Sometimes I feel like things are out of control and that He will let me down. That's why it is so important that I fill my mind with the knowledge that He is watching over me. Feelings are not reliable. But my God is reliable. Even when I do not understand what is happening to me, I can be confident that He is watching over me. I can trust Him.

Verse 5 says that the Lord is my shade. This is a beautiful word picture to me. I am so fair skinned, and I sunburn very easily. The sun is not my friend. At the beach, I sit under an umbrella most of the time. Whenever I am outside, I am looking for shade. I have learned over the years that sunburns hurt and then itch and make me miserable. They can also be deadly. Twenty years ago, I had a melanoma. Thankfully, it was detected early and removed before it spread. I believe that the Lord was watching over me when I ran into a friend at Walmart who told me she had just been diagnosed with skin cancer. I had not been to the dermatologist in years, and this prompted me to go get a checkup. When I think of God being my shade, the image that comes into my mind is the huge walnut tree in the front yard at my Mama Mae's house when I was growing up. My cousins and I spent hours playing under that tree protected from the sun without a care in the world. The memories of those days bring a smile to my face. I felt safe and secure. I'm sure there were things going on that I didn't know about. Financial struggles, troublesome world events, illnesses, deaths, etc. were probably happening that I knew nothing about because my parents shielded me from them. I didn't need to worry because they were taking care of me. As an adult, I am more aware of the issues in the world around me, but I can rest in the shade of God's protection because He is watching over me.

November 16

Ezekiel 39-40
Psalm 122
Proverbs 27:17-18
James 5:1-12

Patience

"Be patient, then, brothers and sisters, until the Lord's coming. See how the farmer waits for the land to yield its valuable crop, patiently waiting for the autumn and spring rains. You too, be patient and stand firm, because the Lord's coming is near. As you know, we count as blessed those who have persevered. You have heard of Job's perseverance and have seen what the Lord finally brought about. The Lord is full of compassion and mercy." James 5:7-8, 11 NIV

THERE HAVE BEEN faithful followers of Jesus throughout the ages who have longed for His second coming. Every generation since His death, burial and resurrection has been looking up wondering when He would return to take us to be with Him in Heaven. This life is filled with pain and heartache. There are moments of happiness and joy in the midst of the difficulty, but no one gets through this life without experiencing problems. During the hard times, we long for a better place. It is natural to long for what we have been promised, life without pain and tears and sorrow. James is reminding us to be patient. As we watch the news and examine Bible prophecy, it is apparent that the Lord's coming is near. Everything is lining up perfectly. We don't know the exact time, but the puzzle is coming together. God is full of compassion and mercy. He does not want anyone to experience the pain and suffering of Hell. His desire is for everyone to turn to Him and accept His invitation of eternal life. He is giving us every possible chance to believe and accept Him. But there is coming a day, a day that He had planned from the beginning of time when Jesus will appear in the sky and call us home.

Just as the farmer plans His life around the seasons of planting and harvest, we are told to plan our lives with the expectation of His return. In every season there is work to be done for the farmer. He does not sit around waiting for the harvest twiddling his thumbs. He sows, tills, weeds, and tends his crop and then he waits for God to send the rain at the right time. He is diligent and when the harvest comes, he will reap the benefits of his hard work. In the face of suffering, Job remained faithful, and God rewarded his perseverance. "The Lord blessed the last part of Job's life more than the first." Job 42:12 (HCSB) As believers, we cannot give up. We must remain faithful, stand firm, and persevere. Then one day, we will hear the trumpet sound and look up to see our Savior in the sky calling us home. What a glorious day that will be!

November 17

Ezekiel 41-42
Psalm 123
Proverbs 27:19-20
James 5:13-20

The Man in the Mirror

"As water reflects the face, so one's life reflects the heart." Proverbs 27:19 HCSB

"Anyone who listens to the Word but does not do what it says is like someone who looks at his face in a mirror and, after looking at himself, goes away and immediately forgets what he looks like. But whoever looks intently into the perfect law that gives freedom, and continues in it, not forgetting what they have heard, but doing it, they will be blessed in what they do." James 1: 23-25 NIV

You will notice that I went back and borrowed a reading from a few days ago in James because it fits so perfectly with our verse today in Psalm. It is necessary to examine our lives frequently to determine if we are living in a way that is pleasing to God. Do our actions match our words? Are we authentic? Is what we say we believe evident in our lives? I think most of us just go through life getting by day to day. We go to church and over the years have formed beliefs consistent with the things we have been taught and experienced. If asked what we believe about most topics we can give the good Sunday School answer, but does our life reflect that answer. Can others tell what we believe without asking?

Do I really believe that the Bible is God's Word? Do I believe that it is my manual for life, that I can find the answers to my questions in its pages, and that God will speak to me through it? If I really believe that, then am I utilizing it? Am I following it, searching it, and doing what it says? Do I trust that God really loves me, He knows best, and He is working all things out for my good? If I believe that, am I putting my complete trust in Him or do I spend most of my time worrying about things I don't have control over and trying to fix them myself? Do I trust Him with my finances, relationships, health, career, etc.? Do I believe that there is a real Heaven and a real Hell and that everyone is destined to spend eternity in one or the other? If I really believe that, have I done everything I can to tell my friends and family about Jesus so that they will not experience eternal damnation? Am I more concerned about being liked and accepted and afraid of being labeled as intolerant or narrow minded, or concerned about the eternal welfare of those I love? I know this is difficult because you don't want to say so much that you turn them away, but it is important that we pray daily for them and ask God to give us opportunities to share with them. Time is short. Speaking the truth in love is hard, but it is possible with the guidance of the Holy Spirit. Let's take this opportunity to look in the mirror and ask God to reveal to us any areas where our lives are not reflecting our faith and then ask Him to help us be authentic.

Ezekiel 43-44
Psalm 124
Proverbs 27:21-22
I Peter 1:1-12

A Living Hope

"Praise be to the God and Father of our Lord Jesus Christ! In His great mercy He has given us new birth into a living hope through the resurrection of Jesus Christ from the dead, and into an inheritance that can never perish, spoil, or fade. This inheritance is kept in Heaven for you, who through faith are shielded by God's power until the coming of the salvation that is ready to be revealed in the last time. In all this you greatly rejoice, though now for a little while you may have to suffer grief in all kinds of trials. These have come so that the proven genuineness of your faith---of greater worth that gold, which perishes even though refined by fire---may result in praise, glory, and honor when Jesus Christ is revealed. Though you have not seen Him, you love Him; and even though you do not see Him now, you believe in Him and are filled with an inexpressible and glorious joy, for you are receiving the end result of your faith, the salvation of your souls." I Peter 1:3-9 NIV

THIS PASSAGE IN I Peter follows neatly our passage yesterday about being authentic in our faith. This is the why behind the need to examine our lives to make sure that we really believe what we say we believe. If we have been born again into a living hope through the resurrection of Jesus Christ, then we have an inheritance that is waiting for us in Heaven. It cannot be taken away. It is sealed and secure. We are shielded by God's power. We may face trials and heartache. We may experience great difficulties in this life, but He gives us the strength and power to endure whatever we face. The difficulties refine and prove our faith. I have said many times that we do not grow in times of ease. The only way to develop faith is to be put in situations where we must exercise it. When we experience God's peace in the midst of pain, we learn to rely on it. We do not grasp the fullness of His grace and mercy until we recognize our own depravity and our need for it. The joy of His presence is not fully known until we experience it in the depths of despair. We cannot know that He is all we need unless we are put in situations where He is all we have.

Those who do not know Jesus, cannot possibly understand how we can love someone we cannot see. It does not make sense that we can believe in and place our faith in someone who we cannot touch and see. How can He give us joy and peace and strength? It logically does not make sense and yet, those of us who know Jesus understand because we feel His presence in our lives. We know His protection and His love. We know His voice and can hear Him leading and guiding us. The more we get to know Him, the more we experience His presence in ways that are just as real as they would be if He was physically in our presence. He is not only with us, but also living inside us. He is the reason we can carry on each day regardless of our circumstances. We know that the end result of our faith is the salvation of our souls that will be fully realized when Jesus returns to take us home. At that time, we will receive our inheritance that is being kept for us, eternal life in the presence of Jesus. We are filled with inexpressible and glorious joy because we have a living hope in Jesus.

November 19

Ezekiel 45-46
Psalm 125
Proverbs 27:23-24
I Peter 1:13-25

Holy

"But just as He who called you is holy, so be holy in all you do; for it is written: 'Be holy, because I am holy.'" I Peter 1:15-16 NIV

HOLINESS IS SOMETIMES confused with piety and arrogance. Christians are often accused of being "holier than thou" and "thinking we are better than everyone else." That should not be the case. As Christians we recognize our need for God's grace and mercy and in humility, we choose to obey Him. We are instructed to be holy, not because we are better than others or think that we are above them, but because we desire to please Him with our lives. We are indebted to Him and recognize that "our lives are not our own, but we have been bought with a price and we should honor Him with our bodies." I Corinthians 6:19-20 (ESV) We cannot have an attitude of arrogance because we know that any good we do is because He is living in us giving us the strength and ability to accomplish His purposes. Gratitude and humility result in obedience to His commands and a desire to glorify Him in all that we do.

What does holiness look like in our lives? I think we have to go back to the definition to figure that out. Holiness is apartness, sacredness, and separateness. When the Bible refers to God's holiness it means that He is separate from us. He is sacred and set apart completely. He is distinct and different from anything or anyone else. He is above all and beyond all. Obviously, we are not capable of that. God is God and we are not. But we are to be set apart. We are to be distinct. We are to be different from the world around us. We are not supposed to blend in. We are supposed to be in the world, but not of it. When people look at us, talk to us, and get to know us, it should be apparent that there is something different about us. Jesus, who is holy, is living inside of us. He makes a difference in our lives. We cannot continue to do the things that we did before He came into our lives. He changes us and sanctifies us. He makes us holy. Holiness is not the same as perfection. God is perfect in all ways. We are not perfect and this side of Heaven we will not be. But we are to be separate and set apart. We have a sacred purpose. We cannot accomplish the things He has planned for us if we are not living our lives in ways that are pleasing to Him. Holiness is a process that begins when we invite Jesus to be the Lord of our lives and continues until we see Him face to face. It is a conscious choice we make daily to obey Him and follow Him instead of giving in to our fleshly desires. May we each strive to be set apart and live lives that reflect the holiness of Christ in a way that others recognize as coming from a grateful and humble heart.

November 20

Ezekiel 47-48
Psalm 126
Proverbs 27:25-27
I Peter 2:1-10

Chosen

"But you are a chosen people, a royal priesthood, a holy nation, God's special possession, that you may declare praises of Him who called you out of darkness into His wonderful light. Once you were not a people, but now you are the people of God; once you had not received mercy, but now you have received mercy." I Peter 2:9-10 NIV

BRIAN WAS ADOPTED as a baby. He has told me that when he was growing up, he told his sister, who was not adopted, on more than one occasion that he was chosen. They didn't have a choice but to keep her, but they chose him. I'm sure this got the reaction he wanted from her which was less than admirable, but it is evidence of a sense of security and belonging that his parents were able to give him. He could not be more a part of their family if he had been born into it. His cousins, sister, and aunt have on several occasions through the years made comments about how our children resemble one of them or about whether Brian will develop some health issue that they have. We laugh and they catch themselves realizing there is no genetic link, but it is amazing to me that they forget he is not biologically related. We can have that same sense of security because we were chosen by God to be His children. At some point in our lives, He chose us, pursued us, and did whatever it took to make us realize we needed Him. The Holy Spirit convicted us and when we accepted Him, He adopted us as His children. We are His special possession. A special possession is protected and taken care of. It is handled with care and given attention. It wasn't an accident that we came to know Him. Out of the seven billion people on Earth, He chose you and He chose me to be His child. Let that sink in.

When we were adopted, we became a part of His family. I am an only child. I don't know what it's like to have brothers and sisters that I grew up with, but I have been abundantly blessed with so many brothers and sisters in the family of God. Together we are His people, a holy nation set apart to glorify Him. We are not alone. We are meant to function as a body of believers, as a family that loves each other and supports each other. We need each other. We need connection and community. We are a royal priesthood. In biblical times, the tribe of Levi was set apart to perform the functions of the priests. They were the only ones who could offer sacrifices on behalf of the people. They presented requests to God. They were the intermediaries. When Jesus offered Himself as the sacrifice for sins once for all, He did away with the need for someone to serve as a mediator. As children of God, we can each go to God on our own. We have access to the throne room of Heaven. We don't have to go through a priest to get pardon for sins or to seek His help. He chose us and He cherishes us. We are accepted. We belong. We can rest securely in His promises as His children.

November 21

Daniel 1-2
Psalm 127
Proverbs 28:1-2
I Peter 2:11-25

Set Apart

"But Daniel resolved not to defile himself with the royal food and wine, and he asked the chief official for permission not to defile himself this way. Please test your servants for ten days: Give us nothing but vegetables to eat and water to drink. Then compare our appearance with that of the young men who eat the royal food and treat your servants in accordance with what you see. So, he agreed to this and tested them for ten days. At the end of the ten days, they looked healthier and better nourished than any of the young men who ate the royal food." Daniel 1:8, 12-15 NIV

Daniel and his friends were teenage boys living in Jerusalem when it was besieged. The brightest and best young men were taken into captivity to Babylon where they were trained and placed into the king's service. They were just kids taken away from their families and their home. They must have been scared and confused. Most of the young men went along with what they were told. We aren't told anything about Daniel and his friends before their captivity, but their actions tell us a lot. They must have been from families of devout followers of God. They had been taught God's laws and were determined not to compromise. We aren't told why Daniel believed the royal food was defiled. God gave the Jews very specific regulations about food. Sanitation and food borne illness were major concerns, but by following God's instructions the Jewish people were able to avoid many of these issues. They were allowed to eat some meat, but not other meat. We aren't told what meat they were served, but it could have been pork or horse which would have been unacceptable. They were also not allowed to eat any meat with blood in it, so it is possible that the blood was not properly drained, or it may have been prepared in a way that was against God's instructions. Whatever the reason, Daniel believed that eating the royal food and drinking the wine would be disobedient to God. It took a tremendous amount of courage to ask the royal guard to allow them not to eat the food given them. And it took even more faith to trust that God would bless their faithfulness. After testing them for 10 days, they were healthier and better nourished than any of the young men who ate the royal food. They had complete confidence in God's laws, and they believed that obeying God would give them success and they were right.

In a foreign land against their will, these four young men set themselves apart. They remained holy when everyone else went along with the crowd. They weren't afraid to stand out and be different. He gave them knowledge and understanding and helped them to excel in all they did. And He gave Daniel the ability to understand visions and dreams. When they came before the king, he found none equal to them. They were faithful in the little things, and we will see in our reading in the days to come that God gave them more responsibility and opportunities to demonstrate their faith and tell others about their God. Obedience and faith please God and result in His blessing and favor on our lives.

Daniel 3-4
Psalm 128
Proverbs 28:3-5
I Peter 3:1-12

November 22

Even If

"Shadrach, Meshach and Abednego replied to him, 'King Nebuchadnezzar, we do not need to defend ourselves before you in this matter. If we are thrown into the blazing furnace, the God we serve is able to deliver us from it, and He will deliver us from Your Majesty's hand. But even if He does not, we want you to know, Your Majesty, that we will not serve your gods or worship the image of gold you have set up." Daniel 3:16-18 NIV

WE ALL LOVE to see the good guys win and get the happy ending. This makes us feel good and gives us encouragement and hope when we are in difficult circumstances. Verses 24 and 25 tell us that the king had three men bound and thrown into the fiery furnace, but when he looked in, he could see four men untied walking around in the fire. I have the image of four men running around dancing, laughing, and smiling. I don't think they were running frantically trying to escape the fire. I think when they saw Jesus in the fire with them, they knew they were safe, and they were rejoicing that they were being rescued. Jesus didn't just protect them from the fire, He was walking through it with them. This is a beautiful picture of what happens in our lives. Jesus does not just send help to us; He is right there going through it with us every step of the way. In verse 27 we see that "the fire had no effect on the bodies of these men, nor was the hair of their heads singed, nor were their trousers damaged, nor had even the smell of fire touched them." This is amazing! The fire was so hot that even the men who threw them into the fire were killed by its heat and yet they didn't even have the smell of smoke on them. I love to sit by a fire on a cool fall evening roasting marshmallows and talking with friends, but I hate the smell of the smoke on my clothes and body after. No matter how far away from the fire you sit, you still end up smelling like smoke until you take a shower. But Shadrach, Meshach and Abednego didn't even need a shower after they got out of the fire. They weren't sweaty, their clothes weren't damaged, and they didn't smell like smoke. A whole book could be written on all the lessons we can learn from this passage, but let's focus on a couple.

Only God can take us through a fire and have us come out on the other side better than we were before. Whenever we go through a season of difficulty, we usually come out of it smelling like smoke. We often are wounded, and we have scars. It is inevitable that suffering and heartache can leave us battered and bruised emotionally and sometimes physically. It is not common to come out of difficulty with no evidence that the difficulty took place. And that's ok because the difficulties shape us and mold us and make us better. My scars are evidence of my growth. I would not trade my scars in if it meant that I had to go back to the person I was before I got them. The lessons I have learned have made me who I am. I don't want to experience the pain again, but I can rejoice that Jesus was with me walking through the fire every time and helping me out of the furnace when it was time to move on. If people can smell the smoke on me, it might give me an opportunity to tell them about Jesus and how He is always with me, even running around in the fire.

The other lesson that I think is crucial that often gets overlooked in this happy ending is what these three men told King Nebuchadnezzar before he threw them in the fire. They were completely confident that God was able to save them from the fiery furnace and from anything the king could do to them. As it turns out, they were right. God could and did save them. But they told the king that **even if** God did not save them, they would not bow down to him or anyone or anything other than the One True God. **Even if.** This historical account, (calling it a story makes it easier to think of it like a fairy tale and not an actual historical event), had a happy ending. They were rescued, but there are many accounts in the Bible of men and women who were not saved. We personally know lots of people who did not get the happy ending. The good guy does not always win. God does not always give us the miracle we want. Sometimes children die of cancer, women get molested, our loved one dies, we lose our job, and what we fear happens. Shadrach, Meshach, and Abednego knew that there was a good chance they were going to die that day. They knew that refusing to bow down to the king would most likely result in a horrible, painful death and yet they also knew that there is a fate worse than death. They believed that their God was the only God and that one day they would face Him and give account for the life they lived. King Nebuchadnezzar could kill their physical body, but he had no power over their soul. God had the power over their eternal fate. An eternal perspective helped them face earthly difficulties. That is key for us as well. Keeping our eyes on eternity puts things into proper perspective while we are here. Any pain and suffering we experience here is nothing compared to the joy we will experience in eternity with Him if we remain faithful. Life is hard sometimes but knowing that we are not alone in the fire and that God is using the fire to mature our faith helps us persevere.

Daniel 5-6
Psalm 129
Proverbs 28:6-7
I Peter 3:13-22

November 23

He Continued

> "When Daniel learned that the document had been signed, he went into his house. The windows in its upper room opened toward Jerusalem, and three times a day he got down on his knees, prayed, and gave thanks to his God, just as he had done before." Daniel 6:10 HCSB

Following the account of Shadrach, Meshach, and Abednego, today we read about Daniel in the Lion's Den. This was many years later, and a different king had come to power, but we find Daniel in the same situation that his friends were in earlier. He was being forced to choose between God and his life. Those around Daniel were watching him and they knew he was a man of integrity. They decided that the only way they could bring him down was to attack him on his faith, so they set a trap. And Daniel did exactly what they expected him to do. He continued doing what he had been doing. He continued praying and praising God three times a day. He knew that they would be watching him, but he didn't shut his window so he could hide what he was doing. He continued in his daily ritual. It is important to note that he **continued** praying. He didn't just get into this crisis and realize that he needed to pray. This was something he did every day. Three times a day he was in the regular habit of going to his upper room and praying and praising God. He had an intimate, personal relationship with God. He did not just pray when he needed something or when he had a problem. I don't think Daniel had any difficulty deciding whether he was going to obey the king's edict. It wasn't a tough choice for him. Like his friends, Daniel believed that his God was the Only True God, and he was the only source of hope. Even if God did not rescue him from the lion's den, Daniel would not worship anyone but God. We can learn a lot from Daniel. If we are spending time in prayer and Bible study daily with God, He gives us the strength and power we need to face any difficulty that comes along. We cannot wait until we get into a crisis to pray. Daily time with Him prepares us for the battle. An athlete or a soldier doesn't wait till the day of the competition or the battle to begin preparing. They prepare for years so that when the battle comes, they are ready to step in and be victorious. If you wait till you see the enemy approaching to get on your knees, you will not be able to stand under the pressure.

We don't know anything about religious persecution in America, but I am afraid the day is approaching when we will be forced to take a stand. We cannot wait till then to get prepared. Daniel did not fight the men. He didn't become indignant or belligerent. He just kept doing the things he had been doing and trusted God to take care of him. We need to prepare to stand firm by developing all the habits now that we will need to be victorious when the battle comes. I think when Daniel was facing the lion's den, he remembered how his friends had been delivered from the fiery furnace. Remembering God's faithfulness to us and to others in the past encourages us and gives us strength to face our difficulties today. We need to boldly tell others about our God and what He has done for us so that we can spur each other on to faithfulness.

November 24

Daniel 7-8
Psalm 130
Proverbs 28:8-9
I Peter 4

Serious

"Now the end of all things is near; therefore, be serious and disciplined for prayer. Above all, maintain an intense love for each other, since love covers a multitude of sins. Be hospitable to one another without complaining. Based on the gift each one has received, use it to serve others, as good managers of the varied grace of God. If anyone speaks, it should be as one who speaks God's words; if anyone serves, it should be from the strength God provides, so that God may be glorified in everything. To Him belong the glory and the power forever and ever. Amen." I Peter 4:7-11 HCSB

I think we would all agree that these are serious times. The times we live in are not carefree and easy-going. We are all looking over our shoulder for the next shoe to drop. There is just a collective sense of dread and anxiety about the future. And it is with good reason. The economy is bad and there is no indication that is going to get better any time soon. We don't know when the next variant of Covid may hit that proves to be deadly to us or a loved one. International tensions are high with conflict breaking out in regions all over the world. Divisions are deepening over racial issues, vaccination status, and political differences. Everyone is walking on eggshells afraid they will say or do the wrong thing. In this passage, Peter tells us what we, as believers, need to be doing in these troubling times. First, we need to be disciplined in prayer. Yesterday we read about Daniel's commitment to prayer that prepared him for the battles he faced each day. God will give us the strength and wisdom to navigate our days if we spend time soaking in His Word and fellowshipping with Him. But we can't just lock ourselves in our houses and pray all the time. We don't need to isolate ourselves and become hermits. After we have prepared ourselves through prayer, then we need to be about the business of living.

Peter instructs us to maintain an intense love for each other. An intense love is not possible from afar. Intense love is personal and up close. We need to be there for each other. We are the hands and feet of Jesus to a lost and dying world. They will know we are Christians by our love, not by shaking our finger at them in condemnation or shouting our opinions on social media. Being hospitable means that we welcome our neighbors into our homes, and we share life with them. And we serve others. In whatever way God has gifted us, we need to be using that gift to benefit and serve others. Now is the time to be serious in our faith. It is not the time to be concerned with our own interests and well-being. God will take care of us. We need to be about God's business because the end of all things is near. When we look back on our lives, we will never regret the time we spent serving and loving others, but we may regret all the time we spent selfishly thinking about our own needs and chasing after things that have no lasting value. And in serving others, we need to make sure that we are giving all the glory and honor to Jesus who gives us the ability and strength to serve. When people look at our lives and examine our actions, they should not think how great we are. Our actions and words should be an arrow pointing at how great and awesome our Savior is.

November 25

Daniel 9-10
Psalms 131
Proverbs 28:10-11
I Peter 5

Firm

"Humble yourselves, therefore, under God's mighty hand, that He may lift you up in due time. Cast all your anxiety on Him because He cares for you. Be alert and of sober mind. Your enemy the devil prowls around like a roaring lion looking for someone to devour. Resist him, standing firm in the faith, because you know that the family of believers throughout the world is undergoing the same kind of sufferings. And the God of all grace, who called you to His eternal glory in Christ, after you have suffered a little while, will Himself restore you and make you strong, firm, and steadfast. To Him be the power forever and ever. Amen." I Peter 5:6-11 NIV

THIS PASSAGE HAS gotten me through many difficult days. I have it in my scripture ring so I can read it whenever I need encouragement to keep going. It reminds me who my enemy is. My enemy is the devil. My difficult boss, rude neighbor, inconsiderate family member, or selfish coworker is not my enemy. It may feel like they are my enemy sometimes, but I have to remind myself that they are just like me trying to do the best they can to get by. Sometimes I am rude and inconsiderate and selfish, too. Sometimes I let the devil win and I give in to my own sinful desires and I don't think about how it will affect others. I don't know what they have dealt with in their lives today or how the devil has been prowling around trying to devour them. Remembering who my enemy is gives me a better perspective. Instead of reacting in anger or hurt, I can examine the situation and respond in love and patience. The devil wants us to react. That is his goal. He wants to cause hurt and division and pain. He thrives on that. If we allow the Holy Spirit to help us use self-control, we can extinguish the fire instead of fanning the flames. We must be alert and attentive if we want to recognize his tricks and resist him.

One of his most powerful tricks is to convince us that we are all alone and no one else has ever faced the suffering that we are facing. He wants us to feel weak and inadequate. That is why it is so important that we are a part of a body of believers. We are stronger together. We are a family, and we must stick together to resist him. The devil has been around a long time. He is smarter than we are. He knows our weaknesses better than we know ourselves. He will lie, cheat, or do anything else it takes to defeat me, but he has no power over the One who lives in my heart. The Holy Spirit can resist any arrow he throws at me. Thankfully, I am not a soldier fighting on my own. I am part of an army of believers. Throughout the world, from every tribe and nation, every race and ethnic group followers of Christ stand arm in arm, linked together by the power of the Holy Spirit. We have a bond with people we have never met and will never know this side of Heaven. We can encourage and support each other through difficult times with a power that we cannot fully understand or explain. Our prayers and words of encouragement can be the thing that keeps them going one more day. And Peter assures us that after we have suffered a little while, Christ Himself will restore us and make us strong, firm, and steadfast. Our suffering will not go on forever. We can make it to the other side.

November 26

Daniel 11-12
Psalm 132:1-10
Proverbs 28:12
2 Peter 1

Everything

"His divine power has given us everything we need for a godly life through our knowledge of Him who called us by His glory and goodness. Through these He has given us His very great and precious promises, so that through them you may participate in the divine nature, having escaped the corruption in the world caused by evil desires." 2 Peter 1:3-4 NIV

Everything we need. Everything. In the Greek that word means everything. Not some things. Not most things. We have everything we need to live a godly life. We are not lacking or deficient. We are equipped. We can do it! This is not some pep talk Peter is giving us to tell us that we can do whatever we set our minds to, and we can accomplish anything we want. Be all you can be! Go for it! He isn't a coach trying to hype us up for the big game. This is much more important than that. Peter is trying to get across the point that we can get through this life, with all its difficulties and temptations, because we are equipped. Jesus Himself has bestowed on us everything we need to live a godly life. We are not too weak to say no to those sinful desires. We are not destined to follow our same old patterns and bad habits. Things don't have to be the same as they have always been. We can be different. We are different. This doesn't happen because we try harder or because of our own power and ability. Goodness, if that was the case, we would be destined to repeat the same patterns of sinfulness for the rest of our lives. We can't make ourselves be good and godly. He knows that. So, He had a better plan. He would come and live in us to help us, strengthen us, empower us, and equip us.

We are without excuse. We don't get to keep rationalizing our sin and blaming it on our past or someone else or "I just can't help it." Those are lies from Satan. We have access to the power of God in our lives. We need to start using it. We have escaped the corruption of the world caused by evil desires so why are we still letting them rule over us? The only power they have in our lives is the power we allow them to have. Satan wants us to believe that we can't resist temptation. He wants us to think that we are weak. He wants us to think that it is arrogant to believe we can live godly lives. Are we going to listen to him? He wants us to fail. His greatest desire is for us to give in and experience public humiliation. Are we going to believe the father of lies who is cheering against us or are we going to start believing our Heavenly Father who loves us and is always seeking what is best for us? Which voice are you listening to? Are you going to keep believing that you can't overcome that weakness, that you can't change, or will you choose to believe that you have everything you need to live a godly life and start pursuing that?

November 27

Hosea 1-3
Psalm 132:11-18
Proverbs 28:13
2 Peter 2

Judgment

"For if God did not spare angels when they sinned, but sent them to Hell, putting them in chains in darkness to be held for judgment; if He did not spare the ancient world when He brought the flood on its ungodly people, but protected Noah, a preacher of righteousness, and seven others; if He condemned the cities of Sodom and Gomorrah by burning them to ashes, and made them an example of what is going to happen to the ungodly; and if He rescued Lot, a righteous man, who was distressed by the depraved conduct of the lawless (for that righteous man, living among them day after day, was tormented in his righteous soul by the lawless deeds he saw and heard)—if this is so, then the Lord knows how to rescue the godly from trials and to hold the unrighteous for punishment on the day of judgment." 2 Peter 2:4-9 NIV

THIS PASSAGE IS an excellent argument against the popular idea that God loves everyone so much that He would not send anyone to Hell. There is a growing movement among churches that Hell is figurative and not a real place. They contend that God, in His mercy and grace will in the end save everyone and we will all eventually go to Heaven. This is heresy. If there is no Hell and no judgment, then there was no need for Jesus to come to Earth and die a horrible death on the cross and raise Himself from the dead. God is omniscient so He knows everything that will happen. If He knew that He was going to just let everyone go to Heaven, there would have been no need for Jesus to come at all. That teaching denies the gospel and it is a lie. Other teaching suggests that the God of the Old Testament is somehow different from the God of the New Testament and the wrath and punishment that we find in the Old Testament no longer exists. This teaching implies that God has changed His mind and He does not have the same divine revulsion to sin that He had in the Old Testament and that Jesus' sacrifice did away with all punishment for sin. Both teachings are unbiblical. Jesus' death, burial and resurrection did not take away the punishment for sin. In His grace and mercy, He took our punishment on Himself and provided a way for us to receive forgiveness for our sin. God's holiness will not allow Him to overlook sin. He hasn't gotten used to it so that He is willing to look the other way. In this passage in the New Testament, we are told that just as God judged the angels when they sinned and sent them to Hell, as He sent the flood to destroy everyone on the Earth in Noah's day, and as He destroyed Sodom and Gomorrah, a day of judgment is coming when everyone will answer for their actions.

For those like Noah and Lot, who have placed their faith and trust in God and who have remained faithful, they will be rescued from destruction, but those who have not trusted in God will face punishment. One day we are going to stand before the Judgment Seat of God. On that day, we will either see our loving Savior and be welcomed into Heaven, or we will face the wrath of God that will send us to an eternity in Hell. Any teaching suggesting otherwise is not just inaccurate, it is dangerous. We are told that in the last days, there will be false teachers who will tell people what they want to hear. We must be discerning and diligently study His Word so that we will recognize the lies when we hear them and are ready to give an answer to the deception.

November 28

Hosea 4-5
Psalm 133
Proverbs 28:14-15
2 Peter 3

Scoffers

"Above all, you must understand that in the last days scoffers will come, scoffing and following their own evil desires. They will say, 'Where is this coming He promised?' 'Ever since our ancestors died, everything goes on as it has since the beginning of creation.' But do not forget this one thing, dear friends: With the Lord a day is like a thousand years and a thousand years are like a day. The Lord is not slow in keeping His promise, as some understand slowness. Instead, He is patient with you, not wanting anyone to perish, but everyone to come to repentance. But the day of the Lord will come like a thief." 2 Peter 3:3-4, 8-10 NIV

Does that sound familiar? I can't tell you how many times I have heard those words. Actually, I think I hear that argument from Christians more than I hear it from unbelievers. Any time you mention the rapture or the last days, people roll their eyes and close their ears. Unfortunately, there have been so many people over the years who have tried to figure out when the rapture will occur and have gotten it wrong that most people have gotten tired of hearing about it and have just stopped watching. We are told to watch and be prepared. Throughout the New Testament, we are admonished to be ready and to be aware of the signs of the times so that we can see the day approaching. We aren't told exactly when it will happen, but we have been given a lot of information about what the world will look like at the time. You only have to turn on the news for a few minutes to see that everything is falling into place. All the pieces of the puzzle are on the table. They just need to be put into their proper place to set things in motion. I have no idea how long that will take, but I am convinced it won't be very much longer.

The alliances between countries prophesied in Ezekiel and Isaiah are forming. Countries that have been at war throughout history are coming together against Israel. All the players mentioned in these prophecies are on the stage ready for action. The prophecies we find in Revelation have always seemed more like something we would find in a fantasy or sci-fi novel than something we would ever really witness. Technological advancements have now made the mark of the beast very possible. Cryptocurrency has made a One World banking system possible in the foreseeable future where people can be prevented from buying and trading if they do not conform to whatever the Antichrist tells them to do. There are wars and rumors of wars every day all over the world. Natural disasters are becoming more frequent. Satan has accelerated his efforts. He is no longer hiding in the shadows. Sin is not only accepted; it is celebrated. For over 2000 years, since Jesus ascended into Heaven, believers have been watching for His return. God is patient. He wants everyone to accept Him.

He is waiting till the last possible moment so that He can give everyone a chance to repent and turn to Him. But there is a day that was set before creation when all the events prophesied in the Bible will happen exactly as they have been foretold. The day is approaching. We do not want to be caught off guard. Until that day, we keep doing what we know to do. We keep serving and working and telling people about Jesus so that we will be found faithful when He comes.

Hosea 6-7
Psalm 134
Proverbs 28:16-17
I John 1

November 29

Confession and Forgiveness

"If we claim to be without sin, we deceive ourselves and the truth is not in us. If we confess our sins, He is faithful and just and will forgive our sins and purify us from all unrighteousness. If we claim we have not sinned, we make Him out to be a liar and His Word is not in us." I John 1: 8-10 NIV

WE KNOW THAT sin separates us from God. We have all sinned and fall short of the glory of God and the wages of sin is death and Hell. If we do not confess our sins and recognize our need for His forgiveness, we are destined to eternal separation from God. If we refuse to acknowledge that we are sinful and in need of His grace and mercy, we are deceiving ourselves. This principle applies to our lives regarding salvation, but it also applies after we are saved. Our eternal destiny is secure, so we are not separated from God in an ultimate sense, but unrepentance and sin cause distance and separation from God in our daily lives. Sin produces fear, turmoil, anxiety, and dread. It wreaks havoc in our lives and the lives of those around us. All sin produces this result, not just "big sins." We have seen the chaos caused by adultery and other sexual sin. We know the destructive power of substance abuse, pornography, gambling, and theft, but all sin damages relationships. Lying produces distrust and distance. Gossip separates friends. Greed and jealousy result in division and unhealthy competition. All of these and a long list of others can result in anger, hurt feelings and broken relationships,

Unfortunately, there is an even more significant consequence of unrepentance and a failure to recognize and acknowledge our sin. Sin creates a barrier in our relationship with God. As believers, when we sin the Holy Spirit convicts us. He points out our sin to us and makes us feel the shame and guilt of whatever we have done that is not pleasing to God. If we confess our sin to Him, He is faithful and just and will forgive our sins and purify us from all unrighteousness. There is no better feeling than the peace we have when we come clean and are forgiven. The relationship is restored, and we can move forward. If, on the other hand, we ignore the conviction and refuse to repent, we start to build a wall. The more we ignore Him, the easier it gets and before we realize it, we have a pretty high wall built up between us and God. We begin to avoid time with Him because we don't want to deal with it. We spend less time in His Word and in prayer. It gets easier and easier to do the things we know we shouldn't be doing, and we do things that we never thought we would do. The distance we feel from God is not because He has left us; it is because we have wandered from His presence. Confession is good for the soul. He is waiting with open arms to welcome us back. No matter what we have done or how far we have wandered, we can always come back to Him. Ask Him to reveal anything in your life that you need to confess and repent and then turn to Him for forgiveness and restoration.

November 30

Hosea 8-9
Psalm 135:1-7
Proverbs 28:18-19
I John 2

Love for the World

> "Do not love the world or anything in the world. If anyone loves the world, love for the Father is not in them. For everything in the world—the lust of the flesh, the lust of the eyes, and the pride of life—comes not from the Father but from the world. The world and its desires pass away, but whoever does the will of God lives forever."
> I John 2:15-17 NIV

DO NOT LOVE the world or anything in the world. Peter is not saying that we cannot have any pleasure in this life or that we cannot enjoy anything that is not spiritual or religious. He is not saying that physical possessions and wealth are bad. The world is filled with beautiful things that God created and beautiful things that He gave man the ability to create. Those things are not bad. The problem is that we tend to get our priorities mixed up. Our passions and desires overtake us, and we begin to focus our attention on pursuing those things instead of keeping our eyes focused on Jesus.

The lust of the flesh is our basic physical desires. This can include sexual gratification but is not limited to that. Physical pleasure can come from food, drink, drugs, exercise, athletic competition, etc. These things meet basic needs that are good when handled appropriately, but when they become our focus, they can become a lust of the flesh. The lust of the eye is the desire to acquire anything and everything our eye sees. The latest fashion styles, jewels, a bigger house in the right neighborhood, a better car, or a vacation that is better than the one my friend on Facebook took all appeal to our greed and jealousy and a desire for more of the things this world has to offer. These things are not necessarily bad things, but when they become the object of our desire, there is a problem. The pride of life is the ambition and desire to achieve great things so that people will think highly of us. The desire to be respected and thought well of is admirable, but the lust for power and position leads to pride and arrogance. These are the three things that Satan offered Jesus in the wilderness. He offered Him food to satisfy His physical cravings. He offered Him all that His eye could see, and He offered Him power and status. Jesus knew that anything this world has to offer is temporary and will pass away. Physical pleasure lasts for a little while, but ultimately just leaves you craving for more. Earthly possessions rust and lose their value. The more we get, the more we want. And power and prestige can be taken away in an instant. Nothing Satan offers has any lasting value. When we keep our eyes focused on Jesus, we can enjoy the things this life has to offer without becoming consumed with them. Balance and self-control are the keys to avoiding a love for the world that leads to destruction.

December 1

Hosea 10-11
Psalm 135:8-14
Proverbs 28:20-21
I John 3

Love in Action

"This is how we know what love is: Jesus Christ laid down His life for us. And we ought to lay down our lives for our brothers and sisters. If anyone has material possessions and sees a brother or sister in need but has no pity on them, how can the love of God be in that person? Dear children, let us not love with words or speech but with actions and in truth." I John 3:16-18 NIV

There are a lot of romanticized notions of what love is that we see in Hallmark movies and popular novels. The giddy feeling when you see your soul mate across a crowded room, the exhilaration of the first kiss that sweeps you off your feet, and then just when you think things aren't going to work out, a miracle happens, and you get together to live happily ever after. Those things make for great television and a good book you don't want to put down, but they have distorted the true meaning of love. Love is not a feeling. The idea that love is some overwhelming emotion that conquers all has led to much disillusionment, heartache, and broken relationships. This is true of romantic relationships, but it is also true of relationships with friends and family. If you believe that love is a feeling, when things get tough and you don't feel happy, you move on to another relationship that gives you that good feeling again. Then when that relationship faces difficulty, you move on again. The reality is that life is tough, and every relationship is going to face difficulty. If your "love" is based on feeling good and being happy, you will go from relationship to relationship, never experiencing the intimacy of true love.

Satan is a master at counterfeit. He excels at providing substitutes that he presents as the real thing. He has done a masterful job of convincing us that love is a perfect relationship where all your needs are met, and you feel happy all the time. Not only is that not realistic, but it is a lie. We have discussed the fact that you must be put in situations where you need patience to develop patience. You must be in situations where you must demonstrate faith to develop faith. I think the same is true of love. If everything is sunshine and roses all the time, I don't think you can develop love. Love is not really love unless it is tested and proven. Love is action. Love is commitment. Love is perseverance. Love is being there through thick and thin, good times and bad. Love is hard. It's not fun. Love is laying aside your own interests and desires to meet the needs of others. Saying "I love you" to someone is nice but showing your love for them is powerful. We all want to be loved like that. We want people in our lives to love us sacrificially no matter what happens. But the question we need to ask ourselves is, "Do I love like that?" Am I loving the people in my life that way? Am I allowing Jesus to demonstrate His love through me? Am I putting aside my own interests and desires so that I can meet the needs of others? Do I love others unconditionally and sacrificially?

December 2

Hosea 12-14
Psalm 135:15-21
Proverbs 28:22-23
I John 4

Because He First Loved Us

"We love because He first loved us. Whoever claims to love God yet hates a brother or sister is a liar. For whoever does not love their brother and sister, whom they have seen, cannot love God whom they have not seen. And He has given us this command: Anyone who loves God must also love their brother and sister." I John 4:19-21 NIV

TODAY'S READING GIVES us the "how" to the reading from yesterday. How do we love others unconditionally and sacrificially? How do we love in action and in truth? When it comes down to it, I am a selfish person. If I examine my motives and my actions, most of the time I don't like what I see. If I am brutally honest with myself, I have to acknowledge that I fall very short of loving like Jesus loved. On my own, I act and think in ways that benefit me. Most of my time and energy is spent on things that make me happy or that will prosper me in some way. The idea of "not looking to your own interests but each of you to the interests of others" Philippians 2:4 (NIV) sounds very holy, but it is very hard. It does not come naturally. We each have an innate drive to look out for ourselves, to protect ourselves. And yet we are told to love like Jesus loved, to seek the benefit of others above seeking what is best for us. I think this verse helps us figure out where to start.

If I love people the way they deserve to be loved, I can usually justify not loving them well. And if people love me the way I deserve to be loved, I must admit that most of the time I would deserve what I get. But that is not what God wants from us. You can't find anywhere in the Bible where we are told that we should love people who love us and treat us well, but we don't have to love people who treat us badly. In fact, we are told to love our enemies and pray for those who persecute us. If our yardstick for how much we love others is based on how they measure up and deserve our love, everyone will fall short. And we will fall short when others are measuring us. So that can't be our standard. We love because we have been loved. The love we demonstrate to others is an overflow of the love that Jesus has shown to us. God loves us perfectly and completely. When we were still sinners, He died for us. (Romans 5:8, John 15:13) His love is unconditional, and nothing can separate us from His love. (Romans 8:38-39, Isaiah 54:10) The only way that we can love others and look to their interests above our own is to recognize that we do not deserve to be loved and yet we are loved fully and completely by our Heavenly Father. John is explaining that gratitude to God overflows in love to others. If we do not have love for others, then we really don't fully appreciate what God did for us. The measure of our love for Him is exhibited by how we love others. Ouch! I'm just going to leave that one there for each of us to examine our own hearts.

December 3

Joel 1:1-2:11
Psalm 136:1-12
Proverbs 28:24-26
I John 5

His Love Endures Forever

"Give thanks to the Lord, for He is good. His love endures forever. Give thanks to the God of gods. His love endures forever. Give thanks to the Lord of lords; His love endures forever. To Him who alone does great wonders, His love endures forever. Who by His understanding made the heavens, His love endures forever. Who spread out the Earth upon the waters, His love endures forever? Who made the great lights—His love endures forever. The sun to govern the day, His love endures forever. The moon and stars to govern the night; His love endures forever." Psalm 136:1-9 NIV

THIS PSALM IS a liturgical hymn. Its words were used in public worship by the Jewish people. The priest or Jewish leaders would say the first part and the people would follow each phrase with "His loves endures forever." In some translations, it reads, "His mercy endures forever." The Hebrew word translated here is "hesed" which we have discussed before. It is the unique and complete love God has for His people. A great multitude of the people of God would be gathered in the temple courts. The priest would exclaim a reason to give God praise and the people would respond loudly proclaiming God's faithfulness. It is known as the "Great Hallel" in Jewish tradition because it gives examples of God's goodness to His people and then encourages them to express a Hallelujah in response. When life seems overwhelming and the world is crushing in around us, the best thing we can do is turn to the One who made the world and everything in it. When our perception of God grows larger, the size of our problems grows smaller. Exodus 15:11, Isaiah 40:25 and Psalm 89:6 all ask the question "Who is like our God?"

One if the most famous prayers by St. Augustine describes our God perfectly. "What then are You, my God? What, I ask, except the Lord God? For who is the Lord besides God? Or who is God besides our God?—Most high, most good, most powerful, most omnipotent, most merciful and most just, most secret and most present; most beautiful and most strong; most stable and most incomprehensible; unchangeable (yet) changing all things; never new, never old; makings all things new, and bringing the proud to (the collapse of) old age; ever acting, ever at rest; gathering, and not needing; carrying and filling and protecting (all things); creating and nourishing and perfecting; seeking, though you lack nothing."[22] No problem we face, difficulty we encounter, or mountain that lies before us is even a challenge to God. My days are in the hands of the One who is in complete control. I can rest in His "hesed" and know that "He is working all things out for the good." His love endures forever. His love for me endures forever.

Joel 2:12-3:21
Psalm 136:13-26
Proverbs 28:27-28
2 John 1

December 4

Everyone

"And afterward, I will pour out My Spirit on all people. Your sons and daughters will prophesy, your old men will dream dreams, your young men will see visions. Even on My servants, both men and women, I will pour out My Spirit in those days. I will show wonders in the heavens and on the Earth, blood and fire and billows of smoke. The sun will be turned to darkness and the moon to blood before the coming of the great and dreadful day of the Lord. And everyone who calls on the Lord will be saved; for on Mount Zion and in Jerusalem there will be deliverance, as the Lord has said even among the survivors whom the Lord calls." Joel 2:28-32 NIV

THIS PASSAGE IN Joel is quoted by Peter at Pentecost and is used to explain the outpouring of the Holy Spirit. He connects the coming of Jesus to the prophecies that the people of his day would have been very familiar with. He wants them to understand that Jesus came to fulfill the Law not to do away with it. Paul quotes Joel in Romans 10:12-13, "For there is no difference between Jew and Gentile—the same Lord is Lord of all and richly blesses all who call on Him, for 'Everyone who calls on the name of the Lord will be saved.'" (NIV) Again, Paul is using passages that they were familiar with to point to the salvation that is found in Jesus and to help them understand that God offers salvation to anyone who will accept Him.

Throughout Joel, he uses the phrase "the day of the Lord" to refer to coming judgment. God revealed to him that there would be a day when judgment would come on the world. In the first chapter he points to a day of judgment for Israel and calls on them to repent and turn to God. He refers to Israel being scattered and a period of persecution and suffering for the Jews because of their wickedness. But then he goes on to speak of a time when the Jewish people will return to Him, and God will restore them and save them. In that day, the nations who support Israel will be blessed and those who turn against Israel will be cursed. Israel is God's chosen people. That has not changed. When the Jews rejected Jesus as their Messiah, God turned His attention to the Gentiles. For the last 2000 years, God's focus has been on the Gentile nations. There is coming a day when His attention will return to Israel, and they will accept Him as their Lord. He has not forgotten them. They have experienced His discipline, but they will be restored. The last verse of Joel tells us that God will avenge His people and that He dwells in Zion. As believers we must pray for Israel. As a nation, it is very important that we stand with Israel. If we turn our back on Israel, we are doomed. God will not bless a nation that does not support Israel. There are numerous verses that give this warning. (Genesis 12:2-3, Genesis 27:29, Psalm 122:6, Isaiah 60:12, Zechariah 1:1-14, 2:8, Isaiah 41:11-12) We need to pray for our leaders to understand the importance of supporting Israel, but it is also important for us to pray for the Jewish people individually. Pray that God opens their eyes to the truth that Jesus is their Messiah so that they will be saved before they have to go through the Tribulation. Many will turn to Him in those days, but many will die during the judgments before they understand and accept Him.

December 5

Amos 1-2
Psalm 137
Proverbs 29:1-3
3 John 1

Teachable and Humble

> "He who is often reproved, yet stiffens his neck, will suddenly be broken beyond healing." Proverbs 29:1 ESV

BY NOW YOU all know how much I love sports. Football, basketball, and soccer are my favorites, but you can probably talk me into watching any sporting event. I love the competition and the excitement of a good game. Unfortunately, when God handed out athletic ability, I think I forgot to get in line because I didn't get any. So, I watch from the bleachers. I have learned a lot over the years from watching games and listening to coaches and athletes talk about great players and teams. One quality stands out in determining the level of success they will achieve. When asked about the secret of his success in basketball, Michael Jordan gave this explanation, "My best skill was that I was coachable. I was a sponge and aggressive to learn."[23] Athletes and teams who reach the highest levels are ones who recognize that there is always room to improve. They are humble and don't think they have it all figured out. They want to learn and are disciplined and dedicated to doing whatever it takes to get better. Talent will take you a long way, but at the end of the day, the ones who reach the top are the ones who are never satisfied with yesterday's win. They are always pushing themselves to be better, try harder, go to the next level. When they reach a goal; they set another one.

This is not only true for athletes. This applies to every area of our lives. Being teachable and humble will help us succeed in anything we do. A willingness to accept and utilize advice will determine the path our lives take. "Stiffening our necks" and refusing to listen to advice will eventually lead to failure. Thomas Edison said, "I have not failed. I've just found 10,000 ways that won't work."[24] Henry Ford said, "Failure is only the opportunity to begin again, only this time more wisely."[25] Everyone who has achieved something great has experienced failure and used it as an opportunity to learn. "Pride goes before destruction, a haughty spirit before a fall." Proverbs 16:18 (NIV) A humble spirit gives God plenty of room to work in our lives. It can be argued that Michael Jordan was the GOAT, the Greatest basketball player Of All Time. And yet he recognized that he didn't know everything. He knew that there was always room for improvement. Most of us will never be able to say that we are the GOAT in anything. But even if we could say that we are the GOAT there is still room to grow. Instead of being easily offended and refusing to listen to advice, may we wisely soak in what we are told, prayerfully examine it, and wisely apply what is beneficial to our lives. Not all advice is useful, but we need to always be open and receptive to those God sends to teach us.

Amos 3-4
Psalm 138:1-3
Proverbs 29:4-6
Jude 1

December 6

Know Your Audience

"Be merciful to those who doubt; save others by snatching them from the fire; to others show mercy, mixed with fear—hating even the clothing stained by corrupted flesh." Jude 1:22-23 NIV

IN THIS PASSAGE, Jude is giving us instructions on how to deal with believers who have fallen away. He is explaining that there are different approaches we need to use with different people depending on the situation and the person. There is not a one-size-fits-all approach in dealing with these situations. In verses 20-21, he says that before we try to deal with anyone who has gone astray, we need to make sure that we are building ourselves up in our holy faith and that we are in prayer. We need to be grounded in our faith so we can stand firm. When we are confronted or made aware of a situation where a fellow believer has either fallen into sin or has been led away by false teaching, we need to spend serious time in prayer for them asking God to give us wisdom about how He wants us to proceed. Sometimes we just need to pray for them. But sometimes God will use us to confront the issue. If we believe He wants us to approach the person, we need to evaluate the situation and ask God to show us what they will be most receptive to. Some people need to be dealt with gently and lovingly. For those who have doubts about their faith, we need to come alongside them and gently reprove them showing them the error of their ways and helping them to turn back to God. They may have been led astray by false teaching that made them doubt things that they had learned. It is important to be patient and to stick with them while they figure it out.

Others, however, may need to be dealt with more harshly. Those who are engaging in unrepentant, willful sin, need to be rebuked. They need to understand the seriousness of their sin and the consequences of their actions. Those who are spreading the false teaching to others also need to be dealt with more aggressively. It may even be necessary to remove them from the fellowship of the church if they refuse to repent. Obviously, church leadership would need to be involved if that step is necessary. Those led astray by weakness and ignorance need to be dealt with differently than those who fall away because of pride and arrogance. A humble spirit is important in dealing with anyone. Love and respect are always received better than piety. It is also important, as Jude explains, to have a healthy fear when confronting anyone about sin. This fear comes from a recognition that we are not immune to temptation ourselves and that, but by the grace of God, we might be in their position of needing someone to confront us. This attitude ensures that we deal with them in the way that we would want to be dealt with ourselves. Confrontation is uncomfortable for most of us, and we would rather not get involved, but sometimes it is necessary. If we truly love people, we cannot allow them to continue in sin or be led astray by dangerous false teaching. We are called to encourage others in their faith. To do that, the bad stuff must be weeded out so that solid faith can grow.

December 7

Amos 5-6
Psalm 138:4-8
Proverbs 29:7-8
Revelation 1

Revelation

"The revelation from Jesus Christ, which God gave to show His servants what must soon take place. Blessed is the one who reads aloud the words of this prophecy and blessed are those who hear it and take to heart what is written in it, because the time is near. 'Do not be afraid, I am the First and the Last. I am the Living One; I was dead, and now look, I am alive for ever and ever! And I hold the keys of death and Hades.'" Revelation 1:1, 3, 17-18 NIV

REVELATION CAN BE a scary book. A lot of people think it is so difficult to understand that they don't even try. I want to challenge you as we finish reading through the Bible in a year to delve into it this month. Revelation is the only book that promises blessings for those who read it aloud, hear it and take it to heart. Even if you don't fully understand everything in it, at least ask God to reveal to you what He wants you to learn from it. Some people believe that we just shouldn't worry about what Revelation says. They read and study all the other books but prefer to just skip over Revelation. God thought it was important to include in the Bible, so we must conclude that He wants us to know the information that it contains.

Revelation was written by the apostle John while he was exiled on the Isle of Patmos. In a dream or trance, he is transported to Heaven where an angel gives him a guided tour of the Heavenly realm. He is given visions of God's End-Times Plan and the angel explains many of the events he sees. To understand Revelation, it is necessary to study the Old Testament prophecies and some New Testament scriptures as well. Revelation expounds on prophecies found throughout scripture. For example, the description of the Antichrist found in Daniel 9 is further developed in Revelation 13. Daniel, Ezekiel, Isaiah, Zechariah, I Corinthians, I Thessalonians and several other books contain information about the events discussed in Revelation. I'm going to give a brief overview of the end time events as I understand them. I am drawing on several different resources for this summary but rely heavily on Got Questions. Scholars disagree on the order of events to come, but this is my understanding of how it will occur.

1. The rapture of the church- Christ will appear in the sky, the dead in Christ will rise first and then those who are alive will join them in the sky. The rapture of the church is imminent and can occur at any time. We are told to be ready and to watch for His return (1 Thessalonians 4:16-18, I Corinthians 15:51-52).
2. The Battle of Gog and Magog- In the first part of the Tribulation, a great army from the north (Russia, and Turkey in alliance with several other countries from

the Middle East and Africa), attacks Israel and is defeated by God's supernatural intervention (Ezekiel 38-39). No country comes to help Israel in this battle.
3. The rise of the Antichrist- When the church is taken away, (2 Thessalonians 2:7-8), a man who is empowered by Satan will gain worldwide control with promises of peace. (Revelation 13:1, Daniel 9:27). The Antichrist will establish a Covenant with many that will begin the Tribulation period. Another man, the False Prophet, will establish a one world religion under the guise of peace and tolerance that will eventually require worship of the Antichrist. (Revelation 19:20).
4. The Tribulation- A period of seven years in which God's judgment is poured out on sinful humanity (Revelation 6-16). During this time, the Church will be in Heaven where the Judgment Seat of Christ and the Marriage Supper of the Lamb will occur (2 Corinthians 5:10, Revelation 19:6-10).
5. The Jewish Temple is rebuilt.
6. The two witnesses appear to preach the gospel in Jerusalem (Revelation 11:3).
7. The seven seal judgments- These occur during the first half of the tribulation.
    a. Releasing of Antichrist on the Earth (Revelation 6:1-2).
    b. Antichrist takes peace from the Earth and causes people to kill each other (Revelation 6:3-4).
    c. Famine, disease, food shortages, slave labor (Revelation 6:5-6).
    d. One fourth of the population of the Earth killed by sword, hunger, death, and the beasts of the Earth (Revelation 6:7-8).
    e. Martyrs in Heaven cry out to God to avenge their deaths (Revelation 6:9-11).
    f. Great earthquake occurs that makes every mountain and island on the Earth move. The sun will become black, and the moon will be like blood (Revelation 6:12-17).
    g. Total silence in Heaven for half an hour preparing for 7 trumpet judgments (Revelation 8:15).

8. The first six trumpet judgments- These will occur during the middle to latter part of the Tribulation.

    a. God rains down hail and fire on the Earth. One third of trees and grass will be burned up (Revelation 8:7).
    b. A great mountain burning with fire (possibly a meteor) is thrown into the sea, turning one third of the sea to blood, killing one third of the creatures in the sea, and destroying one third of the ships on the sea at the time (Revelation 8:8-9).
    c. A great star burning like a torch (possibly another meteor) falls from Heaven on a third of the rivers and springs contaminating them and causing many people to die as a result (Revelation 8:10-11).

    d. God strikes a third of the sun, a third of the moon and a third of the stars so that a third of them are darkened and a third of the day will be dark (Revelation 8:12-13).
    e. The bottomless pit is opened, smoke will rise from the pit making the sun and air dark. Then a swarm of locusts will come out of the smoke. They are told not to harm the grass or plants or trees, but only men who do not have the seal of God on their foreheads. They are not allowed to kill but only to torment for 5 months (Revelation 9:1-12).
    f. 4 demonic angels are released from the Euphrates River to literally kill one third of mankind that is left. They will be leading an army of 200 million demonic spirits (Revelation 9:13-21)

9. The Abomination of Desolation- At the midway point of the 7-year tribulation, the Antichrist breaks his covenant with Israel, and it becomes evident that he is the Antichrist. The Jews are scattered and many of them turn to the Lord, realizing that Jesus is their Messiah. A great persecution breaks out against anyone who has believed in Jesus during the tribulation (Daniel 12:11, Mark 13:14, Revelation 12:17).
10. The two witnesses are killed and lay in the public square for 3½ days while people gloat over them and celebrate their deaths. Then they will rise from the dead and be taken up to Heaven. There will be a severe earthquake destroying a tenth of Jerusalem and killing 7,000 people (Revelation 11:3-14).
11. The seventh trumpet judgment
When the 7th trumpet is sounded there is rejoicing in Heaven because the end is near. Then there will be lightning, noises, thunder, another earthquake, and more hail (Revelation 11:15-19).
12. Believing Jews flee to a place in the desert where God will protect them for 3½ years (Many think it will be to a place called Petra in Jordan) (Revelation 12:6, 13-14).
13. A war breaks out in Heaven- Michael the Archangel and his angels cast Satan down to Earth. He is furious because he knows his time is short, so he wages war against any Christians remaining on Earth (Revelation 12:7-17).
14. The Antichrist will receive a fatal wound and die and be raised to life. The False Prophet will set up an image in honor of the Antichrist and everyone will be forced to worship it, or they will be killed. Everyone will be forced to take the mark of the beast and without it they will not be able to buy and sell (Revelation 13).
15. The seven bowl judgments- the last of God's Wrath to be released on the Earth.
    a. God causes festering sores to break out on the people who have the mark of the beast (Revelation 16:2).
    b. God causes the entire sea to become blood, killing every living creature in the seas (Revelation 16:3).

    c. God causes all the rivers and springs to turn to blood (Revelation 16:4-7).
    d. God causes the heat from the sun to scorch men with great heat and fire (Revelation 16:8-9).
    e. God causes total darkness to fall on the kingdom of the Antichrist (Revelation 16:10-11).
    f. The Euphrates River is dried up to prepare the way for the kings of the east to come to the Battle of Armageddon. Then three demonic spirits are released from the mouths of the Antichrist and the False Prophet, and they go out to all the kings of the Earth to bring them to the Battle (Revelation 16:12-16).
    g. God causes a severe earthquake over all the Earth. The city of Babylon is destroyed, the islands and mountains disappear, and 100-pound hailstones fall from the sky. Then a voice from the temple says, "It is done." (Revelation 16:17-21).

16. The Battle of Armageddon- At the end of the 7 years, all the nations of the world will come against Jerusalem. Jesus will return with the armies of Heaven, placing His foot on the Mount of Olives, and He will save Jerusalem and defeat the armies of the nations fighting for the Antichrist. The Antichrist and the False Prophet will be captured and thrown alive into the Lake of Fire (Revelation 19:11-21).
17. The judgment of the nations- Jesus will judge the survivors of the tribulation, separating the righteous from the wicked (Matthew 25:31-46). The Old Testament saints will be raised from the dead. The righteous will enter the Millennial Kingdom and the wicked will be cast into Hell.
18. Satan will be bound and held in the bottomless pit for 1,000 years (Revelation 20:1-3).
19. The Millennial Kingdom- Jesus Himself will rule the world for 1,000 years. Jerusalem will be the capital. There will be peace and prosperity on the Earth (Revelation 20, Isaiah 60-62).
20. The last battle- At the end of the 1,000 years, Satan will be released from the bottomless pit for a short time, but will be quickly defeated, and will be thrown into the Lake of Fire forever (Revelation 20:7-10).
21. The Great White Throne Judgment- All those in Hell will be brought back, and all the wicked from history will be resurrected to stand before God in a final judgment (Revelation 20:11-15). The verdicts will be pronounced, and they will be cast into the Lake of Fire for eternity.
22. The New Heaven and New Earth- God completely remakes the heavens and the Earth. He will wipe away all tears and there will be no more pain, death, or sorrow. The New Jerusalem will descend from Heaven, and the children of God will spend eternity with Him (Revelation 21-22).

    I know this is a lot to take in, but I wanted to give you an overview before you jump into the book. I'm not going to spend a lot of time in the devotions each day in Revelation. As you can imagine, it is very difficult to do a quick devotional over such heavy material. I may hit a few things, but I'm hoping you will spend time on your own examining it each day. I pray that you will be blessed for reading it as verse 3 above promises.

December 8

Amos 7-9
Psalm 139:1-6
Proverbs 29:9-10
Revelation 2

Known

"You have searched me, Lord, and You know me. You know when I sit and when I rise; You perceive my thoughts from afar. You discern my going out and my lying down; You are familiar with all my ways. Before a word is on my tongue You, Lord, know it completely. You hem me in behind and before, and You lay Your hand upon me. Such knowledge is too wonderful for me, too lofty for me to attain." Psalm 139:1-6 NIV

FOR SOME PEOPLE the idea that God knows everything about them is a scary thought. I think the way you perceive this depends on your view of God. If you think of God as a judge or king sitting on a throne looking down waiting for you to mess up, then this is very scary. If you see God as Santa Claus who is making a list and checking it twice to see who is naughty and nice, then you probably don't want God to know all the naughty stuff you have done or thought about doing this year. But if you think of God as your Heavenly Father who loves and cares about you, you have a different perspective. God knows everything we have ever done, everything we will ever do, all our thoughts, all our hurts, all our motives, our deepest desires, and our deepest insecurities. He knows before we mess up that we are going to mess up. And thankfully, He is not on His throne waiting to zap us and He isn't up there looking down in disgust because we messed up again. He isn't mad at us, and He isn't going to give up on us. He knows the good, the bad and the ugly, but when He sees us, He is filled with love and compassion. He is sad because He knows that what we did will cause negative consequences for us, or that it will take us further away from Him. He is disappointed because He knows that our actions are not what is best for us. He sees all that we can be, and He wants that for us. He does not want us to settle for anything less than His best. He is our biggest cheerleader, clapping when we get it right and proud when we listen and follow His plan. And when we do mess up, He is always there waiting to pick us up and help us get back on track.

As parents, we want what is best for our children, but we cannot always make it happen. They choose their own way sometimes and do not listen to our advice. As human parents, we don't always know what is best. Our motives are good and our love for them is pure, but we can't see the future, so sometimes we get it wrong. That is not the case with God. His plans are always best. What He tells us is always for our benefit. And because He knows what we are going to do before we do it, He often provides a way out for us. He puts a song on the radio at just the time we need to hear it, He sends a friend to give us encouragement, or He calls to mind a Bible verse that tells us what we need to do. Because He knows us so well, He knows what we need, when we need it, and He provides it. Unfortunately, we aren't always listening, so we miss it and sometimes we choose to ignore His prompts. The knowledge that we are fully known, and we are fully loved by the One who has the ability and power to accomplish His perfect plan for our lives is too wonderful to even fathom, and yet it is true. I pray that we embrace the reality and experience all its benefits.

Obadiah 1
Psalm 139:7-12
Proverbs 29:11-12
Revelation 3

December 9

Lukewarm

> "I know your deeds, that you are neither cold nor hot. I wish you were one or the other! So, because you are lukewarm—neither hot nor cold—I am about to spit you out of My mouth." Revelation 3:15-16 NIV

Laodicea was a large and prosperous city that had a reputation for medical knowledge, especially for an effective eye ointment. It was also a banking and commerce center and many wealthy people lived there. It was located on a major highway. In one direction was the town of Colossae. Colossae was known for its cold and refreshing water. A six-mile aqueduct system was built from Colossae to Laodicea to transport the water. Unfortunately, by the time the water travelled the six miles, it was no longer cold and refreshing, but was lukewarm. It also picked up sediment and germs in the aqueduct so that by the time it reached Laodicea, it had a foul smell and tasted bad. In the opposite direction was the town of Hierapolis. It was known for the Baspinar Springs, a natural hot spring that people traveled for miles to visit. When Jesus was talking to the people at the church at Laodicea, He knew that they would understand exactly what He meant when He told them that He wished that they were either hot or cold. The cold water was useful and good and the hot water from the springs were useful and good, but the lukewarm water was not useful and just needed to be spit out. In our cultural understanding we think of being cold as not being saved at all, being lukewarm as being backslidden, and hot as being on fire for the Lord. So, we think that the Laodicean church is just backslidden, but that is not what Jesus is saying. He is saying that cold water is good and hot water is good, but the Laodicean church was not useful at all because it was filled with people who were not even Christians. This is the only church of the seven churches that Jesus wrote to that He had nothing good to say to at all. The other churches had some things they were doing right and some that they needed to work on, but to this church, He had nothing good to say. He treated them like the Pharisees. It looked good on the outside, but in reality, it was nothing more than a social club that talked about religious stuff.

The warnings to the churches were written to specific churches in Turkey in biblical times, but they were chosen specifically to provide warnings to churches and people throughout the ages so that we do not fall into the same patterns of behavior. Jesus' warning to this church is a stark reminder that it is possible to go to church week after week, year after year and never know Him personally. There are a lot of people who go through the motions and look very religious that do not have a personal relationship with Jesus. They have head knowledge but no heart knowledge. In Matthew 7:21-23, Jesus warns that in the last days many will say to Him, "Lord,

Lord." And He will tell them, "Depart from me, I never knew you." (ESV) This is one of the scariest passages in scripture. It is a reminder to examine our own hearts, but it is also important that we take seriously our responsibility to spur one another on and to build each other up in authentic faith.

December 10

Jonah 1-2
Psalm 139:13-18
Proverbs 29:13-14
Revelation 4

Fearfully and Wonderfully Made

"For You created my inmost being; You knit me together in my mother's womb. I praise You because I am fearfully and wonderfully made; Your works are wonderful; I know that full well. My frame was not hidden from You when I was made in the secret place, when I was woven together in the depths of the Earth. Your eyes saw my unformed body; all the days ordained for me were written in Your book before one of them came to be. How precious to me are Your thoughts, God! How vast is the sum of them! Were I to count them, they would outnumber the grains of sand---when I awake, I am still with You." Psalm 139:13-18 NIV

DURING EMILY'S PREGNANCY, we talked often about how Hadley was developing. She and Logan had an app that told them approximately how big she was each week and what body parts were forming and growing. Human development is completely fascinating to me. The minute detail of each step the human body goes through from the moment the egg and the sperm join to the moment that they can leave the mother's body is nothing short of miraculous. All the organs, bones, joints, blood vessels, and other cells that must come together exactly the right way to perform each bodily function cannot possibly be random. If you take any part of the body and examine all the things that must work perfectly for it to fulfill its role, and then you realize that each part not only has to do its job, but it must work with all the other parts of the body to function properly, it is mind boggling. We take it for granted that our thyroid is going to do its job and our liver will do what it is supposed to do. We don't have to tell our bodies to do all the things necessary to keep us alive. To believe that that level of design happened by chance makes less sense than thinking that this computer I'm typing this devotion on was a pile of wires and circuits and it somehow pulled itself together to become a computer. Our bodies are far more detailed and perform more difficult functions than any computer and yet many people do not believe that they had a Creator who designed them. These verses tell us that God knits each one of us together personally in our mother's wombs and that He has all our days planned before we are born. He has a unique and specific plan for each of our lives. There are no accidents. Whether a child is planned by its earthly parents or not, each child is planned by God. He is with us from the moment we are formed and stays with us through every moment of our lives. We are each precious to Him.

 Modern technology has made it possible to see the development of the baby in the womb. When I was pregnant with both of my girls, ultrasound pictures were very limited. The doctor told us what we were looking at and we took his word for it, but it was hard to see what they were describing. The ultrasound pictures we got of Hadley were amazing. You could see her lips and her fingers. We didn't have to be told what we were looking at because the picture looked almost like a photograph. The idea that a baby is not a baby until it is viable outside the mother's womb is ridiculous. We can usually see the heartbeat by the time a woman knows she is expecting. We can see facial expressions on the child that prove that they can feel pain within a few weeks of conception. All the organs, limbs, and body parts are visible in the first trimester. Abortion is a barbaric practice that should not even be acceptable on animals, much less innocent children. Abortion is murder and God takes it very seriously. As Christians, it is our responsibility to fight vigorously for the protection of the unborn. And just as importantly, it is our responsibility to love pregnant women and support them in any way we can. Abortion is not the best option for anyone. The mother suffers from the pain, heartache, and guilt of her choices. The idea that it is a quick, simple solution is not the reality. The abortion industry is making millions of dollars each year through deception at the expense of innocent babies and scared, desperate mothers. We cannot remain silent.

Jonah 3-4
Psalm 139:19-24
Proverbs 29:15-17
Revelation 5

December 11

Never Too Late

"The Ninevites believed God. A fast was proclaimed, and all of them, from the greatest to the least, put on sackcloth." Jonah 3:5 NIV

THE STORY OF Jonah is an amazing picture of God's love and mercy. Nineveh was the capital of Assyria located on the Tigris River. The Ninevites were evil, wicked people who were enemies of Israel. Their destruction would be a victory for Israel, and they deserved God's wrath so Jonah probably believed that punishing them would provide justice. The story of Jonah is unique for several reasons. All the other Old Testament prophets provided warnings to Israel. The Israelites followed a pattern of disobedience that began with a period of obedience and serving God, then they were led astray and worshipped the gods of the people around them, God allowed them to be taken into bondage, they cried out to God, He sent a deliverer, they repented and turned back to God and then the cycle repeated. God used the prophets to warn Israel of the consequences of their sin and to give them an opportunity to repent. This cycle has happened over and over throughout Israel's history. The book of Jonah is different because Jonah was not told to preach to Israel and warn them of coming destruction. He was told to go to a foreign city, filled with wicked people and warn them that if they did not repent of their evil ways and turn to God, they were going to be destroyed. This would have been like God telling us to go to Syria or Iran and tell ISIS that they need to repent and turn to God. Jonah wanted them to get what they deserved so he was not excited about this assignment. This is the first example of foreign missions we find in the Bible. For some reason God had compassion on the Ninevites.

The other thing that is unusual about this event is that this pagan nation listened to Jonah, repented and the whole city turned to God. The only clue about the timing of this event is found in 2 Kings 14:25 which places Jonah during the reign of Jeroboam II. We know from historical writings that he ruled Israel from 786-746 BCE. There was a famine from 765-758 BCE. There was a large earthquake around 760 BCE and during this period the Assyrians lost several battles and were forced to give up territory to their enemies. On June 15, 763 BCE there was a total solar eclipse over northern Iraq which would have passed over the city of Nineveh. We do not know the exact date that Jonah went to Nineveh, but it seems likely that he went to the city right after all these things happened and warned them that God was going to destroy them. God had prepared their hearts and then He sent Jonah at just the right time when they were scared and desperate and would be willing to listen. There are several lessons we can learn from Jonah. God loves all people. He wants everyone to repent and turn to Him. No one is too far gone. If God sends us to tell someone about Him, we need to trust that He will prepare them to hear what we have to say. At that point, it is up to them to respond. We are responsible to tell them and then let the Holy Spirit work on their hearts. We cannot assume anyone is impossible to reach. If they are alive, they still have a chance. We just need to keep praying for them.

God will go to great lengths to get our attention. He sent a famine, an earthquake, war, and a solar eclipse to soften the hearts of the Ninevites, a wicked, pagan people. He knows what it will take to reach us, and He will use whatever is necessary because He loves us and doesn't want anyone to perish. Jonah was not happy when the people repented. He wanted his enemies to get the punishment they deserved. We need to be careful to remember who our enemy is. People are not our enemies. Satan and his demons are our enemies. We may have to ask God to soften our hearts so that we see people the way He does, with mercy and compassion. Throughout the Bible, we find that God gave warnings before He punished. He would have been completely justified if He decided He had had enough and just sent fire from Heaven and annihilated them all. But instead, He gave them a chance to turn from their evil ways and come to Him. He does the same for us. He is the God of second chances and third chances and fourth chances. It is significant to note that just over a hundred years later, the Ninevites returned to their former ways. God sent Nahum to them to warn them, but they failed to listen, and they were destroyed by the Medes. God is longsuffering and patient, but if we reject Him, we will face His wrath.

December 12

Micah 1-2
Psalm 140:1-5
Proverbs 29:18-19
Revelation 6

Revelation/Vision

> "Where there is no revelation, people cast off restraint; but blessed is the one who heeds wisdom's instruction." Proverbs 29:18 NIV

THE WORD "REVELATION" has been so associated with end-time events that whenever we see this word, we think it is referring to the apocalypse. Merriam Webster defines revelation as "an act of revealing or communicating divine truth, something that is revealed by God to humans."[26] The New Living Bible translates this verse, "When people do not accept divine guidance, they run wild." Basically, this verse is telling us that people who do not accept God's guidance do not have purpose and direction. Without the benefit of God's guidance in their lives, they are destined to live a meaningless existence. This seems harsh, but it is true. Solomon, who was the wisest person who ever lived, concluded, "Meaningless! Meaningless! Everything is meaningless." He had obtained knowledge, wealth, possessions, and power and he realized that nothing satisfied him. People who do not have God in their lives are constantly trying to find purpose and meaning. They chase after anything that they think will bring them pleasure. It works for a little while and then they go on to the next thing. They are seeking purpose and fulfillment and never find it. We were created in the image of God and because of that we can never be complete without Him. When we accept Jesus into our hearts, the Holy Spirit comes and fills up places in us that we didn't even know were empty. Let's imagine a glass tumbler is your life. You take a hand full of marbles to represent all the things you try to fill your life with like relationships, work, possessions, money, hobbies, interests, talents, dreams, etc. Fill up the glass with the marbles. It looks full, but if you look closely there are gaps throughout the glass around the marbles. Now take another glass filled with water and pour it in. The water is like the Holy Spirit. He fills up all the gaps. He goes in around our talents, work, hobbies, relationships, dreams, etc. and He fills us to the brim. He completes us. Without Him there will always be gaps.

I cannot imagine going through this life on my own. If I didn't have God with me leading and guiding me, I don't know where I would be. I would be motivated by selfish ambition and led by my emotions. My choices would revolve around seeking pleasure and comfort. I don't know how I would deal with difficulty and disappointment if He wasn't there to comfort and encourage me. If He was not there to help me overcome temptation, there would be no reason not to give in. When I experience pain and suffering, He gives me hope that tomorrow will be better and helps me find purpose and meaning in what I am experiencing. How can you keep going if you don't have hope? We have the benefit of divine guidance. God reveals to us everything we need to live a life of meaning, purpose, and direction and we are blessed if we listen to Him.

Micah 3-4
Psalm 140:6-13
Proverbs 29:20-21
Revelation 7

December 13

Deliverer

"I say to the Lord, 'You are my God.' Hear, Lord, my cry for mercy. Sovereign Lord, my strong deliverer, You shield my head in the day of battle. I know that the Lord secures justice for the poor and upholds the cause of the needy. Surely the righteous will praise Your name, and the upright will live in Your presence." Psalm 140:6-7, 12-13 NIV

LET'S FACE IT. We need a deliverer. We need someone to ride in on a white horse, sweep us up and carry us away from the pain and heartache of this world. Jesus is our deliverer. In every situation we face, He is the only One who can help us. He is our source of hope. One day He will appear in the sky, rescue us, and take us to be with Him. In the meantime, there are many practical ways in which we can experience His deliverance in our daily lives.

1. Jesus delivers us from the power of Satan and his demonic forces. There is a battle that rages all around us between the spiritual forces in the Heavenly realm. Satan is a real and powerful enemy who is prowling around seeking to destroy us. He does not want us to be effective in our spiritual lives and he will do anything he can to weaken our faith and keep us from telling others about Jesus. Thankfully, "the One who is in me is greater than the one who is in the world." I John 4:4 (NIV) Satan has no power over me because the Holy Spirit who lives in me can stand firm against anything he throws at me.
2. Jesus delivers us from temptation. "God is faithful; He will not let you be tempted beyond what you can bear. But when you are tempted, He will also provide a way out so that you can endure it." I Corinthians 10:13 (NIV)
3. Jesus delivers us from fear. Many people today are paralyzed by fear. We do not have to live in fear because He is with us. We are not alone. "Be strong and courageous. Do not be afraid; do not be discouraged, for the Lord your God will be with you wherever you go." Joshua 1:9 (NIV)
4. Jesus delivers us from anxiety and worry. "Do not be anxious about anything, but in everything by prayer and supplication with thanksgiving let your requests be made known to God. And the peace of God, which surpasses all understanding, will guard your hearts and your minds in Christ Jesus." Philippians 4:6-7 (NIV) Not only will He take away our fear, but He replaces it with peace.
5. Jesus delivers us in persecution. We do not experience physical persecution in America, but believers all over the world face it daily. We may face ridicule,

rejection or hate because of our faith. He may not remove the persecution, but He will give us the strength to endure it and to glorify Him in it.

6. Jesus delivers us from the bondage of sin. Jesus conquered sin and death when He rose from the dead. When we accepted Jesus as our Savior, we were set free from the power of sin in our lives. "It is for freedom that Christ has set us free. Stand firm, then, and do not let yourselves be burdened again by a yoke of slavery." Galatians 5:1 (NIV)

7. Jesus delivers us from physical danger. There are examples in the Bible where God delivered people from physical danger. (Daniel in the lion's den, Shadrach, Meshach and Abednego in the fiery furnace, David and Goliath, David running from Saul, Paul in prison, shipwrecked, etc.) Just as He rescued people in biblical times from dangers, there are countless examples of when He delivered people out of danger, and we have no idea how many times He has protected us from danger that we weren't even aware of.

8. Jesus delivers us from the chains that bind us (addiction, selfishness, oppression). You don't have to be locked in physical chains to be in bondage. Drugs, alcohol, pornography, etc. are powerful chains that prevent people from living the life God has planned for them, but nothing is too powerful for God to overcome.

9. Jesus delivers us from illness (physical, mental, emotional). He is the great physician. He knows our needs and He can heal us fully and completely. Sometimes He does that through doctors and medical resources, sometimes He provides a miracle at just the right time, and sometimes we are healed when we enter Heaven and see Him face to face, but we can be assured that He will provide complete healing.

10. Jesus delivers us from death. Everyone who has accepted Jesus into their hearts has been brought from death to life. We were dead in our sin, and we have been made alive in Christ. We have been given eternal life. The moment we take our last breath on Earth, we will be in His presence in Heaven. Our life does not come to an end, it continues in our eternal home.

December 14

Micah 5-6
Psalm 141:1-6
Proverbs 29:22-23
Revelation 8

Requirements

"He has shown you, O mortal, what is good. And what does the Lord require of you? To act justly and to love mercy and to walk humbly with your God." Micah 6:8 NIV

MICAH'S PROPHESIES WARN of destruction for both Samaria, the capital city of Israel, and Jerusalem, the capital city of Judah. As he predicted, Samaria fell to the Assyrians in 722 BCE and Jerusalem fell to the Babylonians in 587 BCE. But Micah also told them that because of God's faithfulness to His covenant with them, He would save a remnant of the people and bring them back to their land. This passage points to a different way of thinking for them. Verses 6 and 7 give us insight into their mindset. They asked what they needed to do to please God. They suggested bringing a burnt offering with year-old calves or perhaps they would need to bring thousands of rams, or ten thousand rivers of oil. By the time of Micah's ministry, the sacrificial system that Moses put into place had been distorted by the priests and religious leaders to control the people. It had also been corrupted by the cultural and religious practices of the nations around them so that they even asked if they needed to offer their firstborn as a sacrifice. This was a common practice by the pagan nations, but Jewish law never included child sacrifices. Micah's answer to them was not what they expected. Basically, he told them that all God required of them was to love God and love people. Jesus gave the same answer when asked what the greatest commandment was. He said, "Love the Lord your God with all your heart, soul, mind, and strength, and love your neighbor as yourself." Matthew 22:37-39 (NIV) The rules and regulations that God gave them were always intended to accomplish those two things. They were supposed to teach them how to love God and how to love people, but they had been turned into a legalistic system that they could not possibly obey perfectly. God has always been more concerned about our hearts than our ability to follow rules. His desire has always been that we follow Him because we love Him and not because we are forced to do so.

Jewish law had very specific guidance regarding justice. Many of the laws and provisions in our legal system are based on the laws God gave the Jewish people. Honesty, integrity, fairness, taking care of the vulnerable, impartiality, and equity are all necessary to provide justice. Acting justly toward others means that we treat them the way that we would want to be treated by others. The word that Micah uses that is translated mercy is the word "hesed" which we have discussed several times. It means kindness, mercy, faithfulness, goodness, and love. We not only need to treat people justly, but we need to be kind, good, merciful, and loving to them. And he says that we are to love "hesed". We aren't just supposed to do it out of obligation, we need to love being merciful and kind to people. Then Micah gets to the most important part. We are to walk humbly with our God. Walking side by side, talking, communicating, and going somewhere implies that we are together. It requires relationship and intimacy. And it also requires humility to recognize that He is the Creator God of the universe, and we are sinful creatures who owe Him everything. We cannot act justly toward others and love mercy if we are not walking humbly with our God. The love and gratitude we experience when we walk with God overflows and is expressed in "hesed" to others. God sees our hearts and knows why we do the things we do. A humble, loving heart has always been what pleases God.

December 15

Micah 7
Psalm 141:7-10
Proverbs 129:24-25
Revelation 9

Hope

"But as for me, I watch in hope for the Lord, I wait for God my Savior; my God will hear me." Micah 7:7 NIV

THE SITUATION THAT Micah found himself in was pretty hopeless. Everywhere he looked he saw only evil. The rulers and judges were corrupt and the powerful conspired together to fulfill their wicked desires. Not one upright person could be found. And there was no reason to believe anything was going to get better. God had told him that judgment was coming. I'm sure he did not want his city to be destroyed. His job as a prophet was to warn the people of what was coming if they did not repent. It grieved him to know that many people would die, and many others would be taken into captivity. Even though they deserved the punishment they were going to receive, he wanted them to repent and turn to God instead. God had told him that He would save a remnant that would one day return to the land He had given them because He is faithful. Even though they broke the covenant over and over and were not faithful, He remained faithful and would uphold His promise to them. Verse 7 is tucked in the middle of his prophecies. In complete confidence and unwavering faith Micah proclaimed, "As for me, I watch in hope for the Lord, I wait for God my Savior; my God will hear me." He trusted that God would do what He said He was going to do to Israel, but God was going to take care of him. He was not worried. He watched and waited because he believed God was going to hear him and protect him.

Does this sound familiar? When we look around today, we see evil everywhere. Our rulers and judges are corrupt. The powerful are conspiring together for their own gain. Thankfully there are upright people still here, but we know that there is coming a day when all the upright people are going to be removed. Things are not going to get better. God has told us what is coming. We don't know when His wrath is going to be poured out, but He has given us a vivid description of the pain and suffering that will occur. As Christians, we feel like Micah did. We are grieved for our friends and neighbors and even people we don't know who are going to experience the horrors of the tribulation. They may deserve the punishment they are going to get for rejecting God, but we want desperately for them to repent and turn to Him. We know that He will save a remnant, all of those who have accepted Him as their Lord and Savior, and in the end, Jesus will return and set up a Millennial Kingdom where He will rule and reign for a thousand years and we will spend eternity with Him. He is faithful and will fulfill His promises to us. So, like Micah, we can proclaim with confidence and unwavering faith that we will watch and wait for God. We know He hears us, and He will take care of us. He will not let us down. We have hope because He is faithful.

December 16

Nahum 1
Psalm 142
Proverbs 29:26-27
Revelation 10

Refuge

"The Lord is good, a refuge in times of trouble. He cares for those who trust in Him."
Nahum 1:7 NIV

"I cry to You, Lord; I say, 'You are my refuge, my portion in the land of the living. Listen to my cry, for I am in desperate need; rescue me from those who pursue me, for they are too strong for me. Set me free from my prison, that I may praise Your name. Then the righteous will gather about me because of Your goodness to me."
Psalm 142:5-7 NIV

CLOSE YOUR EYES and think of refuge. What does that mean to you? A refuge is a place of safety, security, and rest. For a soldier, refuge can be found in a walled fortress or in reaching friendly territory when they are being pursued by the enemy. For a scared child, a mother's loving arms is the refuge they need. When going through a season of difficulty, a few days at the beach or in a mountain cabin may be the refuge that gives us a much-needed rest. For many of us home is our refuge. The world can be a cruel, scary place, but our home should provide a safe shelter where we are loved and taken care of. No matter what the world throws at us, when we get home, we should be able to breathe a sigh of relief knowing that we are embraced and accepted.

We find references throughout the Bible of God being our refuge and strength. It is easy to imagine how a walled fortress or a mother's arms can be a refuge, but how is God our refuge? Examining several references in Psalms gives us insight into how we can experience this as a reality in our lives. In Psalm 91, David proclaims that God is his refuge and fortress. He explains that whoever dwells in the shelter of the Almighty will rest in His shadow. This is an important point. To experience the fullness of God's refuge, we don't just run to Him when we are in trouble. Dwelling with God implies that we are living every minute of our lives in His presence. We don't just try to take care of everything we can on our own and only go to Him for the big stuff. We experience His refuge as we are continually in His presence. This Psalm also demonstrates that God was the first place David went when he had a need. He did not run to family and friends or his own resources and then go to God when he had exhausted all other options. He immediately sought God's help and wisdom. Psalm 57 and 61 both give us a beautiful image of God's presence providing refuge. When the girls were little, we did not let them sleep with us, but sometimes we would wake up and find them either in the floor beside our bed or at the foot of the bed sound asleep. They would wake up in the night scared and come into our room just to be near us. They didn't need to wake us or get in bed with us, just being near us made them feel safe enough that they could go back to sleep. They knew we would protect them from anything that could harm them. Coming into God's presence can give us that same peace. When we are feeling scared and overwhelmed, the best thing we can do is take a moment and enter His presence trusting that He is able to protect us and handle anything that comes our way. Psalm 5:11, 34:8, and 64:10 tell us that God's refuge not only protects us from danger, but it also provides joy, blessings, and peace in His presence regardless of our circumstances.

December 17

Nahum 2-3
Psalm 143:1-6
Proverbs 30:1-6
Revelation 11:1-10

Remember

> "So, my heart grows faint within me; my heart within me is dismayed. I remember the days of long ago; I meditate on all Your works and consider what Your hands have done. I spread out my hands to You; I thirst for You like a parched land." Psalm 143:4-6 NIV

WE DON'T KNOW when David wrote this Psalm. It could have been when he was in the wilderness being pursued by Saul, or when he was fleeing an enemy on the battlefield. Or it may have been when his son Absalom was seeking to kill him and take over his throne, but whatever the occasion, we see that he is in perilous danger. He cries out to God begging Him for mercy. He lays out what his enemy has done to him and asks God for deliverance. He is weary and tired. He doesn't have the energy to go on. His heart is dismayed. We have all been there. Sometimes it just feels like we are under attack, with blow after blow assaulting us from every side. Just when we think things are going to get better, something else sneaks up from behind and knocks us off our feet. What do we do when that happens? Do we give up? Do we put a smile on our face and pretend everything is ok when we are really crumbling inside? Neither of those things are the best option. David gives us a much better example to follow. When he was overwhelmed and scared, he turned his focus on God.

First, he remembered the days of long ago. He reminded himself of all the times God had been faithful to him. He thought of the times when he had been in distress, he remembered the enemies who had pursued him, and how God had protected him and delivered him in the past. He encouraged himself by choosing to recall God's interventions in his life. Then he meditated on all God's works. He not only remembered God's faithfulness to him, but he also focused on God's mighty power, majesty, strength, and ability. This helped him to put his own problems into perspective. To meditate you must take your eyes off your circumstances and focus them on God. David then considered or contemplated what God's hands had done. He knew that God was able to help him, He had helped him in the past, and now he was assured that God would hear and answer him again. It took conscious effort to choose to turn his attention from the peril he was facing and place it on God. We would do well to follow his example. When we forget what He has done in the past, we begin to doubt what He can do in the present. Spreading out his hands to God symbolized letting go. I once heard a preacher say that sometimes we need to physically raise our arms and open our hands to force ourselves to let go of what we have been gripping tightly. Hurt, bitterness, anger, fear, resentment, and anxiety are negative things that we don't want in our lives, but sometimes we have been holding on to them for so long that we don't know how to give them up. God wants to take them from us and let us walk in freedom, but we must open our hands and release them. Thirsting after Him like a parched land is something we experience out of desperation. Coming to the end of ourselves produces an awareness of our need for the wellspring of water only He can provide.

December 18

Habakkuk 1:1--2:3
Psalm 143:7-12
Proverbs 30:7-10
Revelation 11:11-19

The Appointed Time

"Then the Lord replied, 'Write down the revelation and make it plain on tablets so that a herald may run with it. For the revelation awaits an appointed time; it speaks of the end and will not prove false. Though it lingers, wait for it; it will certainly come and will not delay." Habakkuk 2:2-3 NIV

"The time has come for judging the dead, and for rewarding your servants the prophets and your people who revere your name, both great and small—and for destroying those who destroy the Earth." Revelation 11:18 NIV

THERE IS AN appointed time of the end. God is not sitting up in Heaven trying to decide when it would be a good time to send Jesus to rapture the church and start the tribulation period. He knew before He ever created time how many days were on the calendar. He isn't winging it. There is an appointed time for everything that happens. Only God knows what those appointed days are, but they are set, fixed and immovable. God gave the prophets hints that they recorded in Scripture so that we could be prepared when the time comes. He gave Paul and John further revelation about the times of the end. But no one has the whole picture. The people in the early church thought Jesus was going to return in their lifetimes and there have been believers in every generation who have watched for Him. He didn't give us a date because if He had told the New Testament believers that He wasn't going to return for at least 2000 years they would have been discouraged. And there would not have been a sense of urgency to spread the gospel.

If we examine the Bible as a whole, we see that God reveals things progressively. He did not lay out His whole plan to Abraham and Moses. He told them what they needed to know. Then over time He revealed Himself and His plan through the prophets and the other writers of Scripture more fully. The Old Testament pointed to His plan of redemption and the coming of the Messiah, but it wasn't until Jesus Himself came to Earth that the full plan was revealed. People for centuries have been examining the prophecies about the end times. Many of the prophecies have not made sense until modern times. From 70 AD until the 20th century people would not have been able to make sense of the references to the "nation of Israel" because until 1948 there was no nation of Israel. It did not exist. The promises of God to bring them back to their land from all over the world would not have seemed possible. The technology needed to accomplish most of the things in Revelation like the mark of the beast, a one world currency, the image of the beast, and the ability for everyone in the world to see the two witnesses killed and laying in Jerusalem for three days and then resurrected did not exist and could not even be imagined. Someone reading those passages in the 19th century could not possibly have understood them. But now all that technology is in place, and we can understand what those passages mean. There has never been a time in history when Russia, Turkey, Iran, and Syria have been allies, so when the Bible mentions them coming together to invade Israel from the north it has always seemed unlikely, but all those countries now have troops just north of Israel in Syria. While they are not exactly friends, they are allies in their desire to destroy Israel. If we examine all the prophecies in the Bible that have already been fulfilled, there is more than enough evidence to conclude that all the rest of them will happen just as they have been predicted. No prophecy in Scripture has ever been proven to be false. They either happened exactly as Scripture said or they have not been fulfilled yet. We can be confident that every word of the Bible is going to happen at the appointed time. Habakkuk tells us that the revelation awaits the appointed time, and it will not prove false. Though it lingers, we are to wait for it because it is certain to come.

Habakkuk 2:4-3:19
Psalm 144:1-8
Proverbs 30:11-14
Revelation 12

December 19

Fame

"Lord, I have heard of Your fame; I stand in awe of Your deeds, Lord. Repeat them in our day, in our time make them known; in wrath remember mercy."
Habakkuk 3:2 NIV

This is an interesting passage. When we think of famous people, we think of movie stars, athletes, and politicians. Generally, people who are famous are esteemed. They are looked up to. They have lots of followers on Instagram and Twitter because everyone wants to know everything about them. Companies pay them to endorse their products because they know that people want to be like them. If they are wearing a pair of shoes, everyone will want to own a pair of those shoes. If they go to a restaurant, everyone will want to go to that restaurant. We want to dress like them, have the same haircut, go on the same vacation, and do everything like them so that we can be like them. Unfortunately, the things that make people famous are generally external like physical appearance, athletic ability, charisma, etc. People rarely become famous because of their character and integrity. Fame is fleeting. It can happen overnight and then just as quickly it can be gone. A sexual indiscretion is overlooked, but a careless word that is politically incorrect can result in being "cancelled."

Fame isn't a term that people normally use for God. Merriam Webster defines fame as "notoriety, reputation, renown, celebrity, and public estimation."[27] It is the perfect term to refer to God. Jesus is the most famous man who ever lived, and His Father is even more famous. Most people on Earth have heard the name of Jesus. They may have heard it taken in vain, but they have heard of Him. As believers, the most important thing we can do is to proclaim His deeds every chance we get and continue to make Him famous. Satan is trying to convince people that Jesus was a not the Messiah, the Son of God. He wants them to believe anything except that He is the One True God. The more people know about Him, the more they will want to know Him. And the more they know Him, the more they will want to be like Him. In the coming year, let's make it our goal to make Him even more famous by spreading the truth about His love and mercy to everyone who will listen.

December 20

Zephaniah 1-2
Psalm 144:9-15
Proverbs 30:15-17
Revelation 13:1-10

Blessing

"Blessed are the people of whom this is true; blessed are the people whose God is the Lord." Psalm 144:15 NIV

BLESSING IS A good church word. We have the idea that a blessing is a reward we can all expect to receive when we become a Christian. If we behave like good little boys and girls, we will experience God's blessing. But if we do not act like we are supposed to, then we will face God's punishment or removal of His blessing. We are told to count our blessings and make sure that we thank God for all the good things He does for us. So, a life that is blessed is a perfect life where we are happy and healthy and have everything we need. This sounds great, but the problem is that it does not line up with reality. And it doesn't go along with what we find in God's Word. Sometimes bad things happen to people who are living godly lives. And no one goes through life without any difficulty. We all experience trials, problems, difficulties, and heartache. If being blessed means that you always have good in your life, then no life is truly blessed.

A study of the Hebrew and Greek words that are translated as blessed can give us insight into their deeper meaning.[28] The Hebrew word, "asre," translated as "blessed" in this passage in Psalm 144 means "the goodness and abundance experienced when God rewards you for walking in His ways." It includes forgiveness, protection, victory, the benefit of God's presence, but it also includes His discipline and correction. It is a result of a relationship with Him. The difficulties we face produce growth and draw us closer to Him. A life without any problems is not really blessed because it cannot experience the fullness of God that is found in pain and suffering. Another word in Hebrew, baruch or berech, that is translated blessing, means knee, or kneel. The knee is the weakest part of the body, and it expresses the idea that He is our strength when we are weak. Kneeling humbly before Him allows us to experience His blessing in our lives.

The word translated as blessing in the New Testament comes from the Greek word, "makarismos", which means, "to be indwelt by God through the Holy Spirit, and, because of His indwelling to be fully satisfied." This definition has nothing to do with good circumstances. It means that we are fully satisfied despite the difficulties we face. We are filled with joy and peace so that we can endure whatever happens in our lives because of His love and mercy. The blessing we receive as people whose God is the Lord is far better than prosperity and good fortune. It is not based on temporal pleasures or feelings of "happiness." To be blessed is to be satisfied completely. Blessing is not an outward reality, but an inner, spiritual truth.

Zephaniah 3
Psalm 145:1-7
Proverbs 30:18-20
Revelation 13:11-18

December 21

The Antichrist and the False Prophet

"The whole world was filled with wonder and followed the beast. People worshiped the dragon because he had given authority to the beast, and they also worshiped the beast and asked, 'Who is like the beast? Who can wage war against it?' The beast was given a mouth to utter proud words and blasphemies and to exercise its authority for 42 months. It opened its mouth to blaspheme God, and to slander His name and His dwelling place and those who live in Heaven. It was given power to wage war against God's holy people and to conquer them. And it was given authority over every tribe, people, language, and nation. All inhabitants of the Earth will worship the Beast." Revelation 13:3-8 NIV

THE BIBLE TELLS us about a man called the Antichrist who will rule the Earth during the seven-year Tribulation. He is referred to by several different names in scripture including the Beast, the Man of Lawlessness, Son of Destruction, the False Christ, and the Antichrist. We are not told his identity, but we are given several clues about what he will be like. He will be revealed after believers have been raptured so we will not be here while he is ruling the Earth. There will be a future Roman Empire made up of ten countries similar to the European Union. From this power structure will come a "little horn" or an unknown politician who will rise to power very quickly. He will broker a peace deal between Israel and her enemies for seven years. During that time, he will allow the Jews to rebuild their temple and to resume animal sacrifices. Halfway through the seven-year period, he will be assassinated. The False Prophet will breathe life into his body and raise him from the dead in Jerusalem. He will proclaim himself to be the Messiah and will enter the temple. He will commit the "Abomination of Desolation" (Daniel 9:27, 11:31, Matthew 24:15-16). We aren't told exactly what this will be, but it will be something that defiles the temple (perhaps an unclean animal sacrifice, or an altar or statue of the Antichrist to be worshipped.) Whatever it is, it will be so abominable that the Jews will realize immediately that he is not their Messiah, and they will flee into the desert. Satan is a counterfeiter or a copycat. He wants to be like God so he copies what God does to deceive whoever he can. He will require that everyone worship him and that they receive a mark on their forehead or hand to declare their allegiance to him. Below is a list of characteristics he will possess.

1. Physical appearance- Stout and imposing (Daniel 7:20), fierce-looking (Daniel 8:23)

2. There is much speculation about where the Antichrist will come from. Some scriptures seem to suggest he comes from a revived Roman Empire and is Western European. Others suggest he will be Middle Eastern and still others think he will be Jewish. I tend to think he will be Western European, but it is possible that he will have Jewish lineage and still be from Western Europe. Trying to guess who it might be seems pointless because it is likely he is not someone that will be well-known until after the rapture. He is probably behind the scenes and will rise to power quickly.
3. Crafty politician/problem solver (Daniel 9:27, Revelation 17:12-17) He will appear to have a solution to bring about world peace. He will be very charismatic and be able to talk people into following him.
4. Military genius who can deceive people into fighting for him- (Revelation 6:2, 13:4, 19:19, Daniel 11:38-39)
5. He hates God and blasphemes against Him (Revelation 13:5-6, Daniel 7:25)
6. He will display miraculous powers given to him by Satan. (2 Thessalonians 2:9-12)
7. He will die and be resurrected (Revelation 13:3-4) This will be to confuse and deceive people into believing he is the Messiah.
8. He will enter the temple, claim to be God and demand to be worshiped (2 Thessalonians 2:4, Daniel 9:27)
9. He will control the economy (Revelation 13:16-17)
10. Arrogant and boastful, selfish egomaniac (Daniel 11:36, 8:25, Daniel 11:36, 2 Thessalonians 2:4)
11. Satan will give him authority to rule the Earth for a time (Revelation 13:7, 17:12-13)
12. He is going to lose and will spend eternity in the Lake of Fire (Revelation 20:19-20)

The False Prophet is the second beast referred to in verses 11-17. He is a religious leader who will come alongside the Antichrist to give him legitimacy. He will appear like a lamb, but his words are like a dragon (vs. 11). He exercises the authority of the first beast and compels everyone on Earth to worship the Antichrist (vs. 12). He will perform miraculous signs like calling down fire from Heaven (vs. 13). He will make an Image of the Beast and cause everyone who will not worship the Image to be killed (vs. 15). He will require everyone to accept the Mark of the Beast to buy or sell (vs. 16-17). He will be thrown into the Lake of Fire with the Antichrist where he will spend eternity (Revelation 19:20). The Antichrist and False Prophet are utterly evil men who have power because they are indwelt by Satan. They will deceive many including the Jews, but when the Antichrist enters the temple and declares that he is God, the Jews will realize that he is not God, and many will turn to Jesus as their true Messiah. It is not important for us to try to figure out who the Antichrist might be. There are all kinds of guesses about his identity. It is not likely that he is well-known yet. It is probably someone in the background who will rise to power after the rapture. Our focus should be on telling people about Jesus so that they will not be here for his reign.

December 22

Haggai 1-2
Psalm 145:8-13
Proverbs 30:21-23
Revelation 14:1-14

Goodness

> "The Lord is good to everyone; His compassion rests on all He has made. The Lord helps all who fall; He raises up all who are oppressed." Psalm 145:9, 14 HCSB

THE GOODNESS OF God does not fit our understanding of goodness. We think of good as the opposite of bad. We describe people as good because of the things that they do, and we describe things as being good if they are enjoyable to us or satisfy a desire. We would say that a pizza is good if we like the way it tastes, a nap is good if it gives us much-needed rest, or our child is good if they obey us. God's goodness is not based on His actions or His ability to make us happy. God's goodness is His character. Good is who God is. He is morally excellent and everything He does is perfect. His goodness is indescribable and beyond what we can even comprehend. Good began with God. He set the standard for goodness and perfection. Genesis 1:31 says, "God saw all that He had made, and it was very good." (HCSB) His goodness extends to all His creation. He is not just good to His children who love Him. He is good to everyone. He cannot be anything other than good. It is just who He is. As humans, we are not typically good, loving, compassionate, and merciful to people who reject us or treat us badly. God extends grace and mercy to everyone. His desire is that everyone would accept Him, so He forgives over and over. He continues to love faithfully even when He is rejected. Every time we call on Him, He is there to help. Everyone who seeks Him, finds Him. No one has ever exhausted their opportunity to receive His pardon. Everyone who has breath can still receive His mercy. In all human history, He has never said no to anyone who comes to Him with a sincere heart. The serial killer, rapist, terrorist, or child molester who repents and asks for His forgiveness is welcome at the foot of the cross. No one is too far gone. No one is beyond redemption. His goodness is available to all.

His goodness is also generous. It goes beyond practical, physical needs. When we sin, He forgives us. When we are weak and weary, He gives us strength and perseverance. When we are afraid, He gives us courage and assures us that He is with us. When we need wisdom, He gives us clarity and answers. When we fall, He is there to pick us up and help us move forward. When we are oppressed, unfairly treated, or rejected, He raises us up to walk with Him. He provides everything we need every time we have a need. The good that He provides is not always what we ask for because His "good" is perfect. He will not give us anything less than what is best for us. If He always gave us what we wanted, He would not be good because, in His sovereignty, He can see the consequences of His gifts. If He gave us something that is not for our good, then He would cease to be good. His discipline and wrath are just as much an expression of His goodness as His forgiveness and mercy. There is a lady in our neighborhood that walks every day carrying a walking stick. She is older than me, but not elderly. I asked one of our neighbors if she has it because she is unsteady. That is part of the reason, but apparently, she was attacked by a dog a couple of years ago, so she uses the walking stick to protect herself. God's goodness is like that walking stick for us. We can lean on it and use it to steady ourselves on our journey through life. We can rely on His goodness to provide what we need to keep us going and hold us up. We can also use it to protect us against Satan's attacks. We can fight off doubt and worry with confidence in His goodness and mercy. God is good all the time. And all the time God is good.

December 23

Zechariah 1-2
Psalm 145:14-21
Proverbs 30:24-28
Revelation 14:15-20

The Wicked

"The Lord guards all those who love Him, and He destroys all the wicked." Psalm 145:20 HCSB

THE END OF Psalm 145 gives us the other side of God's goodness. Yesterday we discussed God's mercy and compassion. We saw how He is patient and loving and does not want anyone to perish. He wants everyone to come to Him and gives opportunity after opportunity for them to turn from their evil ways and accept Him. He would love nothing more than to send only Satan and his demons to the Lake of Fire in Hell and for every human who ever lived to spend eternity in Heaven with Him. Unfortunately, Satan introduced evil and wickedness into this world and man chose to sin and rebel against God. He would not be good and holy if He ignored it or looked the other way. Romans 3:10 tells us that "There is no one righteous, not even one." (NIV) And Romans 3:23 says, "All have sinned and fall short of the glory of God." (NIV) So, who are the wicked in this verse? If we are all sinners, then we all would have to be included in the wicked who He will destroy. In His love and mercy, God provided the means of forgiveness by offering His Son as a sacrifice for our sins to all who accept Him as their Lord and Savior. (John 3:16-18) When we accept the grace and mercy He provides, His righteousness is imputed to us. (2 Corinthians 5:21, Philippians 3:9) Instead of standing with the wicked, we now stand before Him clothed with the righteousness of Christ. Therefore, the wicked are those who refuse to accept Jesus and stand before Him on their own merit as sinful and wicked. We would like to think that this verse is talking about the bad people like murderers, rapists, and terrorists. But that is not the case. Anyone who has not accepted Jesus as their Lord and Savior is wicked.

God's goodness cannot tolerate sin and evil. He is holy and just and evil is repugnant to Him. If He tolerated sin, He would cease to be good. This is a stark reality, but one that we cannot deny. (Psalm 5:4-5, 15:9) The idea that God is too loving to send anyone to Hell is a dangerous lie from Satan intended to deceive people into thinking that they are ok, and they don't need to worry about their eternal destiny. (Romans 6:23) As believers, we are thankful for His goodness. It protects and provides for us. It gives us hope and peace. But it should also give us a burden for those who do not know Jesus. It should compel us to share His goodness with others so that they will accept His mercy and grace and not face His wrath and judgment.

Zachariah 3-4
Psalm 146:1-4
Proverbs 30:29-33
Revelation 15

By My Spirit

> "I replied, 'I see a solid gold lampstand there with a bowl on its top. It has seven lamps on it and seven channels for each of the lamps on its top. There are also two olive trees beside it, one on the right of the bowl and the other on its left.' So, He answered me, 'This is the word of the Lord to Zerubbabel: 'Not by might nor by power, but by My Spirit,' says the Lord Almighty.'" Zechariah 4:2-3, 6 NIV

GOD GAVE ZECHARIAH a vision of a golden lampstand that was supposed to be in the temple. At that time, Zechariah and the people were rebuilding the temple, so it is logical that God would give him visions about the things in the temple. What was unusual was the two olive trees standing on either side of the lampstand. The temple would not have live trees inside it. One of the tasks of the priests was to keep the lampstand full of olive oil. This was probably not a task they enjoyed because it was repetitive and never finished. They had to clean it, fill it, and replace the wicks over and over. It was necessary, but a very menial task, kind of like making the bed or doing the laundry. Almost as soon as they finished, they had to do it again. In Zechariah's vision, he sees a self-filling lampstand. There are seven pipes to the seven lamps coming from the olive trees, so the lampstand is filling itself and doesn't have to be continually filled by the priests. Zerubbabel had been given the job of finishing the building of the temple, but the work had stalled. He needed encouragement to keep going and get it completed. God's Word to him through Zechariah was that he would not find the ability to finish by relying on human might or human power, but he would find it by relying on the Spirit. The olive trees (olive oil) represent the Spirit of God. They are a continual source of power and strength. If he relied on the resources of the world, they would not be enough to provide everything he needed, but if he relied on the Spirit of God, he would find a never-ending supply.

Olive oil was used for many purposes in biblical times and still has many uses. It has medicinal properties and is used for healing just as the Holy Spirit brings physical, mental, emotional, and spiritual healing to our lives. It was used in lamps to provide light just as the Spirit of God brings light in the darkness. Oil is used as a fuel for fires to bring warmth and to cook over. The Holy Spirit brings warmth and comfort to us when we are in distress, and He provides sustenance to us. He is the bread of life. Oil is used to polish metal just as the Spirit polishes our lives and smooths out the rough edges. Oil is also used in perfume to adorn. The Holy Spirit adorns us with inner beauty as He sanctifies us to make us more like Christ. When we rely on our own power or the resources of the world around us, we will not have everything we need, but when we rely on the Holy Spirit, He will continually fill us and provide for every need we have. We will be able to proclaim that it is "not by might and not by power, but by the Spirit" that we can live victorious lives and accomplish His purposes.

December 25

Zechariah 5-6
Psalm 146:5-10
Proverbs 31:1-5
Revelation 16

The Lord Reigns

"Blessed are those whose help is the God of Jacob, whose hope is in the Lord their God. He is the Maker of Heaven and Earth, the sea and everything in them—He remains faithful forever. He upholds the cause of the oppressed and gives food to the hungry. The Lord sets prisoners free, the Lord gives sight to the blind, the Lord lifts those who are bowed down, the Lord loves the righteous. The Lord watches over the foreigner and sustains the fatherless and widow, but He frustrates the ways of the wicked. The Lord reigns forever, your God, O Zion, for all generations. Praise the Lord." Psalm 146:5-10 NIV

On this Christmas morning, let's take a moment to ponder over the God that we are celebrating today. This passage describes Him well. We are indeed blessed if our hope is in the Lord our God. Our circumstances may not be pleasant, but we have the assurance that our God is with us, and He will take care of us. We are in good hands. He is the Maker of Heaven and Earth, the seas and everything in them. He made it all and if He made it, He is certainly capable of taking care of it and sustaining it. He set the Earth on its axis. He put it at the exact distance from the sun and made it rotate with the precise timing necessary to sustain life for us. He created seasons so that crops could grow and provide the nutrients we would need to live. He created the exact balance of oxygen and carbon dioxide necessary. He created ecosystems that function perfectly. He created the human body to live and breathe and work and grow. We are fearfully and wonderfully made. He is the master architect of it all and He will sustain it for as long as He has planned. He has always been faithful and will be faithful forever.

In addition to creating and sustaining it, He is also intimately involved in His creation. He does not watch it from afar and intervene when He must. He cares for us personally and continually. He gives food to the hungry and He cares for the poor. He protects the fatherless and the widows. He gives sight to the blind and defends the oppressed. He releases people from the prison of sin that has bound them, and He deals with the wicked. This is the God we love and serve. We love because He first loved us. He gave us life and He blesses us beyond what we can even fathom. We are His children, and He is our loving Father. Let us celebrate the birth of our Savior today. O come let us adore Him, Christ the Lord!

December 26

Zechariah 7-8
Psalm 147:1-9
Proverbs 31:6-9
Revelation 17

WWJD

"Speak up for those who cannot speak for themselves, for the rights of all who are destitute. Speak up and judge fairly; defend the rights of the poor and needy." Proverbs 31:8-9 NIV

A FEW YEARS back, there was a phrase that went around in Christian circles. You could find WWJD on bracelets, plaques, shirts, and anything else that retailers could think to put it on that people would buy. "What Would Jesus Do" was intended to make us think in every situation about what Jesus would do if He was in our shoes. I think it was good and it did make us think before we acted. The problem is that if we are going to ask ourselves WWJD, we must spend time figuring out what Jesus really would do so we need to get to know Jesus on a whole new level. Just knowing a few Bible stories about Him and assuming how He would respond isn't enough. I heard a lot of people quote the "let him who is without sin cast the first stone" Bible verse as an excuse to ignore sin saying that Jesus said we shouldn't judge others so we shouldn't get involved. That is absolutely not what Jesus would do. When everyone else left, Jesus did not tell the woman caught in adultery that her sin was fine, and she could just go on and do what she had been doing. He told her to "go and sin no more." Ignoring sin is not loving and it is not what Jesus would do. He did not want to stone her, but He loved her too much to let her continue in her sin. In most situations where we find ourselves, the thing that Jesus would do is get involved. He would not condemn, but He would go alongside them and help them turn from their sin and turn to Him.

Out of the WWJD period came another movement that is referred to as the social justice movement. Many churches have adopted this platform and it has been politicized. We are told numerous times in the Bible to care for the poor, widows, orphans and oppressed, and of course Jesus would do those things. However, many churches have begun to prioritize this over the main purpose of the church. The church's number one mission and the number one priority of Jesus was to provide salvation to the lost. The most important need that anyone has is their need for a relationship with Jesus. They are dead in their sins, and they need to be made alive in Christ. We can feed the hungry, heal the sick and care for the orphans, and we should do those things, but if we don't tell them about Jesus, they will die and go to Hell and those things would have done them no good at all. I know that "we have to earn the right to be heard" and to an extent that is true. However, many churches and ministries aren't getting around to the gospel. They are serving them and then hoping that they will see Jesus' love in them and somehow get saved. I'm just not sure how often that is happening. Also, I often see that God's Word is being compromised to try to reach more people. The social justice movement has watered down the Word to make it more culturally relevant and politically correct. Please don't get me wrong, I am not advocating that we don't serve. Churches should be meeting the needs in their communities. And as individual believers we each need to be serving in some capacity. We can all do something. We just must be careful not to lose sight of our most important mission. Showing the love of Jesus must include telling them about Jesus or it is not loving. As we look to a new year, if you are not serving in your community on a regular basis, I would encourage you to make this a priority. The needs are great. There are a lot of lonely, hurting, desperate people who need the love of Jesus. Whatever your age, physical abilities, time constraints, etc. you can find a way to serve. Help at your local food bank, deliver meals, or write cards to shut-ins, get involved in a prison ministry or a ministry to internationals, help in a Habitat for Humanity home, run errands for an elderly neighbor or a new mom. There are endless opportunities if we just take the time to look for the needs. Do Something! I can tell you what Jesus would do; He would get involved in the lives of the people around Him.

December 27

Zechariah 9-10
Psalm 147:10-20
Proverbs 31:10-14
Revelation 18

The Coming of Zion's King

"See, your King comes to you, righteous and victorious, lowly and riding on a donkey, on a colt, the foal of a donkey. He will proclaim peace to the nations. His rule will extend from sea to sea and from the river to the ends of the Earth. Because of the blood of My covenant with you, I will free your prisoners from the waterless pit. Then the Lord will appear over them; his arrow will flash like lightning. The Sovereign will sound the trumpet; He will march in the storms of the south, and the Lord Almighty will shield them." Zechariah 9: 9-11, 14-15 NIV

THE BOOK OF Zechariah is filled with prophecies about the first and second coming of Jesus. Biblical scholars have identified over 100 prophecies in this short book. Thirty-one were fulfilled with His first coming and the rest are yet to come. Zechariah 9:9 was fulfilled in Matthew 21:2-7 when Jesus rode into Jerusalem on a colt, the foal of a donkey at the Triumphal Entry the week before His death. Zechariah 11 portrays Jesus as a Shepherd for the flock of Israel (Jesus describes Himself as a shepherd in John 10:10-12) Chapter 11 also says He will be detested, attacked, rejected, and betrayed for thirty pieces of silver (fulfilled in Matthew 26:14-16, 27:3-10). Zechariah 12 says that His side will be pierced, and He will become an opened fountain for sin and impurity (fulfilled in Matthew 26:28, John 19:34). Zechariah 13 foretells that His disciples will be scattered when He is smitten (fulfilled in Matthew 26:31). Chapter 13 also says that His two hands will be wounded which was fulfilled when He was nailed to the cross in John 19:18. These are just a few of the prophecies that have already been fulfilled. Zechariah was written when the people of Israel returned to Jerusalem after the long period of Babylonian captivity around 540 BC. The specificity of the fulfillment of all these prophecies over five centuries later and the fact that Jesus perfectly fulfilled over 300 Old Testament prophecies with His first coming is proof that He was indeed their long-awaited Messiah.

When Zechariah wrote this book Jerusalem was in ruins, and the people had no idea what their future held. God used him to give them hope and assure them that He had not forgotten them. He wanted them to know that He had a plan to restore them and bring them back into fellowship with Him. They misunderstood Zechariah's prophecies and those of the other prophets. They were not expecting a humble, gentle, servant king who came to bring peace and offer Himself as a sacrifice. They were expecting a warrior king who would come and conquer their enemies and rule the Earth. They did not understand that He is both servant and warrior. His first coming was not what they expected, and many missed it. Many Jews still do not accept Jesus as their Messiah. They are still looking for a warrior king who will ride in and save them. Jesus came the first time to make peace between God and man. He set us free from sin and death by the shedding of His blood. He is the risen King, and He wants to rule and reign in the hearts of His people. He offers peace and redemption for all who accept Him.

December 28

Zechariah 11-12
Psalm 148:1-6
Proverbs 31:15-19
Revelation 19

The Second Coming of Zion's King

"On that day, when all the nations of the Earth are gathered against her, I will make Jerusalem an immovable rock for all the nations. All who try to move it will injure themselves. The people of Jerusalem are strong because the Lord Almighty is their God. They will look on Me, the one they have pierced, and they will mourn for Him as one mourns for an only child and grieve bitterly for Him as one grieves for a firstborn son." Zechariah 12:3, 5, 10 NIV

"I saw Heaven standing open and there before me was a white horse, whose rider is called Faithful and True. With justice He judges and wages war." Revelation 19:11 NIV

YESTERDAY WE LOOKED at some of the prophecies in Zechariah about Jesus' first coming. Today I would like to examine some of the prophecies about His second coming. Zechariah 12:10 above foretells that one day the Jews are going to realize that Jesus was their Messiah, and they will grieve bitterly. Their eyes will be opened, and they will see that they rejected, denied, and then murdered their Messiah. They will repent and turn to Him and be restored. Revelation 1:7 confirms this. Zechariah 9:10 says that Christ will be the King to rule over all the nations and Jerusalem will be the seat of His Kingdom. Zechariah 12:1-9, and 14:2-3, 12-15 foretell that Christ will fight for His chosen people against all the nations that come against them and save them from destruction. Today's reading in Revelation 19 goes into greater detail about the battle that will take place between Jesus and His enemies. Zechariah 14:4 says that Jesus' feet will stand on the Mount of Olives, and 14:5 tells us that Christ will come accompanied by His saints, the overcomers. Revelation 19:14 confirms this. Zechariah 14:6 talks about a time when everyone left on Earth will go to Jerusalem every year to worship Him and will be sanctified by Him.

When Jesus returns the second time, He will not come in peace. The prophecies about His second coming give a very different picture of Jesus than the humble, servant King who came to Earth as a baby in a manger. When He returns, the trumpet will sound, and He will step foot on the Mount of Olives in Jerusalem to deal with Satan and his demons and destroy evil and sin completely. Anyone who has not accepted Him as their Lord, will face His wrath and will be cast into the Lake of Fire. Then Jesus will rule the Earth from Jerusalem and establish an earthly kingdom for 1,000 years. After that, He will establish a new Heaven and new Earth where we will live for eternity. There are over 1800 references in the Bible to Jesus' second coming.

Seventeen books in the Old Testament and twenty-three books in the New Testament mention Christ's return. One out of every thirty verses in the New Testament teaches that Jesus is coming back. The specific fulfillment of all the prophecies surrounding His first coming gives us confidence that the prophecies about His second coming will be fulfilled exactly as they have been foretold as well. We do not understand all the details, but we have been given everything we need to know to watch in hope for His return.

December 29

Zechariah 13-14
Psalm 148:7-14
Proverbs 31:20-23
Revelation 20

Judgment

"Anyone whose name was not found written in the book of life was thrown into the Lake of Fire." Revelation 20:15 NIV

REVELATION CAN BE very confusing because it is not chronological. John did not record the visions he received in the order in which they are going to occur. He may have received the visions in the order that he wrote them down, but nevertheless, he skips around making it hard to piece together. The order I gave you earlier this month came from the research of a lot of scholars who spent years examining Revelation along with the other prophecies in the Bible. They do not all agree on the exact order, but they are consistent for the most part with only slight variations. There are some misconceptions that I would like to try to clear up related to our reading today in Revelation 20. These are things I did not understand until a few years ago when I did an in-depth Revelation Bible Study related to the Judgment Seat of Christ and when that occurs for different groups of people. This is how I believe it will occur. I am not dogmatic about it, but I think this is consistent with scripture.

At some point in the future, a trumpet will sound in Heaven and Jesus will appear in the clouds. The bodies of everyone who has died who accepted Jesus as their Lord and Savior will raise out of their graves. Their souls are in Heaven with Jesus so their bodies will meet their souls in the sky. Then everyone who is alive at that time who has accepted Jesus will join them in the air and they will all be taken to Heaven for seven years. (I Thessalonians 4:13-18) During that time, they will stand before the Bema Seat of Christ and be judged for their works while on Earth. This will not be to judge whether they will be allowed to get into Heaven. If they are there, their name is written in the Lamb's Book of Life. This will be a judgment to determine rewards in Heaven. I believe that any crowns we receive we will immediately lay at the feet of Jesus because we will recognize that any good we ever did is because of His presence in our lives. We will have pure hearts so any rewards will be received in humility and gratitude. (Romans 14:10, 2 Corinthians 5:10). At the end of the seven years, Jesus will return to Earth, and we will return with Him. There will be another time of judgment where Jesus will judge all the survivors of the tribulation. This is when Jesus will separate the sheep from the goats, the righteous from the wicked. The people who were saved during the tribulation and either martyred or lived to the end will go into the Millennial Kingdom with the other believers. The wicked who survived will be cast into Hell. (Matthew 25:31-46) Many believe that at this time the Old Testament saints will be resurrected and allowed to go into the Millennial Kingdom as well. Satan is bound and thrown into the Abyss and the Antichrist and

False Prophet are thrown into Hell with the wicked. At the end of the 1000-year reign, Satan is released for a short time, finally and completely defeated by Jesus, and thrown into Hell. At that time, all the wicked people throughout history will be resurrected to stand before the Great White Throne Judgment. Jesus will judge them based on their works and they will receive their final sentence and be cast into the Lake of Fire in Hell for eternity. (Revelation 20).

So, there are three different times of judgment for different groups of people. I hope this explanation is helpful and relieves some anxiety about standing before Jesus for judgment. For believers, there should be no fear about the future. Our destiny is secured. We don't have to worry about "not making it in." I do not like "hell fire and brimstone" preachers who try to scare people into Heaven, but this is a stark reminder that everyone will someday stand before God for judgment and those who don't know Jesus will spend eternity in Hell. We need to pray for opportunities to tell people the truth before it is too late for them.

December 30

Malachi 1-2
Psalm 149
Proverbs 31:24-27
Revelation 21

Eternity

"Then I saw a new Heaven and a new Earth, for the first Heaven and the first Earth had passed away, and there was no longer any sea. And I heard a loud voice from the throne saying, 'Look! God's dwelling place is now among the people, and He will dwell with them. They will be His people, and God Himself will be with them and be their God. He will wipe every tear from their eyes. There will be no more death or mourning or crying or pain, for the old order of things has passed away.' Nothing impure will ever enter it, nor will anyone who does what is shameful or deceitful, but only those whose names are written in the Lamb's Book of Life." Revelation 21:1, 3, 4, 27 NIV

REVELATION 21 GIVES us a picture of what eternity is going to be like. I cannot even begin to fathom how beautiful it will be. The description of streets of gold, giant doors made from a single pearl, walls decorated with every kind of precious stone, and no need for the sun or moon because everything is illuminated by God's glory is beyond our comprehension. In addition to all the beautiful things that will be there is the absence of the things that have made this life difficult. There will be no more pain, no more tears, no more illness, and no more death. There will be no sin. There will be no Satan and no evil people who follow Him. There will be no more lies and no more shame. We will not struggle with sin and temptation. We will not need to hide anything. There will no more addiction and no more bondage, no more slavery or racism, and no more sexual perversion. There will be no more war, or hate, or violence. We will experience freedom and complete peace.

We will be in the presence of Jesus. We will finally get to see Him face to face and behold His glory. We will understand the depth of His love for us. I'm not sure if we will get insight about the things we did not understand that happened to us in our earthly lives or if those things just won't matter anymore, but I am confident that we will be at peace with it either way. And we will get to see our loved ones who passed away before us. What a wonderful reunion that will be. Relationships will be restored. We will experience forgiveness and healing and all the hurt and emotional pain will be gone. Dysfunctional family dynamics will be repaired, and we will be able to love and be loved unselfishly and completely. This is the source of our hope. I can only imagine what it will be like as I long for that day and wait in hope and anticipation.

December 31

Malachi 3-4
Psalms 150
Proverbs 31:28-31
Revelation 22

The Wife of Noble Character

"She is clothed with strength and dignity; she can laugh at the days to come. She speaks with wisdom, and faithful instruction is on her tongue. Charm is deceptive, and beauty is fleeting; but a woman who fears the Lord is to be praised." Proverbs 31:25, 26, 30 NIV

The description given in Proverbs 31 of the virtuous woman is a very familiar passage. I think it has the potential to be discouraging because it seems impossible to accomplish. No one can live up to this. So how should we handle it? Do we take one look at it and throw up our hands without even trying or do we run ourselves ragged trying to be this perfect wife? The first thing that we need to look at is who wrote this passage and who it was written to. The passage identifies King Lemuel as the author, but most scholars believe that it was written by King Solomon using a fictitious name. Solomon did not write this passage to women to tell them how to be a good wife. The text tells us that Proverbs 31 was an inspired utterance that his mother taught him. If Solomon is the author, then his mother, Bathsheba, told him these things to advise him on what kind of woman he needed to look for. Knowing what we know about Solomon and his many wives and concubines, he did not listen to his mother or at least he did not heed her advice. He may have written this passage wishing he had listened. This gives us a whole new perspective on this passage. If you are the mother of a boy, you want him to choose well. This is not a specific woman that is being described. It is a compilation of all the traits that this mother wanted in a wife for her son. It is not intended to be a measuring stick for us to use to examine our lives and see how badly we are failing. But we also should not completely ignore it. It is excellent, practical advice given by a wise woman that we can learn from. As we read it, we can ask God to reveal to us areas that we need to work on and then allow Him to guide us in implementing them in our lives. Most of these traits do not only apply to married women. They are qualities that can be applied to the lives of any believer.

1. She is trustworthy. Her husband has full confidence in her because she is honest, and he knows he can trust her in everything, big and small.
2. She is a hard worker, industrious, and resourceful. She is not lazy. She works hard to take care of what has been entrusted to her. Her house is in order, and she is prepared.
3. She is clothed with strength and dignity. Her strength comes from God so she can handle whatever comes her way. She handles herself with dignity in ways that glorify God.

4. She is wise. Her wisdom comes from the Lord. She acts wisely and she gives wise advice to others.
5. She is a good steward of her time and resources. She does not waste what she has been given.
6. She trusts God and acts on her faith. She is confident about the future because she knows that God will take care of her family.
7. Her value is not found in physical appearance or material wealth, it is found in her relationship with God. She is confident, capable, and self-assured because of God's work in her life.
8. She is generous. She reaches out her hand to the needy and extends her hand to the poor.
9. She selflessly serves others. Her focus is not on her own desires and needs, but on meeting the needs of her husband, her family, her friends, and those in need. Her joy is found in loving and serving others.
10. She respects her husband. She comes alongside him and helps him in all he does.
11. She teaches and instructs her children in the ways of the Lord. She disciplines them in love and trains them in righteousness.
12. She is kind, gentle and humble toward others.

The beginning of a new year is an excellent time to examine our lives and ask God to show us what He wants to work on in us this year.

Bible Versions

New International Version (NIV)
Holman Christian Standard Bible (HCSB)
English Standard Bible (ESV)
New American Standard Bible (NASB1995)
King James Version (KJV)
Christian Standard Bible (CSB)
International Children's Bible (ICB)
The Message (MSG)
New Living Translation (NLT)

How To Have a Relationship with God

THE BIBLE TELLS us that we are all sinners. Romans 3:23 says that "all have sinned and fall short of the glory of God." (NIV) And Romans 3:10-12 says, "There is no one righteous, not even one. There is no one who understands; there is no one who seeks God. All have turned away; they have together become worthless. There is no one who does good, not even one." (NIV) Romans 6:23 says, "For the wages of sin is death, but the gift of God is eternal life in Jesus Christ our Lord." (NIV) We cannot save ourselves. No matter how many good things we do we cannot be good enough. We are going to mess up. Jesus is the only person who was ever perfect. So, the first thing we must do is admit we are a sinner, and we need a savior.

But the Bible tells us that God knew we weren't going to be able to be perfect, so He provided a way for us to be saved. John 3:16 says that God loved the world so much (He loved you so much) that He sent His One and Only Son that if you believe in Him, you will not perish but have everlasting life. Romans 5:8 says, "But God proves His own love for us in that while were still sinners, Christ died for us!" (HCSB) The next thing we do is Believe in Jesus. We believe that Jesus was the Son of God who came from Heaven, to be born of the virgin Mary, lived a perfect life, died on a cross and rose Himself from the dead. Now He is in Heaven with God preparing a place for those who have asked Him into their hearts. And one day He will come again to take us to be with Him.

And lastly, we call on the name of Jesus and ask Him to save us. Romans 10:9-10 says, "If you confess with your mouth, 'Jesus is Lord,' and believe in your heart God raised Him from the dead, you will be saved. One believes with the heart, resulting in righteousness, and one confesses with the mouth, resulting in salvation." (HCSB) And Romans 10:13 says, "Everyone who calls on the name of the Lord will be saved." (HCSB)

In summary-

1. Admit you are a sinner in need of a savior.
2. Believe in your heart in Jesus.
3. Call on the name of Jesus to save you.

It is that simple. You don't need anyone else to help. There is no secret formula or special words you have to say. Just talk to Him from your heart. Once you do that, He will come to live inside of you. He will help you, lead you, guide you, comfort you, strengthen you and give you joy and peace that are beyond anything you can understand. He does not promise to make all your problems go away or to give you an easy life, but He will be with you every step of the way and He will give you the wisdom and strength to deal with whatever you face, and you will have eternal life so that when you die you will spend eternity in Heaven with Him.

About the Author

CHRISTY COLEMAN SCHUETTE is a loving wife, mother, grandmother, and follower of Jesus Christ. Christy was born and raised in Arab, Alabama. She is 1987 graduate of Auburn University with a bachelor's degree in social work and a 1988 graduate of the University of Alabama with a master's in social work. Christy now resides in Bowling Green, Kentucky with her family. In her free time, she enjoys keeping her new granddaughter, Hadley, sewing, reading, scrapbooking, cooking, and spending time with her friends and family. Christy has written curricula for Vacation Bible School and Bible studies for many years, and has served in her church through children's, youth, young adult, small group, and women's ministries. She has been involved for several years in local ministries serving the Bowling Green community including Helping Hands Ending Hunger, House on the Hill, and Room in the Inn. Her passion is discipleship and helping others grow closer to Jesus through His Word. In 2021 she started a blog with daily entries to inspire readers to delve into scripture and learn to apply it to their lives. You can find her blog at www.christysdevotional.com.

Endnotes

1. The Baptist Hymnal, Miles, Charles Austin, "In the Garden," pg. 187, Nashville, TN, Convention Press, 1991.

2. Merriam-Webster.com Dictionary, s.v., "simple," accessed February 10, 2020, https://www.merriam-webster.com/dictionary/simple.

3. Merriam-Webster.com Dictionary, s.v. "entrusted," accessed March 9, 2020, https://www.merriam-webster.com/dictionary/entrust.

4. Quote Fancy, accessed March 11, 2020, https://www.quotefancy.com/quote/52859/Franklin-D-Roosevelt.

5. Ernst, Douglas, "Joy Behar Mocks Mike Pence's Faith, Calls His Relationship with Christ Possible 'Mental Illness,'" The Washington Times, February 13, 2018, https://.m.washingtontimes.com/news/2018/feb/13.

6. Renner, Rick, "Tetelestai-It is Finished! January 12, 2021, https://crosswalk.com.

7. Santayana, George, "The Life of Reason: The Phases of Human Progress," Volume 1, Reason in Common Sense, https://www.azquotes.com/authors/12976-George_Santayana.

8. Merriam-Webster.com Dictionary, s.v. "exclusive," accessed May 10, 2021, https://www.merriam-webster.com/dictionary/exclusive.

9. Lifeway.com, accessed June 11, 2021, https://www.lifeway.com/en/articles/women-leadership-spiritual-gifts-growth-service.

10. Merriam-Webster.com Dictionary, s.v. "integrity," accessed June 2, 2021, https://www.merriam-webster.com/dictionary/integrity.

11. Lucado, Max, Cure for the Common Life: Living in Your Sweet Spot, Nashville, TN, Thomas Nelson, Reprint edition, May 2, 2011.

12. The Free Dictionary.com, s.v. "acclaim," accessed July 10, 2021, https://www.thefreedictionary.com/dictionary/acclaim

13. The Baptist Hymnal, Oatman, Johnson Jr., "Count Your Blessings," pg. 644, Nashville, TN, Convention Press, 1991.

14. Cambridge Dictionary.com, s.v. "wisdom," accessed September 2, 2021, https://dictionary.cambridge.org/wisdom.

15. The Free Dictionary.com, s.v. "wisdom," accessed September 2, 2021, https://www.thefreedictionary.com/dictionary/wisdom.

16. The Baptist Hymnal, Whittle, Daniel W, "I Know Whom I Have Believed," pg. 337, Nashville, TN, Convention Press, 1991.

17. Merriam-Webster.com Dictionary, s.v. "refuge,' accessed September 10, 2021, https://www.merriam-webster.com/dictionary/refuge.

18. Merriam-Webster.com Dictionary, s.v. "hope," accessed September 11, 2021, https://www.merriam-webster.com/dictionary/hope.

19. Got Questions, "hesed," accessed September 20, 2021, https://www.w.org/meaning-of-hesed.html.

20. Christian Quotes, accessed September 30, 2021, https://christianquotes.info/quotes-about-faith.

21. Merriam-Webster.com Thesaurus, s.v. "bitterness," accessed October 10, 2021, https://www.merriam-webster.com/thesaurus/bitterness.

22. Fr. William Most, "Excerpts from St. Augustine," 1.4, EWTN, https://www.ewtn.com/catholicism/library/excerpts-from-st-augustine-9962.

23. Quote Fancy, accessed November 3, 2021, https://www.quotefancy.com/quote/867513/Michael-Jordan.

24. Thomas A. Edison Quotes. BrainyQuote.com, Brainy Media Inc, 2021. https://www.brainyquote.com/quotes/thomas_a_edison_132683, accessed November 3, 2021.

25. Henry Ford Quotes. BrainyQuote.com, Brainy Media Inc. 2021, https://www.brainyquote.com/quotes/henry_ford_121339, accessed November 3, 2020.

26. Thomas A. Edison Quotes. BrainyQuote.com, Brainy Media Inc, 2021. https://www.brainyquote.com/quotes/thomas_a_edison_132683, accessed November 3, 2021.

27 Merriam-Webster.com Dictionary, s.v. "fame," accessed November 16, 2020, https://www.merriam-webster.com/dictionary/fame.

28 Biblical Hermeneutics, "blessed," accessed November 20, 2020, https://hermeneutics.stackexchange.com/questions.

CPSIA information can be obtained
at www.ICGtesting.com
Printed in the USA
LVHW020223020622
720196LV00011B/819